# ENGLISH LITERATURE

## VOLUME I

*by Guy E. Smith, Ph.D.*

## About the Book

1. Designed for nonspecialized students and general readers. Emphasis in the main section is on the works that make literature, with biographical and historical backgrounds woven in to make a unified and complete story of the major literary contribution to Western culture.

2. Separate sections of plot summaries of the major works and a dictionary of literary terms to enable the student or general reader to find in a few seconds essential review information about works he has read and definitions which may be difficult to locate quickly in voluminous histories and anthologies.

3. Sections that stand out from the main text, giving careful and detailed treatment of the literary trends and movements as well as the political and social backgrounds within which the types of works are produced.

4. Both in the main section and in a special Chronological Table, relationships are given between English literature and other great bodies of writings in the world literary pattern.

## About the Author

1. Dr. Smith has taught both classical and modern languages and literatures for 25 years. At present teaches in University College, University of Utah.

2. Has published articles in various professional educational journals. Has done translations both from and into Spanish. His modern version of *Celestina* and a novel by Benito Pérez Galdós are scheduled for publication in early 1957. At present he is completing a manuscript in English of the Galdós masterpiece, *Fortunata y Jacinta*. Has under way a project consisting of a series of review handbooks on various of the world's literatures.

# ENGLISH LITERATURE

## To Romanticism
## Volume 1

*with*

Plot Summaries of Major Works
Dictionary of Literary Terms

*By*

GUY E. SMITH, Ph.D.
*University of Utah*

**1967**

## LITTLEFIELD, ADAMS & CO.
Totowa, New Jersey

## ACKNOWLEDGMENTS

Quoted lines from "The Second Shepherds' Play," translated by Homer A. Watt, are from *The Literature of England*,
Vol. I, by Woods, Watt, and Anderson, copyright 1947,
1941, 1936, by Scott, Foresman and Company, and are
used with their permission. *(See pages 199, 200.)*

Quoted lines from "Everyman" are from *"Medieval
English Verse and Prose"* (Modernized Versions), by Roger
Loomis and Rudolph Willard, copyright 1948, by Appleton-
Century-Crofts, Inc., and are used with their permission.
*(See pages 201–203.)*

# PREFACE

A conveniently manageable presentation of a major literature may attempt to crowd into an outline framework as many dates, names, and important facts as possible. The result is a skeleton, with sharply gleaming bones, each in its proper place. Another such work may jump from author to author and from period to period, offering isolated but somewhat complete sketches, rather than a unified story.

This book offers an over-all presentation of the literary story of England for the student or for the general reader. Its single aim is to create an interesting and accurate view of the books that have combined to make the greatest single body of writings in the Western World. It blends the historical facts and the biographical data into a complete story, unified but uncrowded by detail.

## Designed for students and nonspecialists

This book is not designed basically for specialists, nor for those who already possess an extensive knowledge of English literature. It aims to be a handy manual of essential information for the student who needs help in supplementing his reading and lecture notes or who desires a handy unified organization of essential data, or who wishes a quick reference manual wherein he may find in a few seconds a particular fact or definition. The plan will also provide the student with detailed summaries of the major works, thus giving him a reference outline of the books he reads as well as the contents of many important selections he will not have time to read in their entirety. The book is also designed for the nonstudent who desires to acquire a working knowledge of this most important branch of Western culture but

who has not the time to wade through many books and to sift
out the requisite information from many detailed discussions.
And, third, the work would not be out of place as a handy reference manual on the shelves of the specialist in literatures.

### Emphasis on literary works

The major emphasis is on the works that make literature and
whatever additional data can be considered absolutely essential
for an understanding and appreciation of them. This leaves little
room for literary polemics and the amassing of biographical and
bibliographical detail. There is no attempt here to be original
except in plan of presentation. My task has been one of meticu-
lous sifting and elimination of masses of material and to organize
those remaining elements of prime importance into a unified
whole. The final story must be interesting and accurate; it must
provide a complete story, yet elaborate only where the modern
nonspecialized reader will derive the greatest fruits of appreciation and pleasure along with his acquired cultural advancement.
It must bring him stimulus and leading suggestions for further
search and research into the apparently vastly confusing mass of
world literatures. It must show the over-all harmony in all
literatures, aside from the barriers of language, and that the
total fund of the best aesthetic writings of man show few isolated
and single-handed accomplishments, but rather an adaptation
and assimilation of best thought and form from whatever sources,
brought together in new works by the leading literary spirits of
particular epochs and countries.

### Divisions of the manual and their use

The specific plan of this book is as follows:

1. The main body of the two handy volumes gives a continuous presentation of the story of the literary development of England from its beginnings to the present time. Detail is suppressed
to give unity and an uncrowded view of particular periods.
Historical and general cultural notes are used to preface each
period of literary development to provide a picture of the political
and social setting within which the literary men of genius worked
upon the writings which have come down to us as the outstanding
literary contributions of the period.

2. Few of the principal works will be discussed in detail in
the first section. However, as each major work is introduced in
the main body of the book, unless a summary is given there, a

page number in parentheses (248) will indicate that a summary
of its contents will be found in Appendix A. Additional notes of
a critical and comparative nature will be included there when
they would bring additional appreciation or understanding of the
importance of the work discussed. The summaries are arranged
in the order in which the works were introduced into the main
section. They may be located also from the alphabetical index
of the book, where titles are set in italics.

3. As each new literary term is introduced into the first
section of each volume, rather than present an elaborate definition at that point, a single asterisk (*) will indicate that full information relative to this term will be found in Appendix B, in
its alphabetical position. This Appendix will thus provide a
completely detailed dictionary of the terms used in discussing
literatures, presented in nontechnical language. The arrangement
of this section is an alphabetical order with cross references,
calculated to save the student laborious searching for essential
definitions in voluminous histories or anthologies. Many terms,
not actually used in the main section, will also be found here.

4. Appendix C is a handy chronological outline of English
and world historical events and cultural achievements, including
a detailed outline of literary history. The left-hand page gives
items relating to England and the opposite page contains references to major events in the principal Western cultures outside
of England. Many references to English literary chronology will
be included here that were not considered of sufficient importance to the student and general reader to merit space in the
main body of a coverage of this size. These additional items will
not appear in the general index.

5. Footnotes will not be used in these volumes. Occasionally
references will be given in parentheses at the spot where the
additional information is applicable. Statements in this book are
not the original findings of this writer and will not be defended by
bibliographical references except where there is obvious dis-
agreement among critics generally. The book is designed as an
informative coverage of the subject rather than as a guide to
research.

## *A unified review of English literature*

No bibliography, as such, is included. Many pages or, indeed,
the entire two volumes might be made up of reference to the
thousands of excellent treatments of general and particular

phases of English literature. Basic histories, anthologies, and bibliographical guides are available which devote space to such listings. This book is a review of the field of English literature, and as such, has no value as a guide to sources. Each volume is concluded by a complete index. Titles of works are indicated in italics. The index is cross-referenced.

The writer carries no torch for any particular literature. He loves good books, regardless of the original language in which they were written or of the particular political and social temperament in which they were created. He is simply a professor of languages and literatures who believes that the best writings of our great English literary heritage should be known to all.

G. E. S.

# TABLE OF CONTENTS

# Chapter I

# THE AGES BEFORE CHAUCER

## MIGRATIONS FROM THE NORTHLAND

We view all the beginnings of northern European literatures from much the same perspective. They lie in the mists of antiquity and oral folk tradition, far from any contact with any of the great ancient literatures of Greece, Rome, and the Orient. It remains for the specialist to fathom bits of information about them and pass these facts and theories on to us in modern English.

For the first known writings to survive on the isles we know as British come from the northern mainland, there in those icy regions bordering on the North Sea and the Baltic. When the great Roman Empire was crumbling in the south (5th century), these northern peoples were passing through a Heroic Age* of their own, comparable to that of ancient Greece about which Homer wrote. Like the Greeks, these warriors were seafaring peoples and lived their adventurous and primitive existence mid storm and strife, fearing neither elements nor man. Their fears came largely from their deeply ingrained superstitions, creating for them monsters and horrible shapes that could hardly be coped with by the strength and the weapons of mere mortals. The men among them who were able to meet these monsters and live became the epic* heroes and the subjects for their outstanding literary efforts.

It was during the long winter season of ice-locked harbors that these hardy mariners relived their battles and wanderings. There in the halls of the warriors, the *scops* (poets) shaped the adventures of the season into song and the *gleemen* (minstrels)

recited them to the assembled tribesmen and carried them far
and wide into the halls of other friendly groups.

### Anglo-Saxon becomes the language of England

In seeking the earliest writings of English literature we must
look to these Germanic tribes who began to migrate into the
British Isles as early as the fourth century. We possess no
literary works from the early Britons nor from the Roman occu-
pation of the isles. Within a century and a half after the first
migrations, the Angles, the Saxons, and the Jutes had established
themselves as masters of Britain. Aside from Danish invasions
and some settlements in the north of England, the year 900
found most of the petty strife and local bickering completed and
the Anglo-Saxons had established a basic language and culture
that were to provide the predominant factors in the future literary
development of the English race. By this time the land had
become an integrated nation.

### Christianity conquers the Norse gods

During the first years the Germanic tribes kept alive their
warrior traditions and their fierce love of glory and independence
never died out. But Christianity proved more influential than
their fierce warrior gods of the northland. The native Britons
knew Christianity from the Romans before the fourth century
and the faith persisted as a weak thread, being kept alive largely
through the zeal of Irish missionaries. England was therefore
a fertile ground for Augustine when he came directly from Rome
in 597 to establish the Church in England. The naming of
Theodore as Archibishop of Canterbury in 668 marked a definite
triumph in England over Woden, Thor, and the other deities of
the heroic mold.

## MEDIEVAL LITERATURE

The year 1400 roughly marks the end of the medieval* literary
period for England. This date, again, roughly marks a midway
point from the first writings we may call literature to the present
time. Prior to 1400 the originals of writings in England are
hardly readable to us, except through the translation or adaptations of specialists in the ancient languages: Latin, Anglo-Saxon,
Anglo-French (Norman), and Middle English. The literature

of these early periods is neither modern in spirit nor in language. We shall dwell here only on a few of the highlights of the Old English Period (to 1100) and the Middle English Period (1100-1500) and devote two entire chapters to the transition age of Chaucer (who died in 1400), the man who led English letters into the streams of the Italian and French Renaissance* developments and pointed the way into the great modern English periods.

## THE OLD ENGLISH PERIOD (to 1100)

### Anglo-Saxon Writings

The Angles and the Saxons brought their songs and their *scops* to England. It soon became the concern of Christian priests to rework these heroic poems to remove the pagan deities and replace them with Christian references and to tone down the bloodthirsty spirit of the originals. Three such early heroic, or folk, epics survive only as fragments: *Widsith, The Fight at Finnsburg,* and *Waldere.*

*Widsith* is a wandering *scop* who speaks of the lands and peoples he has visited. Either the poem is a composite of several songs or Widsith speaks with tongue in cheek, for he claims personal acquaintance with kings who lived centuries apart. His travels took him into all parts of the known world. He closes with praise of the minstrels' art and assures his audience that a singer can find friends and benefactors in every clime.

*Waldere* remains in two fragments. The first relates how Waldere's sweetheart encourages and prepares him for battle with Guthhere. She assures him that he will either lose his life or gain lasting glory and she has no doubt he will come through victorious as in other battles he has fought.

The second fragment occurs apparently just before the fight. Guthhere praises Waldere's sword. Waldere boasts of his prowess and the fragment ends as he assures Guthhere that victory will fall to him as he is ready, resolute, righteous, and trusts to God for favor.

*The Fight at Finnsburg* fragment begins at a spot where the young king of the Finns awakens his warriors to the realization that their hall is burning and that the Frisians are attacking. They fight for five days and slay many Frisians. At last their leader is slain.

## Beowulf

The great Anglo-Saxon epic poem is Beowulf (195). It is the only surviving full-length heroic poem of the Old English Period. It was composed in the 8th century and was left to us in a manuscript written about 1100. The material for the poem lies in the Heroic Age of the Germanic peoples on the continent and is "national," in an English sense, because it represents the primitive traditions and customs of the ancestors of all these northern seafaring tribes from which the Angles, the Saxons, and the Jutes sprang. The poem, in fact, treats only of Danes, Swedes, and a mystery tribe, the Geats.

We have somewhat over 3,000 lines of the poem, probably a composite of various songs of the *scops* and *gleemen* of the 6th century or before, and it is likely that somewhat unrelated events have been brought together in the version which comes down to us. It is certain that the later composer has Christianized most of the supernatural references and has softened the bloody overtones of the original poems. The poetry is crude and clumsy but has the primitive charm of all early folk literature. We may read it today in a modern English translation and relive in spirit the crude existence of these hardy northern warriors, feel the lonely and damp atmosphere of the tossing seas, the misty, frozen woods, and desolate moors. We may cheer ourselves in the mead halls before the roaring fire and thrill to the tale of the mighty Beowulf and how he helped to bring peace to the land by slaying the monsters that provided a constant threat to the safety of its inhabitants. As we follow this high adventure in a distant and misty, but very real, world of the past, we can forget the rude and naïve artistry of the poem, the rough and graceless monosyllabic verse and think only of the vigor and charm, the simplicity, and fine emotional perception of those ancient warrior poets.

### Late examples of the heroic tradition

We know that the warrior tradition does not end with *Beowulf* among the Anglo-Saxons of England, for we have two fragments from heroic poems of the tenth century, written in the old epic tradition, but referring to events that took place in a more settled and peaceful Anglo-Saxon England. One is _The Battle of Brunanburh,_ celebrating the victory of Anglo-Saxon King Athelstan over the Danish Norsemen and Scots in 937. The other fragment, *The Battle of Malden,* relates a defeat of the English forces by a force of invading Danes in 991. Undoubtedly, many other poems circulated among our Germanic English ancestors in this heroic tradition and it is possible that other manuscripts from this early period may yet be unearthed.

## The Lyric Verse of the Anglo-Saxons

We have some examples, also, of a verse that is more personal, more of an expression of the emotional state of the poet, in this early Anglo-Saxon period. The lyric* poetry of these people reflects a melancholy view of life, a sense of impending fate and threatening nature. Here we find little of the hope that lies in thoughts of a Hereafter. A very early example of this primitive lyric is *Deor's Lament.* As in *Widsith,* the *scop* speaks directly to the hearer (or reader). He is sad. He has been robbed of his inheritance and the favor of his lord by Heorrenda, who has replaced him as the chief court singer. But, as he says, all misfortune passes, and he cites the sorrows caused by love and violence in the lives of other men, and how these things passed. He reflects upon the fact that Our Lord can make the sorrowful happy and can bring the haughty to low estate.

Thus the lyric grew side by side with the epic in the cultural life of those early Englishmen. Each was crude and each contained some of the elements of the other. And when the Angles and the Saxons came to England, they brought the brooding sadness of lonely and wandering northern peoples that was to appear and reappear in the English elegy* throughout the centuries.

In *The Wanderer,* we meet a homeless man whose life is that of an exile, condemned by fate to plough the friendless waves and seek the companionship of the screaming sea birds. Not for him are the comforts of the mead hall and the protection of a king. He recalls his old life of cheer and happiness and how all that fell about him in ruin. Life is like that on this earth where man is a toy for fate to toss about. All earthly things are transitory and fleeting.

In *The Seafarer,* probably of the early 8th century, an old and weary sailor confronts a young man, enthusiastic but ignorant of the trials and tribulations that this hard life upon the sea brings to a man. The old salt curses the sea in one breath, and in the next reveals his love for and feeling of inseparability with it. When at sea he longs for the comforts of land, and when ashore, neither the love of woman nor the lure of the pleasures of the world can satisfy his deep longing to be back upon the rolling waves. Back to the whale road for him and let others have their lives of ease upon the shore!

In a very fragmentary poem, _The Ruin,_ the poet looks upon the ruined buildings of an ancient race and wonders at the pride these men must have felt in their great accomplishments and how little they dreamed then that he would look upon these stones that can no longer even give any identifying characteristics of what their owners were like.

### The Priest and Early Writings

The influence of the priest is evident in all the writings of this early period in England's literary history. It was the priest who wrote and transcribed all the works that have reached us. He considered it his duty to tamper with all matters that were pagan and not in keeping with Christian ideals. Thus a pagan hero, such as Beowulf, is presented to us with a rather hybrid appearance. He reveals the priest's sympathy with an heroic tradition and the supernatural monsters with which the men of fate had to contend, but he refuses to allow the manuscripts to pass through his hands without the interpolation of pious sentiments. The hero must not only be brave; he must be righteous and fight in the name of the Christian Deity.

A good deal of early prose survives from these clerics and all of it is in Latin. Little of this writing would have interest today for other than specialists in medieval history. Outside of the purely theological treatises of the early centuries, this prose consists of history and chronicle.*

### Bede's Ecclesiastical History

The Venerable Bede is the best known of these early Church scholars. He wrote many books on religious matters in Latin. Bede was a careful student and a fountainhead of the knowledge of his times, and he wrote prolifically. From a literary standpoint, he is best known to us through passages from his _Ecclesiastical History of the English People_. It is from this book that we are able to know of the first Christian poet of England: Caedmon. According to Bede, Caedmon was an unlettered cowherd who received divine inspiration to sing of the

Creation and to turn the Old Testament into song. He has been credited by some critics with a number of poems paraphrasing biblical passages. Following in the tradition of the great Caedmon, other anonymous poets have left us poems and fragments of poems from the period, rendering various Old Testament passages into verse.

The first identifiable Christian poet is Cynewulf, who died about 783. Cynewulf, like Caedmon, is steeped in the tradition of the *scop* and applies his art toward the creation of a Christian epic in Old English. Both Caedmon and Cynewulf are shadowy figures at the best and we do not know positively what compositions of the period were actually written by them. But their names are convenient designations for the two successive schools of religious poets, the one active from about 675 and the other lasting until well into the 9th century.

### Early Christian "epics"

These Christian poems are of little interest to the average reader today but many of them have passages with power and grace. They also offer us a curious treatment of biblical personages, Christ being pictured, for instance, as a hero of the stature of a Beowulf. These cloistered poets retained much of the spirit of the *scop* and the *gleeman* and their poems are truly heroic epics, using personages taken from the Christian Bible. One of the most lyrical and imaginative of these religious poems is *The Dream of the Rood* (Cross) (198), from the Cynewulf cycle.

### Miscellaneous Anglo-Saxon Verse

Many of the important anonymous poems of the late Old English Period are conserved in what we know as the Exeter Book, a manuscript collection of the tenth century. *Widsith, Deor's Lament,* and *The Ruin* are to be found there.

In this collection are many riddles in which objects are described in vague and suggestive terms, the objects to be guessed by the reader. Many references to life and customs of the Viking northland are to be discovered among these interesting little compositions. A horn is described as a proud warrior when decked in gems and trappings. Here it travels with the tribe over the seas and there it hangs on the mead-house wall. Sometimes it is full of wine. Sometimes it must swallow the breath of men and invite valiant warriors to assemble or drive away enemies. The description ends with the inevitable: "Ask what my name is."

### Old English lyric poetry

In addition to the riddles, groups of fragments of heroic poetry and other short verse, including remarkable examples of gnomic* poetry, we are indebted to the Exeter Book for our first examples of the love lyric in English literature.

_The Wife's Lament_ is a rather subtle piece in which the wife has been accused by her husband's relatives of infidelity or magic. The husband is forced by the tribal code to banish her to a lonely spot in the woods. She knows that he must be grieving for her and, as she, remembering their once happy home together. She still loves him and thinks that he, even though he thinks her guilty, must still love her. That would make his grief far greater than her own, for she remains firm in her protests that she was faithful to him and has a clear conscience.

_The Husband's Message_ is carved in runes* on a wooden staff and these runes speak the message. This rune stick has carried many a message over the seas to highborn people. Now it brings a message of love from a man exiled from his people and from his beloved wife. It begs her to listen for the coming of springtime in the song of the cuckoo and come to him in a distant land where he has established himself, mid wealth and prosperity, and has many brave warriors who serve him. He cares not for kings' daughters; life is empty for him without his beloved wife.

### Alfred the Great and Old English Prose

We have noted that a great deal of prose was written during the early centuries in Latin. The Anglo-Saxon priests continued this tradition throughout the entire period generally. Most of their prolific work consists of scholarly writing, devoted principally to theology and history. The Venerable Bede produced for us the first of the great historical writings of English scholarship in his _Ecclesiastical History of the English People_ (731). Bede's contributions to didactic writing in Latin is the most notable on the Old English scene until King Alfred came to the throne of Wessex in 871.

### Early European humanism

Alfred devoted his life to two purposes: securing the nation from Danish invasion and internecine strife, and the promotion of scholarship and literature and the establishment of an educational program for his people. Though a frail man, he made great strides forward in both his aims. Alfred learned Latin, but principally in order to be able to translate the great Latin works into West Saxon. He is England's first great humanist and is to be compared with Alfonso the Wise of Castile (mid-13th century), both men representing isolated pockets of genuine humanism* during the long medieval period of intellectual slumber in Europe before the Italian Renaissance.

Alfred himself laboriously translated Boethius' *Consolation of Philosophy,* Gregory's *Pastoral Care,* Orosius' *Universal History,* and Bede's *Ecclesiastical History,* our first monument of English prose (realizing of course that, in a strict sense, literature does not begin in what resembles modern English until the age of Chaucer). In addition to his translations, Alfred's influence is felt in many other directions. He stimulated research and urged the priests of his kingdom to teach the vernacular. He encouraged the keeping of the *Anglo-Saxon Chronicle* and saw to it that the events of his reign were given proper attention in this running record of events which was kept well into the 12th century. Alfred also did much to preserve the oral traditions of his people. He left a book of proverbs and we have record of a *Handbook,* a treasury of his wisdom which has been lost.

### Aelfric and Wulfstan

Others attempted to continue the stimulus toward the creation of a native literature of vitality. Aelfric is one notable name with his *Homilies* and his *Colloquy on the Occupations,* and Wulfstan, with equally didactic* and uninviting treatises, are among those who tried to carry on the work of Alfred. We have noted a resurgence of the epic tradition during this late period. But the language was changing and the Anglo-Saxon rugged heroic and narrowly restricted tradition was grinding to a halt. A period of decadence had set in and there was nothing in prospect to enliven either the stimulus toward a great literature of varied themes and forms or toward the refinements of a great society. The fragment of *The Battle of Malden* (991) is the last gasp of a dying Anglo-Saxon warrior tradition in poetry.

## THE MIDDLE ENGLISH PERIOD TO CHAUCER
## (1100-1340)

### The Invasion from Normandy

The restless Viking Danes, repulsed in their efforts to consolidate permanent gains in England, turned their roving eyes once more upon the continent and took possession of that northern peninsula of France, jutting far out into the English Channel, afterwards known as Normandy. The Norsemen, with the heroic traditions of the hardy northland, showed a remarkable aptitude for assimilating the more refined culture of their southern neighbors, the French. They were barbarians with a strong will to become civilized, and within a century had become thoroughly French without losing their heroic and daring spirit. They possessed all the harmonious characteristics of a people schooled in Spartan bravery and unsoftened by their love of beauty and refined living. They were coolly practical and sensually artistic; they were a rare thing in the world's history, a race of cultured warriors. They had acquired what the Anglo-Saxons lacked: a spirit of romance.

### *England enters a European cultural stream*

In 1002 a Norman-Anglo-Saxon marriage alliance started a series of interrerlationships that eventually led William of Normandy to invade England to press his claim to the kingship. History records how successful was this invasion. Within a very brief period, a new civilization overlaid the Anglo-Saxon beginnings and England had entered the vital stream of southern European medieval culture in other than a purely theological and scientific sense. But the salutary effects of the coming together of the rugged and heroic simplicity of the Anglo-Saxon poetry and the more refined poetic form and the pageantry and gay color of the Norman importations were to lie dormant for almost three centuries while the conflicting and repressive elements of linguistic confusion and a feudalistic society worked themselves out. But the two elements were present, and although they appeared together rarely, never decayed, but awaited the opportune conditions which would allow them to blossom together into a great modern literature.

### Anglo-Norman Life

For three centuries after the decisive Battle of Hastings in 1066, the Norman-French descendants of the Viking Danes controlled England, and French was the official language. A thoroughly French system of feudalism settled over the land. The castles of the Norman overlords rose to dominate the landscape in every direction. It would seem that Anglo-Saxon civilization was dead.

For a century and a half after the conquest, French was the language of literature, of the government and the military, the law courts, and the church. Latin continued to be cultivated along with French, especially in literature and in the church. French became a symbol of refinement and fine living even for the upper classes among Englishmen. But the huge mass of stubborn Anglo-Saxons continued to be faithful to its language. True, its speech was exposed to many systems and practices unknown before in that rude environment. Many French terms entered the Old English speech. When this language again dominated the land, after 1200, it was no longer the Old English of Alfred's day. It was a new English, but hardly yet modern English. It was a fusion of the strongest elements of both tongues, Norman French and Anglo-Saxon, which we call Middle English. But the fusion was a loose one for another century and more. It needed the pen of a strong literary genius to weld it into a form which could serve as a model for future ages of English-speaking peoples. This man was not born until 1340: Geoffrey Chaucer.

The Norman-dominated society was a system of strict feudalism. The King owned the land and distributed it in parcels to the nobles. This distribution continued in lesser parcels to lesser lords. Each lord owed allegiance, paid taxes, and provided men for military service to the overlord above him, and all paid homage to the King.

### *Rise of the feudal Church*

Side by side with the feudal state rose the powerful feudal Church. The King owed allegiance to the Pope. The Pope was thus the overlord of all spheres of Middle Age society in England. The Church developed its own system of allegiances and tribute, on much the same pattern as the state. Church and State authority clashed at times, but by and large, the Church dominated the thoughts and the actions of all men since it spoke with divine authority, and pressure was strong on all sides to force men to heed its admonitions to consider this life but as a severe proving ground in preparation of one's soul for Judgment Day. Only those who had obeyed blindly the Church authorities and suffered would be worthy of the blessings of the hereafter.

The tight feudal system gave way slowly before the growth of trade and industry and before the pressures of stubborn and persistent men who wanted to be free. But it was well into the fourteenth century before the industrial middle class had grown to sufficient strength to impose a spirit of nationalism that would cause the system of feudalism to crumble and yield before a modern atmosphere of individual freedom and national self-respect.

### The Literature of the Norman-French

All the writings of the early years of the conquest were in French or Latin. It was a branch of French literature, brought to England and nourished there for 150 years, to the virtual exclusion of native forms. It is true that the *Anglo-Saxon Chronicle* was continued in Old English and a few priests kept alive the memory of Alfred and the *scop* of the past. But until the reign of Henry IV (1399), the language of the kings of England was French, and the literature, aside from being written in that language, was a courtly and aristocratic literature. On the semididactic side, many fables and religious tales were produced, as well as a few examples of the particularly French *fabliaux*.* Didactic literature is strong, particularly the excellent histories (in French and Latin) which are of unique interest to specialists in historiography.

### From Epic to Romance*

French epic poetry was imported with the first groups of Normans. *The Song of Roland (Chanson de Roland)* was sung at the Battle of Hastings, and the oldest manuscript we possess today of this chief French epic poem was written in England. During the period following the conquest there was considerable traffic back and forth across the channel of these epic themes, some being written in France and others in England. Occasional English imitations of French themes are the only surviving manuscripts today. Notable French writers of the period did a portion of their writings in England, outstanding among whom is Marie de France.

During the early period the epic warrior was undergoing a transformation on the continent. He was becoming a champion of Christianity against the infidel, largely as a result of the Crusades. This new epic hero, the medieval knight, had his softer side also. He had become a lover and begins to perform his deeds for the sake of his lady love. So, gradually, the purpose for the existence of a folk hero takes on a new light. No longer is he out to rid his people of threats from monsters, nor to serve as the supreme embodiment of their national spirit. Now he seeks adventure for its own sake and to prove his personal prowess. The new epic form, the metrical romance,* becomes a rambling tale of adventure, in which robbers, giants, dwarfs, magicians, and fierce beasts are overthrown for the simple sake of adventure, for a damsel in distress, or for a holy Christian cause. The three interests, then, of the romance of chivalry during the Middle Ages were knightly bravery, idealized love, and religious motivation. The metrical romances, being so closely associated with the noble and the luxury-loving priest, and the leisure provided by the long period of comparative peace to develop fine living in the feudal castles, display a wide range of imaginative effects. They are highly colorful and full of pageantry. The supernatural enters the themes in varying and extravagant forms. The influence of the Provençal troubadours and their lyrics is strong, especially in the glorification of mortal woman, as symbolic of the Virgin Mary.

## The "Matters" of medieval romance

The romances have been classified as to three themes, or "matters." The _Matter of France_ concerns Charlemagne and his followers, some real, some imaginary. These, of course, are the most akin in spirit and purpose to the heroic folk epic. The _Matter of Greece and Rome_ was a cycle of tales based upon the medieval concept of the ancient real and mythological heroes of antiquity.

Of the early French "matters," the one of most concern to students of English Literature is the _Matter of Britain_. These poems are French and concern themes which originate on the continent, chiefly in the peninsula of France, adjoining Normandy to the south, known as Brittany (Bretagne). In Brittany many legends had been accumulating concerning a King Arthur and his knights (203). Arthur presumably lived in the person of an ancient king of the Britons who gave battle to the early Saxons, but the Arthur of the romances is legend.

Geoffrey of Monmouth (mid-12th century), in his Latin chronicle called *History of the Kings of Britain,* records the supposed deeds of this ruler and includes several stories about him and his Knights of the Round Table. This chronicle was translated into French and formed the basis for many romances about Arthur, his queen Guinevere, the magician Merlin, and his knights: famous among whom are Launcelot, Tristram, Ywain, Perceval, and many others. Thus, although the stories of King Arthur are French in origin, much of the legend is based upon English sources. And we shall find adaptations, translations, and imitations of the Arthurian cycle of romances throughout the course of English Literature. To English readers, the Knights of Arthur's Round Table are the best known of all the heroes of European romance.

## THE RETURN OF ENGLISH TO LITERATURE

### The English Metrical Romance

A fourth "matter," the *Matter of England,* concerns early Germanic figures (such as *Havelock the Dane, King Horn),* and these romances in Middle English are more in the tradition of the *scop.* The later poems of this cycle (such as *Guy of Warwick, Beves of Hampton)* concern heroes of England.

It is thought by some critics that these poems may be simply late adaptations of much earlier Anglo-Saxon poems or songs of the type of *The Battle of Maldon.* Others consider them to be mostly adaptations of French originals, created as romances for the "common man," tending to appeal to the taste of the Anglo-Saxon vassals rather than to the Norman overlords. And it is true that, in spite of many of the rugged characteristics present that remind one of the poems of the *scop* of Anglo-Saxon England, these Middle English alliterative romances reveal that all the elements of a code of French chivalry have been adopted, even when dealing with ancient continental Germanic settings.

### *Layamon's Brut*

The first writer of romance in Middle English was Layamon, who opens the English cycle with *Brut,* written about 1200. *Brut* is, in reality, a verse chronicle and devotes the first 2000 lines to developing the "matter" of antiquity. When it does bring its narrative to English soil, a great deal of space is given to Arthur, and particularly to the founding of the Round Table.

Many of the rude English romances of the 13th and early 14th centuries are free renditions of French originals and touch upon all the French "matters." It was not until 1375 that the *Matter of England* produced its masterpiece in one of the most provocatively charming of all European romances: *Sir Gawain and the Green Knight*.

## The Medieval Cleric and Literature

Without taking into consideration the heavier types of theological and historical writing done by clerics in Middle English and Latin, there is a great deal of light moralistic writing of a popular vein to be found during the period. These usually short pieces, in prose or in verse, take the form of homilies, proverbs, fables, tales, dialogues, debates, etc. They are composed by men of the Church and directed toward the common people of the time. They have turned up in various manuscript collections in all Christian countries during the Middle Ages. The following are interesting examples of these narratives with a moral purpose:

1. A *Bestiary*\* of the early thirteenth century contains many little descriptions of the customs and habits of animals, to which are appended *significations,* crude allegorical connections between the habits described and some phase of Church doctrine.

In one such item the elephant is described as being large and powerful. Though powerful, these elephant children must be careful of falling, lest they drown in water in attempting to raise their huge bulk again to standing position. The hunter, knowing the elephant leans against trees to rest and scratch, digs a pit and places a false tree beside it. The elephant leans against the tree and falls into the trap. Mother elephant comes trumpeting along and lifts out her big baby with her powerful trunk. Thus Adam fell because of a tree, and Christ, the Heavenly King, raised him up again to an erect state, now humbled and grateful.

2. A very popular device, employed by churchmen to drive home their truths, was the debate or dialogue in which one speaker represents a worldly point of view and the other a moral and otherworldly viewpoint. A notable Middle English debate is the one called *The Debate of the Body and the Soul*, written about mid-13th century. A man lies dead and is destined for Hell. The burning question is the fixing of the responsibility for

the man's awkward position. Quite to be expected, the body
brings forth much the weaker arguments in attempting to fix
blame upon the soul.

3. Other dialogue poems merely argued philosophic questions
of interest and quite often the debate ended without positive
conclusions. The outstanding example of this kind from this
period is _The Owl and the Nightingale_. The form is epic, with
the poet relating what he has overheard between the two birds.
The nightingale starts the quarrel and soon heated speeches fly
back and forth. The arguments bring out the age old conflict
between youth, beauty, brilliancy, and color, on the one hand,
and severity, gloom, and old age on the other. In short, lives of
pleasure and asceticism are compared.

The poet perhaps had real individuals in mind, or perhaps he
was comparing the pleasure-loving nobility with the humble
clerics. If such motives are accepted, this poem could be called
an early satire.*

## Medieval English Drama

Traces of the dramatic may be observed well back into the
Anglo-Saxon period but these could scarcely be called plays in
any modern sense. The story of the real beginnings of a European drama, independent of any connection with the great
dramas of the Greeks and the Romans, must begin in the
Medieval Church. It was here that priests felt the need of giving
life to the Bible for their humble and uneducated parishioners,
especially on certain occasions, such as Easter and Christmas.
All European literatures have left us traces, more or less intact
dramatic units, of the great mass of liturgical drama* that
existed during the Middle Ages. Various countries apply various
terms to these church plays, but the result is the same with
minor distinctions: a little playlet depicting dramatic episodes
from the Bible or enlarging upon the characters of biblical personages, each play having a dramatic structure, a plot, with the
element of conflict more or less pronounced.

### The Miracle Play

In England these little religious plays of the Church have
received the name *miracle* plays* (see also *mystery* play*). As
the liturgical drama became more popular and appealed to wider
audiences, the Church yielded gradually to pressures toward the
inclusion of more and more secular elements. And, as might be

expected, this secularization tended to get out of hand. Elements of burlesque, mockery, and derision intermingled themselves with biblical themes, and comic and vulgar-speaking individuals mingled on the crude stages with divine personages. The industrial guilds and other groups delighted in providing their audiences with periodic entertainments of a mixed secular and religious nature. The marketplaces and public squares replaced the churches as stages. Frequently the public stage was the bed of a large wagon. The secular writers vied with each other for the applause of the crowd.

Throughout Christendom the Church imposed severe restrictions and prohibitions against this sort of secularization during the Middle Ages, but it seems the tide could not be entirely stemmed. In part, liturgical drama had become entertainment for an uneducated mob.

### The Morality Play

The *morality* play* came into being in the 15th century as a result of the increased use of allegory* in medieval teaching (conducted almost always by the clergy and in Church schools). Here the characters become moral abstractions rather than real personages. Various vices contend with virtues for the possession of the soul of man. The morality play gradually became more realistic, historical, and even political. The morality play displayed a somewhat higher type of realism than the comic and vulgar realism which characterized many secular miracle plays. It is a long step from the medieval morality play to modern symbolism in drama, but much of the significance of this crude beginning lies in its effects upon the later development of English drama. In itself, the morality play (and the liturgical drama in general) did not outlast the Middle Ages in England. The Spanish version of the miracle or mystery play *(auto sacramental),* for contrast, enjoyed great popularity as late as the early 17th century.

We know of the existence of specific miracle plays in the early period of the Norman conquest, written in French or Latin. Of the Middle English form, we have many fragments and four cycles, played by trade guilds in several towns of England, totaling more than 100 examples. Critics agree generally that the finest examples of the miracle play and the morality play, respectively, are: _The Second Shepherds' Play_ (199), dating from the late fourteenth or early fifteenth century, and _Everyman_

(201), late 15th century. All the miracle and morality plays are anonymous.

## The Verse of the People

It is always delightful to contemplate a light and fluffy dessert after the heavier courses of meat. It is fitting that this discussion of the beginnings of the modern world's greatest literature should end with fare that is meant to give nothing but simple delight and uncomplicated pleasure: the lyric verse and the ballads* of the common people of the medieval ages in England.

This early poetry cannot be dated and no authorship may be claimed for particular selections. It comes from oral tradition, and like Topsy, it just grew from unknown original forms to those which we have recorded for us. Some of this verse dates from as early as mid-12th century, such as the *"Cuckoo Song,"* which every student has encountered in his public school anthologies. These lyrics and ballads were sung by wandering minstrels of the people and hummed by churls, vassals, and guild members throughout the period of feudalism. The noble usually considered them common and unworthy of his notice. He took delight in more subtle fare provided by the metrical romance. Most of this folk verse changed in form and content through the years, and ofttimes a single ballad has been preserved in a variety of forms. It is likely that centuries passed before many of the thousands of these little poems were recorded. Sometimes, undoubtedly, they were changed and set to music by the collectors. They reached written form mostly in the Renaissance days when the humanists and cultured poets began to appreciate their beauty and value in preserving the total culture of an age gone by. And many of the later poets came to be innoculated with the spirit of bygone folk simplicity and beauty to the extent of incorporating the oral forms artistically in the composition of their more refined verse. But, however many alterations they may have suffered in the process of transmission and recording, they still inspire in us a common sympathy and appreciation of a fine sense of simple artistry that never died out entirely in the Anglo-Saxon during his centuries of feudal subservience.

### *Famed European Ballad literatures*

The popular ballad in the British Isles is one of the most extensive bodies of folk song in the world of literatures. In the Western World, only the literatures of Spain and Germany can claim a similar richness. In England (since we cannot here be concerned with the Irish, the Scots, and the Welsh), the ballad, a simple narrative poem with lyric qualities, covers subjects which range throughout the daily lives of the people, their hopes, their fears, and their tragedies. The ballad was an oral newspaper of actual events. And it told of the epic heroes of a nonwarrior and domesticated folk, the chief of whom in English balladry is a figure who has been well known to every English-speaking child in all of the modern ages. He lives and will continue to live in our imaginations. He was perhaps a man; perhaps his life was simply a creation of the sublimated ambitions of a hard working and poorly compensated Anglo-Saxon people. His name is Robin Hood, of course (203).

> Come listen to me, you gallants so free,
>   All you that loves mirth for to hear,
> And I will tell of a bold outlaw,
>   That lived in Nottinghamshire. . . .

And if one's predilection lies in areas other than the lawless life of Robin's merry band in the green forests of Sherwood, can he say that he might not be tempted to sign on for a voyage with Sir Patrick Spens?

> The king sits in Dunfermline toune
>   Drinking the blude-red wine:
> "Oh whar will I get guid sailor,
>   To sail this schip of mine?"

> Up and spak an eldern knicht,
>   Sat at the king's richt kne:
> "Sir Patrick Spens is the best sailor
>   That sails upon the se . . ."

### The Provençal influence in England

The new Anglo-Saxon poet and minstrel, whatever had been his *scop's* tradition for ruggedness and adventure in the cold and dank forests and on the high tossing waves of the northland, had come to consider himself one with the color and springtime of the English countryside. He has left us many examples where he had learned to express his emotions in lyric poetry, as light and musical as any age of literature has produced. He had inherited much of the pagan philosophy that would blossom full blown in the Renaissance English lyric, a heritage which had come to him from the Provençal school of François Villon in southern France. His Norman cousins had given him something of their love of refined living.

> Cast aside dull books and thought;
>> Sweet is folly, sweet is play:
> Take the pleasure Spring hath brought
>> In youth's opening holiday!
> Right it is old age should ponder
>> On grave matters fraught with care;
> Tender youth is free to wander,
>> Free to frolic light as air.
>>> Like a dream our prime is flown,
>>> Prisoned in a study:
>>> Sport and folly are youth's own,
>>>> Tender youth and ruddy.
>>>>> (Trans. by J. A. Symonds, London, 1884.)

# Chapter II

# THE AGE OF CHAUCER
# (14th Century)

The 14th century was one of great promise for the future of English letters. It produced the greatest English writer before Shakespeare, Geoffrey Chaucer (1340-1400), the figure who towers above all others in English Middle Age culture. But Chaucer's surroundings and contemporaries deserve no little attention for, although well below him, three other literary figures stand higher than all else that the medieval period had produced: The Pearl Poet, William Langland, and John Wyclif.

This century demonstrated that the Anglo-Saxon had conserved intact his heritage from his heroic ancestors and had profited by his forced exposure to the Norman-French refinements in form and colorful content. This chapter will consider that assimilation of culture and the men who prove that the fusion had taken place. Chaucer himself we shall consider in a separate chapter, since he stands alone in greatness and provides the vital link in language and in the assimilation of ancient culture between the medieval and modern times in English literature.

## Historical and Cultural Notes

The century was a turbulent one in the political and economic arenas. The Hundred Years' War (1337-1453), largely prompted by commercial rivalry between France and England, resulted in a series of sea and land engagements between the two countries during the entire age. Victory now rested with the English; now with the French. France won the final battle. Despite the domestic disruptions, the total results of the war strengthened England as a national state, promoted the growth of large population centers and manufacturing, and hastened the end of feudalism.

The plague, or Black Death, swept Europe during the century and reduced entire populations drastically. The effects of the dread Oriental disease upon England was to further the reduction of the population and help kill feudalism as a system. Labor became scarce and guilds gained in power. Rebellions of workers forced several liberal reforms and raised the living standard of the peasant.

A despotic king, Richard II, only added to the turmoil. Riots and all forms of social upheaval were normal everyday occurrences throughout the age. The clergy had become dissolute and the Church had lost a good deal of prestige and power in England. The Pope was accused of conniving with the king of France for political power and the individual churchmen were considered corrupt. There was open rebellion against rigid Church doctrine by John Wyclif, who headed a group known as Lollards in a move for religious freedom. The seeds for a future split with the Church of Rome were being sown in England.

### *A struggle to cast off feudalism*

The age was one of the realistic outlook. It was an age of indecision and confusion; it was also an age of color and action. The old order was bending, but it had not broken. England was still laced into a medieval framework, but it was a structure that was groaning at every seam. Preoccupation with today and this life showed through a crumbling orthodoxy that had for so long preached and enforced a renunciation of the interests of this life on earth. People demanded a bit of enjoyment with their suffering. It was a vigorous age that showed at every step that it was not yet a time to break completely with the past.

English literature advanced as it never had before and demonstrated flashes of genius, none of which was surrounded by a spirit sufficiently dedicated to change to take full advantage of it. Another century was to pass before England matured culturally to the point of realizing that this 14th century had brought its literature into the light and had provided the materials which, though they lay unheeded, could be used as tools by men of genius to shape a truly great body of writings in an English mold.

### Three Principal Contemporaries of Chaucer

Aside from the great contribution of its major writer, the 14th century produced three literary figures of sufficient stature to give this age lasting importance:

1. _The Pearl Poet_. A manuscript of about 1390 contains four poems that show a refinement not yet seen in Middle English verse. The unknown poet, who produced his masterpieces around 1370, is known to us by the subject matter of the first of his poems, called _The Pearl_. One of the finest elegies in English poetry, this long alliterative* lyric poem tells of the father who comes to mourn at the grave of his little daughter, "precious pearl without spot." While there, he sees a vision of her in Paradise. She is grown to maidenhood and (as Beatrice led Dante by the hand in _The Divine Comedy_) she shows her father about Heaven and gradually causes him to lose his grief and become filled with hope. Struggling to follow her further, the father plunges into a stream to reach her—and wakes from his dream, still beside the child's grave. This poem gives English literature its first great elegy.

Two other poems of the Pearl Poet are _Patience_ and _Purity_. These are little homilies in a colorful and glowing verse on the two virtues represented by their names. They deal with various biblical events such as the Deluge and Jonah, the Fall of Man, and urge the reader toward redemption through Christ and the Virgin. The Pearl Poet, however, is much more than merely didactic. He teaches, but does it with a warmth and vitality that the religious poem had not known in previous ages.

The Pearl Poet gives us the masterpiece in the long tradition of metrical romance: _Sir Gawain and the Green Knight_ (209). This long poem is divided into four _fyttes_ (cantos, sections), and employs alliterative long lines combined with short quatrains.* Sir Gawain, of course, is no new figure to literature. His adventures were told in many of the early Norman-French romances of the heroes of Celtic legend.

Here our poet retells a single adventure of the legendary knight and it is his manner of telling it that makes this one of the best of all European romances. Aside from his deftness in handling the monotonous alliteration he introduces beautiful lyric descriptions of nature, humorous episodes, picturesque descriptions of customs of the lords and ladies of the ages of chivalry. Interspersed with his light lyricism are dramatically powerful and fast-moving passages of high adventure and knightly daring. And, aside from the color and pageantry, there is an all-pervading atmosphere of the mystical. It is a moral poem but its moralizing is unobtrusive and hardly noticeable to the reader. It is a fitting climax to the English contribution to the "matters" of the romantic epic of courtly verse. It is a contribution, equal in depth and beauty to the best of the French and German poems, and a poem which will whirl the modern reader, despite himself, through an age of fascination—a world where knighthood was in flower.

2. William Langland gives us *Piers the Plowman,* one of the most important of the contributions of all Western literatures of the Middle Ages. The author is a man whose name has been a subject of literary controversy. But, whether the poem is by Langland or another, or assembled from the efforts of more than one creator, *Piers Plowman* is a great poem and one that was widely influential in its own age. We have forty-seven manuscripts of the poem before the time of the printing press.

### England's greatest early allegory

*Piers Plowman* is a satire which takes the form of allegory. Piers (or Peter) is a plowman in truth, who is the leading figure of a series of visions by the author. By means of these insights into the activities of Piers, the author strives to reveal to us the evils of this world and to teach the road that leads to truth and betterment. All the corruptions of the State and society are held up to view in this series of visions.

The poet, one William, "in a somer sesun, when softe was the sonne," lies down to rest and dreams that all society passes in review before him. All professions and callings reveal themselves to be self-seeking and dishonest. In a second vision, when men beg for a way of knowing the truth, Piers steps forth and offers to show them the way to avoid the Seven Deadly Sins. He points out what each person should do to rectify his own life. Piers, concerned with his plowing, nevertheless takes time out from honest labor to deliver many honest truths about the hollowness of his age, the falsity and hypocrisy of his society and Church.

Piers is a very earthy preacher of salvation. The way out of sin for the individual is a gospel of work. His is the evangelism of the poor and humble priest, intent upon the helping of mankind to help itself. In the last vision, Piers wages allegorical war with Death and Hell and emerges triumphant without other weapons than his true theories of moral action. William, our dreamer, awakens with joy at the victory of Piers and hears the happy pealing of the bells at Easter season.

*The Vision of William concerning Piers the Plowman* is a

sharp contrast with the verse and content of Chaucer. *Piers* is in medieval alliterative verse,

> A fair field full of folk, found I there between,
> Of all manners of men, the mean and the rich.

The author of *Piers the Plowman* gives us the last great example of mastery over this traditional, but usually monotonous, rhythm of the literature of the English race. Langland views the reality of his age from a medieval viewpoint and he does it better than his predecessors. Chaucer avails himself of the new verse forms of the Italian and French Renaissance and views the same realities with a modern eye. Both poets are masters of their respective, but differing, viewpoints.

3. *The Wyclif Bible.* The third notable secondary figure of the age is John Wyclif. Wyclif enters the portals of literature somewhat by accident. He was a churchman, but a reformer with much the same view of his society as had the author of *Piers the Plowman.* He opposed the orthodox views and advocated a division of the powers of Church and State. He wrote many tracts in Latin but sent his "poor priests" out to preach the simple truths of religion in the vernacular. He advocated a simple earthly faith and abhorred pomp and pretense. He was a forerunner of the Reformation with his preachings and his active participation as leader of the Lollard group to protest the powers of the Pope.

### First English translation of the Bible

Wyclif entered literature by giving us the first English translation of the Bible. Undoubtedly Wyclif himself did only portions of the work, but he supervised and coordinated the entire task and the subsequent ages have called it *The Wyclif Bible* (1382- -89). The translation is from St. Jerome's *Latin Vulgate Bible* (383-405). Wyclif's work paved the way for the most famous of the English translations, the *King James Version* in 1611.

The Wyclif Bible brought its translator into literature, since this work set a standard for English prose and thus contributed the same type of pioneering effort toward a modern English prose as Chaucer's work did for verse. Both Wyclif and Chaucer are milestones in the development of the modern English language. Aside from the intrinsic value of what they wrote, the models they prepared in language for the use of the Renaissance writers to come, are inestimable. Only historians of the world's most used language in modern times, English, fully appreciate the linguistical contributions of these two 14th century contemporaries.

# Chapter III

# CHAUCER AND THE TRANSITION TO MODERN ENGLISH

## GEOFFREY CHAUCER (1340-1400)

By the middle of the 14th century, all European literary activity was taking a new and upward leap. The spurt to modern times was under way. There are several high points to be noted. Boccaccio, the first great master of Italian prose, was bringing out his *Decameron* (1353), and Petrarch, the first great master of modern poetry, was at his peak of perfection. Juan Manuel in Spain had already adapted the Oriental tale for modern literatures with his *Libro de Patronio* (1336), and Juan Ruiz had produced his *Book of Good Love* (1343). Froissard, the Father of French Prose, was growing up (age 12 in 1350). Literature in Europe was changing its face and the change was to be a great and far-reaching one. It was a true Middle Age —the Dark Ages were definitely relegated to obscurity, and the light of the Renaissance and the bringing of ancient brilliance into the modern world were beginning to fuse their rays to chase away the shadows of a restricted and barbaric past. In an age of political, economic and social convulsion, literature had begun its mighty ascent in the Western World. And in England, Geoffrey Chaucer was in every way the man of an ideal ability and temperament to hurl himself into this widening and swiftly flowing European stream of the future and to bring before his successors the models that would lead surely to greatness, if and when they gained enough of his far-reaching vision to be able to absorb and avail themselves of it.

## Chaucer's Personal Life

Chaucer was the son of a prosperous wine merchant of London. His father supplied King Edward III and it was probably this connection with the court that brought the son into court life as a page when he was seventeen. He saw military service in France two years later and was captured. He was ransomed by the King and again took up the position of Squire in the royal household.

During the next few years he did a great deal of traveling in Italy, France, and the Low Countries. He occupied several official posts during his lifetime, except for a brief period about 1386-1389 when he was out of favor temporarily and seems to have been in financial straits. He was back on the King's pension, however, from 1389 until his death in 1400.

Chaucer's life shows no extraordinary personal accomplishment, aside from his writing. He was a family man who spent his life as a courtier. He was successful in his official missions but never became rich. That he was diplomatic, pleasant, and efficient are foregone conclusions. He carried out many missions, some secret ones, on the continent and was closely allied with a number of important men of his time.

Considering the regal and diplomatic environment in which he lived, it is a bit surprising to find him so wholly devoted to the cause of the common man. Chaucer wrote of course, not out of necessity for survival, but because he loved to write.

## Chaucer's Literary Life

Chaucer's literary life is commonly divided into three ages: (1) the French period (to 1372), the Italian period (1372-1385), and the English period (1385-1400). These divisions, as most such literary walls, are not to be taken too literally.

1. *The French period.* The court of King Edward III was highly imitative of the court life across the channel, and both at home and abroad, Chaucer soaked up the French literary tradition. He learned the *trouvère* art first hand. One of his first literary interests was to translate the *Roman de la Rose* into English. This long medieval French allegory concerns a rose bush, representing love, which is guarded from the lover's approach by various symbolic powers, giving opportunity, as the poem progresses, for many philosophical and satirical di-

gressions. All but about two thousand lines of Chaucer's work have been lost.

## Chaucer's first dream allegory

The _Book of the Duchess_ is Chaucer's first work of any importance. This is an elegy, written about 1369 (presumably before _The Pearl_), on the death of Blanch, John of Gaunt's first wife. It is written in octosyllabic couplets* and takes the typical medieval form of a dream-allegory. Finding himself in a forest, the poet comes upon a knight in black who moans the death of his lady. The knight describes his lady in great detail and his life with her. It is not until the descriptions are complete that the poet learns that the lady is actually dead. The poet, filled with grief, awakens at the sound of a bell. He has been sleeping all the while with the story of Ceyx and Alcyone in his hand. This story (from Ovid's _Metamorphoses_) is one of the death of a husband and the subsequent grief of the wife. The _Book of the Duchess_ is a conscious imitation of the tradition of the _Romance of the Rose_.

These and various minor poems constitute Chaucer's practice period. In themselves, they are of little value, but they indicate strongly that Chaucer is an English poet who intends to continue in an English tradition and in the English language (he knew Italian and French), while assimilating all that he could of European influence. His metrical schemes are all borrowings from the continent in this period.

2. _The Italian period._ Chaucer's mission to Italy had returned him to England filled with the spirit of the new and unquenchable curiosity he found prevalent there among men of letters. He knew Italian literature, both ancient and contemporary, and he longed to imitate it well in the best English of his time. Four major works properly belong to this period of the poet's activity:

_The Parliament of Foules_ (_Fowls_) (1377-1382)
_The House of Fame_ (c. 1379)
_The Legend of Good Women_ (_c._ 1385)
_Troilus and Criseyde_ (c. 1383)

_The Parliament of Foules_ again shows Chaucer using the form of a dream-allegory, the poet using here his own particular seven-line stanza, known as the Chaucerian stanza* (_rime royal_). While reading a portion of Cicero's _De re publica,_ where

Africanus appears to Scipio in a dream, the poet falls asleep and dreams that Africanus appears to him and leads him to a garden where all the fowls are celebrating St. Valentine's season in convention. One high-ranking eagle and two of lesser rank choose for a mate the most exalted female eagle. Representatives chosen officially to voice the opinions of each branch of the assemblage of fowls debate the issue heatedly and often hilariously. At times actual combat is about to break out among individual members and at other times the august parliament is rocked with laughter at the ridiculous proposals. Only one delegate, the cuckoo, seems to have no contentious spirit and wants to rest content with her mate and let others take care of their own love affairs. This attitude is, of course, attacked as being selfish and showing lack of public spirit.

At last Nature has to step in and halt the wrangling, for the chosen representatives are getting nowhere. Nature decrees that the royal eagle should choose whom she pleases, keeping in mind her obligation to mate within her class. She decides to postpone her decision for one year. As all the other birds have chosen mates, the assemblage breaks up by singing the praises of Nature. The poet is awakened by the clatter of the fowls.

Chaucer, in this poem, is following a French tradition of Valentine verse which originated in the French court during the 14th century, celebrating the festival of St. Valentine and the spring mating season. This poem has been called a political allegory.

_The House of Fame_ again presents the poet in a dream. Here Chaucer follows somewhat the plan of Dante, in that his poet is guided through the House of Fame (somewhere in the heavens) where favor is granted to the undeserving and withheld from the deserving among suitors. Then he is guided through the House of Rumor, which contains men of various callings such as pilgrims, pardoners, courtiers, etc., each group with packets and boxes of lies and false reports, being produced by a sort of a factory. As the poet sees "a man of gret auctorite," the poem suddenly breaks off.

This incomplete poem is in the octosyllabic couplet and shows Chaucer's obligation, notably to Dante and Vergil, but also to French works. It has had various interpretations. It is basically a love-dream allegory and is said to symbolize the coming marriage of Richard II. The poem begins to show the mature Chaucer in his handling of description, but is full of erudite allusions. It is undoubtedly satire but the exact intention of the poet escapes us.

*The Legend of Good Women* (in imitation of Boccaccio's *De claris mulieribus*) is again the dream vision in which the poet meets the God of Love and Queen Alceste. He is accused by Love of being rather cynical in his dealings with loving women. Queen Alceste defends him from dire consequences and suggests that, as penance, he write a series of lives of faithful followers among womankind of the God of Love. Chaucer leaves us eight and a part of a ninth of these lives of "saintly" women (martyrs to Love). The most famous and interesting are those of Cleopatra, Thisbe, and Dido. Very colorful stylistic passages are found in the life of Adriadne.

This long poem gives us the five-foot iambic* line, rhyming in couplets ("heroic couplet") for the first time in English. This became one of the most widely used verse forms in English poetry.

The Prologue to the poem comes to us in two forms and is perhaps the most lyrically beautiful portion of the poem. In it the daisy (sacred to French court poets) is praised in delightful passages of superb lyric description.

The sources cited by authorities for this work run the gamut of the finest Latin, Italian, and French writers to deal with love and the various women chosen by Chaucer for his faithful ladies. Alceste is perhaps his symbolic representation of Queen Anne of England, who died before the poem was completed. And her death is perhaps the reason why the poet broke off his work after 2723 lines, during his ninth life. He planned to include twenty famed women in his legend.

### Chaucer's second greatest work

*Troilus and Criseyde* (213), would have made Chaucer famous if he had written nothing else. Chaucer here delivers the chief fruit of his Italian experience. The story of the young Trojan hero, Troilus, and the young widow Criseyde, and their love, and how she breaks her vows to him by going over to the Greek Diomede, is a story that had many tellings since ancient times and throughout the medieval period. Chaucer is directly indebted to Boccaccio and his *Filostrato,* who treated the lovers in a simple and sensual manner.

Chaucer's book-length poem (8239 lines) in the rime-royal

stanza is, in reality, a novel in verse. Constructed in the best traditions of the courtly love of the romances of chivalry, this work is, in addition, a sustained study in character. Chaucer's study of the unfaithful Criseyde is a masterful one. He lets her reveal herself, but holds himself aloof and does not judge her. We may do that. His delineation of the wily, middle-aged Pandarus, the go-between who arranges the alliance between the lovers, is a masterpiece of modern sophistication. Troilus is a typical medieval hero of chivalry who eventually meets death, not through any error on his part, but because it was fated so.

Chaucer handles his verse with the art of a skilled master. His dialogue is as colorful and witty as any modern comedy. His description of emotional states and physical surroundings are equally superb in the main, though some tedious passages are found. The modern reader can well forget that the setting is ancient Troy, for the poem breathes a modern air in its dramatic development and its psychological subtlety. *Troilus and Criseyde* is the first great long narrative poem in the English language.

Aside from the four poems discussed above, Chaucer's Italian period includes several minor works which further show his abilities in the adaptation of new metrical schemes. They also show that the mind of Chaucer was thoroughly immersed in the Italian and French Renaissance movements.

3. *The English period.* By 1385, Chaucer had already produced enough to grant him lasting fame. But during the final fifteen years of his life he was working upon a more positive immortality, and he shows that all his efforts previously had but succeeded in completing his assimilation of ancient and contemporary continental culture and in giving him a mastery over the English language that was completely modern.

The minor works of his final period show Chaucer employing his French and Italian influences with thoroughly English spirit. He writes ballades* in the French manner and rollicking humorous satirical pieces. His final short piece, *The Complaint of Chaucer to His Empty Purse,* shows the poet frankly and seriocomically begging to have his pension raised by Henry IV, who came to the throne in late 1399.

### The Canterbury Tales

But all these minor works are completely eclipsed by the

Chaucerian masterpiece, wherein the poet sums up his age for all ages, *The Canterbury Tales* (216), the writing of which spread over the final fifteen years of the author's life.

In spite of Chaucer's accomplishments before 1385, it is the fruit of his last years—the tales and the portraits of medieval England—that most moderns connect with his name. For the average modern reader will think of Chaucer first as a teller of tales and a painter of word pictures describing the characters which are associated with them.

The framework for *The Canterbury Tales* was an old one even for medieval England. It is hard to believe that the many Oriental collections of tales were unknown there, in which a group of complete stories are loosely connected by a central theme or plot which holds them together in a sort of a "wheel"* arrangement, the spokes of which are the individual tales bound in a central hub which holds them into a rough semblance of what the early novel was to be like. In Spain, several of these Oriental collections had been translated from the Arabic and Juan Manuel had written his *Libro de Patronio* in 1336. In Italy, the Oriental tales were also known, and Boccaccio had produced his framework of tales in *Il Decamerone* in 1553.

It remained for Chaucer, not to invent the framework pattern, but to adapt it to produce a kaleidoscopic view of his own age and of his own neighbors. And he did it in a work that shows an infinitely greater variety of colorful facets than any of his predecessors in the genre. *The Canterbury Tales* of Chaucer runs the gamut of all ranges of his society, except that which had been treated best by the medieval romance, the lords and the ladies of the feudal castles, the knights and the nobles of the court. Chaucer brought the same degree of color and pageantry into the level he loved best—the English middle class. And, aside from his characterizations, his stories were designed to illustrate the many forms which the ancient and medieval tale had taken in the entire sweep of literatures before his time— the fable, the apologue,* the parable, the myth, the epic and romance, the exemplary tale, the ribaldness and crudeness of the mystery play and the French *fabliau*.

In verse forms, Chaucer reviewed in this work his lifetime of discovery and adaptation. Though most of *The Canterbury Tales* is written in *heroic couplets*,* he also employs his *rime royal*, the *terza rima** of Dante and the eight-line iambic pentameter* stanza. He also employed prose, but this is minor and undistinguished, perhaps because of its close proximity to his brilliant poetry.

His stories are clever and his stories can be dull. They fit the person who tells them. His dull stories (witness *The Pardoner's Tale*) are masterpieces of dullness. The tipsy Miller tells a tale that we should expect from a tipsy Miller—a crude and naughty story, but clever and with a masterful execution. The Prioress is nice, delicate, and good—and her story is nice and the telling is refined. The Knight is chivalrous and fond of adventure, and his story is an artful creation of courtly ideals and of noble speech and action. The Pardoner is a slimy faker and a hypocrite, despite the noble ideals that his habit represents, and his tale and his manner of presenting it is a masterful satire on his kind. (See Appendix A for full development of the tales mentioned in this paragraph.)

Chaucer's sources for the over-all framework, his verse forms, and for the content and structure of the tales themselves are many and varied, ranging throughout known literatures, both ancient and medieval. He did not hesitate to take his material wherever he found it. He used it intact, adapted, or reworked it to suit his purpose. But he always left it for us with his individual stamp of originality of thought and style.

### Summary of Chaucer's Contribution

1. Chaucer introduced verse forms which have endured and have been popular with English poets ever since.

2. His contribution to the language has perhaps been over-emphasized. He used the best language of his day and did not corrupt it. He stands in a transition period as a giant among his contemporaries, and he stands again as a monumental figure just before a century of barrenness in English literature, and hence has ever since been regarded as a model, standing between the old and the delayed Renaissance developments in purity of English usage.

3. Chaucer summed up and recorded better than any other man of his age the medieval traditions. The modern reader looks back to Chaucer when he wants an ordered and interesting interpretation of that age of English life and culture on the levels of which we know the least from most of the writers of the age.

4. Chaucer left a body of writing which, in itself and for

itself, is instructive and entertaining. He loved the story for the story's sake and he knew how to tell it for all ages. His work presents an endless variety both in its appeal to the average reader's emotional range and to the student's appreciation for accurate and finely delineated character portraiture, handled within the framework of the best English of the day. Chaucer reads best, of course, in the original late Middle English and it requires little training to be able to read him so. But he reads well in modernized versions also.

## THE FIFTEENTH CENTURY

The political situation throughout the century is one of general unrest in Europe. It was a century which saw the threats of encroachment of the eastern Moslem upon the west finally and definitely broken. Christianity was triumphant, but the narrow rigidity of the tenets of its Church found increasing challenge from within. A reform is in the air and the orthodox inner circle of Church power strikes out against dissenters within its ranks by scattered individual persecution and by mass suppression of liberal thought through the Inquisition.

### Spread of Italian Renaissance influence

On the intellectual side, the revival of interest in ancient culture and its adaptation to contemporary humanity has flowered in Italy and its effects are rapidly spreading north to France and are soon to touch Spain and England and spark them into feverish activity during the 16th and early 17th centuries. For more than a century Chaucer remains a lone English figure who was thoroughly saturated with this spreading humanism.*

The political and religious scene in England continues to be an increasingly turbulent one. The Hundred Years' War between France and England breaks out anew in 1415 and continues sporadically throughout the first half century. This struggle to throw off French domination and influence simply gives way to an internal struggle for political power past mid-century. The thirty-year conflict (1455-1485) between the houses of Lancaster (represented by the red rose) and of York (white rose) is known as the War of the Roses. The royal family, known as the *Tudor* line, of the house of Lancaster, emerged victorious in the struggle. Henry Tudor became Henry VII in 1485.

The struggle brought much good toward the political and

economic greatness and security of England in that they spelled the end of feudalism, the development of a feeling of nationalism, and the emergence of a strong industrial and manufacturing society. All these things led not only to internal well-being and security but also to a strong external commerce, exploration, and conquest. England was rapidly preparing to challenge the hitherto undisputed power of Spain and Portugal on the high seas.

### English Literature in transition

In literature, the century is usually looked upon, or rather dismissed, as a barren age, with a great deal of writing but little that shows the sparkle and promise of the 14th, or the mature developments of the 16th centuries. It is disappointing to find the English writers were not capable of following in the footsteps of Chaucer, the Pearl Poet, and Langland. And perhaps it was because fifteenth-century writers followed too closely in those footsteps and had too much of the introspective view that the literature of the age results in such unpretentious production and was so palely imitative of the masters of the century before.

The strong elements of literature during this age were the fringe genres that hover around to sweeten the broad aesthetic stream of major writings. The drama was producing strong infants (the miracle and morality plays, the interlude) but no mature adults. The romances and popular tales continued. The didactic writings, both religious and historical, went on as usual. Perhaps the strongest approach to originality and artistry is to be found in the popular songs, carols, and ballads of the common people, all anonymous. These charming pieces never lose their simple and unaffected sweet flavor. The single figures that are usually remembered from this century are those of Malory and Caxton.

### The Imitators of Chaucer

Chaucer's direct influence was strong during the century, both in England and Scotland. Both schools of poets employed every device and trick of the master in a large body of undistinguished writings. There was little of imagination or poetic ability in both groups. And it is strange to note that the writers imitated most the poorest writings of Chaucer—those of his early period. Chaucer's early allegorical poems were reproduced in multiple versions and variations. Some typical titles, taken at random from both schools, will serve to illustrate the type of works produced: *Siege of Thebes, Temple of Glas, The Testament of Cresseid, The Dance of the Sevin Deidly Synnis, The Palice of Honour, The Dreme.* There are many, many others of that ilk, from known writers. England's chief followers of Chaucer are Lydgate, Hoccleve, Skelton, and Hawes. In Scotland the names of James I of Scotland, William Dunbar, and Robert Henryson are outstanding. Many of the imitators of Chaucer's work are anonymous and a great many of these poems were at one time attributed to the pen of the master himself. Specialists have succeeded in discrediting these earlier claims.

## Malory and Caxton

The names of Malory and Caxton are often remembered in association in the development of English prose during the century.

Sir Thomas Malory was an interesting individual who has given us the best known of all the 15th century books: *Morte d'Arthur.* This collection has been widely read and copied although, in truth, it is but a translation and compilation of the main body of the Arthurian legends of the Middle Ages.

Malory was of the upper-class gentry, a knight, and a member of Parliament. Through some quirk in his nature, and being of the house of Lancaster mid the civil strife of his day, he suddenly embarked upon a career of crime and violence that finally led him into Newgate Prison in 1450, where he was to remain during the last twenty years of his life. It was here that his book was organized.

Malory was undoubtedly imbued with the quixotic spirit, for he loved the days of chivalry and looked back upon them with affection. He perhaps determined to perpetuate the most famous of the chivalric writings, those of King Arthur and the Knights of the Round Table, that he might relive vicariously a life that he had missed in his times. Malory did a good deal of translating out of the French. Beyond this, his task was one of modernizing, condensing, expanding, or modifying, and finally, assembling the mass of material in logical sequence. His prose is informal and direct. He tells the stories in a straightforward narrative. His character delineation is as weak as is generally true of the Middle Age romances from which he drew his version of the stories. But, after Malory, and not again until Scott and Tennyson, can one savor better the spirit and the thrills of projecting himself into the days when knighthood was in flower.

Chaucer summed up for us his own age in verse; Malory summed up for us an age already gone by. Malory looks, perhaps with rose-colored glasses and with a wistful sigh, at the ideal man of romance as, in Book 21, Chapter 13, Sir Ector speaks over the dead body of his brother, Sir Launcelot (the spelling has been somewhat modernized):

> . . . thou, Sir Launcelot, there thou liest, that thou were never matched of earthly knight's hand. And thou were the courteoust knight that ever bare shield. And thou were the truest friend to thy lover that ever bestrad horse. And thou were the truest lover of a sinful man that ever loved woman. And thou were the kindest man that ever struck with sword. And thou were the goodliest person that ever came among press of knights. And thou was the meekest man and the gentlest that ever ate in hall among ladies. And thou were the sternest knight to thy mortal foe that ever put spear in the rest. . . .

### A distinguished 15th century printer

William Caxton was England's first printer. He issued Malory's *Morte d'Arthur* in 1485 and printed *The Canterbury Tales* in at least two editions during the century. Caxton himself contributed little directly to English literature. He wrote the preface to Malory's book and did a number of undistinguished translations from Latin and French. His prose is unrefined and ornate at times. His value to the advancement of English culture lies in the fact that he was a businessman who loved books. He perhaps saved works which otherwise might have been lost. He made available to his society and to posterity the books of his century and helped to disseminate widely the raw material of inspiration for the coming waves of humanists—knowledge in an available form.

### The Verse of the People

The ballads, the carols, and the other delightful lyric forms of the common people cannot be divided into the arbitrary periods and ages as the more cultured and ordered literary production of a nation. They spring from oral tradition, and many of the early forms of these short pieces were carried from generation to generation for many years, perhaps for centuries, before they were given written form. Much of this mass of folk literature became a favorite field of study for the humanists of the sixteenth and later centuries and it was only then that it was organized and modernized into the forms with which we are acquainted. Until the 16th century this popular body of literature was recorded only in the memory of the people.

*The Ballad.* We have in written form today more than three hundred themes treated, and more than a thousand versions from the English medieval times of the folk ballad. How these ballads were composed we do not know exactly. Some students of the genre maintain that they were put together in village group gatherings; others hold that each ballad is the separate composition of an individual bard whose identity was lost as the poem traveled from town to town and from mind to mind in memorized form.

Modern literary historians have classified these folk gems under varied themes. The principal cycle includes those so-called "folk epics" dealing with the outlaw Robin Hood and his merry men of Sherwood Forest. Then there is the group dealing with events in English or Scottish history, such as *Chevy Chase,* dealing with the feud-battle between the followers of the English Earl Percy and the Scottish Earl Douglas, in which the noble lords and most of their men are slain in the woods at Chevy Chase.

> God save our king, and blesse this land
>     with plentye, joy and peace,
> And grant hencforth that foule debate
>     twixt noble men may ceaze!

Other divisions include the ballads dealing with love and domestic life, the supernatural, and those episodes retold from the epic and the romance. There are also humorous ballads, the themes of which we can almost imagine from the titles given to them (e. g., *Get up and Bar the Door*).

The artistic ballad, generally speaking, is one of known authorship, usually written deliberately in the style of the ancient folk ballad by a cultured poet of the sixteenth century and later. A charming anonymous ballad of the period is called *The Nut Brown Maid,* and is classified in this category because of its complicated structure.

A fitting conclusion to this brief consideration of the ballad might be a glance at the ballad's method of treating love—perhaps the chivalric ideal of the common people. Sweet William, it seems, had deserted Fair Margaret—

  Fair Margaret dy'd today, today,
   Sweet William he dy'd the morrow;
  Fair Margaret dy'd for pure true love,
   Sweet William he dy'd for sorrow!

## Postscript to the Middle Ages

When the Middle Ages in England came to an end is impossible to determine. The Italian Renaissance, which began about the middle of the 14th century, was hardly known in England during that century, except by Chaucer. The gentry and royalty of the 15th century knew, more and more, the Italian developments and their effects in France, but were children of their political times—isolationists, filled with the desire to throw off all continental domination and to make England great in a commercial and military sense. The middle and lower classes, though freed somewhat from feudalism, were still an unlettered mass.

### *England approaches the modern age*

But the modern age was upon England at the close of the 15th century. The Tudors, mercantile rulers, were in power and the feudalistic minded rulers of an age of chivalry were through. The printing press was in England to stay and Columbus had found a new world. The Church was about to lose its absolute domination over the minds of men—worldliness was about to have some importance in the scheme of life. The Renaissance was banging at the gates and Englishmen were ready to open their minds to it.

# Chapter IV

# RENAISSANCE COMES TO
# ENGLAND (1500-1558)

## What Was the Renaissance?

### *The ancient cultures*

The term Renaissance means *rebirth,* or more broadly, *revival.* The very meaning of the term, then, implies that something died, or very nearly did, and was here reborn. We know now that the great ancient civilizations of Greece and Rome cast their artistic and intellectual influence over the known and geographically restricted civilized world of that time, roughly between 1000 B.C. and 400 A.D. (with exception of the areas with civilizations unkown to the peoples of the old Roman Empire: the Far East, and the civilizations of the Toltec and pre-Toltec, the Maya and pre-Maya, and the Inca and pre-Inca in the Western Hemisphere). This Greco-Roman civilization had not only developed rather complex and workable social, economic and political systems that were highly respected by their known world of influence; it had advanced far in scholarship and scientific discovery, in philosophy, and in the building up of a fund of culture in the arts and in literature. We know that thought and individual action were somewhat free (at least in the upper groups of society) and that, at periods, truly democratic institutions prevailed at least to the extent that they have been workable in modern times. We know that these Greco-Roman cultures decayed from within with the loss of spirit to maintain themselves strong, and were attacked by barbarians from without, and that a Dark Age came over these areas which took these advances in the West and Middle East back almost to the point where they had begun. At least, surface life reflected that fact in, say, 600 A.D. Had this culture, this desire to learn and practice a policy of material prosperity and freedom of thought and discovery died? Had this love for human existence and its potential fruits been stamped out completely? Yes and no. It would perhaps be better to say that it had suffered a stultifying relapse—an earthquake had leveled the buildings and time and neglect had covered it over partially with savage growth—but its evidences were still there, pending a renewal of desire and spirit to look for them.

### Culture in the Dark Ages

During the Dark Ages (roughly 400-1200) that desire and spirit were weak in those same areas. The highly refined Greek and Latin languages still survived and slowly became the bases for the forging of the greatest portion of several vernacular European languages (Spanish, Portuguese, French, Italian, Roumanian, Catalan, Provençal, etc.). The Catholic Church, the institution with almost supreme power over these areas during this period, preserved much of this culture in its archives and its monks and priests copied and preserved this fund of past culture for those few who had the interest to learn or the ability to read. Here and there enlightened monarchs sought to preserve and improve on this fund of semiburied culture (e.g., Charlemagne in France, Alfonso the Wise in Spain, Alfred in England, etc.).

Meanwhile, two areas, isolated from the lands of the Christian Dark Ages, were developing varying degrees of a culture of their own—the Islamic East (569—) and the extreme northland of the European continent (566—). But generally these streams of independent achievement did not penetrate very deeply into the former Roman areas until much later.

### An upswing in cultural interest

The Dark Ages in the west was a time of scant civilization, in the sense of civilization as the ancients had known it. The Middle Ages (latter part of the Dark Ages, 1200-1400 roughly) is scarcely any better in spots, but during this time some areas are showing an increasing tendency to study the ancient classics, to experiment in science, to advance scholarship, and produce secular art and literature. Also, during this time, institutions other than the central Church at Rome are gaining some control over restricted fields of thought and action. And increasingly both individuals and groups are experimenting with worldly accomplishment in literature, philosophy, art, and social ideals. Also the influences of the two independent cultures mentioned above are being communicated into the Christian areas of the south and west. More and more individuals of the one Church are gathering followers in movements that protest the restrictions and rigidity of the mother institution. The Church was more and more showing a tendency to promote, encourage, and stimulate competing institutions and movements: the state, industrialism, commerce and exploration, discovery and colonization, etc.

Change during the Middle Ages was gradual and sporadic. There were bursts of energy and increasing drive to free the mind, but these were isolated and produced but slow results from generation to generation. No ferverish general activity is noted, no general spirit of scholarship and artistic accomplishment takes place, no thoroughgoing upsets of general Church authority are evidenced, no wholehearted devotion of rulers and leaders in favor of a wide split with the past. When this spirit finally took hold of minds of men of intelligence and ability in a large area of western humanity (Italy, about 1350) and turned human intelligence to the feverish search for tools to work with in the realm of scholarship and artistic production, it is labeled the Renaissance. And when this stimulus (or disease, or neurosis, or surge of humanistic thirst for knowledge and a broadening of mental scope and enjoyment of life here on earth) invaded other parts of this European world, we continue to call it Renaissance in those areas.

Something, then, did almost die, not quite, and its rebirth pains were slow and the process was laborious. And when it burst forth into the light, it was not quite any longer as it had been. There was much to add to it that had accumulated slowly, not only in Christian Europe, but the elements that had already infiltrated from the areas where cultural development had not been so restricted (notably the Arabic influences). And man also had the desire and was now free enough in most areas to take all these elements and mold something new in the world—what we call our modern fund of culture.

## *Complex meaning of "renaissance"*

And if Renaissance means only the going back to ancient classics for continued impetus, the Renaissance is still going on! But that is the restricted view, and as we shall see for England, the Renaissance in that narrow sense will explain only a part of what took place there. For in English Literature, Renaissance means not only an exposure to this *rebirth* of ancient cultures, but also the availability of the continental developments from 1350-1536. It means more than that. It signifies the awakening of the potential lying dormant in Englishmen of ability, to take up those tools and combine them with their own abilities and skills to produce a great body of writings—certainly the greatest in the world in the mind of any Anglo-Saxon descendant.

## What Is Humanism?

Humanism is the second term that is constantly being employed to aid our understanding of what happened to bring a modern age upon Europe, so radically different in all phases of life from what had been true in the Dark Ages, and their late division, called the Middle Ages. Humanism and Reformation are the terms used to describe two particular types of revolt which took place simultaneously with the Renaissance. Where the Reformation was a revolt in spiritual matters, humanism was the stimulus which spread through European societies aiming at creation and development of human interests upon a higher earthly plane than that of gross, animal existence.

Humanism, as we use the term today, simply means any view or attitude in which interest in human welfare and enjoyment is considered most important. It is, then, thought and action which give prime consideration to the affairs of men as compared with the supernatural.

In literature we specifically define as humanism that Renaissance revival of classical learning from the 14th to the 16th centuries as opposed to ecclesiastical studies and the continuance of the methods and traditional approach of medieval scholasticism* toward all intellectual activities, artistic, philosophical and theological. Humanism came to be a mental attitude which emphasized the study of man as man and the development of a devotion to those studies most likely to elevate and advance human culture and enjoyment of life upon this earth. Despite the brilliant efforts of many churchmen from the 9th century on (including such great Christian Fathers as St. Augustine and Thomas Aquinas) the approach of the Scholastics had degenerated into quibbling, disputation and verbal subtlety in attempting to formulate a rational view of life to fit a changing world.

Humanism of the Renaissance period is the direct source for

all modern systems of intellectual, scientific, or social development.

## What Was the Reformation?

An understanding of the term reformation* is as necessary to a grasp of the significance of literary developments as is the comprehension of the terms renaissance and humanism. They all are simply labels which we apply to represent the three forces, often fused but always affecting each other, occurring simultaneously in the period between 1350-1620. Of course, any fixed dates are arbitrary and the duration of the general upsurge of changing forces which involve all three movements varies considerably in the various areas of Europe. The important thing for the student of literature to keep in mind is that the three terms represent movements which, together or separately, caused great literary works to be produced.

The Reformation, simply stated, was the rebellion of many European groups against the Church of Rome, reaching a decisive climax in the sixteenth century. After that century, western Christians are to remain divided generally into two general classifications: the Catholics and the Protestants. There were many and complex causes for the rebellions which do not interest us here, for our chief concern only lies in the effects of *renaissance, reformation,* and *humanism* in the production of England's great works of literature.

## *Effects of Reformation upon Renaissance development*

In Italy, the intellectual and artistic phases of the Renaissance did not require the Reformation in order to develop. In other areas these same phases could not have full rein of freedom without its effects being felt. The development of literature in some areas seemed to be more restricted by the general pressure of local authority than in others. At any event, the political, social, moral, and economic struggles of the Reformation movement had their effects upon literatures everywhere. It was only when those situations were favorable to free artistic and literary development that literature could reach a full flowering in any area.

## *Directions of the English Reformation*

In England we have noted (page 25) an early local rebellious movement under Wyclif and the Lollards, resulting in an English translation of the Old Testament. The movement was not widely enough accepted to win permanent effects. This small local attempt at "reformation" failed.

But with the widening horizons of freedom of thought and inquiry, coming from Italy, the small movements multiplied, until in 1521 Martin Luther became the first great name in Protestantism by his open and successful challenge to the rigidity of Church orthodoxy. Followers sprang up from all sides and other leaders came to head groups all over Europe and the British Isles.

The fire was no longer to be controlled, and by the early years of the 16th century was blazing brightly in England. New translations of the Bible began to appear, beginning with the New Testament translation of Tyndale in 1526, and by 1611 there had been eight of them. When, in 1536, Henry VIII broke definitely with Rome and declared himself, in the Act of Supremacy, the head of a Church of England, the Reformation was victorious in England. Many historians assign this (1536) as the date when England entered upon the full stream of the intellectual developments of the Renaissance.

### Renaissance Influences in France, Spain and Germany

From the preceding sections we have seen that Renaissance implies the transition from the Middle Ages to modern times in Europe. It means digging out the surviving culture of the ancients, renewing it, translating its literary pieces into the vernacular languages, disseminating it, copying and imitating it, applying to it knowledge gained elsewhere, adapting it to new situations, and generally, attempting to add to it and improve upon it. But the term means more than that. It indicates to us the changes that took place in the intellectual and moral attitude, the awakening of a spirit of inquiry and the freeing of the minds of individuals from subservience to the dictates of institutions: the Church, feudalism, and the rigid principles of medieval scholasticism.

The Renaissance began in Italy and it is from here that we must trace its influences on the other European nations. The Italian movement began in the first half of the 14th century, and by 1400, Italy had produced the most famous three names in its literature: Dante, Petrarch, and Boccaccio. Italy had now very definitely superseded France as the leader of European literary taste.

## *The slow spread of Italian Renaissance influences*

The rest of Europe was not yet ready. It is true that individuals were enthused by Italian humanism and artistic production. England's notable example, of course, is Chaucer. But he did not start the English phase of the Renaissance. He was a true Renaissance humanist and literary artist, but he was more than a hundred years ahead of his fellow Englishmen in this respect.

France, aside from some individual efforts, did not enter the Italian stream until after 1495. The first real impact there was with Ronsard and other members of the *Pléiade,* shortly after the turn of the century. And by 1535, the master scholar, idealist, utopian, and very earthy Rabelais had produced his *Pantagruel* and *Gargantua,* and the French phase of the movement was in full swing.

## *A Counter-Reformation in Spain*

With the vivid single exceptions of the *Celestina* (1499) and *Amadís de Gaula* (1508), and the poetry in the Italian manner of Garcilaso de la Vega (1531-1536), Spain did not enter wholeheartedly into the foreign streams at all. It is here that the Counter Reformation was the strongest. There is little true humanism in Spain, but there is a strong movement in literature, architecture, and painting, showing strange and powerful nationalistic qualities, which overshadow foreign influences in the latter half of the 16th and the first half of the 17th centuries. Spain became a foremost leader in the Baroque* tendencies of the 17th century.

## *The German reaction toward philosophy*

The politico-religious struggles in Germany overshadowed the weak attempts of individuals to foment a movement following the Italian humanism. In Germany the Reformation movement was strongest and this particular development there is often referred to as a Teutonic Renaissance, producing more philosophy and treatises than literature. Germany also took an active interest in scientific development and writing during the period. But in the aesthetic sense, fine literature was not produced in Germany during the entire period of direct Italian influence. Germany's great literary period was not to come until much later.

## RENAISSANCE BEGINNINGS IN ENGLAND

The Renaissance came late to England. Only Chaucer was directly influenced by the true Italian movement. By 1500, the feverish activity in Italy and France toward the unearthing of the classics, the translation and dissemination of classical knowledge had taken place. The masterpieces of Rome and Greece had already received modern interpretation and could now be read and understood in vernacular languages. The pioneering was completed. They were available for English use.

The English were an island people and early showed some of the withdrawing tendencies observable also in peninsular peoples (notably Spain). They liked to observe, but took some time to make up their minds to participate. Besides, the 15th century was a century of conflict and the warding off of continental domination for England—the Hundred Years' War, the War of the Roses, persecution of the Lollards.

### *Political effects of the Reformation in England*

When the Reformation did burst upon England, its conflicts had more of a tendency to be political than doctrinal. The Tudors had been out of power for a long time in England. When they came back with Henry VII (1485), their position was still precarious. The Tudors practiced a personal rule and were proud and ruthless. They belonged to an industrial family and were bent upon achieving greatness and power for England. And when, with Henry VIII, it came to a matter of bowing his will even to the Pope, the break came, swiftly and suddenly, with Rome. Up to Elizabeth, they tolerated scholarship and humanism, so long as it did not in any way offend the royal will. Henry VIII did not execute Sir Thomas More for his humanism; it was because More's strong faith annoyed him. Elizabeth, Henry's daughter, by Anne Boleyn, was as strong willed and wily as her father, but she was also a scholarly girl and was not personally attractive. With these personal qualities, together with the fact that England now appeared to be secure and strong, she opened wide the gates to scholarship and the development of literature. And in her reign (1558-1603), literature showed astounding development.

## Great Ages of European literatures

The Renaissance beginnings produced Italy's great writers; Spain had its own Golden Age of national and Baroque genius near 1600; a little later France came to the front with a refined form of neoclassicism and a new age of enlightenment*; Germany scaled the heights with its romanticism and its great body of philosophers and composers near 1800. England gave the world a body of literature, bested by none, in her Elizabethan Age.

## Sir Thomas More and the Humanists

The Renaissance came to England as humanism before it showed marked effects in aesthetic writings. A remarkable scholar from Holland, Desiderius Erasmus, spent a great deal of time in England between 1511 and 1514. He taught at Oxford and became intimate with the first group of English humanists to bear a name, _The Oxford Reformers._ Names identified with this group are John Colet, William Grocyn, and William Linacre. These great students had studied in Italy and were principally interested in the reform of learning in England.

Of most importance to us is a student of the Oxford group and of Erasmus, Sir Thomas More (1478-1535). He was the son of a judge and became steeped in the higher realms of humanistic studies. He occupied a number of high public positions and finally became Lord Chancellor (1529). He had studied the Cartusian philosophy, and though he never practiced it, was highy intrigued by the ascetic life. After disapproving Henry VIII's divorce plans (from Katherine) and finding himself involved in the quarrel between the King and the Pope, he resigned his offices and retired to private life. He refused to attend the King's wedding to Anne Boleyn. The King was angry and watched for the opportunity to involve More in some specific act which could be labeled treasonous. He demanded of More an oath to support his Act of Supremacy (1535). More could not repudiate the Pope's authority and was imprisoned and later beheaded.

## The first great modern "utopia"

Of More's many scholarly writings, the one which most places him in the sphere of literature is his _Utopia,_ written in Latin in 1515-1516 and translated into English in 1551. The word "utopia" is Greek for "no place."

All great literatures have their examples of books describing an ideal state. More views the corruption and imperfections of his age and longs for a perfect world. In his political dissertation (which is a romance at the same time), More is thoroughly Renaissance minded in that he is attempting to build up a state which is a work of art.

New World discovery and exploration had given More an ideal locale for his Utopia, an island in the unknown oceans of the Western Hemisphere. In Book I, the very realistic More analyzes the evils of his age in a rather careful but ironic manner. He treats here of greed, self-seeking public officials, unjust taxation, inequalities of distribution of wealth, dishonest and conniving foreign relations, filth and disease—and all the public evils which have, to varying degrees, provided fodder for political and social reformers of all ages. In Book II, the author becomes fanciful and shows a fertile imagination in his witty and clever invention. At times satirical, More projects for us a state with religious toleration, with social heavens, and with physical comforts. Honesty and good faith, of course, prevail. Many peoples today struggle toward, and some have accomplished partially, the "actualities" of More's imaginative commonwealth.

Other humanists of More's time are: Roger Asham, a pioneer in modern English usage, who wrote history, a treatise on English composition, and a number of works on education, the most important of which is *The Schoolmaster* (1563-68); John Foxe, Richard Hooker, Sir Thomas Wilson, and others. These men tended to do their writing in the generation following More and the Oxford group.

## The New Poetry: Wyatt and Surrey

Poetry lagged behind prose in the early years of the 16th century. There was scarcely anything new in English verse from the innovations of Chaucer until the last years of the reign of Henry VIII. And when something vital and spontaneous did come again to poetry it came from a Chaucerian source: Italy's Petrarch. Until Elizabeth came to the throne the names of Sir Thomas Wyatt (1503-1542) and Henry Howard, Earl of Surrey (1517?-1547) are inseparable as representing the twin forces that brought verse forward through more than a century of barrenness, adding to the Chaucerian lyric new qualities of spontaneity and expression of individual emotion that the 15th century had not quite reached. With these two gentlemen of the court, English lyric poetry begins its long career of natural expression that is full and free. And the full impact of newness that these two courtiers brought forward to inspire the sudden outburst of lyrical freshness in the following half century can be realized only when one studies the output of both poets, for one complements the other. Wyatt's verse is simpler and appeals to the individual through its tenderness and sweet melancholy; Surrey leans to a faster tempo and a dramatized imagery. Together, Wyatt and Surrey are sufficient to bring us the realization that at long last Chaucer has been rewarded with his first true disciples.

### The sonnet and blank verse enter English literature

Sir Thomas Wyatt introduced the sonnet* into English and gave it a gentleness of grace, beauty, and simplicity that its inventor, Petrarch, had not achieved.

The Earl of Surrey used blank verse* first in England in his translation of the Fourth Book of the *Aeneid*. He used the so-called "Shakespearean" rime* scheme for a number of his sonnets, the form that was to become so popular with later poets as to almost claim the name of "English" sonnet.

The themes most common to both Wyatt and Surrey are the unkindness of love, the mental and emotional turbulence it brings in its wake, and the faith and constancy of the true lover in spite of all this sweet sorrow.

> . . . But as for me, though that by chance indeed
> Change hath outworn the favor that I had,
> I will not wail, lament, nor yet be sad,
> Nor call her false that falsely did me feed. . . .
> (Wyatt in Sonnet No. 23)

## Chapter V

# THE ELIZABETHAN PERIOD TO
# THE KING JAMES BIBLE (1558-1611)

### Historical and Cultural Notes

When Elizabeth I came to the throne of England in 1558, the conflicts of the past century were not over entirely, but there were signs that a firm and skillful hand could direct England to a destiny of greatness in the world. The ruling hand of Elizabeth proved to have that requisite firmness and skill. During her reign, internal order and individual security were attained for a large portion of Englishmen. A new Church, under the domination of the State, was firmly established, the colonial system was inaugurated, and England became supreme on the high seas. After 1588 (date of the defeat of the Spanish Armada), she was no longer threatened by Spain. France had given up hope of dominating the isles, and in commerce England was challenged only by the Dutch. The feudal system was gone and Renaissance beginnings of the first half of the century had assured that English scholars and literary men were now definitely linked with all the continental founts, flowing from both the ancient and the modern learning. Furthermore, practical and ruthless though she was, Elizabeth was a student herself and had great sympathy with both scholarship and the arts. England, during Elizabeth's reign, came to a period of national unity and spirit, of external respect, and of internal well-being. The pioneering had been done in literature by Chaucer, the humanists, Wyatt and Surrey, and others. She already had a brilliant past in folk literature—one of the most charming of any nation. Her drama had constantly pushed the liturgical toward a definitely secular theatre. England had a queen who was loath to put any restrictions upon literary development, and English literature had all the tools with which to produce a Golden Age.

## Elizabethan Literature: A Summary

The Age of Elizabeth was predominantly one of change and expansion in all phases of life. Man was faced with a new, wider, and richer world. The world, at last, seemed to exist to satisfy man. It was a mass vibration, and in literature, that form which most expressed for the mass this new world view, half fancy, half real, was drama. Drama became the most developed literary form of England's Renaissance and the one genre that was most broadly popular, giving the most powerful and spontaneous expression to the multisided aspects of a newly discovered existence.

It was a great lyrical period, especially in the sonnet and the song. With a rich native fund of medieval popular lyric to build upon, combined now with the Italian innovations, developed by such poets as Chaucer, Wyatt and Surrey, the Elizabethan poetry achieved a gay and glorious perfection.

The third form, in which the greatness of Elizabethan literature lies, is the longer and more learned type of non-dramatic poetry—a Renaissance refinement of the epic-romance-allegory cycles of the medieval literature. In this form Spenser's *The Faerie Queene* is to rival in importance in world literatures the famed artistic epics of Italy: Ariosto's *Orlando Furioso* and Tasso's *Jerusalem Delivered*.

The age produced many great translations from both poetic and prose works of the ancients and moderns of other languages. Otherwise, English prose was slow in developing, and when aesthetic prose was attempted, it tended to result in an awkward and burdensomely artificial vehicle. Great English prose must await the ages to follow The prose of the Elizabethan Age of most distinction is that of voyages and discovery—reports of the widening circle of English power and influence in a rapidly expanding physical world.

## Contrasting Types of Elizabethan Prose

English prose writers of the period were less sure of their instrument than the poets. They romped and played with a variety of experimentations in language and the handling of themes—not yet finding the firm and solid ground of the novel and the essay that was to distinguish English literature of the next periods. Aside from the purely historical and philosophical prose of the age, it is distinguished largely for a deliberate cultivation of artificiality and decorative effects and for its racy narratives of high real adventure and exploration of the broadening horizons of the New World.

The artificial prose was a deliberate cultivation of the fanciful and the romantic by gentlemen of Elizabeth's court. The Queen, vain and unattractive, built around herself a court which was colorful and splendid, but hollow and with a fragile and thin shell. She loved praise and adulation and favored men who showered her with personal compliments. Elizabeth's vanity caused her to attempt to set the fashion and taste for her age. She dressed extravagantly and adored all manner of decorative splendor, both in the physical appearance of her court and in the language and forms of etiquette used there. The deliberately cultivated hero worship of Elizabeth accounts for a good deal of the prose and poetry of these courtly writers.

### English prose acquires ornamented elegance

John Lyly (1554-1606) is the foremost name among those who attempted to mold the English language into an artistic elegance of expression by use of classical ornamentations of all sorts, alliteration,* antithesis,* lavish similes,* and all modes of highly wrought linguistic artifice. He tried to mold a prose as to give the effects of elegantly constructed poetry. He had had the reputation at Oxford of being a clever trifler and his literary reputation lies in his clever trifling with the English language.

The artificial literary fashion which Lyly set has taken on the particular term "euphuism"* because of his two books: *Euphues or the Anatomy of Wit* (1579), and its sequel, *Euphues and his England* (1580). *Euphues* is fiction but its main purpose is the depicting of a new and artfully constructed society.

The story of the first book is set in Italy where Euphues, a dandy of Athens, has come to live a life of "clever trifling." He settles in Naples, which could be London, and runs into one Philautus, who introduces him to his fiancée, Lucilla, who is the daughter of the governor. Lucilla, the promised bride of Philautus, falls in love first with Euphues, but in the end, proves to be a bit fickle, as she winds up by marrying Curio. All this simple triangular intrigue gives Lyly an opportunity to toy with and impose his ideas on friendship, love, and various other questions. He even touches upon education for children. Eventually the two comrades make up and, Lucilla forgotten, they decide to go to England together.

In the second book, Philantus marries in England and Euphues returns to Greece. Elizabeth receives her just due when the two friends have stopped at the house of an old gentleman, on the way from Canterbury to London. Fidus, the old man, tells them of the glories of the Queen. While the two friends are in England, Lyly indulges in much byplay of intriguing situations at the court, the moral of which seems to be that lovemaking in her presence is repulsive to Elizabeth. After Euphues returns to Athens, he pens an epistle* to some Italian ladies, the burden of which is an elaborate praise of Elizabeth of England.

Lyly died in obscurity, but "euphuism" lives today to remind us of this highly ornate and falsified style he set in English, his skillful manipulation of sentence structure to include various conceits, and a play-on-words type of linguistical insanity.

Sir Philip Sidney (1554-86) is a writer who shows us equally well the artificial prose of the Elizabethan Age, but in a different setting than that of Lyly. Sidney was a courtier and an intelligent Renaissance gentleman. He toured the European centers to perfect his education. He was a soldier, a diplomat, and a poet; he was an ardent Protestant. He fell mortally wounded in support of the Dutch against the Spanish at Zutphen.

### Great European pastoral romances

His *Defence of Poesie* (1580) laments the affectation and falsity of English literary style. His chief claim to fame in prose (we shall discuss his poetry later) lies in his pastoral* romance *Arcadia* (begun in 1580). Sidney's work is typical of the Renaissance pastoral, of which the most famous continental examples are Italy's Sannazaro and his *Arcadia* (1504) and Spain's Montemayor and his *Diana Enamorada* (1542-59).

The pastoral is a loosely constructed love plot, interspersed with episodes of various sorts involving rather isolated short stories (the Italian *novella**) and including verse pieces scattered throughout. It was a courtly pastime in the Renaissance for the lords and ladies to be intrigued by thoughts of the pastoral and simple life. They liked to find themselves pictured as shepherds and shepherdesses, roaming the meadows and woods of a rural countryside and tasting the delights of love and the calm carefree life of the woodland glades. Usually the love plot involved very complicated triangles and quadrangles, with the course of true love seldom running smoothly. The plots lead nowhere in particular, but are broken into by colorful and often amusing incidents.

Sidney's style in *Arcadia* is whimsical and varied in spots; it is laborious and dull in other places. But everywhere it is highly ornate and full of elaborate figures of speech. Sidney does not hesitate to vary his story. In the beginning it is a medley of courtly shepherds and their companions, lovely country maidens. As the story proceeds, broken here and there by sonnets and other lyric verse, it takes a decided turn toward the medieval romance of chivalry, with the setting still remaining a rural and imaginative arcadian landscape. Sidney wrote *Arcadia* purely to amuse himself and his sister, the Countess of Pembroke. He was dabbling in Renaissance fancy and color, leading brilliantly to practically no serious conclusion. If one reads such a book with such an attitude, it makes reading for a lazy summer afternoon. One is likely to fall asleep in the midst of it, and that is entirely in keeping with the spirit of such a book. One's sleep should be sound after reading any amount of *Arcadia,* for the material is calculated to clear the mind of any worry, care, or weighty thought.

There were other writers of pastoral romances in the age. The most known are Robert Green's *Menaphon* (1589) and Thomas Lodge's *Rosalynde* (1590), which provides Shakespeare with his plot for *As You Like It.* Green and Lodge vary little from the pastoral traditions set by the Italian Sannazaro. In language, Lyly's "euphuism" prevails.

### The picaresque novel

Thomas Nash (1567-1601) introduces us to still another branch of Elizabethan prose. He wrote satires and allegorical pieces, but is best known for his production of a crude but early historical novel, *The Unfortunate Traveller,* or *The Life of Jack Wilton* (1594). This work is our first English example of the picaresque\* novel, a genre started with the Spanish *Lazarillo de Tormes* in 1553, translated into English in 1569. This Spanish genre of roguery was to have a long line of followers in England. The Spanish picaresque novel was an autobiographical account of a young boy who sought to keep his belly filled by his slyness and cunning, rather than by his honest efforts. As the lad's adventures unroll in episodic manner, the customs and trickeries of the various levels of Spanish life are revealed.

*The Unfortunate Traveller* has the same loose structure as the typical Spanish prototype but is genuinely historical in spots. It is thus not only the first English picaresque novel (developed later with such sureness by Defoe, Smollett, and Dickens) but also the first English historical novel. Nash's style is journalistic and often incoherent, but racy and relatively free from the conceits of euphuism.

Jack Wilton, the hero, or antihero, is an English page boy who tours the continent and finally arrives in Rome. He plays elaborate tricks along the way. He meets famed personages of the day, such as Erasmus, More, and others. He witnesses historical events of the time of Henry VIII, for instance, overhearing Luther deliver his arguments at Wittenburg. All through the narrative are little journalistic bits in terse prose commenting upon customs and interesting bits of gossip. Jack would lead us to believe that Italy was a country in which sin and wickedness resided as normal existence.

### Chronicles of English discovery and exploration

The prose chronicle-like accounts of real adventure and expansion of the English into the trackless seas were written by the adventurers themselves or by more sedentary home dwellers who collected and compiled various accounts, but who wrote with the same patriotic fervor as the participants themselves. One such collection of narratives is written by Richard Hakluyt and its title is typical of those bold and bombastic accounts: *The Principal Navigations, Voyages, Traffiques, and Discoveries of the English Nation, made by Sea or over Land, within the Compass of these 1500 Years* (1589-1600). Hakluyt gives us much of our knowledge of the famed Elizabethan sea dogs, such as Hawkins, Gilbert, Drake, and the Cabots. The first-hand accounts were written by men who participated in the events described. Typical is Sir Walter Ralegh's *The Discovery of the large, rich, and bewtiful Empire of Guiana* (1596).

## EDMUND SPENSER: MASTER OF THE NONDRAMATIC LYRIC

While English prose was to await another age before it could lose its apparent clumsiness and involved structure, English poetry, after 1550, was ready to burst into bloom. Both in dramatic and in nondramatic verse, the Elizabethan Age has never been surpassed for its variety, its depth of charm, its fullness, and its tuneful spontaneity. The lyric was the charm of the English Middle Ages in literature, but it lacked form and serious purpose, and with the full flood of Italian and French Renaissance influences, the English lyric expression knew no bounds to limit its development of freedom, simplicity, ease, and grace, a fullness of depth and sincerity.

In Elizabethan verse, then, mid a multiplicity of great names, two rise to loftier heights than their fellows: in dramatic poetry, the name of Shakespeare, and in nondramatic verse, the name of Edmund Spenser.

## Spenser's Life

Edmund Spenser (1552-1599) was six when Elizabeth came to the throne of England. His father was a London cloth maker. The lad, with a talent for literary genius, was not of the nobility, nor was he born to wealth. His education for greatness was nonetheless a fairly adequate one. His age was the first in England's history where a lower-middle-class mind for genius could exert energy and achieve the polish needed for full expression.

His first education was at Merchant Taylor's school and from there he proceeded to Cambridge. Poor in health and with modest means he pushed himself into every branch of learning, studying Latin and Greek, philosophy and rhetoric. He made friendships with the scholars of his time and drank from every fount of classical and contemporary knowledge available to him.

Spenser leaned to the side of the Puritans in the religious conflicts of his times. He was not bigoted and held himself aloof from all extreme viewpoints. He took his Master's degree in 1579. His education had led him to imbibe equally from the literary past of his own country and from all the continental sources. He had achieved a correctness in English that few of his fellows approached; he was steeped in the past, the chivalric ages, and with his immediate contemporaries.

Spenser never gained wealth or high position. He served in clerkships, as secretary to noble gentlemen, and succeeded in being subsidized to a modest degree by the Court. He was disappointed in all his attempts toward substantial recognition by Elizabeth. After suffering loss of his property in Ireland, as a result of insurrections that were sweeping the land, he fled from that country with his wife and four children, and died suddenly in London at the age of forty-seven, a poor and disillusioned man.

## Spenser, Poet of the Renaissance

By Spenser's time English poetry had exploited its native sources and had added, one by one, foreign innovations. No poet since Chaucer had been at home with them all in combination. The foreign accretions, in the hands of the poets of the early Renaissance, had tended to become stereotyped and still did not have the movement and flexibility of a perfect fusion. A master hand was needed to blend these elements into an English pattern and to draw from the harmonious blend a new vigor and simplicity. Spenser provided the needed genius to make that transition.

His first great work is _The Shepherd's Calendar_ (1579). Until this time he had done mainly translations from Petrarch and du Bellay. Spenser's first famous work was a series of eclogues,* one for each month. The classic eclogue dictated the form for Spenser's work. Each of his lyric divisions come from the mouths of simple shepherds. The months are devoted to the development of various themes, the principal of which is the love of Colin Clout for Rosalind. This theme is dominant in his eclogues for January, March, June, and December. But he deals with many subjects: February is a religious allegory and April is dedicated to praise of Elizabeth, in May he discourses on religion, and October laments the sad state of poetry in his day.

Spenser is deliberately using his classic framework, made famous by Vergil, to create beautiful lyric poetry. His development of ideas and narrative exposition are purely secondary to that purpose. He sets out to put on exhibition a refined usage of all the forms of English poetry, the sonnet, the elegy, the couplet, the eight-line stanzas. His vocabulary runs the range from homely rustic speech to the flowered ornamentation of euphuism. _The Shepherd's Calendar_ is a display case of English poetic meters and composition at the beginning of the period of greatness of the English Renaissance, arranged for display by the greatest master of English since Chaucer, but with the innovations which Chaucer had not known in the 14th century.

## A Spenser Miscellany

It is evident that Spenser had begun plans for his long master-piece, *The Faerie Queene,* at about the time *The Shepherd's Calendar* was published. It was not until 1589 that he published the first three books. The second three books were not issued until 1596. During this period, however, Spenser was writing brilliant verse. Some of these works are:

1. A volume of short verse called *Complaints, Containing Sundry Small Poems of the World's Vanity.* In this volume the poem entitled *Mother Hubberd's Tale,* is an allegorical satire on the evils and vanities of Spenser's world. Written in heroic couplets, this collection of four tales attacks the worldly minded clergy, the corruption of the Court, and other social evils of the day.

2. *Colin Clout's Come Home Again* is a tribute to Sir Walter Ralegh, and contains much autobiographical data, as well.

3. *Amoretti* (1591-1595) is a sonnet sequence tracing Spenser's love and wooing of Elizabeth. He refers, of course, to Elizabeth Boyle, an English girl whom he married in Ireland. The group of 89 sonnets relates the course of his wooing and subsequent marriage. All show the rich talent of the poet in their simple smooth-flowing beauty, as they follow the level as well as the uneven trails through his courtship period. This is one of several sonnet cycles of the age, the most famous of which is that of Shakespeare.

A number of other poems, stretching over a fifteen-year period, show Spenser to be a poet's poet. Versatile and smooth-flowing lines glide from his pen as though from a never-ending stream of reserve metrical beauty of expression.

## Great Allegorical Epic: The Faerie Queene

Spenser was ever occupied with earthly moral relations. He was an artist and evidently, as early as 1580, conceived the idea of a mighty poem in which to expound his views. He was, in fact, dealing with a basic problem of the Renaissance, earthly morality to govern man as an individual and to define his relationships to the State. Spenser, typical Renaissance artist that he was, had yet much of chivalric ideals within his make-up. An age was gone but he was loath to see its high idealism go with it. Therefore, using the medieval allegory as his vehicle, he conceived a plan by which to present, by means of a series of knightly adventures, his scheme for an ideal earthly moral code. The result is incomplete, but brilliant. It is England's first epic* and one of the great works of world literatures.

## Complex allegory in "The Faerie Queene"

*The Faerie Queene* (222) was to have contained twelve books, each book divided into twelve cantos,* each book being designed to show one of the qualities of knightly perfection in Spenser's interpretation of Aristotle's twelve virtues. Each book was to be a complete idealization of an individual virtue, brought out in a framework of chivalric romance and adventure. At the same time, a central theme was to run throughout the twelve books in which the State was to be glorified, along with its ideal queen, Elizabeth.

Spenser wrote only six of his projected twelve books. It is possible that a great deal more of the work was destroyed when his castle in Ireland was burned in Tyrone's Rebellion in 1598.

*The Faerie Queene* is the world's prime example of an extremely intricate allegory. On the surface the book may be read as simply a series of knightly exploits. Gloriana, the Fairy Queen, is holding a twelve-day festival. It is obvious, of course, that Gloriana represents Queen Elizabeth. On each of the twelve days, any stranger in distress may appear before the Queen and request a champion to handle whatever dragon, ogre, evil giant, or other oppressive influence, that is presenting trouble. Spenser follows through only six of these adventures, the champion in each case representing one of the twelve virtues laid down in Aristotle's philosophy. These twelve virtues, then, taken together, represent the ideal moral gentleman. This is the lowest and simplest level of the allegory.

Each adventure is filled with various characters representing various qualities which contribute to and provide conflict for illustration of the major virtue, represented by the champion. For instance, in Book I, the champion, the Red Cross Knight, represents *holiness*. On a higher allegorical level, then, he represents the Anglican Church in England. The Red Cross Knight champions Una (representing *truth*) against the dragon (representing *error*). For the Puritan-leaning Spenser, the dragon represented the Church of Rome.

On a still higher level of allegory, in each of the books appears the Ideal Knight (Prince Arthur) who represents highmindedness or gentlemanliness in the body politic, the State. This knight appears at the most opportune moments to help the elements of virtue (represented by the champion and his companions) in order to aid them in achieving their goals.

So then, *The Faerie Queene* is designed to present interesting tales of high adventure, to illustrate the ideal make-up for the individual to make him into the ideal citizen of the world, to illustrate the ideal political, social, and religious institutions to lead the State to perfection, and to illustrate the ideal State, deserving to embody such institutions and to aid them and the individuals who make them up for their collective and individual welfare and thus to advance its own perfection.

The verse form employed is the invention of the poet and has become famous as the *Spenserian stanza.** This form has been used by many English poets in works which stand in the foreground of the best of English poetry. Burns, Shelley, Keats, Byron, and Tennyson are a few of the romantic school of the 19th century, in which this form was a particularly favored meter.

### An artistic, intellectual, and technical masterpiece

Aside from the charm of the poetry and the entertaining features of the narratives (and the inevitable monotony which sometimes prevails), *The Faerie Queene* is a masterpiece of an imaginative and a very cultured mind. Spenser demonstrates in this work alone that he had intimate knowledge of the best of the world's artistic works as well as the philosophies of all the ages, combined with his power in the poetics involved. Spenser shows a masterful execution of his fusion of such varied and complicated elements. The work shows Spenser, not only as a master of his artistic and intellectual matter, not only as a finished craftsman, but as a human being in his age of conflict, with all the prejudice and bias which that implies in the individual of any age of conflicting ideals and systems.

*The Faerie Queene* is perhaps the world's only half-completed book that ranks in the foremost file of the writings of all times and of all peoples.

### Spenser's Contribution

Edmund Spenser brought intact Chaucer's model for English poetry across two centuries of time, fusing into it the diffuse native and foreign innovations of the intervening two hundred years, giving his successors a new model of perfection to follow.

His verse presents a full procession of the splendors of poetic form and color. It is redolent of the figures, institutions, and ideas of a great age, and for him a new age, not entirely to his liking, in the history of man. It is, at the same time, redolent of the best ideals of the ages past, the ancient and the medieval. Spenser's total verse is artistic perfection, meeting life in conflict and in harmony equally. The content of his verse shows a human creator displaying, for the most part, a new world of pleasant illusion, but at the same time revealing a very real store of equally human disillusion. Spenser is for us the great non-dramatic poet of the English Renaissance.

## Spenser's Contemporaries in the Lyric

Many great English lyric poets live for us in the shadow cast by the greatness of Spenser. Some of these are equal in certain of the elements in which the master excelled. Others are superior to him in certain qualities. It is only in the sum total of all the noble attributes of lyricism that Spenser ranks first in the Elizabethan lyric. Shakespeare is Spenser's equal in every respect and perhaps superior in the sonnet and the song, but Shakespeare's supreme greatness for us lies in a differing, but contiguous, field of literary accomplishment—dramatic poetry and all that this entails in the creation of England's greatest drama. Among the many notable poets who wrote during the later years of Elizabeth's life and shortly afterward, the following are worthy of consideration in even as brief a review as this one.

## The Sonneteers

Among the sonneteers of the age, aside from Spenser, the following are of primary importance:

1. Sir Philip Sidney (1554-1586), aside from his prose contributions discussed elsewhere, was a p⹁⸱t of considerable range. About one-third of his poetry consists of a famed sonnet cycle, containing 108 sonnets and 11 songs, called *Astrophel and Stella* (1591). His sequence is inspired by Penelope Devereux, who divorced Lord Rich and later married the Earl of Devonshire. Sir Philip's fanciful love affair with her continued the development of the Italian sonnet in England. Sidney was one of the first to weave a single theme into a lyric series. Thus he was able to portray psychological degrees of change in the emotional outlook of the lover Astrophel (Star-Lover) for his Stella (Star).

The psychological development, combined with Sidney's flawless rhythm, makes this work one of the greatest first-hand reportings of love, as real as it was noble, in English Literature.

2. <u>Samuel Daniel's</u> *Delia* (1592) and Henry Constable's *Diana* (1592) are other examples of the extreme popularity of the sonnet in Elizabethan poetry. There is nothing in particular to distinguish either collection. Daniel's has some rather bad rhyme in it and an unusual vocabulary, and Constable's is distinguished mainly by the inclusion of some very fine religious sonnets.

### *The greatest sonnet cycle of the age*

3. <u>William Shakespeare (1564-1616).</u> The sonnet cycle of Shakespeare presents the greatest of all the sonnet collections of the age. His sonnets have passed into the realm of universality and they are the most popular of English sonnet verse. Many of them indeed reach a magnitude of poetic conception and many achieve a harmony of thought and emotion that will intrigue readers of all ages.

Shakespeare apparently was writing sonnets from about 1593 until at least the close of the century. They were not published until 1609 and there has been much discussion as to their proper order, since Shakespeare himself evidently did not consider that they would contribute to his lasting fame. Editors and critics are responsible for the order in which they are arranged today.

There are 154 sonnets in the collection. The entire first 126 are addressed to a young man, perhaps a patron of the dramatist, and the final group is addressed to a certain "dark lady." The form of variation from the Petrarchan sonnet has come to be known to us as the "Shakespearean rime or sonnet" and uses three quatrains and a concluding couplet. The quatrains usually pose the question or theme and the couplets provide the poet's conclusion or answer.

*Sonnet 116*

Let me not to the marriage of true minds
Admit impediments. Love is not love
Which alters when it alteration finds,
Or bends with the remover to remove.
Oh, no! it is an ever-fixéd mark
That looks on tempests and is never shaken;
It is the star to every wandering bark,

Whose worth's unknown, although his height be taken.
Love's not Time's fool, though rosy lips and cheeks
Within his bending sickle's compass come;
Love alters not with his brief hours and weeks,
But bears it out even to the edge of doom.
    If this be error and upon me proved,
    I never writ, nor no man ever loved.

## A Great Translator

George Chapman (1559-1634). Chapman was one of the foremost literary men of the age. He did a series of translations from Greek and Roman classics which are still read today with interest. He translated Ovid's *Banquet of Sense* in 1595. In 1611 his famed rendition of Homer's *Iliad* appeared, to be followed two years later by the *Odyssey*. His translations show that Chapman was touched more than a little by the fanciful style of the age; they tend to result in his Englished versions less simple and direct accounts than in the originals. Chapman's fame in original work lies in the continuation of Marlowe's paraphrasing of Musaeus' *Hero and Leander* (published 1598), done in heroic couplets. Chapman added the final four books. Chapman's addition shows a considerably different and more obscure and weighty style than does Marlowe's lighter and more sensuous rendition of the earlier books. Chapman's other production, aside from a few short poems, lies in his contributions as a predecessor to Shakespeare in the drama.

## Michael Drayton: Poet of Variety

Michael Drayton (1563-1631) is in many ways the typical Renaissance writer and is worthy of being considered among the star performers for that very reason. It is the specialist who tends to live in literatures, the man who stands above the crowd of mediocre writers in a particular genre. Drayton was average in his age. He was a literary dilettante—he tried everything and did it all passing fair. He wrote chronicle, pastoral, sonnets, legends, and mythological narrative. He wrote historical romance and many skillful lyrics. He wrote some of the best known ballads in English, most notable being the "Ballad of Agincourt."

Fair stood the wind for France,
When we our sails advance . . .

Drayton's work is voluminous, largely historical and patriotic, inspirational, as in his "To a Virginian Voyage."

> Britons, you stay too long;
> Quickly aboard bestow you!
>   And with a merry gale
>   Swell your stretchéd sail,
> With vows as strong
> As the winds that blow you!

Drayton is undistinguished, but nonetheless is a typical Renaissance literary figure in that he threw himself eagerly into every aesthetic rivulet that trickled into the broadening stream of that new flood of interest in artistic revival and accomplishment in literature.

## The Songsters of the Age of Elizabeth

In 1557 a little collection of *Songs and Sonnets* was edited by a certain Tottel. This pioneer anthology is now known to us as *Tottel's Miscellany*. This book contains the first poems to show a real modern influence of lyric melody, personal expression, and simple rhythm. From *Tottel's Miscellany,* which contained both the lyrics written by gentlemen of the Court as well as the popular ballad rimes of the middle and lower classes, a continuous stream of such song books are known to us. Such glamorous titles as these come from the Elizabethan Age: *A Handbook of Pleasant Delights* (1556), *The Paradise of Dainty Devices* (1576), *The Phoenix Nest* (1593). Much of the material for these collections is anonymous, much is by known authors, and much of the short musical lyric poem of the age (whether in the known collections or not) can be extracted from works of the great Elizabethan dramatists.

### *Development of native verse forms*

The importation of Renaissance verse forms from abroad did not in any sense discourage the native popular stream of musical lyric verse and the catchy ballad meter of the English common people. The foreign importations merely funneled into the native stream and produced short lyric and ballad genres that were both popular and cultured. Otherwise, they simply remained aloof from it and both streams ran parallel courses throughout the age. Many of the charming short pieces were still being composed by unknown poets but much of the popular verse was produced by the great names in dramatic poetry: Ben Jonson, William Shakespeare, Christopher Marlowe, etc. These men were striving to appeal to a popular audience in drama and this vein of cultivated popularity runs throughout the Elizabethan theater and gives us many charming short pieces of lyricism—little musical, clever poems calculated to appeal to every generation of English-speaking men and women who yet retain something of nature and uninhibited emotional fancy as a part of their structure. It would only be a generation of cold, calculating, intellectual machines to whom these little lyric ditties would not appeal.

In the anonymous category, let us consider a few lines, here from "Back and Side Go Bare."

> Back and side go bare,
> Both foot and hand go cold;
> But belly, God send thee good ale enough,
> Whether it be new or old.

And when it comes to marrying,

> If ever I marry, I'll marry a maid;
> To marry a widow, I am sore afraid;
> For maids they are simple, and never will grutch.
> But widows full oft, as they say, know too much.
>
> . . . . . . .
>
> Then, if ever I marry, give me a fresh maid,
> If to marry with any I be not afraid;
> But to marry with any, it asketh much care;
> And some bachelors hold they are best as they are.

The known authors of the Elizabethan lyric are many: Sir Edward Dyer (1550-1607), John Lyly (1554-1606), George Peele (1558-1597), Robert Greene (1560-1592), Robert Southwell (1561-1595), Thomas Dekker (1570-1641), Thomas Campion (1567-1619), and many others.

Occasionally, the great names of the Age of Elizabeth would indulge in such simple delightful fun as to participate in such good-natured and charming banter as this: here Christopher Marlowe (1564-1593) has *The Passionate Shepherd* (say) *to His Love,*

> Come live with me and be my Love,
> And we will all the pleasures prove
> That hills and valleys, dales and fields,
> Or woods or steepy mountain yields.

Sir Walter Ralegh (1552-1618) is not so sure that all shepherd maids might be attracted by such an offer in his *The Nymph's Reply to the Shepherd*.

> If all the world and love were young,
> And truth in every shepherd's tongue,
> These pretty pleasures might me move,
> To live with thee and be thy love.
>
> . . . . . .
>
> Thy gowns, thy shoes, thy bed of roses,
> Thy cap, thy kirtle, and thy posies,
> Soon break, soon wither, soon forgotten,
> In folly ripe, in reason rotten. . . .

The great writers of this age have given us songs that will live forever in English. There is in them a tune, a melody, a simplicity, an individual emotional appeal, a spontaneity, and a charm of imagery that cannot be equaled on an intellectual level. What English heart can fail to thrill at Ben Jonson's *Song to Celia* (1616)?

> Drink to me only with thine eyes,
>     And I will pledge with mine;
> Or leave a kiss but in the cup,
>     And I'll not look for wine.
> The thirst that from the soul doth rise
>     Doth ask a drink divine;
> But might I of Jove's nectar sup,
>     I would not change for thine.
>
> I sent thee late a rosy wreath,
>     But not so much honoring thee
> As giving it a hope, that there
>     It could not withered be.
> But thou thereon didst only breathe,
>     And send'st it back to me;
> Since when it grows, and smells, I swear,
>     Not of itself, but thee.

## THE NEW DRAMA I: FROM MEDIEVAL TO CLASSIC INFLUENCE

### England and Spain lead in European drama

The two major European countries to resist longest the all-enveloping surge of Italian and French Renaissance tendencies were Spain, a peninsula, and England, an island. Both were countries that had a strong folkloric literature in the ballad and in the popular lyric. It is also to be noted that in both countries the liturgical mystery or miracle play ("auto" in Spanish) had degenerated into a crude, but clever, secular drama of the people by mid-15th century. It is also to be observed that both peoples, insular and peninsular, had taken this little secular play to their hearts and flocked into the public squares of every village to see and applaud what was designed more and more to please them. Drama in both England and Spain had strong popular roots before the Renaissance courtly and classical drama had an opportunity to develop. In both countries drama was democratic and popular from the outset. When Renaissance forces did begin to operate in both countries, drama came to the fore in both literatures as a full-blown genre and with a solid tradition of liturgical-secular development. Never since the great ancient Greek period of the theater had the world seen such dramatic activity and such a phenomenal brilliance as in Spain and England in the latter years of the 16th century and the early years of the 17th.

### English and Spanish drama compared

Though development is sudden and fantastic in both countries, a difference is quickly noted in the types of drama to come out of these bursts of feverish activity. In Spain, the Counter Reformation and the continuance of a feudal state kept drama on a very national and somewhat isolationist basis. The classic thread was weak and the Spanish "comedia" catered to local themes with a curious mixture of comedy, tragedy, and religion, often in the same work. In England, with the strong Reformation influence, the popular and the classic tendencies developed side by side, the tragedy and the comedy developed apart but played to the same audiences, and the intellectual and the bawdy became common grounds upon which the noble, the student, and the industrial and farmer classes met and mingled. England's drama of the Elizabethan Age was prolific, popular, and highly diversified. Spain's Golden Age of drama, at the same time, was national and popular with all classes. England's drama was of more universal appeal, since it enjoyed in equal measure classic and medieval folk influences. Lope de Vega, Spain's greatest dramatist, and Shakespeare, England's powerful universal dramatic artists, were contemporaries.

## From Morality Play to Interlude

It has been noted previously (Chap. I, pp. 16-18) that by the late 15th century, the morality play had replaced, and lent some new dignity to, the miracle play. By the end of the 15th century, the term interlude* had come into being. The morality had become highly allegorical and often proved to be rather heavy fare for the crowds in the public squares. The interlude was very short, almost entirely dialogue between two or three characters, with little action or stage setting required. These little skits depended upon clever lines rather than intrigue or stage machinery for their effects. Hence they tended to be comic or farcical. These interludes were used to fill in intervals at banquets, meetings, festivals, etc. Gradually the interlude was used to fill in the intermissions between divisions of the morality plays. Once more the village players had a vehicle for a more coarse and crude humor. The interlude, since the nobility often employed village companies to perform for them during banquets, *fetes,* and other occasions, came to acquire a higher type of writer and one of known identity. Also printing tended now to perpetuate the form. Writers of the day saw in the interlude a splendid vehicle for propaganda and satire.

## *Great writers of the "interlude"*

Henry Medwell, the first known English dramatist, produced an interlude called *Nature* (c. 1495) in which the history of man from babyhood to old age is represented. In it there is much realistic dialogue and humor as man dallies with the Seven Deadly Sins on his way through life. The "sins" tend to be rather lively and not wholly unattractive.

*Fulgens and Lucres* (c. 1491) by Medwell, is the earliest known interlude of a wholly secular nature in England.

Around 1530, John Rastell adapts a part of the Spanish *Celestina* as an interlude. It is likely that, at this time, the Spanish *paso* or *entremés* was also known by Englishmen, since this short secular and farcical type was highly popular in Spain during this age.

The first really great writer of interludes is <u>John Heywood</u> (c. 1497-c. 1580). Heywood was employed in the court of Henry VIII as a musician and entertainer in general. He wrote seven interludes known to us. All are comic and emphasize fast action and lively dialogue.

His best interlude and the masterpiece of the entire genre is *The Four P's* (printed in 1569). This broadly humorous skit satirizes religious practices of a corrupt nature. The four P's are "a Palmer, a Pardoner, a Potycary (Apothecary), and a Pedlar." There is little action and it results in a series of speeches (or debates) between the first three characters mentioned, with the Pedlar acting as judge. He is to determine which of the three can make the most unbelievable and exaggerated statement. It seems that the Palmer wins by asserting that he never saw a woman who was not even-tempered.

Many other writers of interludes are known from this early period of the purely realistic and secular skit-like dramatic vehicle, a definite forerunner of the great Tudor drama to come. After Henry VIII's reign the interlude lost favor with the court, but continued to be produced for many years, largely as a vehicle for satire and debate of current problems.

## THE NEW DRAMA II: CLASSICAL COMEDY AND TRAGEDY

### Comedy from Terence and Plautus

The classical Latin comedy had become a part of English education as early as 1500. There are evidences of many performances of comedies of Terence and Plautus (who wrote about 200 B.C.) in Eton, Westminster, and other English schools. The actors were schoolboys who perfected their conversational Latin in this manner. Schoolmasters had indulged in the pastime of making translations here and there from these Roman playwrights.

Shortly after 1550, there appeared two original English five-act comedies, both fully adapted to English life in regard to setting, theme, and characters, but following closely the art form set by Terence and Plautus. The English full-length drama had appeared at last and with amazing completeness. Both were written by men in close touch with English schools and both plays were soon being performed by pupils. _Ralph Roister Doister_ (224) was written by Nicholas Udall (c. 1505-1556) at Eton, and _Gammer Gurton's Needle_ by William Stevenson, a fellow at Christ's College, Cambridge, who died in 1575. _Ralph Roister Doister_ antedates the second comedy, as it was performed at Eton as early as 1551. As such, it is the earliest known fully developed English comedy.

Both comedies observe the classic Roman theatrical devices. Each is divided into five acts. As in the Roman comedy, the humor is broad and coarse, the language is racy and natural. There is little character development, the personages being merely types. Both are realistic and the verse is simple doggerel.* Both contain merry songs.

_Ralph Roister Doister_ depicts middle-class life in London. It seems that a wealthy widow is engaged to marry a man from her own class when Ralph, good-natured and simple, sets out to woo her also. One Merrygreek acts as a go-between and provides most of the farcical fun by the mixups he creates. After the regular suitor is alienated by reports of the widow's inconstancy, the plot rapidly unravels and he is convinced of the widow's faithfulness. Ralph, Merrygreek, and the happy couple sit down to a feast, the best of friends, as the play ends.

_Gammer Gurton's Needle_ is laid amid village rusticity. It happens that here two widows are involved: Gammer Gurton and Dame Chat. Gammer has lost her one and only needle and becomes persuaded that Dame Chat has taken possession of it. The humor is very broad and coarse in the scenes following. It finally becomes apparent that Gammer had misplaced her needle in the seat of her servant Hodge's breeches as she was mending them. Hodge, sitting down in an hilarious scene, becomes painfully aware that his backside is acting as a cushion for Gammer Gurton's needle.

## Tragedy from Seneca

The first influential tragedy in a modern language was the Italian Trissino's _Sophonisba_ (1515). It was not acted for many years. _Orbecche_ (1541), by Cinthio, founded a school of tragedy in Italy and made a deep impression on Italian audiences with its crimes and shedding of blood. Both these pioneer modern tragedies imitate the classic Greek models of Sophocles and Euripides. In French, the first modern tragedy was Jodelle's _Captive Cleopatra_ (1552). The model here is Seneca, a Spanish

Roman, who wrote his tragedies in Latin about the middle of the first century after Christ.

## Characteristics of early English tragedy

The first Elizabethan tragedy was a Senecan tragedy. There had been a great deal of interest in reading Seneca in the years of Elizabeth's reign, especially among the barristers of the Inner Temple in London. Seneca's plays were never very actable and concerned mainly the philosophic aspects of climactic situations and the tragic consequences, usually very gory ones. They were meant to be read, not presented on the stage. They were stilted and grave. This type of play was not destined to suit English temperament. The English had learned to like a story, a complete story, in their drama, and were little interested in merely a philosophic revelation of the *dénouement* and the gory consequences of the tragic error present in the characters. However, the experimental beginnings of English tragedy were to be definitely Senecan.

*Gorboduc, or Ferrex and Porrex* (226), the first English tragedy, written in blank verse, was performed before Elizabeth in 1562. The play was written by two members of Parliament, Thomas Norton, who wrote the first three acts, and Thomas Sackville, who wrote the final two acts. *Gorboduc* had a political purpose. The two authors wished to use their play to convince Elizabeth that she should marry and bear children to insure the security of the throne for the Tudors. They chose a source from British history for their theme. Their play, then, is not only the first English tragedy, but also a forerunner of the historical play, to be developed in such grand style by Shakespeare and other late Elizabethan period dramatists.

*Gorboduc* is stiff and formal, and otherwise follows Seneca in its division into five acts, the extensive use of the chorus of four old men to advance the plot and to propound ideas. The unities* are not so well observed as in Seneca.

*Gorboduc,* the King, divides his lands between his sons Porrex and Ferrex. At this point the play becomes really Senecan in its gory aspects. Porrex murders Ferrex to acquire all the lands. Ferrex happened to be the favorite son of the mother, Queen Videna. She murders Porrex. The Britons, angered at such royal behavior, murder both the King and the Queen. Thus there is no proper heir to the throne. The common people rise against the nobles, who are forced to choose a king outside the ruling line. This was a hint to Elizabeth not to let the Tudor line become extinct also. (It did, nonetheless—Ed.)

## A "playwriting contest" among barristers

Another group of barristers at Gray's Inn, not to be outdone by the good members of the Inner Temple, continued the tradition of the cooperative writing of tragedy a few years later by the production of the second English play of the kind, also in blank verse. This tragedy, *Jocasta* (1566), is credited to a member of Parliament, one George Gascoigne, who also wrote a good deal of moralizing pamphlets, sonnets, and translations. Gascoigne's *Jocasta* followed very closely the Italian *Giocasta* (1549) of Dolce, which had followed a Latin translation of Euripides' *Phoenissae*. Gascoigne actually wrote only the second, third, and fifth acts. Another member of Gray's Inn did the first and fourth, while a third member wrote the epilogue.

*Jocasta* actually did not advance English tragedy on its way to greatness. It shows less originality than *Gorboduc*. Considerable moralizing has been introduced. After the authors got through borrowing from the Italians, the ancient Greeks, and Seneca, as well as quoting their own moralizing pamphlets, there was little room left for originality. *Jocasta,* the second English tragedy, is undistinguished for much except its position in the foreground of development of Elizabethan drama.

The rivalry continued between the stubborn barristers of the Inner Temple and those of Gray's Inn. In 1567, five different gentlemen of Inner Temple collaborated on *Gismond of Salerne in Love,* copied from Boccaccio as to theme, and thoroughly Senecan as to structure and spirit, though with the addition of much romance.

The Gray's Inn crowd presented *Misfortunes of Arthur* before Elizabeth in 1588. Some seven authors are responsible for this play, including Francis Bacon. Seneca is again the order of the day.

It is to be noted that this Senecan tragedy does not in any sense indicate a taste for that sort of thing among the English people. All the efforts here represent a sort of contest between two groups of lawyers. Nowhere had *Gorboduc* been improved upon and the plays were not performed in public theaters. They were read a great deal by the inner circles of intellectuals and performed for the amusement, edification, and instruction of the Queen, who paid the costs of production.

# THE NEW DRAMA III: PREDECESSORS OF SHAKESPEARE

In the second group of Elizabethan dramatists both the English adaptation of the broad-humored Roman comedy and the imitations of the style and spirit of Seneca by the barristers' groups underwent considerable change. The comedy added romance and delicate lightness with Lyly, Peele, and Greene; the Senecan tragedy received radical modification at the hands of Kyd and Marlowe. These pre-Shakespearean dramatists laid the groundwork for the appearance of the master handlers of both comedy and tragedy.

Marlowe, the greatest English dramatist before Shakespeare, was born the same year as the master (1564), but died as the literature's greatest dramatic representative was only beginning to write (1593). Thus he is Shakespeare's predecessor, whereas, had a dagger not ended his life at the age of twenty-nine, the turn of the century might have seen a pair of geniuses at the top rung of the ladder of fame in world drama.

## Pre-Shakespearean Comedy

John Lyly (c. 1554-1606), aside from the prose romances of *Euphues,* wrote eight comedies. Lyly's gentlemanly use of a language of many colors and flights of rhetorical fancy extended to his ideas of what the English comedy should be like. It should be, above all, moral, and it should be dainty and fanciful. The characters should perform deeds of generosity and delicate tenderness. He maintained all this, for one reason, because the parts in the plays of the day, particularly those of women, were taken by young schoolboys. Lyly, then, is romantic and light (except in language perhaps) and fanciful.

His *The Woman in the Moone* (c. 1584) is his only play in blank verse. All the rest are in prose, but with lyrical passages and songs here and there. This play is a light satire on women. He personifies Queen Elizabeth as his Pandora, endowed with the qualities of the Seven Planets, making her a very variable and changeable woman.

Lyly's other plays are: *Alexander and Campaspe* (1581) in which Alexander the Great renounces his love for a slave girl because she is in love with a painter; *Sappho and Phao* (1584), a light court allegory; *Gallathea* (1587), a charming thing in which two girls, disguised as boys, fall in love with each other. Venus comes along and changes one into a boy and the problem is solved. *Endymion* (1586) retells the story of Cynthia and her love for the shepherd Endymion. *Midas* (1592), a satirical comedy on greed, and *Mother Bombie* (1587 or 89), a rustic theme in a light manner, complete the list.

Lyly's comedies are somewhat plotless. His characters speak in a stilted euphuistic manner, characterized later so beautifully by Shakespeare, who satirized the high-flown euphuism, as have many English writers:

> Taffeta phrases, silken terms precise,
> Three pil'd hyperboles, spruce affectation,
> Figures pedantical.

Lyly did substitute a more subtle and cunning wit for the broad and coarse humor of the imitators of the Roman comedy. His comedies are also known for their charming lyric songs and other musical bits. In *Alexander and Campaspe,* for instance:

> Cupid and my Campaspe play'd
> At cards for kisses: Cupid paid . . .

George Peele (c. 1558-1596) was a ne'er-do-well in his life. He was born in the gutters of London, and in spite of his imaginative powers, an M.A. degree from Oxford, and his many opportunities, never seemed to fit himself into a higher life. He died in poverty and scarcely two steps ahead of the jailer for a series of swindles. Ornamental and flowery poetical diction distinguish his work. His lyrics are delicate and he is a master at the manipulation of blank verse. He had a great sense of dramatic intensity. His great faults are a poor sense of construction and coherency of the whole. He was given to introducing highly irrelevant scenes, disturbing to the continuity of his main themes. His main contribution is an unsurpassed poetry of delicate beauty.

The *Arraignment of Paris* (1581), a pastoral in honor of Elizabeth, takes up the mythological story of the beauty contest of the Greek goddesses, in which Paris awarded the apple to Venus, in preference to Juno and Minerva. The two rejected goddesses had Paris brought before a council of gods to answer the charge of bad judgment. Diana decides the issue by awarding the apple, not to any of the three, but to an unheard-of nymph, significantly named Eliza.

Peele's *Edward the First* (c. 1591) is a lyrical but rather crude historical play. His *The Old Wives' Tale* (c. 1591) is rather incoherently arranged but preserves many folkloric elements, such as nursery rhymes. The play is a satire on romances and is perhaps, despite its looseness, his best play. He also wrote a scriptural play in *The Love of David and Fair Bethsabe,* colorful and decorative, a piece which perhaps influenced Milton's *Paradise Lost* and the French Racine's *Esther.*

In 1607 a popular collection of rather ribald jokes and sayings was published under the title *The Merry Conceited Jests of George Peele.* George Peele, a brilliant versifier, was the François Villon of the Elizabethan Age.

Robert Greene (c. 1560-1592) was a very prolific writer, being accredited with more than two dozen novels and many broadsides,\* tracts, and other forms of popular distribution of the day. Greene was a popular dramatist and it is certain that he wrote a good many more plays than are traced to him. He introduced many innovations into his comedies which gave them a modern touch. He, for the first time, gave women a major place in his plots. He knew how to portray well the feminine character. He mixed various elements of the fanciful and the fantastic into realistic situations. He was an experimenter and tended to overcrowd his plots. His plays tend toward the melodramatic.\* His influence on Shakespeare and his contemporaries was strong.

Perhaps Greene's best play is his prose *History of Friar Bacon and Friar Bungay* (1589), a partly historical piece, in which Greene keeps two well-integrated plots running merrily along side by side. One plot concerns the legendary Friar Bacon, a magician, and particularly the head of brass which the Friar had constructed and which uttered little bits of weighty predictions. The interesting element is that Friar Bacon renounces his black arts before he is irrevocably lost, a contrast to the Faust legend, where Dr. Faustus falls a victim to black magic. The other plot is a light romantic love story.

Greene shows evidence of being influenced a great deal by his contemporary, Marlowe. And both he and Marlowe, in their respective spheres of comedy and tragedy, did much to help shape the great English drama to come.

## Pre-Shakespearean Tragedy

Two dramatists of this pre-Shakespearean period succeed in reshaping the Senecan tragedy to make it palatable to English taste. Not only did these men set an English standard for the adaptation of the Latin tragedy; they laid the framework for the English theater's most masterful field of production.

### A creator of popular tragedy on the Senecan model

Thomas Kyd (1558-1594) is almost universally known for only one play, *The Spanish Tragedy* (229), written perhaps in 1583 or early in the next year. This melodramatic thriller in blank verse immediately caught the fancy of the public. The people flocked to Henslowe's theater to see it and ten printed editions are known prior to 1634. The drama had come back to the people and in a startling different form, which they loved. For during the next century no peoples (with the possible exception of the theater-going public of ancient Greece) had become so drama conscious as the English and the Spanish.

Kyd gives his public a contemporary setting and plot. He continues to use the Senecan devices of the ghost, the declamatory digressions, and the revenge motive, but he pours a bag of tricks of his own into the mold that were calculated to send (and did) chills and thrills through his audiences. Kyd's play is a "tragedy of blood" but executed with the finesse of a seasoned hand that knows just how far to go to keep his illusions from reaching the point of being morbid.

Kyd sets his play in Spain, a country that had set the pace in world exploration and had become England's closest rival. As Kyd's play saw its *première* performance, Spain was planning and collecting stores and taxes to finance a mighty Armada of vessels to storm English shores. And Kyd's play was still going strong when the Spanish Armada went to pieces against the Irish coast in 1588.

His plot is complex and imaginary, unlike the dull monotony of the singleness of purpose of Senecan plots. Kyd is an early master of the unexpected and turns loose all manner of subplot interludes upon the audience. He introduced all sorts of twisted and neurotic personalities to add to his bizarre effects. Kyd has eight murders and suicides, as well as one public hanging, take place before the public gaze. Not content, he piles on other equally horrible and spine-chilling spectacles, as the ripping out of a man's tongue by its roots. His play is a succession of side-show acts, some going on simultaneously with others. There is not a dull moment and little time is allowed the spectator for more than a few short breaths before final curtain.

Most of Kyd's other production is lost, including a *Spanish Comedy* and a play entitled *Don Horatio,* which we know was produced in 1592. But *The Spanish Tragedy* is enough to immortalize the name of Thomas Kyd. We today do not consider it a good play, but we respect the powerful effect it had upon those master playwrights to come, who knew how to utilize Kyd's devices in the molding of mature tragedy.

### Shakespeare's greatest predecessor: Marlowe

Christopher Marlowe (1564-1593), is Shakepeare's greatest predecessor in English drama. The two dramatists were born in the same year. Marlowe loved knowledge and became one of the finest scholars of his time. His views in religion were antipathetic to both Catholics and Puritans alike. His defense of Jews and of Eastern faiths caused him to be called an "atheist" and worse names. He was hailed before the Privy Council for his liberal views. Before the case could be decided, the poet was stabbed to death in a tavern brawl. There are several views of the exact circumstances of his death.

Marlowe's personal life is a record of ideals equal to his superior intellect. He was highly popular with his fellow dramatists and a small intimate circle of friends. His country was in religious conflict, but Marlowe found that the English people were far from accepting as a fellow citizen a man who criticized the ignorance of either side of the conflict. Much of the scandalous libel of the times against Marlowe's name has been disproved by scholars of recent times. Marlowe's character appears to us today to have been on the same high level as his mind and his drama. The Reformation had come to England in the late 16th century, but tolerance and open seeking of the truth had not.

### Marlowe's great plays

Marlowe, in a very short-lived writing career, has left us the greatest dramatic production of English literature to Shakespeare. His contribution to the form and style of the Englished romantic tragedy is great; his models of character development are even greater. In four plays, *Tamburlaine the Great* (c. 1587-1588),

*The Tragical History of Doctor Faustus* (c. 1588-1589), *The Jew of Malta* (c. 1592), and *Edward II* (1593), Marlowe had shown English drama that the secret of greatness in tragedy does not lie in its "blood bath," but in the tragic fault in character and in the elements of inner conflict and its interplay with external circumstance. His themes revolve around one great personality engaged in a mighty struggle to attain a goal, but not quite succeeding because of a tragic fault of character.

Marlowe sneered at the conceits of euphuism and brought the blank verse line to a point of being a powerful vehicle with which to treat an elevated theme with seriousness and conviction. With it he reaches the thundering heights of oratory and murmurs the sweet nothings of young love equally well. His plots are tightly integrated and his mechanical structure and stage devices are blended in to achieve whatever effect the situation calls for with both unity and precision.

Which is Marlowe's greatest play is a moot question and largely a matter of individual choice, for each, to a degree, is marred by minor failures of the author to attain the perfection of the great master, Shakespeare.

*Tamburlaine the Great* (232) is divided into two parts of five acts each. It is a "hero" play in which a Scythian shepherd rises by sheer barbaric power of personality to become a conqueror of kingdoms. His crude but cunning and clever cruel nature is fired by an ever-growing ambition as he achieves success after success. Marlowe's rhetorical lines resound as he drives his remorseless and savage nature higher and higher up the ladder of power and fame. In this play Marlowe's electrifying verse compensates for a rather weak dramatic structure.

In *Tamburlaine*, Marlowe depicts a driving ambition that will not be satisfied; in *The Tragical History of Doctor Faustus*, his theme is an intellect that pushes itself to destroy the laws of nature in order to know more than is given to a human mind to accomplish. The story of the scholar who was willing to sell his soul to the devil in return for power, superhuman knowledge, and pleasure is an old one. It had been a legend of the middle ages. Ultimately, it was to receive its supreme telling in Goethe's *Faust* (1808-1832), more than two centuries after Marlowe. As in *Tamburlaine*, here Marlowe again has an opportunity to deal with human aspiration after the unattainable, the clash of human will and man's fate. The first two acts of the play are magnificent in their intensity and power. The texts, which have come to us, are marred by a good deal of coarse humor that seems quite out of keeping with the taste of Marlowe himself, and was probably added by editors. Again Marlowe reveals an inability in stage craftsmanship.

The *Jew of Malta* again presents a lust for power and wealth, which will admit no obstacles to its path, nor does it hesitate before any methods to attain its goal. The earlier parts of the play reveal Marlowe at his best, but he falls short. This time he yields to the temptation to pull all stops and let blood flow. Before the play ends it has gone all the way toward the Senecan "blood bath" and has degenerated into the "chills and thrills" type of melodrama that Kyd's *The Spanish Tragedy* had shown from first to final curtain. Marlowe's picture of Barabas, the Jew, is his most masterful character portrayal.

In *Edward II,* Marlowe shows that his knowledge of stage technique has grown steadily stronger. From a technical stand-point this is the strongest of the plays; from the standpoint of character development, it is the weakest of Marlowe's plays. He attempts to develop several characters at once, and neglects his central historical figure. He had sacrificed character for tech-nique. His verse also suffered from his drive here for structural perfection. Perhaps, had he lived, he might have achieved both objects.

Aside from two plays of less importance, *The Massacre at Paris* (1593) and *The Tragedy of Queen Dido of Carthage* (1594), Marlowe did translation from Ovid and Lucan. We have noted his *Hero and Leander* (p. 65), which Chapman finished after Marlowe's death, and his lyric *The Passionate Shepherd to His Love* (p. 67).

### *From Marlowe to Shakespeare in English drama*

From Marlowe to Shakespeare is but a step; actually, in time, it is no step at all, for as Marlowe worked on *Doctor Faustus* (c. 1588) Shakespeare was probably writing *The Comedy of Errors* (c. 1589). Both were twenty-nine when Marlowe died in 1593. Shakespeare, building up slowly in sureness of tech-nique and knowledge of verse and character building, was almost ready to give the world his own genius and what he had absorbed of a genius that had been cut short too soon—Christopher Marlowe.

## The Staging of Elizabethan Drama

When Elizabeth came to the throne (1558), she found a company of eight actors of interludes attached to the court. By this time, in England, it was not unusual for gentlemen of wealth and position to have attached to their households private companies of players. It had become a matter of social distinction and the players wore a special livery to proclaim the various houses they served. Gradually wandering companies began to tour the villages, independent of the support of rich patrons. The great indoor, and outdoor, sport of the Elizabethans had become the drama in all its forms. The companies often used their position to steal and plunder, thus gaining for the profession in general the reputation of thievery and dishonesty. The Puritans, opposed to the theater as being an invention of the devil, with actors performing as his instruments, lent their support to the side of much growing opposition to actors.

The amateur status of dramatic performance, however, continued to gain popularity. The schools and universities had long performed the plays of Plautus and Terence as a part of the school curricula. In 1572, an Act of Parliament declared that all companies of players must perform for some responsible patron. Otherwise, actors would be considered rogues and vagabonds and treated accordingly. Unsponsored companies were forbidden to perform in London, by an Act of 1574.

### *"Public"* and *"private"* playhouses

To avoid the city laws, companies began to acquire more or less fictional sponsorships and to erect playhouses outside the city limits, usually in the most disreputable districts. These "public" playhouses mushroomed in the late years of the century, under such inspiring names as *Curtain, Red Bull, Fortune, Rose, Hope, Swan, Globe*. The first was established in 1576 by one Burbage and was called simply *Theatre*.

Playhouses which succeeded in being allowed to establish themselves within the city became known as "private" theaters, and played to a smaller and more select group of playgoers. They often provided seating and artificial lighting. Outstanding among these early "private" theaters were *Paul's Boys* and *Blackfriars*. In the early 17th century, it is interesting to note that Shakespeare's company of players had the controlling interest in *Blackfriar's* the main "private," and the *Globe,* the principal "public," theaters. It is the "private" group, however, that gave rise to the sumptuous permanent structures of the 17th century.

In spite of the Puritan opposition and the generally bad reputation that attended acting, by the time James I came to the throne in 1603, acting had become a profession in England, some companies receiving subsidies from the court and other wealthy patrons and some making their own way by public admission charges. The English people had become theater conscious and were not to be denied their satisfaction of this new form of amusement. The wandering companies continued to tour English towns and generally had better accommodations than had their medieval prototypes, the "pageant" players, when the platform of a large wagon, driven into the public square, served as a stage for the morality and miracle plays. Now these roaming groups performed in inn yards, surrounded by the rooms of the inner court. A somewhat crude stage was erected at one end of the yard and crude galleries were constructed outside the windows of upper rooms to give the more distinguished playgoers seating away from the crowd, which usually stood in the open yard or seated itself on rough benches.

## Details of staging Elizabethan plays

The "public" and the "private" playhouses in London had recognizable distinguishing features other than the location and type of patronage. The "public" theaters had their stages extended out into the "pit" where the poor classes stood on three sides. They were also roofless. Many inside experimental theaters today (university groups, Little Theater groups, etc.) play to small audiences, seated on three sides of the players, and are often designated as "theaters in the round." The *Globe,* the most famous of the Elizabethan theaters in Shakespeare's day would have given the appearance of a round building, flat on the back side. The "private" playhouses, such as *Blackfriars,* had the stage at one end of the hall, the conventional arrangement still.

Other details are interesting. Women, then, as now, used the the theater to display new apparel and jewelry. Often they came wearing masks to conceal their identities, and perhaps to shield their blushes at the coarse humor that often came from the stage or from the "pit." A flag was run up a pole an hour before performance time to let the public know a show was to be given that day. The performance usually took place about two or three in the afternoon.

The stage was larger than the average stage today and only the rear portion was curtained. Often members of the gentry sat on the stage itself to watch performances. Fisticuffs were not unknown on the stage itself between actors and spectators, for this front stage seating was often taken by the inevitable aristocratic hecklers of the day. An upper stage was built across the back to serve for balcony scenes, frequent in the plays of the day. Properties were used, but were often quite symbolic, a crude altar representing a whole church interior, for instance.

There were no women in the casts of plays. Women's parts were taken by young boys, with high-pitched voices if possible. Love scenes, it is obvious, were seldom exploited beyond certain stereotyped and symbolic gestures—the lines had to carry the burden of realism in this department.

### Variety of dramatic production

By the end of the reign of Elizabeth, both "public" and "private," as well as the strictly court theaters were playing a variety of types of production: short interludes, comedies, and tragedies, masques,* allegorical court plays, historical representations, the translated Roman comedy, medieval romance, etc. Musicians enlivened the performances, usually beginning their playing an hour before the first curtain and performing between the acts.

By the end of the Elizabethan Age, English drama was performed, with relatively limited modifications, much as drama is today. And by this time, the English common man could witness some of the best dramatic production of all time. Only Spain equaled the Elizabethan theater on the continent at this early state in the development of the modern theater. And only Spain's three or four top names (Lope de Vega, Calderón, Tirso, Alarcón) could rival England's Shakespeare, Marlowe, and Jonson. And only England's theater continued its greatness, almost uninterruptedly from that day to the present.

### THE NEW DRAMA IV: THE GREAT SHAKESPEARE

"He was not of an age, but for all time!"
— Ben Jonson

The most revered single name in all literature is William

Shakespeare (1564-1616). He used the English language to touch the heights of dramatic art and of universal human psychology and emotional range for all peoples and all times in his plays. He plumbed the depths to which the human soul can sink and he soared beyond the realm of fancy and idealism. He is a universal master of dramatic and poetic literature. What the aesthetic culture of the world inherited from this one pen is limited only by the fact that beauty and fullness in writing are bound by the language in which the creator writes. It is a pity that the works of a Shakespeare cannot be sensed by all peoples as the creations of a Michelangelo or of a Beethoven.

We believe that Shakespeare wrote as many as 37 plays. At least one-half of this number are today immortal gems in the total production of the drama. His name would have lived in our literature for only one of them.

The treatment of Shakespeare in this review book must be inadequate and brief. An appreciation of his greatness, a brief picture of what he accomplished and a suggestion to every reader that Western man's cultural fund is woefully short without an intimate contact with and a feeling for the masterpieces of this English writer is all that a few pages can do at best, and it is all that many pages could do. In our world the facilities and opportunities to communicate with the highest dramatic art of our heritage are many and open to all. The thought and the beauty of Shakespeare have never been censored and they have never lacked those who would lead us to him by every known medium of communicating the past heritage to modern man.

### Controversy over the authorship of the plays

Thousands of books and articles have been written in many languages about this man and his art; the editions of his works would defy count. The performances of his plays, good ones and bad ones, but all with sincere homage to the superb writer of drama, are legion. No actor, nor actress, has been really great until the supreme test of Shakespearean interpretation has been passed. Scholars have spent their lives delving into the plays and into the circumstances and backgrounds clinging to them. Some have tried to prove that Shakespeare is a pseudonym, a "cover-up" for Francis Bacon, that the bard of Avon could not have done that magnificent work and that the great essayist possessed the intellect for it. This writer has no quarrel with this position; he has no wish to reach back in time and transfer deeds to plays which have been the free property of the whole world for almost a half a millenium. And he has no wish to take issue with those who would tell us that the capacity in a particular man for great artistic production is measurable by the minds of modern scholars or publicity seekers; he is merely content to go along with the blind man who also created immortal literature, John Milton:

Sweetest Shakespeare, Fancy's child.

## His Life

The poet was born in the village of Stratford, on the little Avon River. He was baptized in the little village church of Stratford-on-Avon, April 26, 1564, and fifty-two years later he was buried there. His father was a tanner and glover. William attended the local grammar school until he was fourteen, and as he says, picked up "small Latin and less Greek." His formal education was small, but his powers of observation and his faculty of curiosity were great. He did not attend the universities, but he stored up images from nature and life about him.

His father's financial circumstances became more and more strained and William was forced to leave school. At eighteen he married Ann Hathaway, a woman eight years his senior. We have evidence that young Shakespeare was of a full amorous nature. Ann's and his child was baptized six months after the marriage. The marriage did not prove to be an ideal one. It is also evident that he indulged in pranks of various sorts. There is some reason to believe that he left Stratford (between 1585 and 1587) because of the matter of deer stealing from one of the local gentry.

He went to London and soon became attached to the company of actors playing the *Theatre* of James Burbage. He stayed with Burbage as actor, playwright, and part owner for many years.

His life was spent on the stage and behind the scenes. The *Theatre* was razed and the new *Globe* was built. We have records of the young actor's performances and of his friendships and enmities. There is evidence that the more intellectual of the playwrights of the day were a bit envious. George Peele, for instance, leaves us this choice bit of his opinions of the young upstart: ". . . supposes he is as able to bombast out a blank verse as the best of us."

Shakespeare seems to have prospered modestly. He maintained his parents in comfort and bought a good deal of land around Stratford, which he seems to have visited seldom during his busy career in London. He, however, retired to Stratford when he was fifty and died there in 1616. The little village of Stratford-on-Avon is today the world's most famous literary shrine.

### Shakespeare's attitude toward his plays

There is ample evidence that Shakespeare's fellow playwrights were jealous of him and perhaps angered somewhat by his careless and indifferent attitude toward his art. After he had created a masterpiece, he would then seem to forget it. It is only through the efforts of friends that many of his plays were saved. He did not bother to collect and publish them. His First Folio edition of his collected plays was the effort of two friends seven years after his death. This is one of the principal arguments of Bacon supporters, that his carelessness shows a lack of interest in something that was not his own. It is always annoying to ordinary men of intensity and seriousness of purpose to stomach a relatively unlettered genius who tops the work of scholars and collectors of degrees with apparent ease, and then adds insult to injury by taking a lackadaisical attitude of complete indifference toward his accomplishment.

Shakespeare was popular in his day. Crowds flocked to his plays. He had wealthy patrons, and beginning with nothing, he rose to a position among the middle class gentry. And, burning jealousy aside, his comrades respected and admired him. In all the statements made about Shakespeare, before and after his death, by his contemporaries in the Elizabethan theater, one adjective is more frequently used than any other, "gentle."

### Periods of Growth in Shakespeare's Art

*The Experimental Period.* Up to the time of the death of Marlowe (1593), Shakespeare had delved into comedy, tragedy, and the historical play. His pattern was set and he had experimented with most of the devices which he was to perfect in his next period. He was somewhat entangled in the euphuistic speech of his predecessors (it especially shows in *Love's Labour's Lost*. He tried his hand at adaptation of a Plautan comedy *(Comedy of Errors)*. The Senecan horrors intrigued him for a while (*Titus Andronicus*). He tried an imitation in drama of a love romance of the day (*Two Gentlemen from Verona*). And he imitated freely from the earlier chronicle or historical play (*Henry VI*). He delved into the Italianized court play with success (*Taming of the Shrew*).

These early plays were experimental and they were done as well as any of their types had been done, with the exception of the Senecan horror play. They show the same artificiality in spots, the pedantry and the slapstick comedy in other spots, of their predecessors. Character development is on its way for Shakespeare, but he does not achieve any great measure of perfection in it as yet. His language is experimental, florid, and bombastic here, doggerel there, beautifully lyric and simple further on.

*The Transition Period and Development of Originality*. From 1593 to the end of the century, Shakespeare delved little more into tragedy. He perhaps realized his shortcomings and immaturity in character development (in comparison with Marlowe, for instance) and that he did not wish to follow up the traditions of Seneca, Sackville, and Kyd. From *Titus Andronicus* (1593-1594) to *Julius Caesar* (1599-1600) he concentrates upon romantic comedy (and romantic tragedy with *Romeo and Juliet*) and history. He throws his powers of originality into these more easily developed types. Masterpieces begin to flow from his pen at once.

### The first great comedy

*A Midsummer Night's Dream* (1595-1596) proves that he had arrived at his goal in the romantic comedy. It is a dream play with skillfully handled multiple plot sequences. Some of the most charming of the airy characters (Puck, for instance) begin to show up here, and some of the most quotable lines.

> Lord, what fools these mortals be!

And the world has not yet advanced in the jet age to anything comparable to the accomplishments of the saucy Puck.

> I'll put a girdle around the earth
> In forty minutes. . . .

In this period Shakespeare was coasting along a plateau in his career. He did not feel quite ready yet for the hard climbs. He rested, undecided and learning from life and maturity, and produced great light comedies. His great escapist comedies soar in the realms of delight and fancy, touching reality here and there, giving readers and audiences alike untold and delicious thrills, as he trips with light and sure foot through a pleasant world of minor conflicts and light romantic themes. His poetry touches all the delicate nuances of lyricism and becomes lightly philosophical at times, but always the light touch is there, and we know that everything is going to turn out all right. Audiences do not attend *Much Ado About Nothing, As You Like It* (237), or *Twelfth Night* to add to their worries or to strain their emotional cords in following dire conflcting writhings of personality change. They go for beauty of verse, light laughter, visual spectacles, and a wisdom that merely skims the surfaces of thought.

### *The major historical plays*

During the period Shakespeare rapidly produces the bulk of the best of his historical plays (240). Relatively easy and comparatively free from complications of structure and plot development, these historical pieces gave Shakespeare an opportunity to pull the stops of a more thundering type of patriotic verse. He soars to the grandiloquent, and England has never received more resounding or poetic praise from one of its sons.

> The royal throne of kings, this sceptered isle,
> This earth of majesty, this seat of Mars,
> This other Eden, demi-paradise,
> This fortress build by Nature for herself
> Against infection and the hand of war,
> This happy breed of men, this little world,
> This precious stone set in the silver sea,
> Which serves it in the office of a wall
> Or as a moat defensive to a house,
> Against the envy of less happier lands,
> This blessed plot, this earth, this realm,
>     this England.
>
> —King Richard II, Act II, Sc. 1, Line 40

Shakespeare yet felt that dry historical matter, despite the unity, the patriotic appeal, the manipulation of action, and the resounding language, was in need of relief from too much of the same thing. And in Henry IV he thought of the broad Roman comedy, and turned up a set of characters as a background for his superb comic creation, Falstaff. Falstaff is at once fat, cowardly, blustering, a liar and a cheat, and a valiant friend. He is seldom merely crude; there is much wit in his slapstick. The scenes with Falstaff, who plays in and out during the two parts of the play, are in the idiomatic prose of the taverns of Shakespeare's day—lively, colorful, and occasionally a bit hard for moderns to follow. Falstaff was definitely not a man of action.

> I were better to be eaten to death with
> rust than to be scoured to nothing with
> perpetual motion.
>
> —Henry IV, Pt. II, Act I, Sc. 1, Line 249

## Romeo and Juliet

During the period Shakespeare sends his powers of romance a little into the deeper side and gives us one of the world's most stimulating romantic tragedies: *Romeo and Juliet* (1594-1595) (244). The poet had soon conquered the temptation to yield to the ominous threat of Seneca. His tragedy is not to be horrible for the sake of horror. Bloodletting is incidental here and hardly noticeable. The Senecan influences are present but unobtrusive; the revenge motives are toned down into a feud between two families who learn love and reason at last, after paying a frightful price. The Shakespearean play does not cause his audiences to exclaim over the horror of it all, but rather, the pity of it all. The young lover is treated in a light and fanciful way, with the touch of true romantic melancholy. Sentimental lovers of all time have much quotable fodder from these touching scenes.

> Good night, good night; parting is such
> sweet sorrow,
> That I shall say good night til it be
> morrow.

## Great characters of comedy

Shakespeare, now in his thirties, and sure of his abilities in comedy, tries to bring his lightness toward the graver side, the side of reality, and touch tragedy, but so very lightly that no one will get hurt. His *Merchant of Venice* (1596-1597) (248) does just that. And here the poet has his opportunity to experiment with character development. He brings us Shylock, his best development of a personality to date. And here he brings us his second great feminine character, Portia. She is older, a wiser, and a more intellectual woman than Juliet. Three other portrayals of women are to distinguish Shakespearean comedy (women without the tragic potential of his later plays) of this period: Beatrice of *Much Ado About Nothing,* Rosalind of *As You Like It,* and Viola in *Twelfth Night*—a picture gallery of unforgettable women, delicately drawn and varied.

In *The Merchant of Venice* there is substance and near-tragedy. It has romantic love, witty dialogue, and even descends a bit to the broader level with Launcelot Gobbo. The play breathes of the Oriental story in his subtilties of plot: the casket story, the ring story, and the bond story. And, over all, hangs the strongest character of Shakespeare's theater so far, the grasping and crafty Shylock.

*The Period of the Great Tragedies and the Bitter Comedies.* The period of Shakespeare's mastery of the drama, from 1599-1609, is also a period which signals a change in the English mind and spirit. Elizabeth dies (1603) and James I, the son of Mary Stuart, comes to the throne. The Elizabethan Age is on the wane and a new age is beginning. But the change in politics and temperament has no effect upon the genius of the developing Shakespeare, who has now reached his decision that he is ready to give the world great tragedy, within or without the Senecan model.

His plays of this period are of three groups: (1) the Roman plays, including *Julius Caesar, Antony and Cleopatra,* and *Coriolanus;* (2) the comedies (a new and serious type), *Measure for Measure* and *Troilus and Cressida;* (3) the tragedies of *Hamlet, Macbeth, Othello,* and *King Lear.*

### Julius Caesar: foremost Roman play

*Julius Caesar* (c. 1599) (252), based on Plutarch, is noble and intellectual in its conception. Brutus, rather than Caesar, is the central figure. This play is, in essence, a Senecan tragedy, complete with its ghosts and revenge motives, together with many long and philosophical disquisitions. But Shakespeare's treatment is powerfully dramatic and his language is eloquent, but admirably clear.

Hitherto, the great dramatist had only produced one near-perfect characterization, Shylock. But here the personalities of Caesar, Brutus, Cassius, and to a degree, Antony, are clearly drawn. Caesar is boastful, superstitious, and inwardly thirsty for praise and power. Brutus is given the same idealistic hero treatment here as Plutarch gave him. Cassius is slated for the role of villain, but as it turns out, a rather sympathetic villain. Antony becomes Shakespeare's instrument to reach his height of dramatic oratory in the funeral oration speech. Shakespeare, perhaps, already had in mind his intention to use Antony as the foil upon which to develop his greatest feminine character portrayal, Cleopatra. He is given some of the noblest lines in this intellectual, rather than dramatically emotional, play. He is always the foil, however, which Shakespeare uses to develop his idealization of Brutus. Antony, a friend and favorite of Caesar, comes at last to say of Brutus:

> This was the noblest Roman of them all;
> All the conspirators, save only he,
> Did that they did in envy of great Caesar;
> He only, in a general honest thought,
> And common good to all, made one of them.
> His life was gentle; and the elements
> So mix'd in him that Nature might stand up
> And say to all the world, *This was a man!*

### Four world masterpieces of tragedy

In *Hamlet* (1602) (255), *Othello* (1604), *King Lear* (1605), and *Macbeth* (1606), Shakespeare reaches deep into the well-springs of tragedy and gives us four masterpieces of near equal power. Here Shakespeare deals with the tragic elements of conflict of wills, conflict of will with circumstances, and conflict of will with itself. His development of his four great personalities who, by a series of casual and logical episodes, come to disaster in their struggles, is both technically masterful and thoroughly effective. Hamlet's tragic end is brought about through a weakness of will, indecision, and procrastination. This is the tragic fault of his personality. Othello is again the victim of an inner conflict, a clash between the noble Moor's love and his sense of honor. This inner struggle weakens his will to the point of falling an easy victim to the base intrigue of Iago, a lesser man by far. Lear's weakness is his susceptibility to hypocritical praise and adulation. His own pride blinds him to the true values in his circumstances and lets him fall an easy victim to appearances. Macbeth's fault is essentially that of Tamburlaine, a driving ambition. But Macbeth is essentially a man of goodness and virtue and, after his first crime, is constantly seeking peace of mind.

Here Shakespeare creates his most forceful woman character, Lady Macbeth, who is willing to submerge all her womanly qualities to become an unswerving instrument to overcome her husband's weakness in his path to fortune and power. The conflict here, then, is multiple—each playing against the other to push events forward to their inevitable conclusion—disaster for husband and wife. The temptation here is brought from the supernatural world, in keeping with the primitive setting of early Scotland, a people of superstition, of ghosts and monsters, much like the early Angles and Saxons in their misty northland, peopled with beings beyond human ken who controlled the destinies of weak man.

These four tragedies are the most powerful serious production of English drama, and if they do not excel, certainly equal the best examples of serious tragedy in world drama to the present time.[1]

*Antony and Cleopatra* (1607) is a riot of colorful scenes, a masterly portrayal of sensuous luxury to surround Shakespeare's central figure, his greatest characterization of a woman, Cleopatra. The play is loosely constructed but gives a sense of luxury through its very multiplicity of scenes and its double ending, first the death of Antony in the fourth act, then the final act with Cleopatra going alone toward her inevitable end.

Shakespeare's Cleopatra is his supreme effort in the creation of female character. He has made her the "eternal" feminine, full of contradictory qualities. He makes her fickle, shallow, and licentious in one scene; in another part of the play she is faithful, true, and heroic. She is characterized by inconsistency.

### Shakespeare's bitter comedies

Shakespeare is serious now and in the interludes between creating great tragedy he writes three comedies: *All's Well That Ends Well* (1601), *Measure for Measure* (1603), and *Troilus and Cressida* (1603). These are not happy plays, if one con-

[1] A review book of this size cannot delve deeply into the plots of many works that follow the same basic patterns. Only five works of Shakespeare are being included in the Plot Summaries Appendix, plus a view of one of the dramatist's historical groupings. These six digests illustrate the course of perfection that Shakespeare achieved in his major types of production. For the student or general reader who wishes to follow the course of other powerful plots developed by this master dramatist, this writer recommends the inexpensive McGill and Ault: *Synopses of Shakespeare's Complete Plays*, published by Littlefield, Adams & Co., 1954. This handy guide, not only gives full character descriptions and essential data as to sources of plays, etc., but follows in detail, act by act and scene by scene, development of the plots of each of Shakespeare's plays.

siders them in the same light as the airy and delicate touch Shakespeare injects into his early romantic fantasy. But the poet is no longer in the mood for mere frivolity and entertainment. He does not intend tragedy. He wants here to present evil forces that illustrate something broader than merely the tragedy which comes to individuals. He feels the need to present a few of the problems present in the social group. He does this by means of straight stories which have little about them that is amusing, unless one is amused by a wife who must plot with her husband's mistress in order to substitute for her in the dark of night so that she may conceive a child by him and thus keep his love (*All's Well That Ends Well*). *Troilus and Cressida,* of course, is another treatment of the faithless Cressida, and Shakespeare neither spares her nor heroic ideals in his satire. *Measure for Measure,* again, is a picture of degradation, not unusual, nor particularly shocking. It merely arouses a bit of disgust on the part of the reader that there are such people.

Some have characterized these comedies as "dark," or tending to reveal a morbid side to the Shakespeare of this period. It is true that they reveal a bit of the seamy side of life and approach tragedy at various points, but the first two end well. In these comedies Shakespeare does not fail in his poetic perfection. Some of his best passages are in these plays, and Isabella (*Measure for Measure*) is one of his better character portrayals.

In these plays Shakespeare comes as near as he ever did to the social comedy and to serious satire. Here the poet is simply experimenting with a new comedy, which reads very much like a cut from real life as it was lived in the upper circles of society in Renaissance Italy, or perhaps England. They are problem plays and all show carelessness of workmanship, and generally, weakness of characterization. Shakespeare was more concerned in typing his personages than he was of building central character. Taken in their entirety, none are mediocre plays and all leave the sour taste that Shakespeare intended as a reaction to them.

*Timon of Athens* (about 1606) belongs to this period and fits none of the groupings. It is included in Shakespearean collections but is generally believed to be only partly the work of the great dramatist. Another play of the period, *Pericles, Prince of Tyre* (1608), poorly constructed, also is judged to be only partly the work of Shakespeare.

*The Final Period. Shakespeare returns to romance.* The

poet's return to romance in his final three efforts has a touch of a master hand that is playing with drama. It seems that Shakespeare is amusing himself, playing on a lofty plane with noble verse and intricate plot structure, playing with philosophy and calmly mingling ideas with his art. His touch is again light but not feathery as in his previous period of the romantic comedy. It seems that the poet had just never gotten around to trying two or three things in the drama, and he decided to try them now. These last comedies are simply the great dramatist on a holiday.

*Cymbeline* (1609-10) is a romantic tragicomedy which begins with dire threats of disaster and ends with peace and relative happiness. Here Shakespeare is playing with his most intricately woven plot. *A Winter's Tale* (1610-11) welds two separate plots into one play and allows sixteen years to lapse between the third and fourth acts. Shakespeare is indeed toying with dramatic technique. These two comedies contain some of the poet's most delicately drawn women characters.

### Is Prospero a self-portrait of Shakespeare?

*The Tempest* (1611) is Shakespeare's last major play. As in the above comedies, this play deals with the separation of family members, and the reconciliation or the bringing them together again. The poet has the action take place far from civilization, on a tropical isle. Wise old Prospero and his daughter, cast adrift by his brother who wanted his position as the Duke of Milan, have lived in this Western World paradise for twelve years. During this time Prospero has learned the arts of magic and is in full control of his environment when the evil brother and various companions are shipwrecked upon the island. The play has the most airy and the most revoltingly ugly of Shakespeare's supernatural or semihuman characters, Ariel and Caliban. This play is one of the most charming plays for the reader in Shakespeare's repertoire. There is little that is deep and there are few tense situations, but his beautiful poetry carries one along from one surprise to another in rapid succession.

It is hard to believe that there is not much of Shakespeare in his old philosopher-magician, Prospero. It is Prospero who carries a burden of light, musing, and mature wisdom throughout the play—a wisdom which more and more sounds like the poet himself, bidding farewell to the theater, freeing Ariel, the blithe spirit of Imagination, breaking his magic staff, and drowning his book "deeper than did ever plummet sound."

When Shakespeare retired to Stratford-on-Avon to live out the little that remained to him of life mid his boyhood scenes, his plays were written and apparently already forgotten by him. He had lived a full life, he had hurt no one, he had his material possessions, sufficient to provide for his needs, he had presented the world with a full measure of his intellect and his God-granted powers of superior observation and the ability to express the images that he received from nature and human life. It was humanity's responsibility and not his to say if his accomplishment merited life beyond that alloted to its creator.

He quite likely gave no thought to his Prospero, but it is this characterization of Shakespeare, above all others, who uttered for him a fitting farewell to his personal world of the theater—the most important part of his life on earth:

> Our revels now are ended: these our actors,
> As I foretold you, were all spirits, and
> Are melted into air, into thin air:
> And, like the baseless fabric of this vision
> The cloud-capp'd towers, the gorgeous palaces,
> The solemn temples, the great globe itself,
> Yea, all which it inherit, shall dissolve,
> And, like this insubstantial pageant faded,
> Leave not a rack behind: We are such stuff
> As dreams are made of, and our little life
> Is rounded with a sleep.

### A dramatist for the ages

But as long as there is human life and intellect, and a spirit of artistic imagination among us, the contribution of William Shakespeare will not melt into thin air. When it does, our cultural heritage will have crumbled into dust, for Shakespeare has become an integral part of it and inseparable from it, and will go where it goes and will endure in greatness just that long. The Renaissance made possible a Shakespeare in our world; only a new Dark Ages of barbarism could snatch him away.

## THE NEW DRAMA V: SHAKESPEARE'S
## CONTEMPORARIES

### Elizabethan versus Jacobean Drama

Drama in England during the Age of Elizabeth presents many and interesting facets. The great and varied production of one man, Shakespeare, tends to obscure the fact that there were other playwrights of no little ability, working side by side with him and producing plays of equal or near equal merit.

It is in the work of these contemporaries of Shakespeare, rather than in that of the master himself, that one must look to distinguish Elizabethan drama from Jacobean drama. Perhaps, in reality, the distinction is more apparent than real. The fact that James I succeeded Elizabeth on the throne of England in 1603, in itself, would not affect aesthetic writing. But the temper of the new king, the facts that he was a bigot, corrupted, extravagant, and wasteful, and that the English people resented him bitterly, would tend to alter the tone and theme of litera- ture, not the development of technique. The spirit of free will and individualized development was threatened; the spirit of revolt grew in the face of a tightening absolutism. In addition, Puritan ideas (if not Puritanism as an organized group) of morality were gaining ground rapidly and the English mind was turning away from the light and the frivolous. The theater was becoming more and more a symbol of sin and wickedness in the minds of the new and growing puritanical middle class. In 1642 things reached such a state that the playhouses were closed by Act of Parliament. They opened again in 1660 upon a new and freer age.

If the tone of English drama after Elizabeth is different in these same writers, who began their careers before the death of the Queen (1603), it is because of these pressures and in- fluences, rather than any sudden decision to alter the course of dramatic endeavor. English drama did not lose its forward momentum because a queen died; it continued unabated in its surge into the new century, prolific and varied, experimental and seeking new avenues of expression and technique. Its changing temperament can be observed, but it is not a new drama; it is part and parcel of the new drama that had started with *Gorboduc* and *Ralph Roister Doister*. The contemporaries of Shakespeare, all younger than he, are different from the master, yes, but they are so because, basically, they are pursuing the same ideals he was, perfection in dramatic art in directions which individual experimentation led them.

Elizabethan drama therefore goes on after Elizabeth is dead; literary movements do not respond to the flipping of the pages of calendars nor the whims of fate that change the names of monarchs. Elizabethan drama is at its height in the early years of the 17th century and changed, in its concept and execution, slowly, as one generation gave way to another with differing concepts.

## Shakespeare and Jonson compared

Shakespeare had already shown concern with social problems in his later plays; Ben Jonson, Shakespeare's greatest contemporary, a dramatist who begins to write about the turn of the century, shows the restricting influences operating upon his production, less of the freedom and universality of Shakespeare. Shakespeare is a true Renaissance dramatist; everything of freedom and individual direction of will which is bound up in the term Renaissance is present in him. Ben Jonson, a decade younger than Shakespeare, is more a man of his narrowing age, less of a universal figure, more of a representative of a declining Renaissance.

Shakespeare's contemporaries are sometimes divided into groups as to whether or not they tended to follow the "old school" (presumably a Shakespearean school, but more properly, a romantic school). This writer cannot see justification to group these writers as "schools." Shakespeare and Jonson, for instance, were contemporary playwrights and wrote for the same public, but they were writers who observed the events of the turn of the century with ten years difference in their ages. Jonson's popularity, in comparison with a decline in popularity of Shakespeare in the new century, simply attests to the fact that Jonson's temperament was more in keeping with the changing temperament of the immediate future of the English people. In the 19th century the pendulum had swung back to Shakespeare in the world of literature, and Jonson was seldom referred to in literary circles. Today we recognize both dramatists for their accomplishments in the theater, as we live in an age more inclined to look for universal and permanent values.

It is this changing temperament, then, that we must look for in the *Jacobean*, rather than the *Elizabethan*, drama of England. The difference is there but it is not because the continuing stream of dramatists are new men, or any less artists than Shakespeare himself. They simply face a narrowing perspective; they are more of *an age* than of the ages.

## Ben Jonson (1573-1637)

*His Life and Personality.* Few among us have not heard of the unusual inscription on Ben Jonson's gravestone, *"O Rare Ben Jonson."* And, in a sense, it is an appropriate one, for Jonson was a literary rebel and an independent personality. He was opinionated and narrow, and had personal force and drive. In his age he became an arbiter of literary taste and opinion— one might almost say a dictator.

His scholarship was extensive, but not formal. He studied at Westminster School. He was denied entrance to the university and went to work for his father, a master bricklayer. Despite his humble origin, he worked hard to improve his mind, and aspired to become a court poet. In the life of such a dogmatic and bold personality, we should expect to find conflict and clashes with his fellows. Jonson's life is full of them. He killed a fellow actor in a duel, had a number of personal clashes with friends and patrons, was imprisoned twice. He became a Catholic and later renounced his conversion. He became Poet Laureate at the court of King James.

### Jonson: the "classic" dramatist

*His work.* Jonson was classic and refused to tinker with romantic drama. He aspired to imitate Plautus and Terence in his own time and his best plays are just that, cynical and satirical. His mind showed the typical confusion prevalent in English society. He ridiculed and pretended to hate Puritans, and practiced in his literary life what he pretended to hate. In his personal life, he was pagan and gathered around him an entire school of young dramatists at his tavern feasts, all adoring the master, becoming known generally as "the tribe of Ben."

Jonson was a master craftsman and a superb versifier. He had a light touch and could write of love, but with a cynical, whimsical, and satirical approach. His work is not refined or polished, but it is straightforward and drives directly to his objective. Petrarch, to Jonson, is a model to scorn. But, in drama, Jonson stuck to the classical unities* of time, place, and action very closely. He brought a comedy of manners to the English theater and portrays his times in the spirit of classical Roman satirical comedy.

In poetry he wrote love lyrics, elegies, odes, epistles, and satirical allegory. He tinkered with all types. He wrote literary criticism and treated grammar. In the theater, he tried every form but romantic comedy; this he refused to do, but in some scenes of his other plays, *Volpone,* for instance, he shows he could have been master of that genre also. He wrote many masques for the court, he did pastoral drama, he did allegorical comedy. But his main production consists of his comedy of "humours,"* his mature social satire, and his classical tragedy.

### Jonson's comedies of "humours"

*Every Man in His Humour* (1598) is perhaps Jonson's best representative of the comedy of "humours," in which he concerns himself with a sharp analysis of his contemporary society. He strikes out at the foibles and affectation of his fellows. In this play every character has his particular eccentricity (or humour) which molds his personality. It is an interplay of quirks of personality which tend to amuse us today. But Jonson's play attracted an immediate following. This is Jonson's most influential play (though not his best). His "humours" theory, however, influenced playwrights throughout the century.

The following year he attempted to capitalize upon this success by writing *Every Man out of his Humour* (1599). It is not so well integrated as his more successful endeavor, but his characters continue to sparkle as Jonson continues to stir their varied and condemning "humours." For the most part, Jonson succeeds in making his characters plausible and alive, but occasionally one can almost see the strings as Jonson manipulates his disgruntled beings like puppets.

His classical tragedy is weaker than his comedy. He becomes a bit too Senecan and his tragedy seems pale beside the efforts of Shakespeare.

Perhaps his greatest plays are those satirical and realistic toned comedies where he is less concerned with "humours." *Volpone, or The Fox* (1606), *Epicoene, or the Silent Woman* (1609), and *The Alchemist* (1610), (261), are all masterpieces of satiric drama. They have never been equaled since the ancient satirical comedies of Greece (Aristophanes) and Rome (Plautus, Terence), both ancient dramas notable for their satires as well as their tragedy. These three plays of Jonson represent the epitome of social satire in the drama in modern times.

## Summary of Volpone

In *Volpone,* Jonson is concerned with teaching his public that mischief leads to its own miserable consequences. Volpone (Fox), a crafty miser of Venice, and his servant Mosca (Fly), set out to hoodwink as many friends as possible for Volpone's gain and pleasure. Volpone, reputedly rich, has no heirs. The old villain feigns all sorts of sicknesses and the sly servant injects into the minds of each friend the idea that he can easily become the old man's heir. These friends bear such auspicious names as Voltore (Vulture), Corbaccio (Crow), Sir Pol (parrot), Corvino (raven).

Volpone, through Mosca, gets one to change his will in his favor, another to entrust his beautiful wife to him, and all to present him with gifts of jewelry and other valuable articles. But Bonario, Corvino's disinherited son, upsets the scheme by surprising the supposedly-dying Volpone in very youthful antics in the bedroom with Celia, Corvino's lovely wife. Needless to say, Jonson brings all the tricksters and greedy individuals to a sad discomfiting end. The chief magistrate gives us the moral of the play as Volpone is condemned to prison, his properties confiscated:

> Let all who see these vices thus rewarded
> Take heart and learn the lesson. Mischiefs feed
> Like beasts, till they be fat, and then they bleed.

## The Variety of Jacobean Drama

Many dramatists supplied the theaters of London, both "public" and "private," during the period, all secondary in our modern concept, to Shakespeare and Jonson, but each contributing, in his own way, to the mass of dramatic production that survives from this Elizabethan Age and the following transition period. We can only mention a few highlights.

*The Followers of Jonson in the Satirical Comedy.* George Chapman (1559-1634) produced his *Comedy of Humours* a year and a half before Jonson's masterpiece in this genre. His *All Fools* (1599) is another example of the kind. All are stiff and loosely constructed.

Thomas Dekker (1570-1641) produced breezy comedy, full

of rich imaginative character portrayals. His representative effort in a satiric vein was *The Belman of London* (1608). He is lighter than Jonson, a happier man than Jonson.

Philip Massinger (1583-1640) is a master of satire and proves his affinity to Jonson with *A New Way to Pay Old Debts* (1625), which involves spendthrifts, misers, and various unsavory types who, in the end, get their just deserts.

John Marston (1575-1634) is rather violently cynical. His *The Malcontent* (1604) is full of Jonsonian characters.

Thomas Middleton (1580-1627). *A New Trick to Catch the Old One* (1608) satirizes the middle-class society in a somewhat obscene manner.

*The Followers of Shakespeare and Marlowe.* Many playwrights, at least in a part of their production, continued somewhat the lighter serio-comic vein that the purely Elizabethan masters had set.

Thomas Dekker, in *The Shoemaker's Holiday* (1600), treats the London working classes in a romantic vein. He is light hearted and gay and mixes well his realistic and romantic elements, much in the fashion of *Romeo and Juliet*. His realism shows much stronger in *The Honest Whore* (2 parts, 1604-1630), a drama of domestic upsets.

Thomas Heywood (1573-1641) deals with Roman historical plays, with English historical plays, and with dramatic romances. He is very original in his treatments. His domestic tragedy *A Woman Killed with Kindness* (1603) is a very modern and rational treatment of adultery. His plays of middle-class realism, such as this one, are his best. He was to become highly popular in the following century and could be termed a predecessor of Ibsen in world drama.

Francis Beaumont (1584-1616) and John Fletcher (1579-1625) wrote their best plays in collaboration. While Fletcher was the more lyrical and fanciful, Beaumont excelled in craftsmanship and mastery of verse. Their best effort in collaboration is probably *The Maid's Tragedy* (1611), a highly sentimentalized tragedy. There were various other collaborationists during the period, Fletcher with Shakespeare on *The Two Noble Kinsmen* (1613) and on *Henry VIII* (1613). Fletcher and Jonson are thought to have collaborated; also Fletcher and Massinger. The two men, singly, in collaboration with each other, or with others, produced a great number of plays.

*The Melodramatic and Violent Tragedy Group.* Seneca was

not dead in the English theater. Many were the attempts to refine the Senecan "blood bath." Among these noble efforts were:

George Chapman's *Bussy D'Ambois* (1607) and *The Revenge of Bussy D'Ambois* (1613), full of ghosts, philosophy,
and melodrama.

Thomas Middleton's *The Changeling* (1624), a sensational
tragedy of blood.

John Webster's *The Duchess of Malfi* (1612-14), a depiction
of the Italian Renaissance with its world of lust, crime, and
intrigue, full of breathtaking horrors.

These examples are enough to illustrate the age. There is
more of the same. All show more of the serious and the moral
in this later extension of the Elizabethan Age into the reign of
James. The light and the airy themes of Shakespeare's *As You
Like It* are gone. Senecan blood still flows here and there, but in
general, the problem, the social satire, the psychological study,
the quirks of personality caused by the "humours"—these are
the important themes of this transitional age. There is much that
has not been mentioned here; it is a crowded period, for English
drama had surged suddenly into fantastic proportions. It refused
to die, and leapt forward again, once the political and social
situations were calmed somewhat and the English theater-going
public, whose taste for drama has never ceased from early
Elizabethan days, demanded its theater once more in 1660.

## THE REFORMATION AND THE BIBLE

The story of the Elizabethan Age in literature would not be
complete without some mention of the great non-English literary
masterpiece which gained so much of the scholarly attention of
English humanists and reformers during the period—the Holy
Bible, both Old and New Testaments.

We have already noted (pp. 25-26) the early efforts of
Wyclif to make the Bible available in English. As the Reformation picked up force in England in the 16th century, there appeared some eight translations into English. That of Miles
Coverdale was the first complete translation of the entire Bible
printed in the English language (1535). These translations and
adaptations varied considerably in style and in the sources (part
of Coverdale's version, for instance, coming from the German-
Swiss).

### The King James Bible

The most famous of all English translations and the one which has generally governed Protestantism ever since was the Authorized Version of 1611 (usually known as the *King James Bible*). Under James I, some 47 scholars and divines of the day worked 3½ years in close cooperation to bring the massive task to completion. The sources were the many past efforts in English, the Latin Vulgate, as well as Hebrew, Greek, and Syriac versions.

# Chapter VI

# CAVALIERS AND PURITANS
# THROUGH MILTON (TO 1660)

## Historical and Cultural Notes

James IV of Scotland, son of Mary Stuart, came to the throne of England in 1603. Elizabeth had been self-willed and ruthless in minor respects, but the new king was a champion of the Divine Rights of Kings. According to this theory, he was responsible to no one on earth, only to God, and he was the one to interpret that divine will. In addition, the new king was intellectual and stern. A great portion of the Protestant clergy supported him whole-heartedly, in hopes that the Church of England could achieve under him the same authoritative position that the Roman Church had once held in England.

Charles I, James' son (1625-1649), was deceitful and impulsive. Both he and his father considered Parliament merely an advisory body and that the king had no real obligation to it. Both sovereigns dissolved Parliament several times during their reigns. For eleven years, from 1629, Charles ruled without a Parliament. Charles, unlike his father, alienated the Puritans by his frivolity. In 1639 he found himself in a war with the Scotch and was forced to reconvene Parliament. This proved to be the body which eventually tried him for treason and executed him.

### Monarchy versus Democracy in England

In 1641, when Charles refused to sign a bill to create a militia under the control of Parliament, the body barred the King from access to arms and munitions, and Charles called his loyal followers to arms. Parliament immediately declared a state of civil war (1642-1648). At first the Royalists (the Cavaliers, or royal supporters of the court, the Church of England, and the

Catholics) seemed destined to win. But slowly the forces of this Long Parliament, the Puritans (Roundheads), comprising most of the middle-class commercial and artisan classes, won decisive battles until the King was captured and executed in 1649.

England became a commonwealth (virtually a republic), but the best efforts of the Puritans toward a democratic government seemed doomed to failure. In 1653, Oliver Cromwell established a Protectorate and guided England toward tolerance and democracy. But, more and more, he assumed the powers of a dictator, and by the time of his death in 1658, dissention was growing among the Puritans themselves. His son Richard no longer could cope with it. Finally, in 1660, Parliament voted to restore the monarchy, with Charles II. The Stuarts and absolute monarchy were back for another unhappy 28 years.

The results upon the intellectual and cultural atmosphere of this conflict over power and ideals were profound. The tone of both thought and action seemed to line up behind either a Puritan or a Cavalier banner. Even the custom of the cut of men's hair seemed to follow the two standards, the Cavaliers wearing their hair long and the Puritans short, hence the nickname *Roundheads* that was applied to them. The Puritans, at their extreme, considered the Cavaliers to be frivolous and given to sinful thinking and living; the Cavaliers, at their extreme, considered the Puritans to be hypocritical, narrow, and tyrannical.

Actually, despite the waste and personal extravagance of the Stuarts, the country prospered during the period. Trade and commerce increased, and despite internal conflict, England commanded the respect of the rest of Europe. British colonies were established in North America (Jamestown 1607; Plymouth 1620).

Accomplishment on an intellectual plane was tremendous. The tone for a modern England was set in this century of conflicting ideals. The Renaissance had never really brought an enduring set of spiritual values. It was colorful and of inestimable worth to the developing future of human civilization and culture, but it was, in itself, individual and pagan. The Reformation was not confined to one set of values. But, as in all good things which are not subject to basic guiding principles, it embodied many fanatics and unbalanced elements.

Puritan ideas and ideals were to gain the ascendency in English life and thought during this 17th century. But Cavalier ideals, the dying Renaissance, were not to be entirely obscured.

The Puritans were perhaps narrow in their view of a personal morality, but they had a wider view of freedom, both personal and political, than the medieval ages had seen. The Puritans, it must be understood, did not constitute a Church or a religious sect. They represent for us, in their wider and less fanatic aspect, a state of mind, a middle-class rationalism, an attitude of intelligent inquiry, and a scientific outlook. The world, as well as England, needed both elements. And, in conflict and upheaval, both survived to cement permanent values from the past and new ideals for the future.

## *Elizabethan romance becomes tempered by Puritanism*

In literature, the color and the lyricism of the Elizabethan Age continued. But enthusiasm, pagan exuberance, and the lack of restraint of the child with the new toy all of his own, pure romance and adventure, fantasy—these things were on the wane. A new note of intellectual questioning, a seeking of solid foundations in reason and accomplishment, a more serious and settled view, a more dignified and less emotional and spontaneous spirit —these things had come to stay. The bulk of enduring literature was to be products of intellectual and scientific-minded men. Some of the light and airy, some of the charm of the first bloom of Elizabethan writing was to be missed from English literature. The 17th century was to be a many-sided period in the development of a complex and rich body of English writings.

We shall consider the literature of the period from the two principal varying viewpoints, sometimes conflicting and always showing intermingling influences, the Cavalier and the Puritan. The courtly ideal was Spenser and his allegorical interpretations of morality and that enthusiastic spirit of pagan lyricism and they continued to fight their way along, with a good deal of cynicism and irony to be sure, parallel to the Puritan intellectual spirit that was leading to its great proponent—Milton.

## LYRIC POETRY TO 1660

### The Cavalier Poets

Even the gayest of the Cavalier lyric of the 17th century lacks some of the sweetness and fresh charm of the song of the Elizabethan Age. There is grace, technical perfection, and polish about this new verse. There is a sophistication about it, a cleverness, an ironical tone. The lyric is dainty and skillful—

but it is artificial. These gay poets of the Royalty faction feel
a little self-conscious mid the more serious atmosphere of their
age. They are a little on the defensive; they have a little of the
spirit of men who are going to maintain their individuality in
spite of what they feel is a cloud of leveling mediocrity creeping
in upon them. They will be light and airy, and a bit pagan, in
spite of it all.

> Gather ye rosebuds while ye may,
>     Old Time is still a-flying;
> And this same flower that smiles today,
>     Tomorrow will be dying.
>
> —Robert Herrick (1648)

The most perfect representative of the Cavalier lyric poetry is
Herrick. His is the most versatile and musical of the verse of the
period. He was a priest who constantly warred with the pagan
in his nature. He was an admirer of Ben Jonson and was one of
the best loved of "the tribe of Ben." His skill at the short melo-
dious lyric poem is unsurpassed. He is thoroughly pagan and
addresses a dozen different imagined or real mistresses in his
verse. He writes a little song of unearthly fragility one day; the
next day he follows it with an obscene epigram. The same poet
who writes upon Mistress Susanna's feet:

> Her pretty feet
> Like snails did creep
> A little out, and then
> As if they played at bo-peep,
> Did soon draw in again.   (1648)

would then address a long litany to the Holy Spirit:

> In the hour of my distress,
> When temptations me oppress,
> And when I my sins confess,
>     Sweet Spirit, comfort me!
>
>             .   .   .   .   .   .
>
> When the Judgment is revealed,
> And that opened which was sealed
> When to Thee I have appealed,
>     Sweet Spirit, comfort me!   (1648)

### *Herrick's companions in the Cavalier lyric*

Herrick had his companions in this Cavalier lyric verse: Edmund Waller (1605-1687), Sir John Suckling (1609-1641), Richard Lovelace (1618-1658), Abraham Cowley (1618-1667), Thomas Carew (1595-1639), George Wither (1588-1667), and others. They were all well educated, Royalist, lovers of good living and rhyme. They all, like Waller, savored pagan delights:

*On a Girdle*

That which her slender waist confined
Shall now my joyful temples bind;
No monarch but would give his crown,
His arms might do what this has done.

It was my heaven's extremest sphere,
The pale which held that lovely deer;
My joy, my grief, my hope, my love,
Did all within this circle move.

A narrow compass, and yet there
Dwelt all that's good and all that's fair;
Give me but what this ribband bound,
Take all the rest the sun goes round!    (1645)

And, like Suckling, they affect disdain for any who will not agree with them:

If of herself she will not love,
Nothing can make her.
The devil take her!

### *Variety among the Cavalier writers*

The group wrote in all the lyric forms and genres: elegies, odes, masques, allegories, epigrams, poetic satire, epistles, eclogues, pastorals. They wrote comedies, tragedies, and prose works, but mainly they wrote love songs, or little light philosophical bits. Richard Lovelace was perhaps the most serious among them:

Stone walls do not a prison make,
Nor iron bars a cage.

. . . . . .

I could not love thee, Dear, so much,
Loved I not honor more . . .

But, in general, Herrick shows best the confusion of the group and his affected position in the scheme of life and death. In his *The Argument of His Book,* he tells us:

> I write of youth, of love, and have access
> By these to sing of cleanly wantonness;
> I sing of dews, of rains, and piece by piece
> Of balm, of oil, of spice and ambergris;
> I sing of times trans-shifting, and I write
> How roses first came red and lilies white;
> I write of groves, of twilight, and I sing
> The Court of Mab, and of the Fairy King;
> I write of hell; I sing (and ever shall)
> Of heaven, and hope to have it after all.    (1648)

## The Late Followers of Spenser

There were a few poets of the period who attempted to revive the tradition of Spenser and Sir Philip Sidney. They went to the sonnet of the Petrarchan variety, the allegorical romance, and revived the florid style of the allegories and the pastorals of half a century before. These Cavaliers returned to a study of Ariosto, Tasso, and Ronsard. They once again sought to revive the spirit of the Italian Renaissance. We regard this a minor effort of this age of transition; a few names and titles will suffice to illustrate this trend.

Giles Fletcher (1584-1623) wrote *Christ's Victory and Triumph in Heaven, on Earth, over, and after Death* (1610), which tells, in modified Spenserian stanzas, of the victory of Christ over Satan.

Phineas Fletcher (1582-1650) in *The Locusts* (1627), relates, in religious allegory, the fall of Lucifer. It is also a satirical attack on the Jesuits.

William Browne (1591-1643) was a pastoral poet. In his *Brittania's Pastorals* (I-1613, II-1616) he imitates Sidney's *Arcadia*.

George Wither (1588-1667) wrote satires and pastorals. His *Abuses Stript and Whipt* (1613), in riming couplets, flays the vices of the Court.

## The Metaphysical Poets

The term "metaphysical" (as applied later by Samuel Johnson to this group) would indicate a poetry that expresses a deep and personal religious sentiment. The poets are employing lyric verse to express their spiritual experiences and inward religious emotions. These poets were mystic,* but their verse differs from true mysticism in that there is not present in it the simple sincerity of true mystics. The mysticism of this group springs from the intellect and reflects the scientific and theological argumentation and terminology of the age. The language of the group is a studied and an abstruse subtlety of twisted metaphor, conceits, and syntactical violation. There is much cynicism and irony in this group of "metaphysical" poets; the term (in reality coined by Dryden and appropriated by Johnson), which is an apt one for the expression of religious feeling and emotion by this group, is both abstract and abstruse and abounding in elaborate subtleties of thought and expression. It was a group more desirous of parading its intellect than in expressing the sincerity of its message. It is a group that stands between the paganism of the Cavalier and the Puritan in the century. It was a group touched by the extremes of both sides.

Most of the group were connected with the ministry. Some were Catholics, some had changed from one sect to another, and some were Protestants; all were intellectual and scholarly.

### Donne: greatest of the intellectual poets

John Donne (1573-1631) is the originator and the greatest of the group. His verse embodies all that is good and all that is bad in the entire production of the school. He is the intellectual poet *par excellence*. There is little melody in his lyricism. He writes from his introspective view, involving the reader in science, metaphysics, philosophy, and theology. This, together with the new "euphuism" of his language, makes Donne a poet difficult to understand and appreciate.

Donne's life is one of indecision. He spent a rather wild and dissolute youth at Oxford and Cambridge. He went on several naval expeditions, one to Cadiz and one to the Azores. He became a lawyer and was discontent with this career. He then turned to poetry. He married without the consent of the girl's parents and was imprisoned for a time. He spent several years in poverty. At last he was ordained priest in 1613 in the Church of England, and received his Doctor of Divinity in 1615 from Cambridge. He became famous for his sermons and was made Dean of St. Paul's in 1621.

Donne apparently was not anxious to have his verse published. It circulated in manuscript during his lifetime, but was not pub-

lished until two years after his death. It immediately became the
delight of young poets who imitated it freely. He was thus un-
wittingly "father" of a school of poets. His name has been a controversial focal point for much criticism of this "metaphysical"
verse. He has been called the "father" of a whole breed of
fantastic poets.

Donne did, indeed, seem to start a contagious influence in English poetry. His poetic eccentricity and obscure and fantastic
thought and imagery permeated English poetry for almost a century. His far-fetched and overflown metaphors seemed to affect
poets, who at the same time they complained of Donne and his
taint, followed in his same path.

### European practitioners of the "baroque" style

It has also been a controversial issue as to whether Donne
acquired his affected and "conceitful" expression from the
Italians or the Spanish, since both Marini of Italy and Góngora
in Spain were practicing the same intricate and flowery poetic
style in the same age. This "baroque"* style of writing in English literature is almost invariably laid at the doorstep of John
Donne. Sir Edmund Gosse (1849-1928) said, in his *Seventeenth
Century Studies* (1883): "For sixty years the evil taint of Donne
rested on us, and our tradition is not free from it yet. He is the
father of all that is exasperating, affected, and 'metaphysical' in
English poetry."

Donne's *A Hymn to God the Father* will illustrate very well
the "metaphysical" poetry of the group:

> Wilt thou forgive that sin where I begun,
>    Which was my sin, though it were done before?
> Wilt thou forgive that sin through which I run,
>    And do run still, though still I do deplore?
> When thou hast done, thou hast not done;
>    For I have more.
>
> Wilt thou forgive that sin which I have won
>    Others to sin, and made my sins their door?
> Wilt thou forgive that sin which I did shun
>    A year or two, but wallowed in a score?
> When thou hast done, thou hast not done;
>    For I have more.

> I have a sin of fear, that when I've spun
>   My last thread, I shall perish on the shore;
> But swear by thyself that at my death thy Son
>   Shall shine as he shines now and heretofore;
>     I fear no more.

Other poets who wrote principally on religious themes during the period and generally employed the language and introspective spirit of John Donne, are: George Herbert (1593-1633), a priest, whose theme is mainly the love and glorification of God; Henry Vaughan (1621-1695), a physician, who introduced themes from nature into his devotional lyrics; Richard Crashaw (1613-1649), a Catholic, more ecstatic and fiery than his contemporaries.

## THE PROSE WRITERS TO 1660

### *Ornate richness continues in English prose*

Early prose in English seems to us today rather quaint, involved, and clumsy. Unlike the lyric verse of the period, most of which has continued to be as sweet and fresh to succeeding generations of readers as when it was set down, the prose of most of the writers seems to have gone stale, to be highly artificial. The ornate style of early prose is noted as early as Malory (p. 38) and simply becomes more ornamented and flowered with Lyly, Sidney, Nash, Hakluyt, and Ralegh (p. 54) in the Elizabethan Age.

And in this new period of transition, with the English novel still over the horizon, English prose had not yet assumed a modern form, clear, concise, and lucid. It was still in a formative state, quaint, formless, heavy, and fanciful. It was still too full of "euphuism," the soaring fancies of the Renaissance, and its discovery of Latinized inversions and hyperbolism,* hardly suited to English. We must wait until after 1660 for the masters who will give us models of ease and clearness, of simplicity and realism in prose style.

However, the Elizabethan and transition prose, with its sweeping imaginative formlessness, with its crescendos and clashing rhythms, with its allusions, its antitheses, its fanciful conceits and eloquence, has much to recommend it. A taste can be acquired for Elizabethan prose, and once acquired, it can be a delight for a modern to forget terseness and simplicity for an hour and soar with Burton, Browne, Walton, or Ralegh—and with Sir Francis Bacon, who is the exception that proves the rule.

## Francis Bacon and the Essay

Sir Francis Bacon (1561-1626) stands almost alone in his age, and he stands squarely in two ages, the Age of Elizabeth and in the Puritan Interlude. Bacon is the outstanding intellectual of both ages, a brilliant scientist and philosopher, the creator of the English essay, and one of the most dissolute personalities in English Literature. (And there have been some who say that he wrote Shakespeare's plays.)

Bacon entered Trinity College, Cambridge, at the age of twelve. His father and uncle were in high position in the court of Elizabeth and the brilliant lad seemed born into high position. By the time he was seventeen he was master of several languages and of most of the world's knowledge in politics, history, philosophy, and science. He was, in addition, versed in the law. He was restlessly ambitious and threw himself into state affairs with a vigor that soon earned him a reputation as a statesman. He had all the intellectual zest and the ruthlessness of moral character that Renaissance statemanship signified.

Under James I he reached the position of Lord Chancellor, the highest legal office in England. He held almost all the titles of honor and distinction granted by the court. He was personally extravagant and wasteful and lived a gay and expensive life. Disaster came to Bacon in 1620 when he was impeached for taking bribes. This was hardly an unusual procedure for public office holders of that time, but Bacon, surprisingly, confessed to "corruption and neglect." He was stripped of his position and titles, fined and imprisoned, and denied the right to serve the state again. The king released Bacon, who retired to private life and spent the remaining five years of his life writing. For the advancement of literature and scientific philosophy, this period of enforced leisure was a boon, for during this period he produced much of his great writing.

### The scientific and philosophical works

Most of Bacon's heavier works were originally written in Latin. They all have excellent English translations. He was not a scientist himself, but devoted himself to the development of scientific method. Perhaps Bacon did not invent the inductive reasoning principle of scientific inquiry, but he gave it established modern expression which has been followed ever since. His inductive method of reasoning (from observation of specific facts leading to the formation of general laws and principles) has been the guiding method of scientific research to the present day. The medieval scientists worked from an assumption or a general principle and amassed facts to support it (deductive reasoning).

Bacon's most important scientific and philosophical titles are: *The Advancement of Learning* (1605), *Novum Organum* (1620), in which his inductive method is examined. *The New Atlantis* (1627) outlines his scientific utopia.

## Bacon's Essays

Bacon is known in literature for his essays.* The term "essay" came into the vocabulary of literature from the *Essais* of the Frenchman Montaigne (1533-1592). The Frenchman's thoughts on life are expressed in an informal and facile conversational style. Where the essay of Montaigne is warm and humane, the prototype of Bacon is cold, compact, and emotionless.

The number of Bacon's essays grew from 10 in 1597 to 58 by 1625. In subject matter they deal with the ethics of public and private conduct, with statesmanship and with the passions, virtues, and personal interrelationships of human beings. One of his best titles is *Of Studies,* in which he tells us:

> Some books are to be tasted, others to be swallowed,
> and some few to be chewed and digested.

In his essay *On Adversity,* Bacon offered advice which came to be only too true in his own life:

> . . . prosperity doth best discover vice, but adversity
> doth best discover virtue.

> Prosperity is not without many fears and distastes;
> and adversity is not without comforts and hopes.

Bacon wrote on many subjects, *Of Truth, Of Travel, Of Goodness, Of Gardens,* and even *Of Marriage and Single Life:*

> He that hath a wife and children hath given hostages
> to fortune; for they are impediments to great enter-
> prises, either of virtue or mischief.

> Wives are young men's mistresses, companions for middle
> age, and old men's nurses.

### Qualities of Bacon's writing

Bacon's essays are objective and logically constructed. They are terse and epigrammatical. They are compact and stimulating. He is the exception of his age and his diction is more clear, crisp, and firmly knit than any other writer of his age. He rejected entirely the conceits and the imagery of the other English writers of his times. But Bacon is scientific and bloodless. He is terse, pointed, and impersonal. His content is sententious and reminiscent of sermonizing evangelism. He lacks the warmth and glow, the feeling of kinship and geniality, the personal and intimate tone that the great Montaigne radiates from every page. The two first great essayists of modern literatures present a very sharp and interesting contrast. They are both great, and they both can be listened to, even today, with profit and pleasure.

### The "Character" Essay

The term "essay" to describe a literary type is new with Montaigne and Bacon, but short prose discussions of various topics had been written long before these men had employed the form so masterfully. During the first quarter of the 17th century, a group of writers, Puritan clergymen all, devoted their leisure to the writing of little prose bits called "characters." The "character" was a short sketch of human character in which a person is endowed with a certain quality or characteristic. This particular quirk of character is responsible for the person's actions. The "character" described in detail the actions and everyday dealings of the person, all to be traced back to his basic quirk of personality. Thus they are little psychological case studies on a rather imaginative pseudoscientific plane. This "character" essay was a fad which was popular during the first quarter of the century (see also the theater of "humours" of Ben Jonson and his contemporaries, p. 100). The "character" was influential not only in the development of the essay but also of the novel.

The chief writers of "characters" were clergymen. Joseph Hall (1574-1656) adapted the idea to English prose. The originator of the form was the Greek Theophrastus, who died in 287 B.C. He had invented the type in his *Characteroi,* which contained descriptions of men, both good and bad, from a depiction of their characteristics and actions. This book appeared in Latin in 1592 and in English in 1616. Hall's collection was called *The Characters of Virtues and Vices* (1608).

Others who developed the literary type were Sir Thomas Overbury (1581-1613), whose *Characters* (1614) embodied all ranges of English society from the country gentleman to the dunce. Following and improving upon his predecessors, John Earle (1600-1665) issued his collection called *Microcosmographie* (1628). This book was highly popular and is considered the best group of sketches to come from this fad in 17th century prose.

## Puritan Whimsey and Eloquence: Burton, Brown, and Walton

### *Burton: The Anatomy of Melancholy*

Robert Burton (1576-1640): One of the most interesting of the rambling, individualistic prose styles characteristic of the age is found in *The Anatomy of Melancholy* (1621) of Robert Burton. Burton was a widely read scholar, having delved into every branch of human knowledge. He was interested in the unusual and he produced one of the most unusual books of all time. The enormous volume (almost a half a million words) is a veritable treasure house of endless quotations, little essays on all branches of learning, wit, paraphrases from the Bible and other sources. The basic skeleton theme of the book is an analysis of the causes and symptoms of various kinds of melancholy and various practical suggestions for curing each kind. It is an exhaustive volume of the most quaint odds and ends of knowledge. Its style is leisurely, pedantic, and imaginative. It is the only book of its kind ever produced. It is a whimsical masterpiece of an encyclopaedic mind that, though scientific and modern, leaned nostalgically backward toward medieval speculative hair-splitting dialectics.

### *Browne: Religio Medici*

Sir Thomas Browne (1605-1682), like Burton, had a mind that was scientific and scholarly, and at the same time mystic and dreamy. He was a melancholy spirit who was filled with unconquerable skepticism. The modern and the medieval are mixed in Browne in about the same proportions as they are to be found in Burton.

His first work, *Religio Medici* (Religion of a Physician) (1642), is a confession of his own rather mystical creed. As he says, "I love to lose myself in a mystery." Like Burton, he is a dreamer, an intelligent dreamer, but no man of action. His prose style is solemn and eloquent and possesses a rich majesty, a grandiose display of stately words and phrases. Browne, like Burton, had tolerant views, detested controversial issues. He preferred the Church of England but had little care how other men worshipped. He believed that religion should be a joy, "I fear God, yet am not afraid of him."

His *Urn Burial* (1659) comments on various methods of burying the dead. This gives him ample excuse to wander off into various philosophical and imaginative reflections on life. His diction in this book, as in his others of lesser importance, is rich in the elevated but colorful language of his age.

## *Walton: The Compleat Angler*

Izaak Walton (1593-1683) is another of the quaint style and the quiet dreamy humor. Walton was an ironmonger in London. He was a Royalist and a loyal member of the Church. Like Burton and Browne he was a peaceful man and avoided the contentions of his times. He wrote a number of biographies of churchmen during his career. He is known to us, however, through his hobby, fishing. He was an ardent fisherman and had acquired about all there was to be known of the sport in his time. His book *The Compleat Angler* (1653), was at once recognized as a complete guide to the art of the rod and line, but it has become famous for its purely literary values. It is one of the most charming books on the great out-of-doors ever written. It is full of descriptions of nature, life at the roadside inns, conversations along the fishermen's paths. He has fishing tales, both tall and short, verse and song, and a multitude of hints on how to achieve peace with oneself and nature. The style of his miscellany on fishing and the backgrounds for fishing is unusually lucid and has a quiet charm that has been equalled rarely in the prose of any language. It is pastoral prose at its best.

## The Theological Writers

Of the writers on purely religious matters, only two merit mention here, and these two are among the best of the prose stylists of the period: Thomas Fuller (1608-1661) and Jeremy Taylor (1613-1667).

Fuller, a Royalist and a churchman, had a ready wit and was given to coining puns. In addition to his books of history and biography, we have such titles as *Good Thoughts in Bad Times* (1645), *Good Thoughts in Worse Times* (1647), and *Mixt Contemplations in Better Times* (1660). These are collections of little moral meditations, full of quotations and paraphrases from scripture, and little anecdotes. His prose sparkles with whimsical humor and imaginative wisdom.

Taylor used an eloquent and resounding language. His style was flowery and colorful. His message was tolerance, charity, and Christian conduct. His *Rule and Exercises of Holy Living* (1650) and *Rule and Exercises of Holy Dying* (1651) are his most famous series of lectures. He was one of England's foremost preachers of all time. He was broad, gentle, and eloquently charming in his brilliant prose.

## JOHN MILTON: THE GREATEST PURITAN POET

John Milton (1608-1674), the greatest name in English poetry after Shakespeare, produced the only English epic poem which is a true rival to the poetic dignity attained by Homer and Vergil in the ancient literatures. And where Dante gave us the spiritual summarization of the Middle Ages, Milton successfully does the same for the Protestant Reformation; both were concerned with the destiny of man in differing social and intellectual environments.

### Four giants of English poetry

Chaucer, Spenser, Shakespeare, and Milton, each supreme and immortal in English poetry, are to us giants of the past, but giants that have guided the course of the development of English into the position of possessing the richest aesthetic literary expression in a single language. In poetry Chaucer's human and earthly descriptions are unequaled; Spenser's rich allegorical fancy carried the imagination to its poetic limits; Shakespeare probed with lyric variety into the wellsprings of the souls of universal humanity; Milton carries the aesthetics of the intellect to poetic perfection. Psychological penetration on a humane scale was Shakespeare's forte; Milton's greatness is in his equally universal joining of the intellect with the spirit of mankind. Shakespeare appeals to the senses and the emotions; Milton appeals to the intellectual and to the aesthetically cultivated reason.

## Milton: blend of the Renaissance and the Puritan

Milton's major poems were written after 1660, after the Restoration of the Stuarts to the throne of England. The early life and the mental and moral preparation of this great poet lie in an age of intense political and ideological conflict. Milton's preparation made him enthused with Renaissance romanticism; his profound spirituality and intellectual thirst made him Puritan and philosophical. Mellowing age and physical infirmity made him see that a perfect harmony could be brought from his conflicting sources of experience, both so agreeable to his mind and senses. In his last years, he employed his technical poetic perfection to the task of bringing us the last burst of enthusiasm from a dying Renaissance, with all its color and individuality, combined with the weight and depth of Puritan thought and ideals. Never since has an English poet so succeeded in harmonizing these two indispensable, but varying, poles of artistry and intellect. To appreciate his great work, we must look into the life of the man, and into his background of wide experience in his earlier periods of accomplishment.

### Milton's Life and Work

*The First Period, Formative Years.* Milton's father was a scrivner and a well-known music composer. The family was Puritan, in good financial condition and highly respected. Milton was denied no opportunity that the educational system of the day afforded. He studied at St. Paul's and Christ's College, Cambridge. He perfected himself in disputation, Latin, and Greek, at which he won top honors. He took his Master's in 1632 and went to live at his father's new place of residence, a few miles outside of London. The next six years were spent in the study of mathematics and music. He also made a study of the Bible, the Talmud, and other theological writings. He did tutoring and some versifying in Latin and English.

During this formative period, the poet produced, in addition to minor verse, four pieces that began to show promise of the developing genius. These poems are *L'Allegro* and *Il Penseroso* (1631-34), *Comus* (1634), and *Lycidas* (1637). *L'Allegro* (the joyful man) and *Il Penseroso* (the thoughtful man) show contrasting moods. They are idealized visions, and in reality autobiographical, since they depict the two sides of Milton's own spirit. The one shows the poet beholding the outer world, the brightness of nature, and taking joy in the activities of life about him; the other shows him introspective, quiet, and dreamy, meditating upon the meaning of life.

### Comus and Lycidas reviewed

*Comus* is a masque, written for a musician friend of Milton. *Lycidas* is an elegy, written in memory of a college friend, who was drowned. The poet represents himself and his dead friend as shepherds, as was traditional in ancient literatures and in the revived Renaissance masques and eclogues. He calls the sea nymphs and the gods of the wind to task for causing his fellow shepherd's death. He invokes Poetry and Learning to mourn over his friend. And, lastly, he invokes St. Peter.

Both *Comus* and *Lycidas* begin to show traces of Milton's grandeur of expression to come. They have the elaborate color of Spenserian verse. But his diction is stiff and irregular, harsh and uncertain in places.

These two poems give much insight into the mind of Milton at this point of the formation of his mind. Both forms are classic and exploited by the gay courtly poets of the Renaissance. But Milton adds something. In *Comus,* he has two brothers search in the forest for their lost sister, who has been taken prisoner by Comus, the spirit of Revelry. But the poet makes the sister save herself from violation by her virtue, while the Attendant Spirit tells the audience: "Love Virtue; she alone is free." Milton, a true Puritan, is here attacking the court party in his belief that it is corrupt and sinful—lacking in the necessary virtue demanded by the Reformation middle class.

In *Lycidas,* Milton goes further. He adds St. Peter to his list of mourners for his dead friend, to mingle with the pagan mourners. Not only does he present us with a strange company of Christian and pagan mourners, but he puts in St. Peter's mouth bitter words of denunciation of the worldly churchmen of the day.

> . . . such as for their bellies sake
> Creep and intrude, and climb into the fold?

The young Milton was burning with the virtue of a reformer,

and for the next twenty years of his life, he was to thunder forth and sharpen his language in denunciation of public and private evil.

In April of 1638, Milton embarked upon an extended continental tour to complete his education. He returned some fifteen months later. This brings to a close Milton's first, or formative, period. He is thirty-one years of age.

*The Second Period, Prose.* When Milton returned from his European travels he did some teaching in small private schools. He wrote his *Tractate of Education* (1644) in the form of a letter. The program he outlines would be a rather ambitious one for the average student of today.

### Milton discusses divorce

About this time Milton married Mary Powell, daughter of a Royalist gentleman. He was thirty-five and she was seventeen. The union was unfortunate. Very shortly after the marriage she returned home on a visit which seemed never to end. Members of her family, however, sought refuge in Milton's house when the Powells were ruined as a result of the defeats that Charles was suffering. The exact status of the relations between Milton and his wife at this time are not known; anyway, the literary consequences are more interesting. Milton wrote (1643) *The Doctrine and Discipline of Divorce, Restored to the Good of Both Sexes,* in which he argued that marriage is a private affair and should be dissolved at the will of either party. This horrified the Episcopalians and the Presbyterians. In 1644, he lashes out in his thundering prose once more and retracts not a single word. He was denounced from pulpits all over England. Later the same year he issued his *Judgment of Martin Brewer,* backing up a pamphlet supporting divorce by a fellow sympathizer. In 1645 two other pamphlets appear in which our author (no poet in this period) refutes all arguments against him.

### Milton discusses freedom of the press

Parliament, meanwhile, had passed a law requiring all publications to be censored by a board. Milton had, of course, violated this act. He was called upon to explain and he replied in his most famous prose work, an oration addressed to Parliament, which is known as *Areopagitica, a Speech of John Milton for the Liberty of Unlicensed Printing, to the Parliament of*

*England* (1644). This is not only a protest against the censorship but a famed plea for free expression of thought. It has become, for both Britains and Americans, a pillar of defense of freedom of speech and of the press.

> Give me the liberty to know, to utter, and to argue
> freely according to conscience. . . .

The case against Milton was carried no further.

## Milton discusses the rights of the people

After Charles' execution, Milton wrote *Of the Tenure of Kings and Magistrates* (1649), in which he argued that it was the right of people to terminate the rule of tyrants by any means they saw fit. It was published two weeks after Charles was beheaded. It was a stern-toned work. Milton was hired by the Commonwealth government and titled Secretary of Foreign Tongues.

In 1649, appeared a book called *Eikon Basilike,* a work which supposedly was the autobiography of the dead king and elaborated upon his pious character. Parliament called upon Milton to answer it. He did so, paragraph by laborious paragraph, in a work called *Eikonoklastes* (1649). It was bitter and personal, and its intent was to smash all the appealing arguments which had been built up in regard to the good and holy qualities of Charles. Its very title is Greek for "idol smasher."

Milton, in his official position, continued to answer pamphlets which came out from time to time in defense of Charles. In 1652 he lost his sight. In the same year his wife Mary Powell died, leaving three daughters. Apparently Milton was not particularly interested in their welfare. He married again in 1656. The second wife died in childbirth fifteen months later. Milton wrote one of his most touching sonnets to this wife whom he seems to have regarded more affectionately than he did his first wife:

> Love, sweetness, goodness, in her person shin'd
> So clear, as in no face with more delight.
> But O as to embrace me she enclin'd
> I wak'd, she fled, and day brought back my night.

## Milton pleads for separation of Church and State

Cromwell died in 1658 and the Commonwealth was on its last legs. Milton published several pamphlets in this and the following year, pleading for a separation of Church and State and attempting vainly to wield his pen to stay the Restoration. But it came in spite of Milton and the weakening will of the people to resist it. It is difficult to understand how Milton escaped the dire consequences of his having been so openly opposed to the King's return to power. He was blind; he had Royalist friends. He was allowed to go into retirement and was persecuted only to a minor degree.

*Milton's Great Period (1660-1674).* Milton married a third time in 1663. Elizabeth Minshull was a good woman who took care of the poet as he set about producing his claim to everlasting fame. He wrote a good deal of prose and odds and ends of verse, but three poetic works are responsible for making this man the most famous link between the Puritan spirit of his age and the pagan and individual spirit of the high Renaissance: *Paradise Lost* (finished in 1665), *Paradise Regained* (1665-1667), and *Samson Agonistes* (1668-1670). The latter two works were printed together in 1671.

Milton lived quietly during these last years. His daughters ignored him, and when he died he left all his remaining possessions to his wife. He apparently had enough left to live comfortably and to provide his wife with sufficient to live out her life. She lived until 1727.

Milton was a disillusioned man. He had thrown himself against the windmills of his times, and like Don Quijote, had been tumbled to earth. He was austere and battled with a steadfast singleness of purpose for what he considered the right. He refused to be imbued with the cynicism and the shallowness that surrounded him in his late years. He was moral, but maintained to the last that Puritan morality did not exclude earthly pleasures. He was not fanatical. He maintained that a good man could be a Puritan and at the same time be an artist and a man who loved life. He refused to yield to a narrow-minded ignorance. He had insuperable intellectual strength, a grim tenacity of purpose, a thorough preparation in language and poetic inspiration, and he determined to give mankind something to cause thinking men to appreciate artistry, intellect, and morality, blended into single works. He succeeded in this noble purpose only too well and died quietly on November 8, 1674.

## The greatest English epic poem

*Paradise Lost.* Milton had planned to write an epic poem for some years. He sought an heroic subject, and for a while considered the legend of King Arthur. But Arthur seemed to him to be too much of the mists of irreality to be good epic material, for, to Milton, a subject of sufficient nobility of range to form the basis of a work of such grandeur and scope must be believable to succeeding generations. To the Puritan Milton there came at last his most logical subject, the fall of Adam, and consequently the fall of man. His subject, then, would not only challenge his poetic abilities; into this theme he could pour his entire scope of knowledge and philosophy, for his poem would demand much more than the story of any earthly hero. Here he would be dealing with drama on a stage of sublime proportions. Only the great Dante had ever tackled successfully a theme so vast in his *Divine Comedy* (begun c. 1307). Dante had touched the strings of medieval spirituality and had made them vibrate through the ages in his immortal interlinking tercets*; Milton's project called for an equally resounding summary of the spirituality of a modern Puritan age of intellectual morality, and he chose the English blank verse as his sounding board.

### Milton's story of Genesis

For *Paradise Lost* (263), Milton chose the Bible story of Genesis, but he worked upon it with the full freedom of his powers of interpretation and imagination. His task was of much greater scope than merely to retell the story of the garden of Eden. The actual temptation and fall of Adam was a minor episode in his scheme for giving to mankind a message of imperishable sublimity through concrete, but vivid, imagery of powerful language—a message which was to

> . . . assert Eternal providence
> And justify the ways of God to men,

Milton was cultured and a poet of insuperable perfection; his work is therefore, a cultured and artistic production of one man's command of the elements that went to make it up. It is an artistic epic* poem, rather than a cumulative result of folk tradition. It employs all the sources of culture that man had built up to the time it was written, the classical Greek and Roman, the Eastern Hebraic tradition, the Western Renaissance sensory impressions combined with the new morality of the Reformation. It was the deliberate work of one man and its effects must be as personal and far reaching among other men of Western intellect through the ages as Milton's impressions were to him.

Milton's subject was religion and Western men have passed through varying dogmatic interpretations of religion. They have disagreed and divided from each other on interpretations of Milton's basic theme. There have been, therefore, many criticisms of Milton's poem that have had little to do with the artistic and intellectual greatness of the work. No criticism is leveled at the sublimity and grandeur of his blank verse; no criticism is aimed at his herculean accomplishment in integration and clear delineation of character and idea. That Milton produced England's greatest artistic epic, no one would deny; that he equaled the dignity, in English, of the classic epics of the ancient world, likewise, hardly anyone would dispute. That the reader or the critic agrees or does not agree with his treatment of Genesis, Adam, Eve, or Satan, is vastly unimportant to aesthetic appreciation of a supreme masterwork of English and world literatures. If these things are important, then artistic appreciation and values have indeed become subject to strange laws in our age of reason.

## *Plan of Paradise Lost in brief*

Milton's epic is divided into twelve books. In the first, we witness the hurling of Satan and his angels from Heaven and the building of their great council chamber, Pandemonium. In Book Two, Satan is chosen to seek out the new world that God has created and introduce sin into it. The next part shows God accepting the Son's offer to ransom Mankind. Meantime, Satan has passed through the spheres and has reached earth.

Satan conceals himself in the garden and witnesses the happiness of Adam and Eve. Gabriel discovers Satan and evicts him from the garden. In Books Five and Six, Raphael is sent by God to warn Adam of his danger. Raphael relates to Adam the entire story of the battle in Heaven between the good and the evil spirits. In the next part, Raphael explains the purposes and the methods employed in the creation of the world. Adam then relates (Book Eight) his life in Paradise, how he talked with God, and how he met and loved Eve.

In Book Nine, Satan, in the guise of a serpent, induces Eve to eat of the forbidden fruit. She, in turn, persuades Adam to partake of it. Book Ten is the great judgment of man. Sin and Death come to dwell upon the earth. The Son comes to earth.

Satan returns to Hell where all the dark angels are turned to serpents. Adam and Eve sorrowfully prepare to leave their Paradise and both offer up prayers for forgiveness.

In the final books, the Son intercedes for his fallen human charges. Michael is sent to lead the couple from the garden and he shows Adam a view of the future of the human race. In the final book Adam sees more of the vision of the future. He takes hope in the coming of the Messiah, his death and resurrection. Adam and Eve slowly leave the garden as the fiery sword closes the gates to Paradise to them:

> Some natural tears they dropped, but wiped them soon;
> The world was all before them, where to choose
> Their place of rest, and Providence their guide.
> They, hand in hand, with wandering steps and slow,
> Through Eden took their solitary way.

## Human and divine conflict in Milton's epic

Milton struggled all his life with his awareness of the pleasures of this world and with his stern Puritan principles. One can sense both, breathing from every page of *Paradise Lost*. It is not simply a theological tract set in good poetry; it reflects the eternal human struggle of all ages for all men. This is the greatest and the grandest nondramatic poem in English. Milton's poem is human and it is divine. He failed, as every human must, to bring his Puritan ideas entirely into accord with his desires and feelings as a human being. He made Satan a great character; he had to be as strong as the reality of temptation. Milton did not need to spend equal effort on the development of God; the victor was too well known to all readers of Genesis, and the ultimate judgments were foregone conclusions. Milton made Satan great to show against what odds victory was achieved. He made Adam and Eve as himself and an idealized concept of what he had hoped his first wife might have been. He wrote a poem, the very theme of which is controversial among Western men, and he succeeded in maintaining a balance between his Protestant intellect, his humanist curiosity, and his Renaissance sensuality. His being was a blend of all three. He employed the medium he believed most capable of solving man's problems —the intellect; he couched his exposition of goodness and evil in a medium of beauty which was never imitated in English poetry. And in his chosen form he conformed to the highest of epic traditions; he wrote the last of the great literary epics. He employed the most dignified of poetic media to give the greatest possible dignity to the theme of most noble proportions in the spirit of Western man.

### An epic poem of the temptations of Christ

*Paradise Regained*. This shorter epic poem follows the Gospel of Luke and concerns the temptation of Christ as it is set down there, with Milton's imaginative powers being given full sway over the details. This work, of course, is not of the proportions of *Paradise Lost*. It is completed in four books.

Milton varies his method in this second epic of temptation. He employs the same grandeur of verse as in *Paradise Lost* but he introduces to a much greater extent the dramatic form. Most of the work is in the form of a dialogue between Satan and Christ. In a sense, this is more of an intellectual epic than the first. The byplay of argumentation demands a more subtle dialectic. Milton has here succeeded in making of his work a mental exercise for his readers. The conflict is purely a spiritual one. Milton saw the fall of man as having resulted from Adam's yielding to temptation. The greatness of Christ is to the intellectual Milton more of a conquest of equally appealing temptation than to any amount of suffering on the cross. Christ, the Son, must prove perfect obedience to God's command, where mere man, Adam, had proved weak. This is the essence of *Paradise Regained*.

Book One shows Satan being made aware that Christ is proclaimed the Son of God. He fears for his power over man and hastens to consult with his fallen angel hosts. They conclude that he now has a greater task than he undertook in the garden, that of tempting the Son of God himself. God in Heaven knows of the scheme and promises not to interfere, but to let Christ be free to yield or to resist. Christ is lured into the wilderness by divine impulsion, and while this is going forward, he meditates in a long soliloquy on his early life and aspirations. He spends forty days in the wilderness in fasting, preparing for his trials, when Satan appears in the guise of an old peasant. He tries various minor temptations which Jesus refuses to heed.

In the Second Book, Satan tries every temptation of a material import that he can invent. He sets a sumptuous feast before the hungry Jesus, he shows great hoards of wealth. Christ ponders on the nobility of poverty and resists all temptation in this direction. Satan gives up a second time.

Book Three shows Satan attempting to make Christ false by holding out to him untold paths to glory and fame. He fails and turns to the theme of earthly power, offering the assistance of his angel hosts to gain power for Christ on earth. Jesus rejects all military force in achieving goodness in this mortal world.

The last book reveals Satan persisting in his design. He shows Jesus the glories of Rome and guarantees to set Jesus up as the supreme ruler of all the world, providing that Christ will fall down and worship him. Failing in this, Satan offers Christ the totality of wisdom, showing him ancient Athens and the domains of intellectuality that could be his. Finally, Satan admits defeat in all temptations. Leading Christ to the top of the Temple at Jerusalem, he bids him prove his divinity by plunging from the height. But it is the tempter himself who loses his balance and falls, howling, into the void, while angels minister to the needs of Christ, who has resisted the ultimate of temptations and has proved that he is capable of saving mankind.

### Milton's greatest work of art

*Samson Agonistes.* Milton ended his career with a form that he had long dreamed of writing—a sacred tragedy. He chose the tragedy of Samson, as recorded in Judges 13-16. In many ways Milton here is recording much of his own disillusion. Like Samson, he had contended all his life with Philistines. He had even chosen his wife from among his earthly enemies and had suffered sadness and loneliness as a consequence. Now he sat, lonely and blind and defeated, amid his lifelong enemies, suffering their scorn and listening to their frivolous shouts of triumph. Milton made this work pulsate with his tragic bitterness.

*Samson Agonistes* is Milton's greatest work of art, coming near in grandeur to the great Greek tragedians: Aeschylus, Sophocles, and Euripides. He had succeeded in bringing over to English pentameter* blank verse the calm dignity of the Greek hexameter*; his life was now filled with that same tragic gravity of Greek serious drama, and he knew how to record it in his lofty and mature wisdom.

### Summary of Samson Agonistes

Milton here employs the form and devices of Greek tragedy. He uses the chorus and holds rigidly to the classic unities. His story concerns Samson's final day on earth, his recovery of God's favor. Samson is blind and alone, the slave of the Philistines. He appears first to us, seated before his prison, bemoaning his fate. The chorus joins him in emphasizing his weakness and the pity that he should have fallen so low from his former position of strength:

> Now blind, dishearten'd, sham'd, dishonour'd, quell'd,
> To what can I be useful, wherein serve
> My Nation, and the work from Heav'n impos'd,
> But to sit on the household hearth,
> A burdensome drone; to visitants a gaze,
> Or pitied object . . .

Manoah, Samson's old father, comes to see him and remarks upon the shame of the pagan celebration going on that day among the Philistines, a celebration invoked among them by Samson's very sin. This provocation acts as the first of the elements which arouse in Samson an inspiration to put forth one more mighty effort to redeem his self-respect and to save his soul.

Samson is then visited by Delilah, his deceitful Philistine wife, who pleads for forgiveness for delivering him into the hands of his enemies. He is untouched by her wiles.

Next comes Harapha, who represents brute strength. The giant athlete taunts the blind Samson and demands that he come to witness the feast. Samson now thirsts for revenge more than ever.

An official arrives to demand that Samson appear before the orgy of the Philistines and demonstrate his famous strength for their entertainment.

In Act Five, Manoah arrives to announce hope for Samson's release from slavery, just as news is being spread that Samson has died in his final act of pulling down the walls of the temple about the heads of the Philistine assembly. All are dead, and Samson has gained back his salvation by his herculean final act on earth.

The final line of Milton's great classic tragedy is fitting as a closing to his career and to his life, "And calm of mind all passion spent." And the world gained immeasurably from the spending of his final passions, a poetry never equalled in grandeur of style, a blank verse that thundered and rolled, flowed as a mighty stream and trickled as a tiny brooklet at the will of the master, with a music that changed cadence with the changing images that sprang from his fertile imagination and deep wisdom.

## Milton's Friend: Andrew Marvell

Andrew Marvell (1621-1678) was a friend, a companion in ideals and a poet who glanced upward in admiration to his superior in Puritan poetry. He and Milton stood alone in their age; they are the "school" of Puritan poets.

Marvell, like Milton, was intellectual and a man of broad education. He likewise was a mixture of Renaissance man and Puritan. He also hated contention and pleaded for tolerance. He, with Milton, was placed high in public office during the Commonwealth. Unlike Milton, he, being a member of Parliament, voted to return Charles II to the throne. Though of the party in power and in opposition to its principles, he was less bitter and more diplomatic than his friend. In spite of his biting satire against the government he remained in Parliament until his death.

### *Toward a classical spirit in English poetry*

His poetry is both Cavalier and Puritan. It has not the warmth of Spenser's verse, but it has the same color and sparkle. It has the satirical and the ironically witty touch of the Cavalier, and it has the intellectual coolness of wisdom of the Puritan. And it leans at times entirely toward the form of the classic Horatian ode. At other times, it is full of the conceits of a John Lyly. His production more truly contains the forms of the past, the present and the future than the production of any poet in his age.

Marvell wrote verse; he was a pamphleteer and a satirist. *To his Coy Mistress* is Cavalier in spirit. *The Nymph Complaining for the Death of her Faun* is as artificial and full of "euphuism" as anything Lyly or Sidney wrote. His nature poems, such as *The Garden,* are sweetly lyrical and simple:

> While all flowers and all trees do close
> To weave the garlands of repose!

In his *Horatian Ode upon Cromwell's Return from Ireland,* Marvell is stately and classic. His best prose satire, *The Rehearsed Transposed* (1672), attacks the corruption he finds in the Restoration government.

Marvell is closer than Milton to the next age—the age of a

new classicism. And he is the first master to project himself into that age with the verse form that was to become the favorite of the classic Pope, the couplet*:

> The grave's a fine and private place,
> But none I think, do there embrace.

# Chapter VII

# THE NEOCLASSICAL AGE
# (1660-1750)

## Historical and Cultural Notes (1660-1702)

Eighteen years of civil war and the Commonwealth were over, and on May 29, 1660, Charles II came back to London as King of England. Charles was rather tolerant and easy-going. He believed in high life and extravagance for himself and his court and was little concerned how others managed their own lives. His principal antipathy was the Puritan tradition. He leaned to Catholicism and believed in the divine right of kings, but bitter experience had taught him not to press his ideas too far into a course of action. During his reign England became more democratic than ever before. Parliament gained in power and definite political parties took shape, the "Whigs" and the "Tories."

England advanced her sea power, and colonization in the new world was on the increase. London was rebuilt after the devastation of the Great Plague of 1665 and the Great Fire of 1666. Known as the "Merry Monarch," Charles stood for stability and order. He restored court life to a semblance of what it had been under the early, but more colorful, Stuarts. "Live and let live" was at least the outward appearance of life in England.

### *An era of religious, political, and commercial conflict*

But the Dissenters, the Puritans, the Anglicans, the Cavaliers, the commercial classes, and the aristocracy, were more and more at each others' throats, and by 1679, the country was near civil war once again. There was much political argumentation, and debate was conducted on a fiery plane.

Charles died in 1685 and James II, his brother, was King. James reverted to early Stuart policy with a vengeance. He dismissed Commons and prepared to initiate a reign of terror if necessary to enforce his whims. He lost the support of almost every sector of society; even his own Tory party turned against him. He continued to act according to his stubborn will, converting Protestant seminaries into Catholic ones, replacing high officials with Catholics, dismissing Oxford professors, turning a deaf ear to the will of Parliament, and generally stirring up a hatred which seemed to portend more bloodletting in the country.

### Death of the "divine right" of kings

William of Orange, James's son-in-law, rose against him and all England seemed to rally to his banner. James fled to France and Parliament declared that he had abdicated. William and James's daughter, Mary, were now the joint rulers. The revolution had been a bloodless one and became known as the Glorious Revolution of 1688. The theory of the "divine" right of kings in England was dead forever. William III and Mary II ruled until 1702, when William died. Their rule was marked by great strides toward a government by the people. Parliament became supreme; the cabinet form of rule was inaugurated. A bill of rights was adopted, and toleration of conflicting faiths was the order of the times. The Bank of England was chartered and financial stability and material prosperity were known as never before.

## THE NEW CLASSICAL LITERATURE: 1660-1750

During approximately the 90 years following the return of Charles II to the throne, the literature of England was dominated by a new spirit of classicism,* known usually as neoclassicism.* In rather inaccurate divisions this period may be classified in two parts:

I.  The Restoration Period, 1660-1700
II.  The Triumph of Classicism, 1700-1750

These two divisions are also known sometimes as the *Age of Dryden* and the *Age of Pope* from the two figures who are the dominating writers of each of the fairly equal divisions. And from 1750 to 1798 one might again hazard two divisions:

I. The Decline of Classicism, 1750-1784
II. The Rise of Romanticism, 1784-1798[1]

## Restoration and Renaissance Compared

Milton was the final burst of the greatness of the English
Renaissance; he was at the same time Puritan, moral, and intellectual. He was a true transition writer. He presented us with
the colossal grandeur of the lofty intellectual, with all the color
and sensuality of a Spenser. And Milton's final effort, *Samson
Agonistes,* was, in form and substance, pure classical tragedy.

English literature's period of dallying with pure romanticism
and pagan lightness was over for a while. In politics and in art,
England had become classical in a Greek and Roman sense.
In doing so, literature had passed through a transition period
of Puritan writing, which appealed only to the few, and the
cynical irony of the Cavaliers. The Restoration brought English
letters back into its more normal course of development.

The Restoration period, however, was not to be a continuation
of the Renaissance. The Elizabethan Renaissance period was
one in which fancy was permitted to roam into the worlds beyond
human ken. There were no limits upon the imagination. A new
world of artistic endeavor and experimentation was open for
the exploration of both the here and the beyond. Nothing was too
fantastic to be considered and nothing which was considered
was to be barred from exploration. The imagination was pagan
and undisciplined and knew no restrictions.

### *Renaissance and Puritan "otherworldliness" compared*

Now, in the Restoration period, there was an inclination to
accept the reality of the present, to write objectively of circumstances as they were. Both Renaissance and Puritan thought
were otherworldly. Renaissance thought was pagan, fanciful,

[1] This *Review of English Literature* will treat, in Volume I, the approach to
romanticism* as an adjunct to its final chapter on the declining neoclassicism. The
first chapter of Volume II will again treat, in a different approach, the same brief
period. As this book is basically designed to fit the normal divisions of two-
semester college survey courses and the existing two-volume history-anthology texts,
this dual treatment of this brief period appeared to have logical justification. This
writer notes that some year-course surveys and some anthologies divide at about
1784 and others at about 1798. The student who studies a declining classicism must
be acutely aware of what is taking its place; equally, the student who, perhaps after
a lapse of time, begins the second portion of his study of English literature with
romanticism, should be made freshly aware of what this new literary movement is
replacing. The dual treatment of this brief period may, then, be skipped by the
student who pursues his compete survey continuously throughout the year. Or, it
may bear repeating and, for that reason, will be dealt with from somewhat differing
perspectives in these volumes.

and experimental; Puritan thought was tied to the mandates of the supernatural, as represented in Reformation orthodoxy. It was a conflict (and therefore a mixture) of these two aspects of otherworldliness that we have observed from Donne to Milton, from Jonson to Marvell. The Restoration attempted to restore some of the lightness to literature, but the result is artificiality. The tone is cynical and the humor is ironical wit. The tone is elegant and the audience is the intellectual sophisticates. There is nothing here for the common everyday middle-class Englishman, who is serious and likes his literature to be of the world he knows.

## From subjectivity toward objectivity

The age of the Restoration is, in literature, false and clever, but the undertone is one that is leading to an objectivity of observation of reality. It is leading to a great genre in English literature: the novel. In science, the Restoration concerns itself with details of investigation, not generalizations and broad principles. In the political arena, there is no fancy, only discussion of the realities of the moment—it is an earthly consideration of what is being done and what can be done now with what we have. Conservatism is the rule. Individual initiative and experimentation on the political and social planes are eyed with suspicion. Expression of the individual must be bound by the limits prescribed in the social conventions of the time. Everywhere, in politics, in commerce, in religion, in the aristocracy or in the middle class, in moral conduct in general, rules must be set up for living together in accordance with reason and common sense. Enthusiasm must be thus disciplined.

And the literature of the time more and more reflects this. It had a definitely serious side and concerned efforts to fix the stability of the state to an ever greater degree. If it was light and experimental, it was written by and for a very restricted segment of the public; it was aristocratic and fashionable within the limits of the court and the small and elite groups of west-end London.

## A literature of aristocratic manners

Writers no longer were free agents of their fancies. They agreed upon rules and principles, both in poetry and in prose. In theme, they were concerned with the molding of society into an integrated group with like ideas and like dress and mannerisms. They were concerned with details of manners and dress, of life among the prosperous middle class groups. As to form and style, the criterion was the writers of the past; not the frivolous and pagan Renaissance past, to be sure, but the more settled and disciplined past, the classic past of Greece and Rome. These new writers looked with a new eye at old established forms and styles; they were *neo*classic. And they looked with favor upon new masters who best represented this tendency toward discipline in literary production; in the Restoration they looked to John Dryden (1631-1700) and, as the *classic* fever became endemic in English literature, they looked to Alexander Pope (1688-1744). They now spurned the individualistic, the fanciful, the experimentative, and the enthusiastic hot flushes of the *romantic* Spenser and Shakespeare. They could bring themselves to look no further back toward the ages of shallow frivolity than to Milton. He stood on that border line, half tainted to be sure, but with one side turned to the new enlightenment.

### A new Augustan Age for literature

The Restoration was the beginning of the rise of classicism; the age to follow was to become its Augustan age—wholehearted devotion to the time of Caesar Augustus in Rome—that Golden Age of Roman literature from about 30 B.C. to 14 A.D., the age of Vergil and Horace, and of the age just preceding, the age of Cicero and Lucretius. And it was this age in Roman literature that had gained its discipline from a still more ancient Golden Age—that of ancient Greece.

### Influences from France

The Golden Age of French culture corresponded to the English Reformation, about 1660-1690, and it was a classical age. As we have observed, the influence of France on English literature was tremendous since 1066. And France was a funnel through which much of the Italian Renaissance influence reached England.

In France the political situation was more settled during the period from the death of Elizabeth to the return of the Stuarts in 1660. There the reaction against the colorfully romantic aspects of Renaissance literature had set in sooner than in England. A powerful influence on French writing was exerted by one François de Malherbe (1555-1628) in the direction of rationalizing the forms of art and in directing French literature toward general rather than individual sentiment. He was anticipating Dryden and Pope when Cavaliers and Puritans were beginning their contentions in the early years of the 17th century.

And with the coming of the Restoration the great masters of French neoclassicism, Corneille and Racine, were already producing masterpieces based on classic tragedy, and Molière was producing realistic and social comedy.

## French neoclassicism influences world literatures

Charles II and many of his supporters spent years of exile in France before 1660 and many of these exiles were thoroughly imbued with the new classic spirit there. When classical models came to govern English literature, they came in large part, not directly from antiquity, but in imitation of French models. This was true of the new classicism in other countries also: Holland, Spain, Germany, Italy, United States, and Spanish America. Neoclassicism, on a world scale, was basically a spread of French classicism, with each literature asserting its native peculiarities and with each group of writers asserting its own tendencies, more or less, to return directly to Greek and Roman works for inspiration. But, the total result was that world literatures, by the early years of the 18th century, were dominated by the ancients, and France had led the way.

## THE RESTORATION PERIOD: DRAMA

The dominant aspects of Restoration literature were drama and satire. Both forms were looked upon with high favor by the court of Charles and encouraged in every way possible. Most of the dramatic production of the age was written for aristocratic audiences. Drama was no longer to be directed to the insatiable craving of the masses to be entertained, as in the days of the "public" theaters of the Age of Elizabeth.

We have noted that the Puritan influence had caused the theaters to be closed in 1642. From the early days of Elizabeth's reign until this time, dramatic production in England was on a colossal scale, and though it changed slowly in tone and theme from Elizabethan (Tudor) through the Jacobean (Stuart) periods, its production continued uninterrupted, being continuously in demand at both "public" and "private" theaters. The English hunger for dramatic entertainment was seemingly insatiable. It is true, however, that the great Elizabethan drama of Marlowe, Shakespeare, and Jonson had degenerated into plays of sensationalism and melodrama before the closing of the theaters. It is also true that dramatic production of a sort did not entirely cease after 1642. Little playlets of humorous import (called "drolls") were produced and presented privately. Masques continued to be favorite entertainment of the nobility on their private grounds.

## English theatres re-open

Drama was again officially sanctioned some two years before Charles II came to the throne. The first production is England's first attempt at opera, *The Siege of Rhodes* (1568), by Sir William D'Avenant. Immediately after Charles ascended the throne, two companies were licensed, the Duke of York's Company (managed by D'Avenant) in 1661 and the King's Company in 1663. Elizabethan plays were revived, but soon a new flow of dramatic efforts supplied the repertoires of these and newly created Restoration theaters. Drama was back on the boards in England.

## Restoration Plays

A Stuart king was back on the throne but the new plays were not the Stuart plays of the ante-1642 years. The audiences were now almost exclusively confined to London and to fashionable society. The Puritan middle class was still hostile to drama. The fashionable society of London demanded plays redolent of the refinement and the elegance of the French taste in manners and dress.

The plays, then, reflected a gay and dissolute society. They were cynically witty and reflected the artificiality of the frivolous. Puritans and puritanical leanings became the chief butt of ridicule in these sophisticated pieces. The plays all reflect a reckless abandon and a suave blasé society. They were designed for presentation to the world of London fashion and aristocracy.

## Types of Restoration plays

There are three types of Restoration play: *the heroic play, the tragedy,* and *the comedy.*

*The Heroic Play.* This was the most elaborate and elegant of the Restoration drama and was short-lived in popularity. The decade between 1664-1674 saw the principal flowering of this particular exotic form. The dialogue was almost invariably in rimed couplets and was particularly extravagant in its ranting and bombastic tone. Everything about the *heroic play* was extravagant. The scenery was expensive and gaudy and the staging was complex. The plot structures were equally complicated and involved. There was an utter lack of reality about this early phase of the Restoration drama.

This form dealt with a portrayal of the complexities of love and of mighty deeds. It was rooted deep in the Senecan tragedy, with its attendant wordiness and philosophy. It was an insincere fad, and even the Restoration sophisticates soon tired of it.

An outstanding writer of *heroic* plays was John Dryden (whom we shall treat fully under his more enduring writings). Dryden's plays had all the faults general to the period, but they were better done than most. Dryden, the greatest Restoration writer, had sufficient time left over from his more enduring satire and critical work to write more than thirty plays. His *The Conquest of Granada* (1672) is one of his best in the *heroic* mold, abounding in wild lawless passion, unnatural characterization, and in elaborate and crowded scenes.

His *The Indian Queen* (1664, in collaboration with his brother-in-law, Sir Robert Howard) is an interesting example of the color and exaggeration that attended the genre. Here the historical Aztec ruler of ancient Mexico, Montezuma, is presented as the low-born general of the Inca (historically in Peru in South America). He does battle against the Mexicans, and as a reward asks for the daughter of the Inca. Being refused on the basis that he is of low birth, he joins the enemy, but is discovered to be of royal blood after all. After harrowing scenes of persecution, lust, suicide, and all manner of sensationalism, the lovers are united. The audience is treated to every possible exaggeration of the theater before the final curtain falls.

Another writer of the type was Roger Boyle, whose *Herod the Great* (1694) is outstanding.

In 1671, the Duke of Buckingham (and others) wrote *The Rehearsal,* which is a burlesque *heroic* play, directed against Dryden. This satirical play is one of the most famous of parodies or burlesques in English literature.

*The Tragedy.* The English classical tragedy of this early period replaced the *heroic* play and was more realistic. It tended to employ blank verse (as in Elizabethan tragedies) rather than the rimed couplets. But there were basic differences here from the tragedies of Shakespeare. Here there was no intermingling of comic scenes with the tragic. The classical unities were observed. There were no subplots. The aim was noble dignity and this took from Restoration tragedy a great deal of color, variety, and humane characterization. There was much imitation of the great French tragedian, Corneille, but without his genius.

One of the best of the Restoration tragedies was *All for Love* (1678), again by Dryden. This was the story of Antony and Cleopatra, with additions and corrections by John Dryden. This is Dryden's best effort in the drama.

Thomas Otway (1651-1685) invoked pity from audiences with his heart-rending tragedies. His emotional scenes were profound and the handkerchiefs of his fashionable audiences were soaked at the conclusions of such plays as *Venice Preserved* (1682) or *The Orphan* (1680).

_Restoration Comedy._ It is in comedy that the age is best represented. If these plays do not accurately reflect actual life among the fashionable, they at least give us the genuine spirit of the group. These plays were witty and brilliant. They were devoted to depicting the speech, the interests, the dress, and the manners of the times. The characters are almost always the people of fashion, and the scenes, the drawing rooms, the salons, the coffee houses, and the streets of London. These comedies reflect the very shams of the people who flocked to see them. They perhaps could be termed immoral. They held social institutions, such as marriage, up to ridicule. They attacked conventional living from every clever angle.

Comedy was the popular type of drama throughout the period and the Restoration's greatest dramatic output lies in this clever, but naughty and artificial, play of social intrigue. A few of the outstanding writers and their particular approach are:

William Wycherley (1640-1715), who is the master of the double meaning of his times. He is the most cynical dramatist of the age and his plays contain the sharpest-edged satire. *The Country Wife* (1672) is one of his best sardonic comedies. It has all the elements of the best (or worst) of Restoration comedy. It is pornographic, witty, racy, vigorous, and daring. Wycherley's plot is, in part, borrowed from Molière, but his atmosphere is that of the moral corruption of the court of Charles II. *The Plain Dealer* (1693) is of fine, integrated structure, and its characters are well drawn. It is one of the best of English comedies of this light artificial type. It concerns a sea captain who discovers the lack of fidelity of his mistress. He is aided by Fidelia, who eventually proves to be a proper wife for our captain, named Manly.

William Congreve (1670-1729) is noted for his comic master-pieces. His plays are lighter and more polished than those of Wycherley. His dialogue is impudent, graceful, and easy. *Love for Love* (1695) is one of the best of the comedies of manners. It is a satire on the vices and foibles of the age, has a well-integrated plot, and sparkles with ready wit. *The Way of the World* (1700) (270) is the acknowledged Congreve masterpiece and certainly is representative of the best of the Restoration comedy of manners. It is perhaps the best technical accomplish-ment of the entire school and has the usual Congreve store of subtle wit. The author is often more concerned with being witty than in developing his plot.

One might mention any number of other foppish writers of this artificial comedy of manners: Sir George Etherege, Sir Charles Sedley, Sir John Vanbrugh, all bright and scintillating, all cre-ators of the farce comedy which pleased their fellow dandies and their ladies.

George Farquhar (1678-1707) was the last of the school and the least like his fellows. He shows a transition influence toward a more sane drawing room comedy. His plots are more real and seem less like something simply to be endured as a foil for the playwright's sparkling, but shallow, wit. Farquhar died at twenty-nine as he was showing a considerable skill in developing a genuine comedy of manners with a more believable reality than had obtained among his contemporaries and predecessors.

Farquhar's best play was *The Beaux' Stratagem* (1707). This comedy displays a simple directness and genial humor which would come as near pleasing a modern audience as anything the school produced. The play is unusual in that it is not laid in a London or Bath setting. It presents a picture of middle-class life in a small English village. It is bustling, risqué, and witty, but a more serious note predominates and the characters are some-what likable.

### Puritan reaction against Restoration drama

If Farquhar could have continued this type of production, perhaps the English comedy would not have declined to such a low level in the early 18th century. In Farquhar's last years the Puritan middle class had again asserted itself against the immorality of Restoration plays. Jeremy Collier (1650-1726), a drama critic, brought a storm of criticism down upon the drama of the age with his *A Short View of the Immorality and Profaneness of the English Stage* (1698). His charges are bold and he does not hesitate to cite names and instances to support his shafts of criticism. Dryden, one of the butts of Collier's bitter charges, himself admitted that there was much truth in the criticism. Collier's work is as extreme in the one direction as the Restoration drama was in the other, but his and other criticisms during the following twenty-five years spelled the doom of the carefree abandon of Restoration foppery in drama. When drama returned to a minor semblance of favor in England with Goldsmith and Sheridan, the comedy of manners showed the effects of the moral and social forces that brought an end to the Restoration flaunting of convention and social institutions.

## JOHN DRYDEN: THE RESTORATION'S CHIEF WRITER

### *A professional man of letters*

John Dryden (1631-1700) was a professional man of letters and his work includes every kind of writing popular in his time: satire, narrative, argumentative and lyric verse; tragedy and comedy in drama; literary criticism and other pamphleteering prose. Dryden was a writer who influenced the other writers of his time, and in a sense, set the standards for all. He was the first English writer to determine fashion in literature. His direct influence was strong in his own age and reached well into the following century. He learned the use of the closed couplet from a predecessor, Edmund Waller (1605-1687), and he cultivated it into a form which dominated more that a hundred years of English poetry. He set the pace in the heroic play, the tragedy and the comedy of manners of the Restoration Age. He took the conceits and the flowery clumsiness out of English prose and gave it an efficiency of directness which it had never succeeded in reaching before his time. Thus he set a model for correctness for both prose and poetry for his successors.

*His Life.* Dryden was a serious and an intellectual master of his dedicated task—and his task was a deliberate one—to succeed in literature in a material sense. He devoted forty

years to it and he succeeded in dying poor, but making the
name of Dryden immortal.

He was born into a Puritan family. His first poem was a
eulogy of Oliver Cromwell. Six months after this was written,
Charles II came to the throne and Dryden immediately penned
eulogistic verse, dedicated to Charles. He proved to be not only
a poet, but a diplomat, for Charles made Dryden Poet Laureate
and Historiographer Royal. When James II came to the throne
in 1685, Dryden became a Catholic and was in favor again, until
the Revolution of 1688. He lost position and wrote, then, purely
for a living. He was a political and religious opportunist, and as
such, reflects for us the temper and the spirit of this Restoration
age.

### *Dryden sets the tone for 18th century literature*

Dryden was educated at Trinity College, Cambridge, and married into the nobility. His life was a successful one and full of
royal honors, despite the fact that he came from Puritan and anti-
monarchical stock. He changed with the tides until 1688, and
thenceforth he refused to budge from his Catholicism or his
hatred for the new regime of William III. He died rather ob-
scurely of gangrene in 1700. But he had set the tone for 18th
century writing and his bones were placed in Westminster Abbey
with those of Chaucer and he was to have shortly a monument
erected to his memory by the new classical generation that followed in his literary footsteps.

### Dryden's Poetry

*His Satires.* Dryden was a master of the political satire in
closed couplets. Critics are divided as to which is to be accounted
Dryden's best work, his poetic political satire or his prose
literary criticism.

From 1681 forward, England was torn by religious and political controversy (largely with regard to the succession to the
throne). In 1678 there was an attempt to force a bill through
Parliament to exclude Catholics from the throne. This would
have denied succession to Charles' son James, the legitimate
son. The Whig leader, the Earl of Shaftesbury, was the sponsor
of the bill. The whole idea was to pave the way to the throne
for the king's illigitimate son, the Duke of Monmouth, who was
an ardent Protestant. Shaftesbury was, of course, imprisoned
for treason.

The King, angered, bade Dryden commemorate the affair with an appropriate work. The result was three of Dryden's most notable allegorical satires in heroic couplets.

## Dryden's chief satire: Absolom and Achitophel

*Absolom and Achitophel,* (1681) makes use of the biblical story (2 Samuel, 13-18) to tell how Achitophel (Shaftesbury) tempts Absolom (Monmouth) to rebel against King David (Charles II). Dryden's poem is vituperative and dignified. He paints satirical portraits of all parties concerned and scolds here and praises there in magnificent verse, according to the poet's political leanings. His description of Shaftesbury is typical Dryden satire—sharp, exaggerated portraiture, but somewhat accurate and fair, nevertheless:

> Of these the false Achitophel was first;
> A name to all succeeding ages curst:
> For close designs and crooked counsels fit;
> Sagacious, bold, and turbulent of wit;
> Restless, unfixed in principles and place;
> In power unpleased, impatient of disgrace:
> A fiery soul, which, working out its way,
> Fretted the pigmy body to decay,
> And o'er informed the tenement of clay.
> A daring pilot in extremity;
> Pleased with the danger, when the waves went high,
> He sought the storms; but, for a calm unfit,
> Would steer too nigh the sands, to boast his wit.
> Great wits are sure to madness near allied,
> And thin partitions do their bounds divide;
> Else why should he, with wealth and honor blest,
> Refuse his age the needful hours of rest?

*The Medal* is a follow-up satire on Shaftesbury, after Parliament had released the Earl and had given him a medal. *Mac-Flecknoe* (1682) is a very personal satire on a fellow poet, one Shadwell, who had dared to answer Dryden's *Medal.*

Later, after Dryden had become a Catholic, he turned his attention to writing in defense of the Roman Church. In 1687 he turned some of his satirical barbs toward the Church of England in *The Hind and the Panther*—the milk-white innocence of the Hind being the Roman Church and the Panther representing the Anglican Church.

*Miscellaneous Works.* We have already noted (pp. 140-

142) that Dryden was the most copious producer of Restoration drama. He also wrote a good deal of political and religious verse. He wrote three operas and did a number of translations from ancient Latin writers.

## Dryden's Critical Prose

Dryden's prose rivals his poetry as a major influence on the literature of the ages after him. His prose mainly consists of various essays appended as prefaces, prologues, or dedications to his plays. These are critical literary discussions concerning many phases of English and foreign letters. He is somewhat prejudiced, of course, in our modern view, but by and large he is very accurate and acutely intelligent in his observations. He would rank Restoration drama above Elizabethan drama, but a man in Dryden's position and in his times would hardly be expected to do otherwise. He was a pioneer, not only in prose style but in English literary criticism.

His essay *Of Dramatick Poesie* (1668) is outstanding among his prose works. This essay is written in the form of a Socratic dialogue between four persons. It concludes that the English stage of his day is superior to that of the French. He ranks modern writers above the ancients. He further concludes that Elizabethan color and extravagance is inferior to the elegance and orderliness of French drama. In discussing Elizabethan drama, Dryden makes exception of Shakespeare:

To begin, then, with Shakespeare. He was the man who of all modern, and perhaps ancient poets, had the largest and most comprehensive soul. All the images of Nature were still present to him, and he drew them, not laboriously, but luckily; when he describes anything, you more than see it, you feel it too. Those who accuse him to have wanted learning, give him the greater commendation: he was naturally learned; he needed not the spectacles of books to read Nature; he looked inwards, and found her there. I cannot say he is everywhere alike; were he so, I should do him injury to compare him with the greatest of mankind. He is many times flat, insipid; his comic wit degenerating into clenches, his serious swelling into bombast. But he is always great, when some great occasion is presented to him; no man can say he ever had a fit subject for his wit, and did not then raise himself as high above the rest of the poets . . .

Quantum lenta solent inter viburna cupressi.
(as cypresses tower above low-reaching bushes)

## Dryden's Contribution

Dryden brought uniformity, precision, and regularity into English poetry. His poetry, generally, lacks imagination; his contribution is chiefly to form. He is artistic, smooth, and clear. Where English poetry had had ample models of color and unbridled imaginative flow, it now had a model of compactness and orderliness.

Dryden is one of the few great critics in English literature. He is the first writer to make a general and concise critical summary of most phases of England's literary past.

Dryden did much to eliminate the excessive baggage that had characterized English prose up to his time. He demonstrated that English was capable of being handled so as to give clear, direct, and concise expression. After Dryden, English had a model with which to develop great prose, both in didactic and in aesthetic directions. The English disease of artificial decoration was shown an antidote and the superb development of prose in the age after Dryden shows that there were writers who recognized Dryden's contribution in bringing about the necessary assimilation process. English now had sufficient examples of its capabilities in creating colorful and imaginative imagery, and with Dryden, in telling the story or the facts with concise clarity.

## Minor Poetry in the Restoration

The lesser poets of the Restoration followed very closely in the footsteps of Dryden. They were Court Poets, successors of the Cavaliers, and their tone was satirical and flippant.

Samuel Butler (1612-80) was the outstanding satirist below Dryden. His fame rests entirely upon *Hudibras,* an incomplete mock heroic poem of over ten thousand lines, issued in three parts from 1663 to 1678. It is a coarse doggerel verse in iambic tetrameter* couplets. The principal butt of its biting, but brilliant, satire is the Puritans.

## *Hudibras: An English Don Quijote*

The general design for Butler's work was the Spanish *Don Quijote*. Sir Hudibras (a name borrowed from *The Faerie Queene*) and his squire Ralpho set out in burlesque knightly fashion to enforce the laws of a Puritan Parliament, aimed at the suppression of the amusements of the people. Hudibras is a Presbyterian and Ralpho is an Anabaptist. Hudibras, in his madcap career, demonstrates all of the hypocrisy, sanctimoniousness, and intolerant vices laid at the door of the Puritans by the courtiers. Needless to say, Hudibras, like Don Quijote, is buffeted about considerably.

*Hudibras* was very popular in Butler's day and has survived for its depiction of the spirit of the times. Butler's work lacks the dignity of that of Dryden, but is interesting for its outlandish rime and its cutting bufoonery.

Others who wrote satire are: John Oldham (1653-1683), whose *Satires upon the Jesuits* (1681) is an attack upon that order; the Earl of Rochester, John Wilmot (1647-80), whose *Satire against Mankind* is a cynical but impartial scolding of the human species. Wilmot, in his *Epitaph on Charles II,* characterized the chief figure of the Restoration as a man "who never said a foolish thing, nor ever did a wise one . . ."

## DEVELOPMENTS IN RESTORATION PROSE

The literature of the Restoration brought a number of varying developments in English prose. No period, until the 18th century novel, brought such fertile growth. All prose writing of the period tended in the same direction—a new clearer and more concise style for English serious writing. Dryden was only one of several writers of the period who strove to bring order and compactness to prose expression. All, in one way or another, were setting up models for the great novelists and essayists to come. English prose was about to shake off its burden of flowery conceits and its clumsy approach to ideas. We have noted the clarity and precise expression embodied in the literary criticism of Dryden; time now to consider one by one the notable directions that English prose took in the declining years of the seventeenth century.

### Philosophy: Hobbes, Locke, and Newton

Science and a rational approach to mankind's problems distinguished the most dignified of nonaesthetic writing.

Thomas Hobbes (1588-1679) was a materialist, who is distinguished most, perhaps, for his *The Leviathan* (1651), written in a clear and concise style. Hobbes believed in absolute monarchy as the best form of government. He believed that the citizen should submit all his powers of action and thought to this arbitrary absolutism for his own maximum good.

John Locke (1632-1704), whose most read work is an *Essay Concerning Human Understanding* (1690), had a more weighty style, but still succeeded in presenting his ideas clearly. He maintained in this work that all knowledge is of experience and sense perception. He rejected all bases for the existence of innate ideas (introspection, inspiration, vision, etc.) and assumed the mind to be as a blank sheet of paper upon which nothing would appear unless it had been received through ex- perience. He is, in this sense, the founder of modern empiri- cism.

Sir Isaac Newton (1642-1727), usually connected in the average mind today with the famous apple episode which made him conscious of the law of gravitation, was a mathematician and one of the world's greatest scientists. His *Principles* (1687) defines his discoveries in motion and gravitation.

## Literary Criticism

There were a number of other literary critics in the age in addition to the master, Dryden. All took the same general view, that the neoclassic writing was superior to anything that had gone before.

Thomas Rymer (1641-1713) is interesting in that he is a contrast to Dryden in his literary evaluations. Dryden tried to be fair in his age; Rymer was shortsighted and narrow in his application of the principles of Aristotle to tragedy. His *Short View of Tragedy* (1693) is indeed a short view. In it he con- demns Shakespeare, saying of *Othello,* for instance, "a bloody farce without salt or savour." But there is salt in his terse sentence structure.

We have noted Jeremy Collier's *Short View,* in regard to an evaluation of Restoration drama (p. 143).

## History, Religion, and Miscellany

In addition to the above, there were nonaesthetic prose writers of all sorts in the age. Sir William Temple (1628-1699) wrote of English history and published several political works, of which *The Character of a Trimmer* (1688) is a self-portrait in which he defines a political middle-of-the-roader of his times. His *On Ancient and Modern Learning* began the famous controversy, the "battle of the books" which Swift pursued with such success in the next generation of writers. Temple's style is very pointed and epigrammatic.

Religious writers abounded among the bishops and archbishops of the day. Rationalism was beginning to prevail in this field. Common sense and ethical behavior were preached, rather than evangelism and soul-stirring enthusiasms.

Abraham Cowley (1618-67) wrote brief prose essays in the manner of Montaigne. His style was easy and far less rigid than that of Bacon upon such subjects as *Of Myself, Of Solitude, Of Greatness,* etc.

## The Diaries of Evelyn and Pepys

Something new came into English prose with these two famous keepers of personal accounts of what went on about them. We owe a great deal of our knowledge of the intimate details of the social intercourse of the Restoration to the notes of John Evelyn (1620-1706) and Samuel Pepys (1633-1703).

Evelyn was a Royalist and a scholarly man who wrote a great number of tracts and essays, and did translations. A most interesting collection of his letters and diary, called *Memoirs* (published 1818), covers the period from 1640-1706. He gives good intimate portraits of the leaders of the Restoration times as well as of William III. He describes places and events and defines the fashionable world in an impersonal and leisurely prose.

Pepys' *Diary* (published 1825) covers the period 1660-1669. Pepys is more intimate than Evelyn, describing his love affairs and intimate thoughts in a clear and racy style. He is a true gossip and loves Samuel Pepys, perhaps, better than any other human being. He gives excellent pictures of the Great Plague, the Great Fire, and other events of importance in the period covered by the *Diary.* He tells what he likes and what he dislikes with pleasurable frankness. It is a delight to read Pepys —it puts one at a most convenient keyhole looking into the heart of intimate life in the Restoration and into the mind of a most whimsical Mr. Pepys, who was there and records it for us with personal comment.

## Idealistic and Realistic Fiction

Since the poetical romances and prose heroic legends began in the early Middle Ages, mainly stemming from the French, there had been successive waves in European literatures of these highly idealized narratives of chivalry (and the later equally idealized pastoral narrative). And since *Lazarillo de Tormes,* in Spain, there had been an ever-increasing stream of picaresque realistic narrative at the other extreme.

## Review of early English fictional prose

In England, we have followed this stream of French romances and have seen them Englished in many versions. We have observed many written on the "matter" of England. In the Elizabethan Age we observed the imitations of the Italian pastoral. In the picaresque realistic vein (aside from the translations from the Spanish), we noted the isolated *Life of Jack Wilton* (1594) of Thomas Nash. Before the Restoration, English prose was "ill" suited for the development of picaresque realism.

Following a new surge of French romances (mostly idealizing historical events with long allegorical excesses), we find many English versions cropping up in the 17th century. These are reworkings of existing French and English romances and all are given to overcrowded detail and digressions of all sorts, mingled with a syrupy sentimentality. All characterization is an extreme, the good people are "divine" and the bad people are "vile." All were dull in the extreme and merit no mention except to record a craze or fad which attracted the fancy of the fashionable society of England in the age.

## A European reaction against idealized fiction

More worthy of mention is the realistic reaction to the idealized narrative. It began, again, in France with Sorel, Boileau, Molière, and others, whose burlesques of the romances were translated into English, along with Cervantes' *Don Quijote* (trans. 1612, 1620), and Rabelais (trans. 1653). This all set off a stream of English "scandal" fiction, taking the guise of private letters which purported to tell actual occurrences. Notable is Mrs. Aphra Behn's *Love Letters between a Nobleman and his Sister* (1684), which went through several editions.

A wave of rogue, or picaresque, fiction began during the same period, relating in disconnected episodes, horrible and hideous crimes, and earthy indecent adventure. An example of one of the best (or worst) of these tales of anti-heroes and heroines was written by Francis Kirkman in 1673. Its title is sufficiently explanatory of the contents: *The Counterfeit Lady Unveiled,*

*Being a Full Account of the Birth, Life, Most Remarkable Actions, and Untimely Death of the Famous Cheat Mary Carleton, Known by the Name of the German Princess.*

The results of these excesses, both on the idealistic and the realistic sides, were not wholly bad, for much was there to be learned from these popular and fashionable extremes of literary experimentation by the later and more sane writers of narrative prose and verse, both realistic and romantic. Much progress was made during this period toward the birth of the English novel, fully developed and sturdy.

## A Great Religious Allegory in Prose

Mid the mass of prose narrative produced in the age by the fashionable writers of romances and tales of roguery and crime, appeared the humble and unique masterpiece of imaginative prose that was to outlive them all. *Pilgrim's Progress* (published 1678), was written by an unlearned Puritan, John Bunyan.

Bunyan was the son of a tinker. After he had learned to read and write at the village school of Bedford, he entered his father's trade. He was drawn into the Civil War at the age of sixteen on the Puritan Parliamentary side. On returning to his village, Bunyan underwent a personal religious crisis as a result of his reading of religious tracts. He soon joined the Dissenters and began to preach in 1653. When the Restoration came, attention of the authorities was drawn to this humble village preacher who attracted such large crowds. He was imprisoned for preaching without a license.

In prison he wrote his *Grace Abounding* (1666), his own spiritual autobiography. He was released in 1672; three years later he wrote the book that was to be read by more English speaking people than any other, with the exception of the King James Bible, *The Pilgrim's Progress From This World to That Which is to Come*. This book was eventually translated into more than 100 languages.

*Pilgrim's Progress* (1678) (272) is a simple prose allegory of the basis of Protestantism—the doctrine of salvation by grace. It records the journey of Christian, a plain man, from the City of Destruction to the City of God, recording all the woes and temptations that Bunyan had passed in order to reach a peace of mind in Puritan faith.

## *Bunyan and Milton compared*

Milton's *Paradise Lost* is an epic of Puritanism on an intellectual and external plane; Bunyan's simple prose tale is also an epic of Puritanism, but in its inner and spiritually emotional state. The two together form the epitome of the artistic production of the Protestant Reformation, the one work in grandiose verse and aimed at the scholarly mind, and the other a manual of devotion for simple folk.

Bunyan is a man of the people who is speaking to them in a language that they can understand, of the terrible doctrine of damnation and salvation:

About the midst of this Valley, I perceived the mouth of Hell to be, and it stood also hard by the wayside. Now, thought Christian, what shall I do? And ever and anon the flame and smoke would come out in such abundance, with sparks and hideous noises . . . that he was forced to put up his Sword, and betake himself to another weapon, called All-prayer. So he cried in my hearing: "O Lord, I beseech thee deliver my soul." Thus he went on a great while, yet still the flames would be reaching toward him: Also he heard doleful voices, and rushing to and fro, so that sometimes he thought he should be torn in pieces, or trodden like mire in the Streets.

## *Bunyan's bases of appeal to Protestants*

Bunyan is simple, direct, and natural in his approach. His book is imaginative and intense with an evangelistic excitement. His allegorical wanderings are simple and most unlearned readers know what he means by the Slough of Despond, the Valley of Humiliation, the Delectable Mountains. No one can fail to appreciate the character of Lord Hate, Faithful, Mr. Money-less, or Mr. Great-heart. It is this vivid homely characterization, the imaginative narrative, and the simple allegory, that make this book symbolic of the sincere religious emotional experience of untold numbers of Protestants throughout the ages. It is a good and lively tale, even for nonbelievers. Bunyan is a born story teller and takes any reader with him on his interesting journey.

## THE TRIUMPH OF CLASSICISM (1700-1750)

### Historical and Cultural Notes

William III fell from his horse in 1702 and died. Anne, daughter of James II, came to the throne. England was soon plunged into the War of the Spanish Succession. The son of James II tried to gain the throne with the aid of France. The Peace of Utrecht in 1714 made it clear that England was to continue to settle her succession problems at home without continental interference.

Anne died that same year without heirs. Parliament had insisted since 1701 that Anne's successor should be a Protestant. When Anne died, the only eligible candidate was George, son of the Grand Duchess Sophia of Hanover, Germany, granddaughter of James I. George I came to the throne of England at the age of fifty-four, speaking only German. He took as little interest in the government as did his son, George II, who reigned from 1727-1760. England's government was in the hands of ministers and Parliament during more than fifty years.

England and Scotland became united under the name of Great Britain in 1707. England, during the period, participated in a number of European wars, as well as the French and Indian War in the Americas. It was a turbulent period in politics, with the Puritan Whigs in power most of the time. The strongest political figure of the time was Robert Walpole, premier from 1721 to 1742. Walpole was a Whig politician of unusual ability, though unscrupulous and stubborn. England acquired, politically, more and more of a spirit of tight nationalism during the period.

### A changing British society

In the social sphere, a moral tightening was taking place. It was no longer popular to hold Puritan principles up to ridicule. The middle class was taking over, and in many respects, it was not a pretty sight. Brutality and mob violence were common in the age. Health and sanitation were practically unknown in London. It was an era of filth, of petty crime and lawlessness. It was a period of suspicion and tale-bearing. The French Montesquieu, in comparing the English with the French of the age, said: "In France, I become friendly with everyone; in England with no one. In England, you must do as the English do, live for yourself, care for no one, love no one, rely on no one." It is a harsh judgment, but apparently basically true.

Industry and trade prospered. There was slowly developing a rich industrial middle class. This class aped the manners of the gentry. Good taste and form were rigidly imposed in a uniformity which either punished or ostracized exception. Coffee was introduced into England in 1652 and the English "coffee houses" flourished. These public cafés were the centers of gossip, political and literary bickering, and gambling.

## The Literature of Neoclassicism

### *The triumph of middle-class Puritanism*

In literature, this Augustan age was a triumph for conformity to established principles, set by the masters of form and style, idols of the upper middle class reading public. It was an age of neoclassicism, and this rigid reign continued unchallenged until the death of its supreme arbiter, Alexander Pope, in 1744. There was humor in literature, but little gaiety and laughter. It was a literature of correctness and controlled elegance. Excesses of imagination or color were frowned upon. Objectivity, rather than subjectivity, was the order of the day. There was little of emotion, of man's personal reactions to nature. On the stylistic side, form was superior to idea, and the best form was that of the ancient arbiters of fashion in literature in Augustan Rome. And when Pope spoke of Nature as "At once the source, and end, and test of Art," he was referring to a rational and careful intellectual concept of right (disciplined) principles of thought and conduct. In England it was a triumph of middle-class Puritanism, without the color and waning Renaissance influences of a Milton, nor yet the carefree wit and conceit of a Dryden. It was a rigid mold that produced a great literature of its kind: the essay, the novel of social manners, critical argumentation, social satire. It was an age of realism, cold calculated conventionalism, abstract expression, and perfect poetry in dead marble patterns—largely in the chill of the rimed couplet.

In this section, we shall consider only strictly neoclassical writers of the period 1700-1744; we shall then devote a section to the decline of classicism from 1750-1784 and the circle of writers who hovered around Samuel Johnson, vainly attempting to carry on the tradition of an anachronistic and artificial classicism. We shall consider the rise of the English novel from 1740-1800 in a separate section, for the novel, from its inception, marked a departure from classical standards and became more and more individualized and romantic as the century wore on. A discussion of the beginnings of the novel, therefore, is a logical step toward our last section in this volume, the rise of English romanticism, in the last years of the 18th century.

## Master of the Rimed Couplet

*Leader of Neoclassicism: Alexander Pope.* The greatest
of 18th century poets and the supreme examplar of English classical literature was Alexander Pope (1688-1744). He remains
for us the flower of the age: the symbol of English neoclas-
sism is the age of Pope. His form was elegant and his poetry was
perfect heroic couplets. His style is brilliant and provides a
dazzling framework for his wit, satire, and sparkling stock of
epigrammatic philosophizing.

Pope was a Roman Catholic and found himself ill served in
a Protestant environment. He was denied the best of English
higher education and could not hope to attain any office in the
government. A private education, a puny physique, and an
acute consciousness of the obstacles he confronted in his age,
gave Pope a driving urge to succeed as a man of letters. He
drove himself to perfection in his studies, and by the age of
fifteen had read widely in ancient and modern literatures. He
had written his four pastorals (1709) in imitation of Vergil and
had become thoroughly settled upon his future classical course
by the age of twenty-three, when his *Essay on Criticism* (1711)
was published. This poem reiterates his concept of the principles of neoclassical art as laid down from Aristotle, through
Horace and Boileau. He lays down, one by one, the rules for
critics of his age, and for the most part they followed them.

## Pope's mock-heroic epic masterpiece

Pope, short in stature, constantly ailing and hunchbacked,
became an irritable and sensitive man. There is nothing of
sentiment or of genuine feeling about the great works of Pope.
They are great because they are perfectly polished specimens
of brilliant wit. But they are coldly inhuman—Pope had the
genius of being charmingly inhuman in his verse satire. The
first of his two masterpieces, *The Rape of the Lock* (275), was
written between 1712 and 1714. It is the most sparkling of English verse satire. It is, perhaps, world literature's chief example
of the mock-heroic epic, a burlesque of the dignified form and
the weighty theme of the epic poem.

Pope's poem has a tongue-in-cheek nobility and is written
in masterful couplets. Pope chooses a subject of infinitesimal
importance and gives it exaggerated grandeur. It seems that
the theme has basis in fact: one Lord Petre surreptitiously

snipped a lock of hair from the head of the unsuspecting Lady Arabella Fermor. Pope's friend, John Caryll, worried over the ill feeling that had been aroused among members of these two Catholic families over the Lord's impudent act, begged Pope to write a poem to attempt to smooth the troubled waters. The result is a masterpiece of social satire in which the petty vanities and affected artificiality of high society are held up to ridicule.

### Philosophy in verse

Pope's other masterpiece and his most quotable poem is his *Essay on Man* (1732-34). In this philosophic discussion in matchless couplets, Pope attempts an application of common sense to problems of the universe and the life of man. It is written in the form of four epistles. The first concerns man's place in nature, the second, individual ethics. The third epistle concerns the origin of society and man's relation to it. The last epistle delves into the founts from which man's happiness springs.

Pope expresses the belief that everything exists as a part of a perfect plan and his advice to man is:

> Know then thyself, presume not God to scan,
> The proper study of mankind is man.

Pope's philosophy is not systematized, nor is it new. He is simply recording for us the scraps of philosophical ideas of his time. The enduring value of the work is its fine bits of superb epigram, its wealth of quotable truths or titillating thoughts, recorded in brilliant phraseology. When a modern says, "to err is human, to forgive divine," "fools rush in where angels fear to tread," "a little knowledge is a dangerous thing," or "hope springs eternal in the human breast," he little realizes that he is mouthing lines originating in Pope's *Essay on Man* and *An Essay on Criticism*.

### Elegant translations of the Iliad and the Odyssey

Pope, as Chapman before him, did translations of the *Iliad* and the *Odyssey*, which proved to be the most profitable of literary ventures. His royalties, on these works alone, enabled him to live out his life in modest comfort. Pope used his brilliant heroic couplet in these translations, and like Chapman, failed to find the simple dignity of Homer's verse.

Pope's other works are many. His *Moral Essays* (1731-1735)

are philosophical discussions of character and riches; his *Dunciad* (completed in 1743) is a satire on literary people against whom Pope had a grudge; his *Imitations of Horace* (1733-1739) is a series of satires on contemporary manners, in the style of Horace; his *Eloisa to Abelard* (1717) is an heroic epistle, perhaps the tenderest writing to be found in the brilliant hardness of Pope's poetry, in which Eloisa renounces her love for Abelard in favor of God.

## A Famed Pair of Literary Collaborators

*Periodical Literature: Addison and Steele.* Joseph Addison (1672-1719) and Richard Steele (1672-1729) are the most famous pair of literary collaborators the world has known. Born the same year, schoolmates, these men, though they wrote separately, share joint importance in the history of the essay.

Addison and Steele left Oxford together, and for a while, their lives followed differing paths. Addison soon rose to high position, entered Parliament, became secretary to two high lords in successive years, and married a countess dowager. He was a scholar and tended to be a bit stiff in his early writing.

Steele did not graduate from Oxford. He entered the army and rose to captain, was cast out by his family, and eventually wound up as a fashionable loafer in the coffee houses. In 1701, he wrote a satire on undertakers and lawyers, called *The Funeral* or *Grief a la Mode*. Steele wrote several sentimental plays (while Addison wrote one coldly stiff tragedy), spent what he earned lavishly, and eventually founded *The Tatler* (1709), a newspaper that appeared three times a week. *The Tatler* was highly personalized journalism, consisting mainly of essays, and purported to be impartial. Its avowed purpose was to expose sham and falsity and to report on subjects of general interest. It had a rather decided Whig leaning.

### Masters of the familiar essay of manners

About this time Addison joined Steele, and their essays began to appear jointly. In 1711, *The Tatler* was abandoned and the two friends started *The Spectator,* which appeared six times a week and was more impartial in its political views. This paper concentrated upon manners and morality. Together the two editors wrote hundreds of intimate essays which did much to mold public opinion of their time. Addison and Steele set the tone and the quality for the journalistic familiar essay in English.

Their subjects covered a range of interests from literary topics to five o'clock teas. They invented a fictional circle of characters to represent various classes of English society, the most famous of whom was Sir Roger de Coverley, a Tory country squire.

*The Tatler* and *The Spectator* had an enormous influence upon not only the future of the intimate and conversational-type essay of England, but upon the periodical production of all Europe. Addison and Steele did much to demonstrate that satire could be moral, gentle, humorous, and highly interesting, even to the groups of individuals being lectured. *The Spectator* suspended publication in 1714 and both editors tried various other periodical ventures, but none that succeeded in equaling the quality or the popularity of their joint enterprises.

Addison was more classical and learned. He did much to cultivate a middle-class taste for literature. Steele's style was more of the intimate chatty variety, humorous, but always on a moral and disciplined plane, though tinged with sentimentality. Together they gave the periodical essay dignity and a place in literature. *The Spectator* had succeeded in its printed intention to bring "philosophy out of closets and libraries, schools and colleges, to dwell in clubs and assemblies, at tea-tables and in coffee-houses."

### English Literature's Most Bitter Writer

*A Prose Satirist: Jonathan Swift.* Swift was a direct contrast to Steele, with his mellow good humor, and to Addison, with his easy urbanity. Jonathan Swift (1667-1745) was intellectual and bitter. He loved men as individuals, but he hated mankind collectively, and he wrote with a pen tipped with vemon of the institutions of man. He is the greatest of the English satirists.

Swift was born and educated in Dublin. His father had died before his birth and Swift faced poverty with his mother. He attended Trinity College in Dublin, and afterward became a personal secretary to Sir William Temple.

Swift was a proud and sensitive person and grew restless in his humble position. However, he remained until Temple died in 1699. He had entered the ministry in 1694 but soon was back at Temple's side.

Temple, a literary scholar, was participating in the current controversy in European literatures over which valued most, the ancient or the modern books—the quarrel between tradition and

modernism, originality, and authority. The arguments had been
flying back and forth since the early years of the century in Italy,
France, and England. Swift had observed the literary conflict
for some time, and in 1704 he published his first two satires,
both mature and finished works, partially concerning this one
question: *The Tale of a Tub* and *The Battle of the Books*.

### Swift's satires in praise of traditional learning

*The Tale of a Tub* is considered one of Swift's most mature
satires and one that illustrates his ironical wit as well as any
work he did:

We of this age have discovered a shorter and more prudent
method to become scholars and wits, without the fatigue of reading
or of thinking. The most accomplished way of using books at
present, is two-fold; either, first, to serve them as some men do
lords, learn their titles exactly, and then brag of their acquaintance.
Or, secondly, which is indeed the choicer, the profounder, and
politer method, to get a thorough insight into the index, by which
the whole book is governed and turned, like fishes by the tail. For,
to enter the palace of learning by the great gate, requires an expense
of time and forms; therefore men of great haste, and little ceremony,
are content to get in by the back door. For the arts are all in a flying
march and therefore, more easily subdued by attacking them in
the rear.

Swift builds up his praise of the ancients by the simple device
of ridiculing the moderns. The main portion of this satire, however, is a reckless and brilliant condemnation of the petty divisions in religion. His flaying of institutionalized religion has
caused him to be criticized as irreligious, but this is hardly fair.
Swift is sincere and strikes at the evil he considers men do to
pure religion in their organizations for worship. He considers
that man degrades every pure idea he touches and converts
an admirable thing into something which is horribly distorted
to suit his selfish ends. Swift, himself, was a member of the
clergy of the Church of England when he published the book.
Later in life, Swift was astounded at his early capacities: "Good
God, what a genius I had when I wrote that book!"

*The Battle of the Books* is more directly a defense of ancient learning and a direct attempt to uphold Temple's views.
It takes the form of a mock-heroic epic of a war that breaks
out between ancient and modern books in the St. James Library.

Neither side wins but Swift is obviously supporting the ancient forces.

### Swift's later years

While Swift was secretary to Sir William Temple he formed a lasting friendship with a young girl, Esther Johnson, whom he referred to as Stella. From 1710 to 1713 he wrote his *Journal to Stella,* a very intimate, tender, and playful series of letters in which he records many of his personal thoughts and doings.

Swift worked as secretary to Lord Berkeley in Ireland for a while after Temple died in 1699, and remained for ten years as pastor of a small church near Dublin. He went over to the Tory faction and found himself at personal odds with his old Whig friends Addison and Steele. He was made Dean of St. Patrick's Cathedral in Dublin in 1713. He remained in this position until mental illness overcame him in 1736. He became insane in 1741 and died four years later.

For a period of fifteen years from 1710, he was one of the most influential men in the public life of his times. He wrote many political pamphlets and essays. His many writings in this period cover religious questions, industrial issues, state matters, social evils (he wrote a *Modest Proposal* in 1729 in which he proposed that the excessively numerous poor children of Ireland cease to be a burden upon their parents, by becoming food for the rich), analyses of elements of political spirit, and some biting satire directed at his enemies. He wrote some verse, the most distinguished of which was his long poem entitled *Cademus and Vanessa* (1726). Apparently a Vanessa Vanhomrigh was in love with him. She died in 1723 and his Stella died five years later. Swift was perhaps secretly married to her; no one knows for sure the exact nature of their relationship over the years.

### England's supreme literary indictment of humanity

*Gulliver's Travels* (1726) (277), Swift's masterpiece of satire, is the bitterest indictment of mankind ever written and is one of the world's most charming children's books. It appeared under the title *Travels into Remote Nations of the World, By Samuel Gulliver,* and is divided into four books. Children, of course, are exposed only to modified versions of his first two books— adventure stories of Gulliver's travels into the land of the pigmy Lilliputians and to that of the giant Brobdingnagians. These, stripped of a few elements not essential to the stories, are charming, innocent, appealing little tales.

But with all its trappings, the entire work is a bitter, but clever and witty, satire on the vices, pettiness, and utter hypocrisy of man and the institutions he creates. It is ironical and diabolical in its tone. Swift's style is simple, direct, and precise. Swift was a master of irony; to say a thing in such a way that the reader would take an opposite meaning from that which the words conveyed, was his most developed skill as a satirist. His was an all-consuming moral indignation. He hated mankind for its complacency in the face of its own obvious hypocrisies and he set out to deliberately make men indignant. He states his purpose is "to vex the world rather than divert it." He does both for the reader who is receptive to a blisteringly clever and ironic expression of ideas, even if those ideas be directed against the group and the institutions to which such a reader belongs. Swift at times was coarse; at others, he was fascinating and charming. But one is always aware that this master satirist was coldly controlling his expression and that behind his pen was a mind that was subject to a terrible emotional pressure. He defined his purpose in life and writing in a letter to Pope, in 1725:

I have ever hated all nations, professions, and communities, and all my love is towards individuals: for instance, I hate the tribe of lawyers, but I love Counsellor Such-a-one, and Judge Such-a-one: so with physicians—I will not speak of my own trade—soldiers, English, Scotch, French and the rest. But principally I hate and detest that animal called man, although I heartily love John, Peter, Thomas, and so forth. This is the system upon which I have governed myself for many years. . . .

## A Creator of Autobiographical Romance

*Daniel Defoe*: *Precursor of Realistic Fiction.* Daniel Defoe (1661-1731) was a middle-class Dissenter, son of a tallow chandler. He became a butcher, a merchant, a secret agent, a journalist, and a very prolific writer of more than 200 pamphlets of various sorts. Defoe was venturesome in business, but careless, and made and lost several modest fortunes.

In his satires, Defoe, like Swift, was master of the ironical approach. In *The True-Born Englishman* (1701) he ridicules the idea of racial superiority. In other essays of the kind, he discusses commercial problems of the day, flays ecclesiastical intolerance, or pleads for better educational facilities for English children.

## An approach to the modern novel

The importance of Defoe to us, however, lies in the direction of the novel. Defoe wrote a number of long prose narratives which were somewhat between the old picaresque novel and a more modern realistic novel. Defoe has a homey, down-to-earth style, and usually winds up his narratives with a considerable amount of moralizing. His structure is loose but he had the gift of telling his story in a shallow, slipshod, but robust, manner. He is not a great novelist, but he is the first English writer of novelistic talent. He has little sense of character development. His novels give the illusion of reality in the manner in which the author strings together a long series of factual adventures or episodes. He approached the novel through a first-person relation of his principal characters. His narratives could be called autobiographical romances. Some of the lesser Defoe titles are: *The Life, Adventures and Piracies of the Famous Captain Singleton* (1720), which took place along the African coast; *The History and Remarkable Life of Colonel Jacque, Commonly call'd Jack* (1722), the autobiography of a pickpocket; *The Fortune and Misfortunes of the Famous Moll Flanders* (1722), the romance of a prostitute who is, at the same time, a pickpocket; *Roxana, or the Fortunate Mistress* (1724), the story of a courtesan among the aristocracy. Defoe's most voluminous output in the novelistic vein is of lower-class or criminal types. He always attends to the moral reform of each of his protagonists after the series of highly adventurous or scandalous episodes is concluded.

## Robinson Crusoe: a famed adventure narrative

Defoe's masterpiece, and one of the world's most famous books, is *The Life and Strange Surprising Adventures of Robinson Crusoe, of York, Mariner* (1719) (281). Defoe had little artistic talent but was a careful observer and recorder of factual realism. Here he picked a narrative which made full use of those powers and required little artistry to keep his account racing along in a lively manner.

His hero is a shipwrecked mariner, cast up on a supposedly deserted island and practically the entire first part is devoted to this man's long struggle with his environment to survive and to build up a private civilization of his own. The story is factual and could well be dull, but the reader becomes fascinated with the ingenuity of this lone individual against nature and receives much vicarious satisfaction in following Crusoe's trial-and-error discoveries and projects. Modified versions of the book have been indispensable reading for young boys during every genera- tion of English and Americans to the present time.

### Poetic satirist of politics and manners

*The Poetry of John Gay*. Aside from Pope, the only other major poet of this era of prose, is John Gay (1685-1732). Gay wrote a good deal of bucolic works in both blank verse and the heroic couplet. His *The Shepherd's Week* (1714) is a realistic pastoral in a mock Vergilian style, describing English country life. *Trivia, or the Art of Walking the Streets* (1716) is bur- lesque classicism, but turns out to be a very realistic picture of manners in London. His *Fables* (1727-1738) are witty and among the best English attempts in this form.

Gay's most famed works are his two ballad operas, *The Beg- gar's Opera* (1728) and *Polly* (1729). Each is satirical and lampoons the political foibles of the time. Sir Robert Walpole comes in for his share of ironical lampooning. There is little plot in either opera, but there is much clever dialogue, some good lyrics, and a great store of witty jabs at political life. Per- formance of *Polly* was forbidden in London. *The Beggar's Opera* was sensationally popular and is the best of English comic operas to the days of Gilbert and Sullivan.

# Chapter VIII

# BEGINNINGS OF THE
# MODERN NOVEL (1740-1800)

## Historical Notes

The novel,* in its modern acceptance as a recognized art form, existed only in restricted meanings for us prior to the 18th century. This form, which presents a sustained story that is not historically true (but might be), became a fixed factor in European literatures of the late 18th century and blossomed into a permanent and predominant genre in 19th century literatures. The novel became, for 19th century literatures, what drama had been in the 16th and 17th centuries. Today this form is accepted as the most popular and the most important type of literature.

### *Famed ancient narrative accounts*

The novel had existed, of course, in its basic framework of telling a story or stories of fictional nature in the ancient and the Oriental literatures. The tales of ancient Egypt, the Indian and Persian stories of the *Arabian Nights* variety, existed several centuries before Christ. In the late Greek period and in Roman literature are to be found several examples that roughly approach the structure of a modern novel: Longus' *Daphnis and Chloë* (a long pastoral Greek romance of the 4th or 5th century), Apuleus' *The Golden Ass,* and Petronius' *Satyricon* (both Roman satirical picaresque romances of the 1st and 2nd centuries).

### *Origins of the modern novel*

But it is from Italy that the name and form of the modern novel derives. There, as early as the 13th century, anonymous

prose tales (called "novella" "something new") were circulated. And this was true also of Spain, where Arabic collections of tales (bound together by a crude framework or "wheel"
arrangement) were translated into Spanish in the same century.
The 14th century saw the great collections of European tales.
The Italian "novella," or short story, continued to be popular
in all European literatures throughout the Renaissance period,
which also saw many long and loosely constructed episodic
novels of the pastoral or picaresque variety. And the medieval
romance began its prose career as early as the 13th century in
France, mainly in translations of Latin romances. There are,
then, many precursors of the general form and content of the
novel before the 18th century.

The particular aspect of the 18th century beginnings of the
modern novel was to bring together these various elements,
a unified plot structure, characterization, an atmosphere of
reality, a modern narrative idiom, into a definitive literary vehicle which aimed to make the public mind familiar with great
or stimulatingly entertaining ideas, presented in an appealing
and integrated prose narrative form. Thus the modern novel
in its 18th century beginnings was simply a dilation of the
"novel" (short story of the "novella" variety). And the major
European literatures were all producing this new form by the
beginning of the 19th century.

### English Precursors of the Novel

One might say the English novel originated in the prose
tales, anecdotes, and legends from European and Oriental
sources, in the Latin collection *Gesta Romanorum* (about 1295),
in Malory's *Morte d'Arthur,* in Sidney's *Arcadia,* in Lyly's
*Euphues.* The first real resemblance to a modern novel is Nash's
*The Unfortunate Traveler,* but the language in this imitation of
the Spanish picaresque novel is not a modern English prose as
yet.

The new surge of prosified French romances and the rogue
fiction of the early years of the 17th century are the first major
contributions in a modern English idiom. Defoe's *Robinson
Crusoe, Moll Flanders,* and other autobiographical narratives,
and Bunyan's *Pilgrim's Progress* have the modern language and
the air of realism and romance, but are still loosely connected
series of narrative episodes, rather than integrated and unified
narratives. Character building is also crude in these direct

precursors. The "character" writers of an earlier day and the familiar essays of the type produced by Addison and Steele are also contributors to the elements requisite to the creation of sustained narrative development in the finished artistic creation which we know as "novel."

## The Big Four in English Novelistic Beginnings

### Richardson, Fielding, Smollett, and Stern

_Samuel Richardson (1689-1761)._ _Pamela,_ or _Virtue Rewarded_ (1741-1742) (284) is the first regular modern English novel. Its author was a London printer who, at the age of fifty-one, was asked by friends to issue a volume of model letters "in a common style" which could be used by the public as models for personal correspondence. The result is a story, told in a series of letters, of the virtuous working girl, Pamela. The modest Richardson soon found that he had gone a bit beyond composing a manual for letter writing—he had composed the first great novel of character in world literatures.

Richardson had married twice, both times to daughters of printers. His first wife died, giving birth to her sixth child. His second wife survived her husband by twelve years and also had given him five children. That Richardson knew feminine psychology can hardly be doubted. He was accustomed to reading aloud to circles of young women of taste and refinement and was frequently called upon by individual women to compose their love letters for them. He was gratified in the extreme to find himself the object of widespread feminine admiration as a result of the circulation of _Pamela._ He understood women and was a careful observer of the workings of the feminine mind. His men characters are definitely less well characterized.

### Pamela: England's first novel of character

Pamela is an honest girl who works for Mr. B, a designing businessman. Through Pamela's intimate correspondence the reader is led through a series of attempts on the part of the rascally Mr. B to seduce her. She loves the wretch but will not allow her virtue to be defiled. Eventually she causes him to see the worth of such sterling virtue. They marry and many more of Pamela's letters reveal her happiness and tribulations as a wife and mother, her husband's shortcomings, and his second and permanent realization that he had been given a jewel of virtue as a life companion.

Richardson's novel is revolutionary in many ways. It is a novel, completely in epistolary form. It is a sentimental novel; it is a novel of character. It is also a psychological novel and a novel of manners. Richardson is a pioneer in the field of characterization and the pursuit of a moral purpose throughout many pages. The episodes are all an integral part of his character and plot development. The author's style is clear and simple.

### Clarissa Harlowe

Richardson again employed the letter technique in the creation of his second sentimental romance, *Clarissa Harlowe,* or *Virtue Triumphant* (1748) (284), usually conceded to be the Richardson masterpiece. Here Richardson experiments further with feminine psychology. He goes beyond his first attempt by making Clarissa more of a spiritually virtuous girl than Pamela (who was conscious of material gain in female virtue).

Clarissa allows herself to be seduced by the villain, Lovelace, under the influence of dope. She refuses to marry him, preferring to die instead. Lovelace has repented his act, but is slain soon in a duel with a relative of Clarissa.

Richardson delves deeply into sentimentality in his second novel and shows his ability to arouse a sense of pathos in his readers and gives a very refined and sure treatment of the emotional crises of his heroine. There is little humor in this book but his character portrayal is a very live one of the girl, and is not so weak as usual in the case of the vile deceiver, Lovelace.

*Clarissa Harlowe* was immediately popular in France and Germany, especially influencing Rousseau's *La Nouvelle Héloise,* written also in the epistolary form.

Richardson's third novel, *Sir Charles Grandison* (1753) is less well done. It is filled with moralizing. He attempts to handle too many characters and tries to introduce a multitude of side plots. In addition, he characterizes men less well than he does women.

Richardson had shown the way into the human heart through cold print. He had paved the way for the presentation of human beings, instead of types, in fiction.

<u>Henry Fielding (1707-1754).</u> Richardson's life and personal emotional and sensitive nature admirably suited him for his role in appealing to the sentimentality of his public. Fielding, no less

great as a character portrayer, was talented in a different direction. Fielding tended to the comic, the satirical, and the healthy human traits of character.

Fielding was nobly born and educated at Eton. His familiarity with the ancient classics is evident in his books. He studied law but finally turned to playwriting. He wrote a number of moderately popular farces and burlesque tragedies. His political satire caused him to be banned from the theaters. He returned to law, and to earn an adequate living for his family, to the writing of novels.

Fielding was anything but sentimental and his reading of Richardson's *Pamela* sent him into gales of laughter. His first experiment in the novel was indeed a novel one. He created as his central character a fictitious brother to Pamela, named Joseph. Joseph, it seems, has the same difficulties as Pamela; he spends his time defending his virtue from designing females. (This novel provoked the gentle Richardson to characterize Fielding's effort as "lewd ingraftment.")

### *Joseph Andrews: a comic masterpiece*

*The History and Adventures of Joseph Andrews* (1742) presents admirable portraits, albeit comic ones. Fielding soon forgets that he set out to burlesque Richardson's novel and turns to the serious purpose of turning out a comic masterpiece. He succeeds admirably. He presents us with a real novel of character and manners. In particular, his Parson Adams and Mrs. Slipslop are immortal. Joseph is, of course, a parody of Pamela and is scarcely believable. He provokes our laughter and that is precisely what Fielding intended that he should do. But Parson Adams becomes a lovable comic English replica of Don Quijote.

It seems that Joseph is being pursued by Lady Booby, Pamela's sister-in-law, and the fate of his virtue hangs in the balance. But, after definitively spurning her overtures, Joseph finds himself discharged from the aristocratic household. He starts out to visit his sweetheart, a humble girl named Fanny, who has also just been discharged from the Booby household. On the way he meets the parson and they set off together on a round of quixotic adventures.

Meanwhile, Fanny sets out for London and is rescued from a would-be seducer by the kindly parson. Joseph and Fanny are reunited, but both are soon arrested for theft, at the instigation of Lady Booby.

For a while it seems that Fanny is Joseph's sister, which makes them both very sad, but the error is soon discovered along with the news that Joseph is really the son of a country gentleman. Joseph and Fanny are married and Lady Booby is thwarted and forced to seek some less virtuous object for her licentious affections than Joseph Andrews.

Parson Adams is Fielding's masterpiece of character creation. He is a good man, fond of food and drink, and with a hatred for hypocrisy and meanness.

Fielding handles his situations like a master dramatist. His action is lively, his humor is delightful (if at times a little rough), and his style is racy and direct.

Fielding then wrote *The Life of Mr. Jonathan Wilde the Great* (1742), portraying the life of a dissolute rake. The book is a satirical biography, for he follows his Jonathan from his youthful career as a master pickpocket until he eventually becomes a count. From here Fielding has his character continue to practice knavery until finally the *great* Jonathan is hanged.

Fielding is using his central character to satirize politics, pretense, and vice in all forms. This is a strong picaresque satire.

### Tom Jones: greatest early English novel

Fielding's masterpiece is *The History of Tom Jones, A Foundling* (1749) (287). It is conceded to be the best English novel before the 19th century and one of the best realistic novels in the language. Many characters are woven in and out in this well-constructed work. All are real and are sympathically portrayed. *Tom Jones* is a truly great novel of all time.

Tom is left as an infant in the bedroom of the kindly Squire Allworthy. The boy's parentage is a mystery which hangs over the events all through the work. Early in the novel Tom is separated from his sweetheart. In his wanderings to find her Tom meets many interesting people and has adventures in every possible English setting. Needless to say, he finally finds his Sophia and discovers himself to be the son of the Squire's own sister.

*Tom Jones* gives an admirable picture of both country and town life of mid-18th century England. Fielding's main strength in this novel lies in his skillful manipulation of a multitude of characters and details, all neatly woven into an integrated plot.

*Amelia* (1751) is Fielding's last novel. This is more of the Richardson type, sentimental and moralizing. It is less satirical than his other works. It has an excess of social propaganda, dwelling constantly upon the cruelties and corruption among the lower magistrates and constables of London. As a novel, it is inferior to his other productions. His pictures of London slum life, however, are very real and anticipate the great Dickens.

In connection with Fielding, mention should be made of a very witty, but cuttingly satirical, novel called *An Apology for the Life of Mrs. Shamela Andrews* (1741). Shamela uses every trickery in the feminine arsenal to get her master to marry her. The author's name was given as Conny Keyber, but many assume that this is Fielding's first novel.

## A precursor of Dickens

*Tobias Smollett* (1721-1771). Smollett was a Scotchman of a very irascible temper who, after being apprenticed to a surgeon in Glasgow, joined the English navy and spent several years in the West Indies. He returned to London and took up practice as a surgeon. As a sideline, he wrote satirical plays and history. His first novel was *The Adventures of Roderick Random* (1748), a rogue or picaresque novel of a rambling sort. It is cynical and episodic, with little character development.

Smollett is realistic, and at times shows his genius for character portrayal, but his personal ill nature shows through at all points. He is a shrewd observer but without the artistry of either Richardson or Fielding.

*Roderick Random* is the first English novel of the sea and its shipboard chapters are the best. His *Peregrine Pickle* (1751) presents a lovable old sea dog, Commodore Trunnion. This novel is also of the picaresque variety and abounds in coarse realism.

Smollett then wrote two novels, one a romance of roguery and the other a satire, obviously patterned on *Don Quijote*. His *The Expedition of Humphry Clinker* (1771) is his most mature work. His sharpness is also mellowed a bit here. His character development and his powers of observation are employed to better advantage here than in his earlier novels. It is another novel which takes the form of letters. It lacks the sentimental digressions of Richardson's works and is more fast moving and direct.

There is a great deal of broad comedy in the work and less of the nagging sort of satirical wit that characterizes the writer's other works. In a sense, the novel is autobiographical, for Smollett was ill in Italy when he created his Matthew Bramble.

Bramble is a sick old bachelor, who travels for his health, accompanied by his old maid sister, a servant girl, and his niece and nephew. Smollett died shortly after he finished this work.

Smollett is weak in plot structure but is unsurpassed among these early masters of the novel in his presentation of detailed items of speech, mannerisms, and character traits. He is noted also for having introduced the sea as a backdrop for the English novel and for carrying his action into continental settings. He is a precursor of the type of a novel that Dickens was to make so famous in the next century.

### An omnibus masterpiece of psychological fiction

*Laurence Sterne (1713-1768)*. Laurence Sterne was a humorist, and the basis for his humor is surprise and the sudden revelation of the unexpected. In his masterpiece *The Life and Opinions of Tristram Shandy, Gent* (1759-1767), his protagonist tells the story. The story he tells is a nine-volume collection of oddities that add up to one of the most amusing books ever written. It is a complex, almost structureless mass of humorous sentimentality, yet it is orderly and altogether a very delicate and finished artistic production. Piece by piece, it is chaos; as the pieces drop into place, it reveals unification and a superb sense of the order of disorder. It is an insane masterpiece. The very eccentricity and wild surprises, the leaping from subject to subject are all held together by a masterful foundation of character building.

*Tristram Shandy* is in reality a collection of whimsical and humorous memoirs. It is the mind of an eccentric man, revealing the minds of equally eccentric personalities. That man is Tristram Shandy, or he is Laurence Sterne. The author himself was a churchman, who had his own particular notions of how life should be lived on this earth and practiced them. He was given to philandering and to associating with strange personalities in life. All of Sterne's frivolity, both mental and actual, goes into his book. Some would say that the book is no novel at all; but it certainly fits into no other classification.

Sterne loved the pleasures of life and indulged himself in many of them. He loved fox hunting and racing. He read avidly, particularly in the oddest and the most whimsical writings he could lay his hands on. His own imagination led him into fantastic pursuits and his Tristram leads his readers through the same strange series of antics that Sterne lived or dreamed.

Sterne's book was highly popular in his time and has never lost its value as good entertainment. To the ordered and logical novels of his predecessors, Sterne added the illogical and the fantastic of human reality.

## A fantasy of human reality

Sterne gave the world its first real psychological novel. His is the depiction of the internal goings-on of an entire group of personages that surround Tristram himself, revealing the inner workings of the stream of consciousness that flows through his individuals: the old Mr. Shandy, Corporal Trim, Uncle Toby, the romantic Widow Wadman. It was a new penetration into character development and this represents Sterne's greatest contribution to the novel. He showed the future writers of novels that character development is not necessarily an ordered and cut-and-dried formula. Human character does not develop that way in life. It follows ordered patterns sometimes, and other times it follows its own tangents and whims. And *Tristram Shandy*'s characters do just that for many, many pages—and they become immortal memories to one who will follow them along.

Sterne's other novel is *A Sentimental Journey through France and Italy* (1768), which is a sort of sentimentalized autobiography. It is written in the same brilliant and complex style as *Tristram Shandy* and is filled with the same humorous insanity. The sentimental element is perhaps too predominant, but Sterne's journey was itself filled with sentimental encounters with members of the tender sex.

## Minor Novels of the Century
### The century's most popular novel

The Vicar of Wakefield (1766) (291). A novel of melodrama and domestic pathos became, in the long run, the most popular novel of the century and one which has persisted in finding readers ever since: *The Vicar of Wakefield* by Oliver Goldsmith. Goldsmith was a member of Samuel Johnson's "circle" and one of the most prolific and versatile writers of the age of a declining classicism.

Goldsmith was poor, and moreover, profligate with what he had. Johnson liked him despite his scatterbrained ways. One morning Johnson went to Goldsmith's quarters, in answer to an urgent message from his friend, to find that Goldsmith's landlady had had him arrested for unpaid rent. Johnson found that Gold-

smith happened to have a manuscript of a novel ready. He sold
it for his friend for the sum of sixty pounds. It became the most
widely read and the most often reprinted of the novels of the age.

*The Vicar of Wakefield* is a sentimental romance and presents,
in an age of rationalism, an interplay of the ideal and the real
that has a charm which has never become dim since Goldsmith's
day. Its appeal is to the noble and the generous nature of the
reader. It is melodrama but is a thriller of the quiet, domestic
sort. The novel might be called a "tear jerker" for it is full of
calamity and is constantly playing upon the refined sensibilities
of the sympathetic reader. One is led to pity the poor Primroses
from the start, as clouds gather about them and complexity upon
complexity is piled up until all seems in vain for poor Dr. Primrose, his wife Deborah, and his five children. But suddenly the
clouds clear and all is joy at the end of the book.

It is a weak novel structurally but an appealingly charming
one. It provides thrills of the quieter sort. Goldsmith shows us
virtuous people and how they can endure misery with fortitude,
how they can bow their proud necks to adversity and rise again
to smile. It is a moral lesson in fortitude and the ability to stick
it out when troubles come.

### A novel of social satire

*Evelina* (1778) of Fanny Burney (1752-1840) is a novel of
manners. It is a realistic picture of family life and reflects accurately a social atmosphere. It is refined and delicate satire,
full of detail of a social nature.

Fanny Burney was a shy girl, daughter of a music teacher.
She served Queen Charlotte as maid and keeper of her ward-
robe. She wrote a *Diary* (1768-1778) which is photographic of
the life and manners of the circle within which she moved. She
gives intimate details on dress, industrial conditions, poverty,
and peculiarities of the great figures of her times. She was an
intimate of the inner circle of Johnson. She is a surface painter
of character. The reader is intimate with the outside appearances
of her characters, but actually knows little of their nature.

### Masterpiece of the "Gothic" romance

*The Castle of Otranto* (1764) of Horace Walpole is a fine
example of the Gothic* romance, which became highly popular
during the last years of the century. "Gothic" as employed in
this novel is perhaps synonymous with "barbaric." The neo-

classical writers looked upon the medieval times with disdain and they created all sorts of fantastic and horrible situations in their "historical" novels of this period. The form was created as a sort of amusement in this ordered age, but lived on to become a serious genre with the romantic writers of the following century.

Walpole's *Castle of Otranto* is laid in the 12th century and is filled with harrowing and fearful experiences. An air of the supernatural and the fearful hovers over the entire course of the plot. The horror begins when Conrad, son of the Prince of Otranto, is found crushed to death beneath an enormous helmet, as he is about to marry Isabella. The Prince, having no heir, determines to marry Isabella himself. About this time the portrait of his grandfather climbs down from the wall and detains him. It all finally resolves itself through the startling revelation that the Prince is a usurper of the throne after all and the rule really belongs to a Theodore. Theodore ultimately, of course, marries Isabella. Meantime, the castle falls down, there are earthquakes, arms and legs appear in strange places, and blood drips from the nose of a stone statue, etc.

This wild romantic tale was written by a neoclassic who himself never did any more thrilling thing than to sip tea with his courtly friends and gossip about the absentee members of the circle. The genre became very popular and many "Gothic" tales were written in the last years of the 18th century. This form was gradually refined into a more subdued and authentic historical romance by the end of the century. Sir Walter Scott was to take this form and refine it into the best of medieval romances the modern ages have seen in literature—but that is a story for our second volume of the Age of Romanticism in the 19th century.

# Chapter IX

# THE STRUGGLE FOR LITERATURE NEOCLASSICISM and PREROMANTICISM (1750-1798)

## THE DECLINE OF CLASSICISM (1750-1784)

### Historical and Cultural Notes

George II died in 1760 and his grandson came to the throne as George III. He ruled until 1820 and his reign proved to be a period of notable transitions for England in politices, social and economic structure, and in the arts. Thirty-two of the sixty years of the reign of George III were to be war years.

The new George was not inclined to allow the government to be managed by ministers and Parliament. He was the last sovereign in England who tried to regain much of traditional power which the Stuarts had exercised. George did not intend to go as far as the "divine rights" principle of the Stuarts, but he did intend to control Parliament. And for a time, through the granting of royal favors to the great lords who controlled masses of voters, the king did gain a semblance of control.

In 1760, England was at her peak of prestige in Europe up to that time, with her American colonies and her new empire in India. By 1783, England had lost her American colonies and much of her former European influence.

### Rise of the factory system

However, despite these reverses, middle-class prosperity was on the increase and industry boomed throughout the period. It was a period of enormous industrial and social revolution. England's factory system, with the invention of new and labor-saving devices and machines, and the new scientific developments in agriculture, were gradually causing a new division in society into capital and labor classes. The aristocratic nobility was suffering loss of prestige and power in the face of the rising wealthy industrial class.

Following the loss of her colonies in America, Parliament regained control of the domestic situation under the very able statesman, William Pitt the younger, and was headed once more for a more stable and democratic control, a system that was not again disrupted basically to the present time.

When England entered the 19th century, the French Revolution had been fought and ideas of liberty, equality, and fraternity permeated the conversation in every meeting of two or more Englishmen.

### *Growing social unrest*

But England again faced wars, first with the Republican armies of France in the last years of the old century and with the Imperial armies of Napoleon in the first years of the new century. Again she was at war with the newly created United States in 1812. George III lived to see peace come again to England, but at the expense of the masses. The country was deeply in debt, a small landowning and manufacturing class had become rich, while the farm-labor and factory-worker classes were on the verge of starvation. It was an era of turmoil, politically and socially; it was an admirably prepared ground for the flowering of the seeds of rebellion and individualism in ideas. A growing romanticism was taking enormous strides forward, banishing into the shadows the classic 18th century.

### Signs of a Dying Classicism

Pope and Swift were the last of the great neoclassicists. The man who was to dominate literary taste in the age to follow (1750-1784), Samuel Johnson, was to step down slowly from his position (not in words, but in the qualities evident in his production) as a classicist and show himself moving toward the new pressures of subjectivity and individualism. Johnson was more of a great personality than he was a great writer; he was the last great Tory personality and lives in literature largely because he represents the quintessence of Toryism.

### *An individual spirit returns to writing*

Neoclassicism could not live long among Englishmen; it was brilliant but artificial to the core. No literature can long survive without feeling. One eventually tires of irony and satire, of entertaining himself with fact and science and philosophy. Johnson, in his late years, had begun to yield to sentimentality and emotion; he began to let his principal followers speak for themselves. A generation of cold and lifeless poetry had caused a nostalgia to permeate the English middle class—a longing for some of the personal charm and life of the days of Elizabeth. The beautiful in nature (not the philosophical systematized "nature" of Pope) and the tender goodness and sentimentality in literature were missed more and more by readers. Reason, during this age, was slowly being eaten into by a growing sensibility.

Of course, the process of change was gradual, and to a large extent, classicism continued to prevail to the end of the period as the dominating external appearance of literature; from 1784, that external appearance of literature was to be romanticism, with much of the neoclassicism remaining. But everywhere in literature were demonstrations of a growing restlessness with order and conventional technique, a search for more freedom of expression and a greater naturalness in approach to human emotion and to the beauties of an external, but real, nature. Essayists, historians, and philosophers were still in evidence, but satire and cleverness of phraseology were disappearing, and in their place were appearing a more humane drama and prose narrative, and a growing lyricism in poetry. People were looking for reality in the novel, a humanity that they could recognize and appreciate.

## Signposts of a transition period

Briefly, these signs were evidence of the transition from neoclassicism to romanticism on the English literary scene:

1. A growing hostility toward classic productions and imitations, which manifested itself in a lack of sales for this type of work among the middle class reading public.

2. A neglect of the ancients, such as Horace. Their imitators and translations of originals were being less and less discussed and read. On the other hand, Shakespeare and Milton were being talked about with enthusiasm.

3. A reviving interest in the medieval ages in England and in the exotic East. Translations of tales such as *The Arabian Nights* were best sellers.

4. Increasing interest in the English landscape and in the real economic and social problems of the English people. People

wanted to read of the life and scenery of their own country. They wanted some idealization, yes, but they were sick of Greece and Rome.

5. The shift from interest in classical France and other modern classical leaders on the continent.

6. A search for novelty in ideas, themes, and styles for expression.

7. The neoclassical writers produced a literature for an aristocratic and intellectual public; the new writers were looking to the demands of a rising bourgeoisie.

8. A new glorification of the individual artist, apart from his production. Artists felt more and more a restless desire to cater to this public adulation, to depart from their objective serenity, by projecting more and more of their own personalities into their works. More and more literary works were becoming subjective in their approach to the world of aesthetics.

## The Last Master of English Literary Taste

*Samuel Johnson: A Great Literary Personality.* Samuel Johnson (1709-1784) wrote for a living, was fat and amiable, and a superb talker. His satire did not contain the barbs and the ironic bitterness of Swift and Pope. He demonstrated a more humane satire in his *London* (1738), a city which he really loved in spite of its vanities and sins, his *Vanity of Human Wishes* (1749), another satire in the heroic couplet about the foibles of human life, which he also loved.

A 19th century literary critic (Gosse) said of Johnson: "He talked superb literature freely for thirty years, and all England listened." And in a sense, Johnson invented much of the vocabulary with which he talked. He compiled the first of English dictionaries, and his *Dictionary of the English Language* (begun 1747 and published 1755) is full of the personality of Johnson, some words being defined much as they are today and others being the compiler's personal and prejudiced self—"*Oats:* a grain which in England is generally given to horses, but in Scotland supports the people."

He also wrote a so-called novel, *Rasselas* (1759), which is a didactic romance, written in a week's time to provide funds to defray the expenses of the funeral of Johnson's mother. And he wrote a good deal of biographical sketches, political commentary, issued an edition of Shakespeare's plays, and a great many periodical-type essays (in *The Idler* and *The Rambler)* on voyages, meditations, and personal impressions of the world around him, as refashioned by Johnson.

Johnson was a "coffee-house" personality *par excellence.* Through his imposing geniality, he was a leader in all literary discussions. He was, in short, a most interesting and entertaining personality. And he was the self-styled and undisputed czar of his literary age—an age that was dying—a neoclassic age.

### Biography of a man and of an age

James Boswell (1740-1795) wrote a *Life of Johnson* (1791). Boswell was a constant companion of the "grand old giant" and records the antics of his hero in an intimate biographical style. The book is intensely interesting and tells us more than the life of Johnson. It gives us an intimate portrait of the life of one Boswell and of the noble struggle of a dying classic pomp and grandeur.

### Oratory and history

*The Johnson Circle; Burke and Gibbon.* Edmund Burke (1729-1797) was a great English statesman and orator. He enters literature through his very eloquent and polished political essays. He is classical, but manages to be highly colorful. He can be extremely tender, and he can be a fiery furnace of bombast, all in the same speech. His logical structure and organization put his essays on a par with the best of their kind. He was a conservative and strove brilliantly for conciliation with the American colonies. Of interest to students of American history, and anyone who likes good oratory, are his *On American Taxation* (1774) and *On Conciliation with America* (1775).

Edward Gibbon (1737-1794), another of Johnson's famous "circle," has gained enduring fame from his superb *The History of the Decline and Fall of the Roman Empire* (1776-1788). It is a masterwork of prose and organization. It has the truly rational approach to historical writing, and is in itself more than history and more than mere neoclassicism; it is a classic work of prose literature for all time.

### Great Irish writers of the age

*The Johnson Circle; Oliver Goldsmith (1730-1774).* Also rubbing elbows with the famous friends of Samuel Johnson, Garrick, the great actor-producer, Burke, the great statesman, Gibbon, the famed historian, and Sir Joshua Reynolds, the famous portrait painter, was a merry and coarse Irishman, equally artistic, but of a somewhat differing personality: Oliver Goldsmith.

Goldsmith was one of the most versatile writers in English literature. He was novelist, dramatist, poet, and essayist and was equally an artist in all four genres. He was also a hack writer who kept the pot boiling with any sort of writing that would bring in a penny.

He was, in turn, a doctor, lawyer, teacher, actor, and writer. Restless and profligate, Goldsmith toured Europe and turned to hack writing finally for steady, but slim, income. Goldsmith could not keep money and was constantly threatened with imprisonment for debt. In addition, he drank and gambled.

Johnson recognized Goldsmith's talent and stuck by him as friend and adviser, although he did not approve Goldsmith's personal habits. Boswell refers to Goldsmith as "a coarse and vulgar" person. Goldsmith was perhaps the only member of Johnson's circle who was not afraid of the blustering master.

Goldsmith turned out some of the most charming works in English. His *Vicar of Wakefield* was the most popular novel to come from his century. Goldsmith's essays are collected in two volumes (1762) under the title, *The Citizen of the World: or Letters from a Chinese Philosopher Residing in London.* There are here 123 intimate essays on every conceivable phase of middle- and lower-class life in the England of Goldsmith's time. He has an easy style and is full of gay, but quiet, humor. He is a link between Addison and Lamb in the familiar essay. There is true satire, sharp but not bitter, and a whimsical charm, rare in a careful observer such as Goldsmith.

### She Stoops to Conquer

He wrote two plays, one of which ranks with the best that the age produced. *She Stoops to Conquer* (1771) (295) has lasted in popularity to the present day. This play is robust, but sane and moral. It is as sprightly as a Restoration drama, but does not depend on Restoration licentiousness for its effects.

Goldsmith's dialogue is racy and the situations still amuse audiences. Goldsmith wrote the play to satirize sentimentality and produced a work which became a masterpiece of ironical comedy. It does not have a well-integrated plot and the sequences are somewhat ridiculous, but it has a full-blooded headiness that never fails to delight audiences.

## A great sentimental poem

In addition to his other accomplishments, Goldsmith wrote poetry. His rimed couplets bring us one of the quietest and most charming of English poems, *The Deserted Village* (1770).

Goldsmith is thinking of his boyhood days in a little Irish village when he pens this memorable picture of a little rural hamlet, whose inhabitants are leaving as industry moves in and spoils the rustic simplicity:

> Sweet Auburn! loveliest village of the plain,
> Where health and plenty cheered the laboring swain,

His descriptions are sentimental and nostalgic:

> The hawthorn bush, with seats beneath the shade,
> For talking age and whispering lovers made!

Goldsmith's villagers are also memories of the "good old days" for the author, when, as he looks back, social evils were far distant threats and rustic simplicity lived on, unaware that unwelcome change was just over the horizon. His rural preacher, for instance, was as unspoiled as the others:

> Remote from towns he ran his godly race,
> Nor e'er had changed, nor wished to change, his place,
> Unpracticed he to fawn, or seek for power
> By doctrines fashioned to the varying hour;
> Far other aims his heart had learned to prize,
> More skilled to raise the wretched than to rise.

Goldsmith wrote a poem that all city folk, who hark back to a simpler life, can read with sentimental sighs. It is a backward look toward a utopia and it is written in an artless poetry. Gone here are the brilliance and the biting fire of the wit of a Dryden or a Pope. Sentimentality had taken over the rimed couplet.

## The foremost dramatist of the century

*The Johnson Circle: Sheridan* (1751-1816). Richard Brinsley Sheridan was born in Dublin. His father was active in the theater there. Young Richard studied law in London but spent the early years of his career in the theater. By 1780, when he was elected to Parliament, his plays were written and he did not enter the theater again. But this was enough to make him the foremost English dramatist of the 18th century.

Sheridan produced two of the three best-known English plays between the Restoration and the late nineteenth century. Like *She Stoops to Conquer* of Goldsmith, Sheridan's *The Rivals* (1775) and *The School for Scandal* (1777) are satires on eighteenth century manners.

Sheridan is more skilful in stage technique. Otherwise, there is little to choose between the three plays. All have restored the witty dialogue of Restoration days, but minus the indecency prevalent in that age. All three attempt to satirize the sentimentality, the artificiality, and sham of the neoclassic society. All have retained their popularity into this century. All three plays make capital of the ludicrous situation and the injection of comic artificiality into their characterizations. All three are clever and amusing; none leaves a bitter taste or worries an audience into serious thought. Their only purpose is to produce the sympathetic smile one moment and rollicking laughter the next. And, given fair casting, they will not fail to do just that in any segment of English-speaking society today.

### The School for Scandal and The Rivals

*The School for Scandal* (299) is usually considered the better of Sheridan's only two plays discussed today (he wrote five) because of better plot integration and a more clever handling of incidents. Its satire is more of an exposure of the malicious hypocrisies of high society than it is a parody of sentimentality. The play borders, at times, upon serious drama, but Sheridan never lets it go quite that far out of the realm of farce. He keeps up the mock-comic atmosphere, while skirting around reality. He thus heightens the effectiveness of his social satire.

*The Rivals* (296) attacks sentimental artificiality with a whole battery of unforgettable characters, all extravagantly caricatured and comic, but all impressive as real people. The dialogue is certainly as witty as any Restoration play, but there is no undertone of irony and malice. The effect is simply hilarious fun.

## THE RISE OF ROMANTICISM (1784-1798)
### Signs of Romantic Revolt

On the eve of the 19th century, it is evident that a general revolution in society and its arts is well under way. The public temper and the individual mind were changing and a modern man was rising out of his assimilation of past experience of groups. He was governed by two sentiments, a democratic one and a philosophic one. Man, as an individual, had learned from a period of rationalism that, to rise economically or culturally, he had to reform dogma or destroy it. He was prepared to endure certain excesses in order to achieve freedom for the individual. He felt himself to be scientific minded and rational. His classic nature told him to be generous and tolerant with the past; his awakening sensitivity told him to be as rebellious as necessary to achieve this new freedom.

In literature, the signs of this new age grew strong in the last years of the 18th century and the last great English literary figure of the waning classic century, who did not live to see the full flowering of his own individual romantic traits permeate the entire structure of English literature, was Robert Burns (1759-1796). Burns is England's most lonely literary figure, a man who was a full-fledged romantic, but who died just shortly before the "romantic school" was proclaimed.

We have noted the signs of a dying classicism. These are some of the characteristics of the infant that was to replace it—a nascent romanticism—a child of old Elizabethan stock, but a child of a later generation, conscious that times had changed and that a new rationalism and a new scientific approach are integral parts of his being and must be lived with, or rebelled against. This first child began to rebel mildly; his children rebelled violently and set the new "romantic" banner high above the "classic" one over English literature.

### The normal course of English Literature

English literature was slowly returning to its more normal course. The English mind, from Anglo-Saxon beginnings, had been inimical to complete logical neatness and order, to imposed form and artificiality. It had been emotionally inclined and imaginative from the beginning. And in Elizabeth's day, emotion, color, and imagination had had a great field day. The English temperament, despite its scientific and rational conditioning, was rebelling and was edging toward a full scale "movement" of inspiration.

### Rebellion of the individual

Logic and rationalism had brought the English middle and

lower classes to a realization that they too must be a part of life and culture. Industrialization had given them a taste of what lay above, economically. Their brief conditioning to views of the startling revolutions in France and to the new ideas of liberty, equality, and fraternity called up an immediate emotional reaction. They demanded a literature of emotion and one which exalted them. They were feeling like individuals. In literature, this sudden burst of emotional and sensory perception on a mass scale results in romanticism in writing.

The young writers, filled with this new atmosphere of the worth of the individual, came to believe in themselves and sought to project their genius in writing. They wrote first to please themselves, to bolster their ego. The writer's object was not to be just a little more precise, to be a little more witty, to be a little more bitterly satiric than his fellows, who were being guided hitherto by the same structural and thematical restrictions. The new writer wanted freedom of expression, novelty of idea, and his own choice of materials. He wanted to write about life as he saw it, whether or not he conformed to social or literary convention. He wanted a new sensation to go forth from his pen, presented in a new form.

## New definitions of "nature"

Such rebellion in literature began to show itself in two directions. The writer first identified himself with external nature, and then with his own very human nature. "Nature" by the definition of a classic, such as Pope, Dryden, or even Johnson, would no longer serve. Each writer now has his own standard for reaction to nature. And these early romantics showed themselves according to the two general reactions which would come from quiet or violent human natures, both in rebellion. Some wrote with a wild irregularity; others wrote in a startlingly calm simplicity, if their natures were such as to react with melancholic or sad manifestations of rebellion. The new literature, then, tended to be wildly gay and joyful, wildly violent and adventurous; or it tended to be quiet, sad and melancholic in spirit, nostalgic, and sadly philosophic. But it was an expression of individuals, not a calculated and intellectual expression of conformity to settled standards that would admit no deviation.

In time and space, the new romantics were filled with their sensations resulting from nature about them, physical nature, and their own natural reactions. But the past also was a foreign ground to explore and they projected themselves backward in time with avidity, to bring into the present the joys and the life that their ancestors must have enjoyed in this nostalgically created utopian time when man struggled against a raw environment and an exotic, if brutal, human nature. The city man and the studious-minded writer found their material in another direction—the simple folk and their unaffected and hence natural expression in the ballad and the song. And some of these new discoverers of "nature" looked into the future and dreamed of what things could be like, and they wrote down their aspirations in glowing projections of the imagination. Some were thrilled by examining the natures of other human beings, and the nature of masses, and setting down their humanitarian views for society.

### A common misconception of the term "romantic"

Almost all the young writers thought they had discovered their most natural functions in nature and they exalted the opposite sex as the supreme complement for their own nature. Marriage was a social institution and hence unnatural; thus marriage is largely ignored by the great group of romantics, except in its larger and more "natural" sense, a marriage of spirits, a marriage of souls, a marriage of bodies and of minds. The term "romantic" has come to mean only this aspect of the new revolt to many minds and has come to be synonymous with this aspect of the movement, largely because the predominant theme of popular romantic writing became an idealization of a beloved object—usually always a member of the opposite sex. But in its essence, the term "romantic," as applied to literature, means any revolt against discipline, any inspiration as opposed to orthodoxy and convention.

In England the direct approach to romanticism was mainly in lyric poetry and in the novel. Chapter VIII has discussed the sentimental and the "Gothic" aspects of the novel. We have noted the elements of sensibility, of nostalgia, and of the individual approach in our discussion of the classic writers who felt a bit of the new breezes. We shall now consider very briefly the young poets who, while being born in a world of neoclassicism, felt the new spirit of individual freedom for inspiration even stronger—the generation of writers who immediately preceded the full bloom of romantic flowering in English poetry. In Volume II, this same generation will be considered again briefly as we pass from the 18th century to the full-fledged romantic movement in the early 19th century.

## The Mid-Century Preromantics

### *A return to the Renaissance*

*The Imitators of Milton and Spenser*. James Thomson (1700-1748) is the earliest in the group of poets which forms the vanguard of the great movement of romanticism in English letters. Thomson was the first of the poets for more than two generations to study and record impressions of nature. Using the blank verse of Milton, he records his impressions in a collection called *The Seasons* (1726-39). In the preface to his *Winter* he sounds the challenge to poets to follow him: "Poetry once more (must) be restored to her ancient truth and purity." He urges his fellow poets to consider the works of Nature as the most elevating and noble motives for poetic enthusiasm. Thomson's observations are keen, but his verse is rather a humdrum recitation of observed detail rather than sweet lyricism. He is a precursor of Wordsworth, but he is no Wordsworth in his skill at making details of nature live and breathe in the heart of his readers.

In his *Castle of Indolence* (1748) Thomson uses the Spenserian stanza to tell of the enchanted castle in the land of Drowsyhead, ruled over by gentle Indolence.

The early imitators of Milton included Edward Young (1683-1765), Thomas Parnell (1679-1718), and Robert Blair (1699-1746). These are melancholy poets who dwell on death and immortality in verse that is reminiscent of *Il Pensoroso* of Milton. Young's *Night Thoughts* is representative, in that it dwells upon the brevity of life. It comments upon the hollow certainty of the grave and the tragic uncertainties of life that leads to the grave. Young's verse is rhetorical and pompous in spots, with occasional flashes of magnificence and color. But mostly, this "graveyard" school of poets reflects a gloomy mood.

There were a number of imitators of Spenser in the century. Some approached the color and warmth of Spenser, but mostly the verse of this group is undistinguished when compared with that of their master of the 16th century.

### *A return to "folk" literature*

*Chatterton, Collins, and the "Ossian" Poets*. Among the best poets of mid-century are those of the "antiquarian" school, those who went beyond mere imitation of Milton, Spenser, and Chaucer. This group sought themes of remote and unfamiliar nooks and corners of the past. They delved into the folk ballad and song of the medieval period, attempting to create in their poetry the impression that it was resurrected or unearthed from a dim past.

Thomas Chatterton (1752-1770), a precocious lad, began to write when he was twelve. Much of his poetry was supposedly the work of one Rowley, a priest of the 15th century. The lad's verse is astounding when one realizes that he was scarcely more than a child when he was creating such forgeries as *The Bristowe Tragedy* and *Ballade of Charitie*. He took poison at the age of nineteen.

About this time there appeared a number of collections of poems, supposedly the work of one Ossian, a figure of the dim Gaelic past.

William Collins (1721-1759), in addition to his odes in a semiclassic vein, is noted for his long *Ode on the Popular Superstitions of the Highlands* (1749). He attempts here to stimulate interest in the native folklore of Scotland. His poem plays around among all sorts of fairy-world figures of medieval highland superstition. This interest in the supernatural and the mysterious, the remote and exotic past, and the strange half light of dreams in which his figures stalk forth, reveal Collins as a harbinger of something that English poetry had seemingly lost in the age of neoclassicism:

> In pageant robes and wreathed in sheeny gold,
> And on their twilight tombs aërial council hold.

### Melancholy and sentiment in verse

*Gray and His Elegy.* Thomas Gray (1716-1771) was a scholar and his early poetry is of the classical school. But gradually he leaned to the "graveyard" group and his verse begins to ponder life and death in melancholy tones. His very quotable and ever popular *Elegy in a Country Churchyard* (1751) causes Gray to live on today in anthologies and in the minds of millions of English-speaking adults who memorized in school such lines as:

> The curfew tolls the knell of parting day,
> The lowing herd wind slowly o'er the lea,

The plowman homeward plods his weary way,
And leaves the world to darkness and to me.

. . . . .

Full many a gem of purest ray serene
The dark unfathomed caves of ocean bear;
Full many a flower is born to blush unseen,
And waste its sweetness on the desert air.

## Immediate Precursors of the Romantic Movement

As the 18th century draws to a close, four transitional figures stand out, proclaiming the victory of a new freedom in English poetry: Cowper, Crabbe, Burns, and Blake. They all belong to the 18th century, except Blake; but both Burns (died 1796) and Blake are full-fledged romantics. They are among the greatest poets in English literature, but both are isolated and lonely voices in that they were *of* a movement, but were ignored *by* it.

### Poet of sensitivity

<u>William Cowper (1731-1800)</u>. Cowper was a sad figure in real life, and his verse is a study in melancholy. He spent his life alternating between fits of gayety and mystical exaltation and periods of deepest emotional depression. At last he became insane at the age of fifty-two.

Cowper was a sensitive soul who, between his spells of melancholy and religious fervor, wrote a great deal of verse, painting the landscapes, the seasons, and everyday objects about him in simple, realistically animated verse. He was a mystic who sketched his visions and religious impressions in sensitive but shallow verse. His nature poems are a meandering series of rather photographic impressions of rural simplicity. His long poem *The Task* (1785), in Miltonic blank verse, is a series of pictures of nature and her moods that proves the poet to be truly humanitarian and sympathetic with all natural creatures, but it also proves him to be more of a descriptive essayist in verse than an accomplished artist of depth of feeling. Cowper's poem is a revelation of simple truths, simply stated, but without the warmth and the passion of the great nature poets that follow him.

### A humanitarian poet

<u>George Crabbe (1754-1832)</u>. Crabbe was another of the humanitarian-realistic group of preromantic poets. Crabbe pro-

fessed to be neoclassic and persisted in following Pope in the use of the heroic couplet in all his verse. His poetry, however, is far from being artificial. His treatment of human life and nature betrays a genuine realism that Pope could never achieve with the rimed couplet. Crabbe is sincere and direct and does not idealize nature, as Cowper, but insists upon presenting his pictures faithfully and with little ornamentation.

Crabbe's personal life had been a cruel one of poverty and squalor. Disillusioned with his career as a physician and later with the ministry, he began to take opium. Many of his poems reveal his rambling thoughts under the influence of the dope.

Crabbe was a misfit in his social environment and in his poetry. He was faithful to the neoclassic school and professed to hate the romantics. He had strong convictions of the moral responsibility of the individual but he had no confidence, at the same time, in the goodness of human nature. His mind was as though suspended between two opposite poles of thought and he could not join either extreme wholeheartedly, nor could he harmonize the conflicting impressions in his spirit.

### Crabbe and Goldsmith compared

He, like Cowper, lacked deep feeling and passion. His heroic couplets could describe faithfully but could not seem to touch the heart of his themes of nature and man. His long poem *The Village* (1783), written in anger at what he considered the falsities of idealism presented in Goldsmith's *The Deserted Village,* reveals a true realistic portrayal of village life and types. He shows true sympathy with the simplicity and the poverty of his villagers, but it is a calculated humanitarianism and his descriptions are devoid of feeling or idealism. Crabbe is a true transitional figure—equally influenced by the classic 18th century and by the romantic 19th.

### Greatest of the Scottish lyric poets

*Robert Burns (1759-1796).* With Robert Burns, true romanticism begins for English poetry. Despite commentary by historians upon his private life (he was given apparently to both women and drink), Burns was a true artist and a genuine romantic. He is one of the most-loved English poets of all time. He touched the wellsprings of human feeling as no other poet of the British Isles had done since the Renaissance.

Burns's childhood was a period of hard work and poverty. His parents were Scottish peasants who wrested a meager living from the rocky soil. His father died in 1784 and Bobby Burns found himself at the head of the family. During the hard years ahead, he managed to study and to write of his everyday impressions and experiences. No experience was too intimate or too minute to be recorded in his immortal verse. He married and gained an appointment as tax collector. He eventually gave up farming entirely and spent the remaining years of his short life as a tax collector. He died at the age of thirty-seven after several years of acute physical pain, probably as a result of his childhood hardships.

Burns is the greatest of Scottish poets and composer of one of the most charming collections of simple songs that can be assigned to one pen in all world literature. Despite his life of toil, Burns had time to love life, and perhaps he loved women and intoxicating beverages too well.

### Burns the satirist

A good deal of Burns's poetry is satirical. He hated narrowness and despised religious smugness and hypocrisy. The churchmen of his neighborhood were scandalized at the barbs Burns sent their way in his verse. In *Holy Willie's Prayer,* for example, he portrays an actual elder in a nearby church, who maintained his holy orders despite proven thievery and carnal sins. He follows "Willie" through the words of his prayer to the Lord to visit damnation to others for the same sins which, in the prayer, "Willie" confesses to and thanks the Lord for the bounty he has received. In Burns's poem the good elder seems to take delight in the idea of Hell—for others:

> I bless and praise Thy matchless might,
> What thousands Thou has left in night,
> That I am here before Thy sight,
>     For gifts and grace, . . .

### Unadorned lyricism

Much of Burns's charm for us lies in his Scottish brogue and in his simple, unadorned, folk manner of presenting his little themes of homely philosophy. Nothing is too small or unimportant to serve him as a subject. He addressed one poem *To a Louse,* another *To a Mouse,* whose home has been disturbed by his plowshare:

Wee, sleekit, cowrin, tim'rous beastie,
O, what a panic's in thy breastie!
Thou need na start awa sae hasty
    Wi' bickering brattle!
I wad be laith to rin an' chase thee,
    Wi' murdering pattle!

I'm truly sorry man's dominion
Has broken Nature's social union,
An' justifies that ill opinion
    Which makes thee startle
At me, thy poor, earth-born companion
    An' fellow mortal! . . .

Bobby Burns's poetry ranges through every emotional experience. His verse is always personal. It is full of sentiment, but is never overly sentimental or false. Whether he satirizes, describes a simple rural scene, or bemoans the inequality of men, his tones always ring true and sincere. His style is never elegant, but always musical and simple. His tone is spontaneous and warmly emotional. He was versatile and could treat any theme simply and delightfully. And he was never more sweet or more appealingly simple than in his little lyric poems of love:

O, my luve is like a red, red rose,
    That's newly sprung in June.
O, my luve is like the melodie,
    That's sweetly played in tune.

As fair art thou, my bonnie lass,
    So deep in luve am I,
And I will luve thee still, my dear,
    Till a' the seas gang dry.

Till a' the seas gang dry, my dear,
    And the rocks melt wi' the sun!
And I will luve thee still, my dear,
    While the sand o' life shall run . . .

### A great English mystic poet

<u>William Blake (1757-1827)</u>. William Blake was a painter and an engraver. He was also a mystic and lived much of his

time among his world of visions and spiritual communications. Some of his verse is, for that reason, hard to comprehend. But the bulk of Blake's verse is as delightfully lyric and imaginative as that of any of the romantic poets. His best poetry is contained in the two collections: *Songs of Innocence* (1789) and *Songs of Experience* (1794). The first collection has a childlike freshness; the second, while still retaining his delicate lyric harmony, begins a search into the darker reaches of man's existence. His later verse became more mystical, abstruse, and symbolic.

Blake broke absolutely with all the artistic traditions of classicism. He was more of a true revolutionist than Burns. His style was entirely his own and his expression was utterly unconventional in his age. His verse has all the nuances of Elizabethan poetry, combined with a musical cadence that is Blake's own.

Blake was a solitary figure in his time. He resented the fact that the "romantic school" did not recognize him. He showed all their qualities in his verse while they were mere children. But in his time, Blake was eccentric and a man who saw visions. His verse was ignored until years after his death. Today we recognize Blake and Burns as two of the best of English poets and the only two thoroughgoing romantic poets of the 18th century.

### *Approach to a Great Age of English Romanticism*

Blake is a proper breaking point for a two-volume consideration of English literature. He spanned a world of English lyric poetry—from the childlike harmony of the folk lyric to the abstruse ideas of a Donne. His poetry possesses the color and the imagery of the brightest moments of the Renaissance and the intellectuality and the spirituality of a Milton. Blake stood on the brink of a new age of greatness for English literature and he was, in his production, in every way a part of it. His verse reflects the long, long way that English poetry had come from *Beowulf,* in form, in language, and in spirit—and his lines indicate what the student and the general reader of today may view in the artistic accomplishment of the fruitful 19th and 20th centuries of English literature:

> To see a World in a grain of sand,
>     And a Heaven in a wild flower;
> Hold Infinity in the palm of your hand,
>     And Eternity in an hour.

And with Blake, this writer may well wonder if small volumes, such as this, can ever really come near to telling the story of the devotion to the principle of "Man doth not live by bread alone" of these artists of our English literary heritage in their efforts to hold up to us a mirror in which we may see, crystal clear, the great expression of ideas and emotions, set down in clear, explicit symmetry of beautiful language:

> Can wisdom be put in a silver rod,
> Or love in a golden bowl?

## *Appendix A*

# PLOT SUMMARIES
# OF MAJOR WORKS

In the following section a digest is given of at least one example of each type of major literary production of the period discussed in this volume. The summaries, together with critical notes, are geared to the main historical section and aim to present a rather full idea of the content of longer works, not discussed in detail in that section, in order not to disrupt the continuity of the critical and biographical material. The best representative examples of works of English literature to the 19th century are included, as well as the varying treatments of literary themes in the different ages of English literary development. The page numbers indicate the location of the discussion of the literary and social backgrounds in which the particular work or plot material was created.

## 1. Beowulf
### (Anglo-Saxon heroic folk-epic poem)

*Page 4.* The Danes, under Hrothgar as king, have built a great hall called Heorot and are happy for a while in it. The king sits amid his warriors, eating and drinking and listening to music and song. But their pleasures are short-lived for, in a marsh nearby, dwells Grendel, a fiend from Hell and of horrible strength. Grendel enters the hall one night and devours fifteen of the warriors and carries away fifteen others to his den under the filthy waters of the fen. This slaughter is repeated the second night. However brave they may be, there is nothing for the poor Danes to do but to desert their rich and comfortable hall and live in the cold and damp woods at night. For twelve years they dare not sleep in the hall lest they be snatched away by the evil monster.

News of the frightful terror travels to the neighboring friendly land of the Geats (perhaps the Swedes). Beowulf, the mighty warrior of the Geats, selects fourteen of his sturdy men and crosses the sea to Heorot. He is welcomed by Hrothgar. Beowulf is determined to pit his mighty strength against Grendel and rid the Danes of their dread fear. After feasting throughout the evening, Hrothgar and his warriors leave the hall and Beowulf and his men settle down to wait in the darkness.

No sooner do Beowulf's men sleep:

> Then from the moorland came / under misty hills
> Grendel gliding on / God's wrath did he bear . . .

Before Beowulf could move, the monster had devoured one of his companions. But, not long did the creature have his way, for our hero seized one of the monster's arms, and after a terrible struggle, tore the arm from Grendel's shoulder. The monster disappeared, bleeding and dying, into the fen. And Beowulf's fame was assured for all time to come for immediately a *gleeman*:

> Who saga and song / of the olden deeds
> Could well remember / took up this tale
> Of the coming of Beowulf / weaving in this feat . . .

But the rejoicing of the Danes and Geats was to be brief. For, the very next night, Grendel's mother enters the hall and carries off one of Hrothgar's nobles. Beowulf and his companions track the monster to the marsh where they see the victim's head and stains of blood upon the waters of the mere. Beowulf takes the finest sword of the group from Unferth, Hrothgar's chief warrior, and plunges into the waters.

It takes our hero an entire day to sink to the bottom, having to dispute every fathom with slimy water creatures. Grendel's mother, seeing him approach, seizes him and drags him into a cave where the water does not enter. Unferth's sword, fine as it is, bends against her hide, so Beowulf struggles with his bare hands until he spies an old rusty sword of the giants upon the wall. He manages to get it and hacks off the evil creature's head. He sees Grendel, dead or dying upon the floor, and cuts off his head also. Taking Grendel's head, he dives upward through the bloody waters. The poison from the blood melts the metal of the sword and he arrives at the surface with only the jeweled hilt in his hand.

In the meantime, Hrothgar and the Danes, seeing the bloody waters, have given him up for dead and have gone back to the hall. Beowulf's sorrowful, but faithful, companions pull him from the water and they rejoin Hrothgar for feasts and songs of rejoicing. During these feasts the *gleemen* sing of many deeds not only of Beowulf but of other warriors of the age, including those of the Battle of Finnsburg (see p. 3).

Soon Beowulf returns over "the whale-road" to the land of the Geats. After many years he becomes their king and reigns wisely and well for fifty years. When he is an old man, a slave Geat fugitive from justice, by accident, takes refuge on a burial mound and discovers there a fabulous treasure. He brings a golden goblet to Beowulf.

It seems that a fierce dragon had made his home in this burial mound of some ancient and forgotten race and had slept there in a cave for three hundred years. He awakens and discovers the goblet missing. Breathing fire, he swoops over Beowulf's land, burning everything in the path of his searing breath, including Beowulf's own hall.

Old man that he is, Beowulf determines to rid the country of its fiery scourge. With a shield of iron Beowulf advances to the mouth of the cave and challenges the dragon to come forth. With smoke and flame, the dragon obliges him. Beowulf's men flee for safety into the woods. Only one brave young man, Wiglaf, rebukes the cowardly warriors, and himself, rushes to aid his king. With Wiglaf's help, Beowulf slays the dragon. The wounded old king looks upon the treasure, gives Wiglaf his armor and the king's golden collar. Then he expires of his burns. Wiglaf rebukes the warriors for their cowardice:

> / Death is more good
> For any noble man / than cowardly life . . .

Beowulf's body is burned in pagan funeral rites. The warriors build a mound over the ashes of their hero and bury the treasure with him. And, high on a cliff, overlooking the wide "sealbath," is the mound:

> That sea-faring men / soon in future time
> 'Beowulf's Barrow' call / in their sea-steeds
> Over the mists of ocean / from afar to view come . . .

## 2.  The Anglo-Saxon Christian Epic Poem

*Page 7.  The Dream of the Rood (Cross),* written in the Cynewulf cycle, around 800.

The poet dreams that he sees a cross. It is beautiful and shining and bedecked with bright glittering jewels. Also it is surrounded by radiant light and blood is dripping from it. It is the True Cross. Our poet is afraid, for he is stained with sin. As he watches, the rood speaks:

> Long years ago / I cannot forget . . .
> As a cross I was raised / my King I lifted up
> Lord of the Heavens / dared I not fall down . . .

And the rood continues to relate the story of the Crucifixion, the Descent from the Cross, and the Resurrection. The cross tells of how it is now honored by men who are the servants of the Lord. He bids the poet to tell this vision to other men:

> Bid I you now / Oh, man, beloved
> Sing you this sight / to others in sin . . . .

The rood speaks of the Judgment Day when the Lord will come on earth. He bids none to have fear who bear the best of signs, the Holy Cross. Here the rood ceases to speak and we presume the poet awakens from his dream at this point and begins his testimonial of how the dream has changed his life and caused him to become devoted to the cult of the True Cross.

### *Most lyrically beautiful of the Christian Epics*

The last lines (to 146) hardly harmonize with the even structure of the rest of the composition and were probably added by another than the poet. This poem is perhaps the most lyrically beautiful of all the so-called Old English Christian epics, and is certainly representative of the best among the many poems produced by priests in the tradition of the *scop* during this age. It shows great imaginative power. Aside from the last lines, the poem makes an organic whole, without the unnecessary digressions that characterized most religious poems of the time.

### 3. The Miracle Play

*Page 17. The Second Shepherds' Play,* about 1400. Manuscript
now in the Huntington Library in California. From the Wakefield (or Towneley) cycle of some 32 plays.

It is Christmas Eve. As the play opens Coll, a shepherd, is
tending his sheep on a cold and lonely moor. He is complaining that the gentry rob poor shepherds and hold them in slavery.
Gib, the second shepherd, enters, also bemoaning fate. His
complaint is that he is married and his will is not his own. His
wife was once gentle and sweet; now she is a shrew. Daw joins
them, also lamenting. He swears that the weather has never
been so bad since Noah's time. The three shepherds are singing
to sweeten their souls as Mak joins them.

Mak has the reputation of being a thief. In fact, Daw finds
Mak wearing his cloak as he enters and snatches it from him.
Mak appeals to their sympathies by telling how he is mistreated
at home and the shepherds consent to let him stay with them.

When the shepherds are asleep, Mak lets the audience know
that he is going to work a spell upon them and steal a sheep.
He does so and takes the fat sheep home to his wife, Gill. They
hide the ewe in a cradle. Mak goes back and lies down with
the three shepherds to ward off any suspicion they might have
of him.

When they wake up, Mak makes certain that he does not
leave until the shepherds are aware that he takes nothing with
him:

> Pray you look up my sleeve, that I steal naught,
> I am loath you to grieve, or from you take aught . . .

When Coll, Gib, and Daw miss their sheep they hasten to
Mak's cottage. He bids them search but not to awaken the new-
born babe in the cradle. On the matter of having children in
season, he philosophizes:

> . . . we must drink as we brew, and that is but reason . . .

Needless to say they do not find the sheep. As they walk
away, they remember that they left no gifts for the babe. They
return and Daw discovers their sheep in the crib:

> Give me leave him to kiss, and lift up the clout.
> What the devil is this? He has a long snout . . .

Mak swears that an evil spirit has snatched away their child and replaced it with a ewe. Not taken in by this, the shepherds toss Mak in a blanket and leave him groaning on the ground.

They return to the moor and lie down to sleep once more. An angel appears and tells them that they must go to Bethlehem to see the babe who is born to chase the Devil from the world. Singing, they agree to go to Bethlehem, even though they be wet and weary. Gib recalls that the child had been foretold:

> They prophesied by clergy, that in a virgin
> Should he light and lie, to atone for our sin . . .
> Save our race from woe,
> For Isay said so . . .

Led by the star, the three shepherds enter Bethlehem and go to the stable and kneel before Mary and the Child. They present their three gifts, a bunch of cherries, a bird, and a ball. Mary blesses them and bids them tell of the Saviour:

> May He keep you from woe:
> I shall pray Him so;
> Tell it forth as ye go,
>    And think upon this morn . . .

Coll, Gib, and Daw go forth singing, and here ends the Shepherds' Pageant . . . .

### Best of the secularized liturgical plays

This piece gives us the fully developed secularized liturgical play of the Middle Ages. As the plays of this type were presented on a raised platform, or wagon, in the public squares of the towns, the realistic, slapstick scenes were presented on one side and the biblical scenes on the other. This little bit is a masterpiece of the crude farcical production that the liturgical drama had become in the hands of the guilds. As a Nativity play, of course, it is an absurdity. But it is highly representative of the humor and of the everyday complaints, the rough lack of any refined sense of propriety, the blending of the crudely comic and the serious—on the level of the man of the people in 14th-15th century England.

## 4.   The Morality Play

*Page 17.  Everyman,* about 1508.  Author unknown.  A moral allegory.

A messenger speaks to the audience and calls attention to the fact that everything in life is transitory and that man must ever look forward to death.  Sin may look sweet in the beginning but causes the soul to weep when the body is again clay.

God then speaks and complains that man has forgotten His lessons and the Crucifixion.  He decrees that Everyman must die and summons Death to carry out His purpose.

Death receives his instructions from God.  He is to go to Everyman and bid him take a pilgrimage in the name of God. Death sees Everyman and reflects:

> Lo, yonder I see Everyman walking;
> Full little he thinketh on my coming;
> His mind is on fleshly lusts and his treasure,
> And great pain it shall cause him to endure
> Before the Lord Heaven King . . .

Death delivers his message and Everyman is inclined to protest.  Death refuses to listen to excuses despite Everyman's pleas that he is not yet ready.  Convinced that there is no way out he receives Death's promise that he can select any companions he wishes to accompany him on the journey.

He first meets Fellowship and asks him for his company. Fellowship is ready for anything that promises a good time or gain, even murder:

> . . . if thou wilt eat, and drink, and make good cheer,
> Or haunt to women, the lusty company,
> I would not forsake you, while the day is clear . . .

When Fellowship hears the complete story, he is a bit more reluctant and goes back on his first promise to accompany his friend.

Everyman approaches Kindred.  His cousins and kinsmen all are great in promise:

> In wealth and woe we will with you hold,
> For over his kin, a man may be bold . . .

But, again, when they find how great is Everyman's need, his kindred back away from their first generous offers. Even his favorite cousin would go, but—"I have the cramp in my toe . . ."

Everyman has always depended on Goods. But Goods gives him no hope of any companionship in adversity. Everyman begs, as he cannot see himself taking a long journey without Goods. Finally, he grows angry:

> Oh, false Goods, cursed thou be!
> Thou traitor to God, thou hath deceived me,
> And caught me in thy snare . . .

Everyman has failed with all his friends but Good-Deeds. Good-Deeds, it happens, is willing but is too feeble to make the journey, being laid low by his sins. He knows of Everyman's plight and has great sympathy with him. He recommends a visit to his sister Knowledge.

Knowledge offers to go with Everyman, and takes him to Confession:

> Now go we together lovingly,
> To Confession, that cleansing river . . .

Everyman, at the behest of Confession, determines to rid his body of sin:

> Now of penance I will wade the water clear,
> To save me from purgatory, that sharp fire . . .

At this, Good-Deeds rises from the ground, well again, and offers to help Everyman add up his good works. Knowledge smiles, knowing Everyman is now in good hands.

Wearing a new garment of sorrow, Everyman gathers new companions for the journey: Discretion, Strength, Beauty, and the Five Wits.

On the way they stop at a priest's hut and Everyman receives his last rites. Everyman gains the knowledge that, despite the fact there are bad priests on earth, man's best hope lies with them and he must pray that the priests he meets be good ones.

One by one, Everyman's companions have to leave him. Only Good-Deeds can face Death. Everyman is most reluctant to see his Five Wits leave him. But, here at the edge of the grave, Five

Wits says that he can be of no help now. At the last moment, Good-Deeds sums up the truth for Everyman:

> All earthly things is but vanity:
> Beauty, Strength, and Discretion do man forsake,
> Foolish friends and kinsmen, that fair spake,
> All fleeth save Good-Deeds, and that am I . . .

So Everyman surrenders himself and an Angel clears his record:
> Thy reckoning is crystal clear.
> Now shalt thou into the heavenly sphere . . .

### Finest of the morality plays

Everyman is the finest of the morality plays. It is entirely free from the crudities and vulgarity of the secular miracle plays. *Everyman* is modern and has been revived many times in our century by amateur and professional groups. Like all the morality plays, of course, its basic purpose is to teach moral truths. And the best thing one can say for a piece of literature that teaches, is that it conveys its lesson with simple effectiveness.

### 5.   Arthur and Robin Hood: Greatest English Legendary Heroes

*Page 14 et seq. The Arthurian Legend* is a term used to designate the mass of material (the so-called *Matter of Britain*) that accumulated during the medieval period, revolving around the figure of King Arthur and the Knights of the Round Table. A good deal of oral folk tradition on this theme was probably in existence before Geoffrey of Monmouth listed Arthur as a King of Britain in his *Historia Regum Britanniae* (1137). It is thought today that Arthur was probably a Welsh leader of the Celts who fought against the Germanic invaders of Britain in the 5th century.

Whoever he was in history, the stories and deeds of this figure grew into a great body of romantic tradition. Innumerable poems and prose tales grew around this theme until, in the 15th century, Malory (p. 37) organized the cycle of Arthurian legend in his famous *Morte d'Arthur*. The many English and American writers, to the present day, who have gone back to Malory's collection for inspiration, include Tennyson, Morris, Swinburne, Mark Twain, and John Erskine.

### Arthur: feudal ideal of the nobles

In medieval courtly literature, Arthur's court became the principal theme for the metrical romance in England, France, and Germany. Only the theme of Tristram and Iseult competed with the Arthurian legend in the French and German medieval romances. Arthur and his knights represented nobility, the heroes who warmed the hearts of the feudal lords and ladies and who fought for the traditions of this high-born and materially endowed group. In modern times, of course, when literature became democratic, Arthur has become a romantic hero for everyone who reads.

*Page 19. Robin Hood cycle.* Side by side with the noble Arthur and his Round Table knights, sprang up the other great name among English legendary heroes, Robin Hood. Robin became the principal theme treated in the folk ballad of medieval England. We possess more than 300 ballads which treat of the popular outlaw and his own particular type of Round Table, the Merry Men of Sherwood Forest. Robin became the hero for the Anglo-Saxon vassal and a favorite theme for his own literature—a lowly hero who robbed the rich and gave to the poor. The first mention of Robin in cultured literature was by William Langland in *Piers Plowman* (1377), (p. 24), where the author has his allegorical figure of Sloth say:

> I cannot tell my pater-noster, as
>    the priest it singeth:
> But I can rimes of Robin Hood and Randolf
>    Erle of Chestre.

The Robin Hood cycle has been collected and retold in prose by many writers and forms a charming romantic tale for children (and adults) today. Robin Hood appears in many later works romanticizing the English middle ages, such as *Ivanhoe* of Sir Walter Scott.

There are many guesses as to whether Robin was real. One conjecture is that he was the last of the Anglo-Saxons to hold out against the invading Normans in the 12th century.

### Robin Hood: knightly ideal of the people

The Robin Hood cycle tells us much of the folk mind in England at the close of the middle ages. He was the ideal of the people, as Arthur was of the gentry and the nobility. He was the yeoman supreme, as Arthur was the ideal knight. Robin was religious, but hated monks. He was a protector of the weak and the poor. He was gallant and a follower of the free life, an adventurous and brave, but humble, soul.

We summarize here, very briefly, the outstanding episodes and characters of the *Arthurian legend* and the *Robin Hood cycle*.

### *King Arthur and the Knights of the Round Table*

King Uther loved Igraine, the beautiful wife of the Duke of Cornwall. In a war the Duke was killed and Igraine was with child by Uther and the magic of Merlin. Subsequently, Uther and Igraine were married and Arthur was born their lawful child. After Uther's death, Merlin hid Arthur for fear the lords would destroy him.

When Arthur was eighteen he proved his might by removing a sword imbedded in a stone. Tradition had proclaimed that the man who could remove this sword and thrust it in again was the rightful heir to the throne. After repeating this feat various times and defeating several petty kings, the Archbishop of Canterbury conceded that Arthur should be king over all Britain. He married Guinevere and received, as a wedding gift, the Round Table and one hundred knights. He set up his court at Camelot.

Various legends relate how Arthur received his famous sword Excalibur from the hand of the Lady of the Lake, how he won many notable battles during his reign. Merlin, the magician, was his constant adviser and companion in many adventures and state affairs.

Various of Arthur's knights now begin to become famous through their own deeds. Sir Launcelot becomes the first knight of the Round Table in valor and in sterling character. Young Tristram is pictured as a Knight of the Round Table and his adventures are related in the Arthurian cycle. Thus the independently begun legend of Tristram and Iseult began to intermingle with the Arthurian legends.

The legends began to treat of the secret love between Launcelot and the queen. Guinevere is represented as noble and stately, but coquettish and coy. She sends her lover, Launcelot, on many dangerous missions and almost drives him mad with her taunts. On one of these adventures, he is tricked into lying with Elaine, daughter of King Pelles, who bears the child who is to become the noblest and the purest of the Knights of Arthur, Galahad.

After Galahad grows up and proves his right to a seat at the Round Table, the Knights have become interested in seeking the Holy Grail (the cup from which Christ drank). Sir Galahad, through his bravery, combined with his purity and resistance to temptation, finally succeeds in seeing the miracle of the Grail.

Later, after many adventures and magical feats, in which Merlin is always the sinister and scheming figure of a wizard behind the power of Arthur, the legends begin to show signs of decadence. More tragedy and dishonor now come to the Round Table. Enemies rise on every side and Arthur becomes suspicious of Launcelot and his own wife. He sends a party of knights to kill Launcelot. All the party are slain except Modred, the natural son of Arthur, who becomes the Judas of the Arthurian legend. Launcelot saves the queen, who is about to be burned at the stake. They retire together to a castle.

Arthur attacks the castle and the Pope is forced to intervene to arrange a truce between the King and Launcelot. Launcelot and his followers go to France where he becomes king. Arthur invades France to overthrow this man who had once been his favorite knight. In his absence, Modred seizes the throne of Britain and tries to compel Guinevere to become his queen. Guinevere escapes and takes refuge in the Tower of London.

Meantime, Arthur returns to England to drive the traitor from the throne. Modred and his false knights are driven back to Canterbury, where a meeting is arranged. At the truce parley, a knight draws a sword to kill a snake. This causes the nervous knights to fall upon each other. Arthur kills Modred and receives his own death wound.

Arthur, on his deathbed, bids Sir Bedevere return Excalibur to the Lady of the Lake. After trying to conceal the sword twice, Bedevere finally throws it out into the lake where a hand rises and receives it. Arthur is carried to the water's edge where a mysterious barge receives the body of the dying king. Arthur's step-sisters, heavily veiled in black, seat themselves in the barge. The barge is rowed away to the Vale of Avelon where, it is predicted, the King will be healed. All Britain awaited the King's return throughout the ages.

Launcelot, meanwhile, rushed to avenge his former king. He found that Arthur had departed in a dying condition, that the queen had entered a nunnery and that Modred was dead. He retired to a monastery to live out his life in penance and prayer. When he heard the queen was dead he bore her corpse to Glastonbury, where some legends told that Arthur's bones had been laid, and laid her body at her husband's feet.

Launcelot died six months later and his brother Sir Ector, delivered over his body the eulogy (p. 38) which has described for the ages the ideal knight of medieval England.

### Robin Hood and the Merry Men of Sherwood Forest

Young Robin was a great archer. On passing through the forest to attend a shooting match he was challenged by a royal gamekeeper to test his skill on a deer. Not loath to allow such taunts to pass unaccepted, Robin killed one of the king's stags and was forced to flee into the forest to escape the keepers. One of the keepers shot at him and Robin returned the arrow, killing the keeper.

Now facing the death penalty if caught, Robin sought refuge in Sherwood Forest. Soon other homeless and persecuted men joined him and Robin became the leader of the band. The Sheriff of Nottingham offered two hundred pounds reward for his capture, dead or alive.

Thus begin the adventures of the outlaw, Robin Hood. His personal encounters are many. One day he met a huge man crossing a narrow footbridge. Robin, going the opposite way, refused passage to the big man, and the two went at it right merrily with their long staffs. Robin tumbled the huge man into the stream and gained his most loyal follower, Little John.

The stories are told of how many tried to catch Robin and failed. The sheriff, desperate at being rebuked by the king for failure to capture Robin and his merry men, clad in Lincoln green, proclaimed a shooting match. Robin and his trusty lieutenants went in disguise. Robin, in the guise of a ragged stranger, won the golden arrow by outshooting everyone. He sent the foiled sheriff a note of thanks.

Robin's merry men continued to rob rich travelers through the forest and to help the defenseless and distressed among the rural population.

Once, disguised as a butcher, Robin persuaded the sheriff to buy a herd of the finest meat. Robin took the sheriff to claim his purchase and showed him a herd of the King's finest venison on the hoof. Needless to say, the sheriff vowed once more to bring Robin to grief.

Once Little John, in disguise, actually worked for the sheriff for six months. When he grew bored with eating the sheriff's food and pretending to chase Robin Hood, he went back into the forest, taking with him the sheriff's own cook.

One of Robin's most lovable men was Friar Tuck. Robin and his men had heard of a rich monk, named Tuck, who lived nearby. Resolved to rob him, they had come upon a strange monk, singing down by a stream. Robin persuaded the monk to carry him across the river. The monk, who was in reality Friar Tuck, dumped Robin in the middle of the river. After a furious battle which Robin finally won, the two became fast friends and Friar Tuck became a faithful member of Robin's band.

The queen proposed to the king that they have a contest in which she would pit three archers against the best in his royal army. He accepted with glee and picked the very best archers he had in the realm. The queen secretly brought Robin Hood, Little John, and Will Scarlet to London. When the King's men would send an arrow into the bull's-eye, Robin would simply split the opponent's arrow with his own. The king was angry at the hoax but was forced by the queen to give Robin and his men safe conduct back to the Forest of Sherwood.

Many other adventures are told, of how Allan a Dale is helped to win his fair Ellen from the wicked squire, of how bishops and earls are forced to divide their funds with Robin, of how the sheriff gets fooled time after time, and of how Robin gains a sweetheart, Maid Marian, who could shoot almost as true as he.

Once King Richard I, the Lion-Hearted, enters the forest with six of his retainers and they best Robin and his men at all their games. The King reveals his identity and pardons Robin Hood and his men.

Robin, who in reality was the rightful heir of the Earl of Huntington, who had been dispossessed by corrupt lords when Robin was a boy, is restored to his title and estates. He soon wearies of this life, however, and returns to the outlaws of Sherwood Forest. John, the new king, and the sheriff of Nottingham are angered and send a posse of men into the forest to roust out the outlaws. Many men are killed, including the sheriff.

Robin, ill and sad, drags himself to the priory of Kirk Lee, where his cousin is prioress. Instead of bleeding him properly through a vein, the crafty woman, in sympathy with the king, opens an artery and leaves him locked in a room to bleed to death:

> He then bethought him of his bugle-horn,
>   Which hung low down to his knee;
> He set his horn unto his mouth,
>   And blew out weak blasts three.

Little John hears them and breaks down the door, finding his beloved leader dying. He helped Robin to the window, where the outlaw shot his last arrow to mark the spot where he wished to be buried. His merry men disbanded after his death, but their fame has lived on:

> Here beneath this little stone
> Lies Robin, Earl of Huntington,
> None there was as he so good,
> And people called him Robin Hood.
> Such outlaws as he and his men
> Will England never see again.

## 6. The Middle English Metrical Romance

*Page 23. Sir Gawain and the Green Knight,* presumably written by the unidentified Pearl Poet, about 1370. Of the many Arthurian romances of the age in French, German, and English, this relation of the strange adventure of a nephew of King Arthur is the most modern in language, the most artistic in poetic conception, and one of literature's most charming representatives of the courtly epic or romance.

The story relates how King Arthur and the Knights of the Round Table are celebrating the Yule season at Camelot. The festivities are at their height when a knight dressed in green, and mounted upon a green horse, enters the hall. He was a huge man with a green beard. He loudly challenges any knight in the hall to trade blows with him. Arthur's knight can have the first blow now, to be delivered with the stranger's huge Danish axe. According to the terms, the stranger will take his blow one year later at his own castle in a distant land.

The young and inexperienced Gawain accepts the challenge, and taking up the knight's mighty axe, prepared to deliver the blow. The stranger kneels and bares his neck. Gawain swings

and the Green Knight's head rolls across the floor, spurting
blood on the feet of the spectators as it moves.

All stare in consternation as the giant stranger, bleeding pro-
fusely, nimbly leaps after the head and recovers it. Holding
it on high, he leaps upon his horse and is about to leave, when
the head suddenly speaks and identifies its owner as the Knight
of the Green Chapel. It bids Gawain be there at the appointed
hour the next New Year's Day to receive his blow, or forever
be branded a coward among brave men.

The months roll by:

> For though men at feast, make merry and drink,
> A year's soon o'er, ne'er stops, ne'er returns,
> The start and the end, seldom bring the same,
> Thus men this Yuletide, and after this the year,
> Each of the seasons, following one after another,
> After Christmas joy, comes crabbed Lenten time,
> With fish for flesh, and other and simpler fare.
> And then Nature's weather, with winter doth duel:
> The cold backs away, and clouds themselves upraise.
> Warm, sweet showers, of Spring rain doth fall,
> And wets the fair fields, and flowers there spring,
> Ground and groves all, in garment of fresh green.
> Birds ready their nests, singing all the while,
> For soft summer's solace, that cometh anon
> > Over all Nature.
> > And blossoms swell and blow
> > In rows, colorful and bright;
> > And notes most lovely flow,
> > With wooded splendor bedight.

And the months roll by, and with autumn, Sir Gawain departed upon his adventure. After many hazardous encounters
along the way, he finally comes to a great castle among a forest
of oaks. It is Christmas Eve. He seeks shelter and is welcomed
by the lord and his lovely young wife. They tell him that the
Green Chapel is nearby.

During the evening Sir Gawain is royally entertained. The
lady of the castle, who is radiantly beautiful, makes a special
effort to be nice to Gawain during the evening. The lord assures
Gawain that the Green Chapel is only two miles distance and
that he can easily keep his appointment by leaving early on
New Year's Morn. Gawain relaxes and decides· to remain
through the week. The lord of the castle, who hunts during the

day, proposes that Sir Gawain rest at the castle and keep his lady company while he is away. He proposes to give Sir Gawain all the game he manages to obtain during the day in exchange for any gifts which the young knight receives at the castle. Sir Gawain agrees to go along with this agreeable wager.

Here Sir Gawain's period of temptation begins, for no sooner is the lord away the next morning than the charming hostess, in scanty attire, enters his bedroom and makes love to him. But Sir Gawain resists. As she leaves, after long hours of conversation, she kisses him. That evening when the lord returns he presents the noble young knight with the fine venison he has gained from the day's sport. Sir Gawain gives him a kiss, saying that is the total that he has been given at the castle that day.

The next day the lord is in the forest early, pursuing the wild boar that day. And the enchanting lady is back with Sir Gawain, coming upon him in bed and seating herself beside him in her revealing garments of silk. Gawain parries every approach with knightly courtesy, but giving no ground from his ideals of chivalry and chastity:

> "Why, you have forgotten what I taught you yesterday in the most obvious manner I know."
>
> "What was that?" asked the knight, "for, surely, I know not."
>
> "Why, I taught you of kissing," murmured the fair lady. "It is but courtesy in every knight to claim kisses when he knows he is the favored one."
>
> "Please cease such speech, dear lady," the strong knight replied. "I dare not do that for fear I be repulsed. If I asked and were refused, it would have been wrong to ask."
>
> "Oh, my heavens," exclaimed the lovely dame, "you could not be refused. You are strong enough to take what you please, that is if any were so rude as to deny you."
>
> "Yes, by God," Gawain said, "you argue well. But force in my land is considered discourteous, as well as any gift that is not given with good will. I am at your command to kiss as you please. Begin when you like and stop when you are through."
>
> The lady gracefully bends low and sweetly kisses his face . . .

Sir Gawain remained chaste this day in spite of his opportunities to be otherwise. In the evening the hunt has again been successful and the lord presents the youth with his boar. It seems that Sir Gawain was compelled to kiss the lord twice on this occasion.

The third day the lady bestowed three kisses upon Gawain

and persuades him to accept a silken girdle which she tells him will preserve him from mortal harm. Meantime, the lord was on the track of the wily fox with his hounds. After a merry chase, Reynard is cornered and loses his glossy coat to the lord of the castle. When the lord entered the castle that evening, Sir Gawain rushes up to him and kisses him three times and receives the fox skin. After an evening of feasting and entertainment, they all retire. Early the next morning Sir Gawain departs. He has made no mention of the girdle.

On the way to the Green Chapel the servant tries to persuade the knight to turn back. On approaching the Green Chapel, they could hear the Green Knight, sharpening his axe. After exchanging greetings, the youth bares his neck to receive his blow. He flinches as the axe descends and the Green Knight withholds the blow. He reproves the youth for his timidity. Gawain swears that he will not swerve aside again.

The giant again lifts the axe and starts to bring it down. Sir Gawain does not move a muscle. The Green Knight hesitates and this time Sir Gawain reproves him for cowardice. The giant swings but the edge only cuts through the outer skin and a muscle or two of Sir Gawain's neck, spilling a little blood in the snow. He quickly leaps to his feet and declares that he has repaid the debt.

The Green Knight leans on his axe and laughs. After praising the noble youth's courage, he reveals himself as the lord of the castle. He declares that Gawain escaped the first two blows because he had kept to his agreement during the first two days at the castle. He drew blood the third time because Gawain had failed to reveal the gift of the girdle. The Green Knight, in league with King Arthur's half-sister, had planned the whole affair to test the valor and courage of King Arthur's knights. A beautiful lady of their acquaintance had agreed to help them by tempting the brave knight who should accept the Green Knight's challenge. Sir Gawain had come through with flying colors except for the one small fault of keeping the girdle and that was understandable because of his love of life.

As Sir Gawain returns to Arthur's Court, he gazes with shame at the girdle and vows that he will keep it with him forever to remind him of the one time that he had yielded to a weakness of the flesh.

King Arthur's court laughed heartily when Sir Gawain related all that had happened All the lords and ladies vowed that each of the Knights of the Round Table should thenceforth wear a circlet of bright green silk. And it seems that ever afterward, the knights who wore that symbol achieved mighty deeds of valor and remained pure in heart and actions.

## Most charming of the metrical romances

*Sir Gawain and the Green Knight* is a true gem in a genre that produced, perhaps, hundreds of examples during the ages of knighthood and the courtly ideal. The greatest charm of the poem is not the story itself but its many delightful descriptions of a wild nature, the customs and paraphernalia of knighthood, and the colorful pageantry of court life. Its descriptions of the three day of hunting are little masterpieces in themselves. There is little monotony or repetition in the entire 2500-odd lines of the poem. It is fast moving, logical in construction, colorful, and filled with vivid detail. It is generally considered to be the best surviving Middle English romance. There are many good versions in anthologies in modern English. This writer prefers the prose translations to any that have yet appeared in verse.

### 7.   Geoffrey Chaucer: *Troilus and Criseyde*
### A chivalric romance of antiquity

*Page 31. Troilus and Criseyde* was written about 1385-1386. Its locale is the Trojan War, around 1200 B.C., with its characters acting in accordance with the best traditions of the romances of chivalry of the Middle Ages. The verse is the rime-royal. The result is a novel in verse, that can be enjoyed by any modern reader.

At the time when the Greeks were beseiging the ancient city of Troy, Calchus, a Trojan astrologer, saw by the stars that the city was doomed. To save his own skin, he betook himself to the Greek camp, abandoning his beautiful daughter Criseyde, who was recently widowed. The young lady was given permission by Hector to continue to dwell in the city without fear that her father's treachery would cause her harm.

One April day the Trojans gather in the temple to give thanks to the gods for a bright spring season. Troilus, the young son of King Priam, was among them. Also present, in her widow's black was Criseyde:

Among thise othere folk was Criseyda,
In widows habit blak; but natheles,
Right as oure firste lettre is now an A,
In beaute first so stood she, makeless.
Hire goodly lokyng gladed all the prees.
Nas nevere yet seyn thyng to ben preysed derre,
Nor under cloude blak so bright a sterre

As was Criseyde, as folk seyde everichone
That hir behelden in hir blake weede.
And yet she stood ful lowe and stille alone,
Byhynden other folk, in litel brede,
And neigh the dore, ay undre shames drede,
Simple of atir and debonaire of chere
With ful assured lokyng and manere . . .

Troilus had been scornful of young lovers until that moment.
But when he saw the lovely widow, he was smitten sore with
her beauty. Fearing to have hope, he spends his energies by
day in fighting the Greeks. By night, he sings sad songs and
groans under the pain of love.

His older and worldly wise friend, Pandarus, came upon him
in this sorrowing state and learned the truth. Criseyde was
Pandarus' niece. The wily uncle decided to bring the two young
people together. He spent some time trying to persuade Criseyde
that Troilus had pure intentions toward her. Gradually he
brought her to the point of meeting Troilus at the house of a
friend.

After some time had passed Pandarus decided that things
had come to the point where Troilus could possess the young
widow. He invited Criseyde to dine with him and concealed
Troilus in the house. A storm arose and it was necessary for
the girl to stay the night at her uncle's. By means of sly per-
suasion, the uncle brought his niece and Troilus together that
night. And after that, they met many times at Pandarus' house
Each time they exchanged vows of eternal love. By day Troilus
was invincible on the field of battle; by night he was the fault-
less lover.

But their joy was foredoomed for dark days ahead. A number of famous Trojans were captured one day by the Greeks
An exchange of prisoners was arranged. Calchas persuaded
the Greeks to ask for his daughter in exchange for one of the

Trojan warriors. At the Trojan council Hector, Troilus' brother, opposed the exchange but the vote went against him. Troilus was in the deepest of despair as Criseyde made ready to depart for the Greek camp.

At the parting of the lovers in Pandarus' house, Criseyde, broken hearted, promised that she would remain faithful to Troilus and would persuade her father to let her return to the city within a few days. The lovers part, and on neutral ground the exchange is effected. Diomede, a handsome young Greek, leads Criseyde away to her father.

Impatiently, Troilus waits ten days and Criseyde does not return. By the tenth day Criseyde was convinced that Troy would fall. Diomede, meantime, was bending every effort to win her for himself. Without hope of seeing Troilus again, she gave herself over to him.

Troilus wrote to her again and again. Her replies renewed her protestations of love for him, but she stated that she could not return to the city. The war went on; Hector is killed by Achilles. Troilus finally guesses the truth. And one day, on the battlefield, he saw pinned to Diomede's armour his own brooch which he had given to Criseyde. He now knew life was hopeless for him. He fought with Diomede during succeeding days without either of them gaining a decisive advantage over the other. At last, one day, Troilus was killed by the mighty Achilles. His spirit floated into the spheres and laughed at the vanities of the earthbound existence far, far below:

> Such end hath, lo, the love of Troilus!
> Such end hath, lo, his great worthiness!

### First of the great English narrative poems

*Troilus and Criseyde* brought a freshness and a modern spirit to English narrative poetry that it has never lost. And, since Chaucer's day, the two legendary lovers have been dealt with in three famed British narrative poems: by the Scottish Henryson in the 15th century, Shakespeare in the Elizabethan Age, and by Dryden in the 17th century.

There are several verse and prose translations into modern English. But a scrutiny of the two rime-royal stanzas quoted here from the original poem shows that, with Chaucer, Middle English was donning a modern dress.

## 8. Geoffrey Chaucer: *The Canterbury Tales*
### Portrait gallery of medieval England

*Page 33. The Canterbury Tales* was written in the last years of the 14th century, consisting of a prologue and twenty-four tales, held together loosely as one narrative. Here the prologue and five representative tales are digested.

### The prologue

Whan that Aprille with his shoures sote[1]
The droghte of Marche hath perced to the rote,
And bathed every veyne in swich[2] licour,
Of which vertu[3] engendered is the flour . . .

. . . . . .

Bifel that, in that seson on a day,
In Southwerk at the Tabard as I lay
Redy to wenden on my pilgrimage
To Caunterbury with full devout courage,
At night was come in-to that hostelrye,
Well nyne and twenty in a companye,
Of sondry folk, by aventure y-falle[4]
In felawshipe, and pilgrims were they alle,
That toward Caunterbury wolden ryde . . .

Chaucer here begins his observations of these twenty-nine acquaintances at the Tabard Inn. All are bent toward the same goal, a pilgrimage to the shrine of Thomas-a-Becket at the cathedral at Canterbury. Every middle-class station in 14th century English life is represented: a knight, a poor parson, nuns and priests, a pardoner, various tradesmen and craftsmen (merchant, reeve, cook, plowman, haberdasher, shipman, innkeeper, yeoman, etc.), the professional men (clerk of Oxford, doctor of physic, sergeant of law, etc.). Here, then, are gathered representatives of the upper middle-class gentry, the tradesmen and the craftsmen of the guilds, the clergy (both good and bad), the common worker, and the liberal professions. Each pilgrim's character is described in detail, physical appearance, and a careful delineation of habits and customs—in short, here is a veritable portrait gallery of 14th century English society.

---

[1] sweet, [2] such, [3] strength or power, [4] brought together.

The Prioress is particularly appealing with all her qualities of delicacy and goodness, her intelligence and good grace. And, especially at the table did she show her fine breeding:

> At mete wel y-taught was she with-alle;
> She leet no morsel from hir lippes falle,
> Ne wette hir fingres in hir sauce depe.
> Wel could she carie a morsel, and wel kepe,
> That no drope ne fille up-on her brest.
> In curteisye was set ful muche hir lest.[1]
> Hir over lippe wyped she so clene,
> That in hir coppe was no ferthing[2] sene
> Of grece, whan she dronken hadde hir draughte . . .

## The plan for The Canterbury Tales

After dinner, the host at the Tabard Inn suggested that the poet and he become a part of the company. He further suggests that, to lighten and make pleasant the journey, each shall tell two stories going and two others returning. The story judged to be the best shall earn for its teller a fine dinner upon their return to the inn.

So it is agreed. The next morning they travel southward. And, upon the way, lots are drawn, and the first turn falls to the noble and chivalrous knight. The host acts as director of the story-telling and calls upon each, as his lot falls, to begin his tale. The stories reveal every type of narrative form known to literature up to Chaucer's time, with exception, of course, of the drama in its dialogue form. It is interesting to note that the worst efforts are contributed by Chaucer himself. He begins a verse burlesque (*Rime of Sir Thopas*) of the doggerel rhymes of knightly adventure, typical in his day, and is stopped by the host, who does not recognize the obvious satire that Chaucer is attempting. The poet then turns to prose and substitutes a dreary sermonizing tale—"a little thing in prose," "a moral tale," which bores the entire company.

In all, only 24 of the contemplated 128 tales are actually told before Chaucer abandons his plan. It is interesting to note that all three of the century's famous European collections of tales (Juan Manuel: *El Libro de Patronio* and Giovanni Boccaccio: *Il Decamerone*) failed to include anything near the number planned by their authors.

*The knight's tale.* A tale of chivalric adventure in which two knights of Thebes, cousins, are captured by Theseus, Duke

---

[1] desire, [2] smallest trace.

of Athens. Palamon and Arcite, the captured knights from the Theban royal household, are imprisoned for life.

The beautiful sister-in-law of Theseus was accustomed to walk in the garden beneath the tower in which the two brave youths are imprisoned. They both fall in love with her at sight. When Arcite is released because of an old friendship with a noble in Theseus' household, he decides to stay. He disguises himself under another name and works in the Duke's kitchen so that he may have an opportunity to see Emily, the Duke's sister-in-law.

Palamon, after 7 years, escapes and hides. He and Arcite meet and agree to fight it out the next day in full armour. Theseus separates them and decrees that they shall meet a year hence in formal tournament, each with his supporting retinue of one hundred knights.

The tourney is quite a grand affair. Arcite and his knights are declared winners after Palamon is captured. However, the victor is thrown from his horse and is mortally hurt. Arcite dies in Emily's arms after the two knights make up their differences. The dead hero receives typical burial ceremonies of epic Greek heroes.

The years pass and at last Theseus persuades Emily to accept Palamon as her husband.

*The miller's tale.* A direct contrast to the tale told by the knight, this is a ribald and naughty tale that shocks the more delicate members of the company. The miller is a bit drunk on ale when he tells it.

There was a rich carpenter of Oxford who took in boarders. One of these was a poor student named Nicholas. He is described as being as sweet as "licorice or ginger."

And it seems the carpenter had recently wed a beautiful young girl. He watched her and worried most of the time that she would deceive him. The girl is described in the most glowing of lusty terms by the tipsy miller.

Nicholas lost no time and made violent love to the young wife, Alison. Also a young dandy from the town, named Absalom, was taken with the beauty of the girl, but Alison preferred the poor student.

Nicholas had a plan to trick John, the carpenter, so that he could spend the night with Alison. He convinced John that a second flood would sweep over the earth. John rushed up into the attic and began cutting holes in the flooring, rigging up tubs with supplies, etc., so that they could get away when the waters came suddenly. Meantime, the two young lovers took full advantage of his absence from the nuptial bed. John, weary from his work, fell asleep in the attic.

Near daybreak, Absalom sneaked up to the bedroom window and urged Alison to let him come in to her. She could not get rid of him unless she gave him a kiss. For the sport of it, she backed up to the window and the lad kissed her backside.

Angered, Absalom vowed vengeance. He got a hot iron and returned, demanding another kiss. Nicholas, to get in on the fun, backed up to the darkened window opening and received the hot iron for his pains.

He screamed for water to cool his burning backside. This awoke John, who thought the flood was upon them. He jumped into a tub, cut the ropes, and fell through to the bottom floor.

The young rascals ran into the street screaming. The neighbors laughed themselves sick when they looked upon the saddened John, Nicholas, and Alison.

*The pardoner's tale.* This is satire on the malpractice of priests who use the exemplary story to play upon the superstitions of the ignorant folk. In the prologue, the pardoner explains to the company that the moral of his tale is, "money is the root of all evil." He offers his services to the entire company to cleanse them of sin.

In Flanders all the young people were indulging in excesses of eating, gambling, drinking, dancing, and visiting brothels.

One early morn three of the drinkers vowed vengeance upon Death, who apparently dwelt in the neighboring town, since a good friend of theirs had just died there.

The three dissolute young men stagger off to find Death and kill him. On the way they insult an old man who tells them that Death is beneath a certain tree in the forest. Instead, they find there a great pile of gold.

They decide they had better guard the gold until night. They draw lots and the youngest among them is sent into town for food and drink.

While he is away, his two comrades plan to kill him upon his return. He, in turn, plots to kill his companions. He puts poison into two of the bottles of wine he is bringing back.

When the youth returns, the other two attack him without delay. In the ensuing struggle, one of the men pulls out a dagger and kills the companion who had gone for the food. Exhausted from the exercise, the two rascals drink the wine and are poisoned. Thus, all three of the revelers had, in reality, found Death beneath the tree.

*The prioress' tale.* As might be expected, the dainty Prioress is concerned with the religious tale. She is concerned only with the moral effects of her "miracle of the Virgin" and does not think in terms of personal gain or of the psychological effects of mass evangelical zeal.

In rime-royal she relates how, in a great city of Asia, there was a little group of Christians who had a school. A widow's small son was in the primary grade. And, as the older children were singing *Alma Redemptoris* in Latin, he listened and learned the song. He knew not what he was singing, but he sang the song in a loud voice as he passed on his way to school through the quarter of the Jews.

The Jews, angered at this sacred song, seized the boy, slit his throat, and threw him into a pit. The widow waited up all night but her little boy did not come home. She went out searching throughout the town, but no one had seen the child.

At last, she passed near the pit where the poor boy's body lay. Suddenly, through the slit throat of the child came, loud and clear, the notes of *Alma Redemptoris*. The amazed Christians gather up the broken body of the child and carry it to the convent. When the boy was placed upon the altar he told the monks the reason he could go on singing the beautiful notes of *Alma Redemptoris*. It seems that the Virgin had come into the pit and laid a pearl on the child's tongue, causing him to continue singing, though lying there with his throat slit.

Needless to say, the wicked Jews were hunted out and killed by the authorities.

*The nun's priest's tale.* This is the outstanding example of the animal fable, filled with clever humor and sharp and witty dialogue.

Once there was a widow who possessed a beautiful rooster, named Chanticleer. "In the field of crowing he had no peer." He lived with his seven hens in the widow's barnyard.

Partlet, his favorite wife, became worried one night when Chanticleer dreamed he was being chased by a fox. She insisted it was all just a dream and what he needed was a laxative.

The next morning he was out in the long grass when he suddenly saw the fox. He was tempted to fly screeching away, but the fox soothingly told him that he was a friend and that he had entertained his relatives many a time in his house. He assured Chanticleer that his father was quite a singer. He wondered if the son had inherited the divine gift of his father.

Chanticleer closed his eyes, bared his throat, and crowed. The fox grabbed him by the throat and started to carry him away. The hens raised quite a clatter and the widow came out to see what was the matter. She, her children and the hens, the donkey and all the barnyard animals made such noise that no one could have heard himself think for miles around.

This terrible noise worried the fox, who was sensitive and jumpy-nerved. Chanticleer suggested that he yell to them and tell them to shut up for they could do nothing for poor Chanticleer. The fox opened his jaws to do so and the rooster flew up into a tree.

The fox tried to cajole him to come down by using his ·most dulcet tones, but the cock had learned his lesson and his vanity had been dulled by experience:

> . . . curse me for a dunce,
> If you fool me like that more than once . . .

And the fox, equally chastened, had learned to keep his mouth shut.

### *A human comedy of the late Middle Ages*

*The Canterbury Tales* is a human comedy of the age of Chaucer. Every literary trick is employed by the poet to give variety and spice to his narratives: humor, bawdiness, pathos, drama, moral example, romance. His verse forms run the gamut of his European experiences from the rhymed couplet to the eight-line iambic pentameter. He even uses prose but it is pale beside his lively manipulation of verse forms.

*The Canterbury Tales* is as an anthology of medieval literature. The tales represent the range of writings from the moral tale to the *fabliau* (the farcical and bawdy tale), from the romantic epic to the satire, from the folk tale to the classical legend. He touches the thoroughgoing realism of the man of the soil in one tale to rise to the supernatural and the weird in the next. He is, in turn, didactic, dramatic, prosaic, tragic, comic, narrative, lyric—in short, he is everything that life presents and his people are an highly aesthetic representation of what life around him offered to the one with an eye to see, a will to appreciate, and an ability to record. Chaucer had them all more than a century before anyone else in England.

## 9. Edmund Spenser: *The Faerie Queene*
Renaissance allegorical epic

*Page 61. Spenser's plan:* Spenser, in a letter addressed to Sir Walter Ralegh, indicated that his over-all purpose was to "fashion a gentleman or noble person in vertuous and gentle discipline." He projected twelve books, each of which should present a main character representing one of twelve virtues, all of which would be embodied by the central figure of knightly perfection, Prince Arthur, who would appear in all the books. The very complex allegory would proceed on three levels: (1) the allegory of the virtues of the individual and the vices that beset the Christian soul seeking perfection, (2) the allegory of Spenser's times, portraying the struggle of the religious ideals of the Reformation, (3) stories of adventure and romance to carry each of the allegories, each having as central figures of perfection Prince Arthur, the perfect knight or gentleman, and Gloriana (Queen Elizabeth), the perfect symbol of the good State.

Spenser's framework for the entire poem would involve a twelve-day feast at the Court of Gloriana (Elizabeth, the champion of Protestantism). Each day a distressed person could appear before the Court and ask for a champion. Each book would describe the particular adventure involved in overcoming the evil or vice which was represented in the petition for help. Spenser completed only six of his projected twelve books.

### Book I.

A Gentle Knight was pricking on the plaine,
Y-cladd in mightie armes and silver shielde,
Wherein old dints of deep wounds did remaine,
The cruell markes of many' a bloudy fielde;
Yet armes until that time did he never wield;
His angry steed did chide his foming bitt,
As much disdayning to the curbe to yield:
Full jolly knight he seemd, and fair did sitt,
As one for knightly giusts and fierce encounters fitt.
. . . . . .
A lovely Ladie rode him faire beside,
Upon a lowly Asse more white then snow,
Yet she much whiter; but the same did hide

> Under a vele, that wimpled was full low;
> And over all a blacke stole shee did throw:
> As one that inly mournd, so was she sad,
> And heavie sate upon her palfrey slow;
> Seemed in heart some hidden care she had,
> And by her, in a line, a milkewhite lambe she lad.

Thus the Red Cross Knight (representing Christian Holiness) rides forth to aid the fair Una (representing Truth or the True Faith). Una had brought the armour, upon which was the symbol of a Holy Cross in red, and had explained to Gloriana that her parents were being besieged in their castle by a dragon (representing Error), which had laid waste to her father's domain. Young George, a humble youth but of noble birth, had craved the first adventure. Finding that the armour fitted him perfectly, Una accepts his aid and Gloriana knights him as the "Knight of the Red Cross."

On the way the Red Cross Knight enters a cave and slays a fierce dragon (Heresy). Later he is put under a spell by the evil magician Archimago (Hypocrisy), who persuades him that Una is a false harlot. In disgust, our hero departs and meets Sansfoi (Faithlessness) and Duessa (representing Mary, Queen of Scots, the symbol of Papacy). Under the influence of the false Duessa, the Red Cross Knight is drawn into one snare after another by characters representing Pride, Idleness, Gluttony, Envy, Avarice, and Wrath. Finally he is defeated by the giant Orgoglio (False Pride) and imprisoned in a dungeon.

Meanwhile, Una is wandering alone in the wilderness and is saved from other animals by the Lion (Courage). She undergoes harrowing experiences with Lawlessness, Superstition, Stupidity, and with the dread Archimago, who has put on a disguise to represent the Red Cross Knight. Finally Una meets Prince Arthur, a personification of chivalry, who secretly loves the Faerie Queen and does good deeds in her name. They reach the castle and rescue the Red Cross Knight, defeating the giant.

After recovering from his wounds, aided by Faith, Hope, and Charity, the renewed champion rides to Una's castle and slays the dragon. Una's parents are overjoyed when Una and the Red Cross Knight are married. The champion does not linger long by the side of his love, however, as he must return to serve Gloriana for the remainder of his term of service, six years.

Book II. Sir Guyon (representing Temperance) sets out with

Prudence, or Abstinence, to rescue a lady who is reported to have been despoiled by none other than the Red Cross Knight. This, of course, is a frame-up between Archimago and Duessa, but the good knights meet and clash in fierce combat. Finally, they recover their good sense when they see the sign of the Virgin Mary on each other's armour.

Guyon goes on to slay a wicked witch, and together with Arthur, he enters the Castle of Alma (representing Temperance) to rescue her from enemies. Finally Temperance is made secure and the enemies are sent under heavy guard to Gloriana.

Book III. Britomart (a female knight representing Chastity) succeeds in saving Amoret (representing Female Devotion) from the clutches of Busirane (representing Illicit Love).

Book IV. Two knights, Combel and Triamond (representing Friendship) cross paths with Britomart, from Book III. This book is intended to present a Platonic form of love in contrast with the sexual love discussed in the former Book. Here the Blatant Beast, or Slander, is given his first defeat.

Book V. Sir Artegal (representing Justice) sets out to defend Ireland. Her enemies (liars, scoundrels, and braggarts) are finally brought to justice, with Arthur having to act as mediator, to keep Envy and Detraction, aided by Slander, from upsetting the delicate balance of Justice.

Book VI. Sir Calidore (representing Courtesy) finally catches up with the Blatant Beast (Slander), the famed defamer of knightly character. Calidore muzzles the last deadly enemy of the Faerie Queen's Court, and brings him to Gloriana's feet. But the dread beast escapes and is again at large when the Sixth Book ends.

### 10. Nicholas Udall: *Ralph Roister Doister*
#### First English classic comedy

*Page 72.* The first full-length comedy in English is a play written to be acted by schoolboys. It was probably first presented early in 1553. Patterned after the Roman comedy of Terence and Plautus, this play is a true slapstick farce, full of horseplay and simple situations. The characters and the incidents are modeled closely after the Roman comedies, but the setting is completely English. The atmosphere and the crude native humor are distinctly descended from the broad humor of the miracle plays of medieval times.

## Act I

Ralph Roister Doister, a rather well-to-do and blustering young blade, has bragged many times of his loves and acts of bravery to Mathew Merrygreek, a gay and carefree young parasite, who sponges on Ralph. Ralph, for him, is "chiefe banker for meate and money." The cowardly Ralph now says that he is in love again, this time with a rich widow, Dame Christian Cunstance. He cannot imagine that she might fail to fly into his arms, as he prides himself on being a regular devil with the ladies. Merrygreek, agrees to help him win the widow.

Merrygreek gets together some musicians and they go to serenade the good Dame. Ralph waits on the sidelines. Some servant women (Madge Mumblecrust, Tibet Talkapace, and Annot Alyface) come out of the house and laugh and talk with Ralph. He gets old Madge, "a girl . . . scarce yet three score year old" on his side by trying to kiss her. She agrees to deliver a love letter to her mistress. When she does so, Dame Cunstance is annoyed and does not open the letter. She reminds her servants that she is virtuous and engaged to Gawin Goodluck, who is away at sea.

## Act II

Ralph sends his servant boy with gifts to the widow. Madge is finally persuaded to deliver them. The widow is angrier than ever and bids the servant women never to accept gifts from strangers.

## Act III

Merrygreek goes to find out how the gifts were received. He is admitted to the good Dame's presence and delivers Ralph's proposal for a wedding ceremony with the widow the following Sunday. She spurns the proposal. When Ralph hears the news, he falls into a blubbering fit. Merrygreek persuades him to buck up and face up to the widow himself. Ralph blusters around and swears to kill the widow and all her servants. Merrygreek laughs at his bragging. Together, with musicians, they again go to Dame Cunstance's house. The good woman comes out and tells Ralph to stay away from her. Merrygreek had previously gotten his hands on the letter Ralph had written. He altered the punctuation and the spelling so that it now carries insulting terms. When the widow finally decides to read it, she gets quite the opposite impression from it than Roister Doister had intended.

## Act IV

Sym Suresby, a sailor in the employ of Gawin Goodluck, calls upon his master's promised bride. He arrives as Roister Doister and Merrygreek are trying to explain to the widow about the trick that had been played in regard to the letter. Sym hears enough to convince him that the widow is playing fast and loose with his master. He leaves hastily to tell the tale. The widow is furious, and in the quarrel, Ralph threatens to come back with his men and burn down the house.

Dame Cunstance enlists the aid of her friend Tristram Trusty, and with all the servants armed with kitchen utensils, they await Ralph and his forces. Merrygreek comes and decides to join them in the fun. When Ralph arrives, he is routed by the widow and the servants, armed with pots and pans. Ralph is now sure that the Dame is a dangerous Amazon and probably killed her first husband. He renounces his suit.

## Act V

Gawin Goodluck comes to demand an explanation. Dame Cunstance, supported by Tristram, convinces him that she has not been untrue but is still "the pearle of perfect honestie." Merrygreek returns to beg the widow's forgiveness for his pal Ralph. The reconciled couple decide to have a dinner the next day and they invite Merrygreek and Ralph Roister Doister to share it with them.

At the end of the play the entire cast sings a song dedicated to Queen Mary.

## 11. Norton and Sackville: *Gorboduc, or Ferrex and Porrex*
### First English classic tragedy

*Page 73.* The first regular English tragedy follows the structure of the tragedies of the Spanish-Roman Seneca. This play, by Thomas Norton and Thomas Sackville, was performed before Queen Elizabeth in January 1562. It is the first English play in blank verse. Previous efforts had been in a sort of rimed doggerel. These two distinguished lawyers had written the play as a gentle hint to Elizabeth that she should marry and provide an heir for the throne. The play was laid in the reign of a legendary king of early Britain and was of current political import for thinking Englishmen of the day, who feared revolution and bloodshed over the succession to the throne at the death of Elizabeth, the last Tudor.

## Act I

The *dumb show* brings on six wild barbarians, clad in leaves, who try to break a bundle of sticks. They fail, but each breaks single sticks quite easily.

Gorboduc, the last Briton in the line of descent from King Brut, decides to divide his kingdom between his two sons, Ferrex and Porrex. He calls in his councilors and states his desire to retire from rule and urges that his plan will benefit the country. Arostus, the chief adviser, thinks the plan good for the peace and prosperity of the kingdom. Others urge that the king wait until his death to permit the sons to assume full power. Still others point out that normally the eldest son rules and that such a divided kingdom cannot help but bring trouble. The king is stubborn and resolves to set his plan into execution immediately. He gives Ferrex, the elder son, all of the realm south of the Humber River, and to Porrex, the younger son, he metes out the lands north of that river.

A *chorus* of four ancient Britons compare these events with the symbolic pantomime of the sticks. In union there is strength; in division, weakness.

## Act II

The *dumb show* portrays a king being offered a harmless cup of wine by a sage old courtier. He refuses it, but eagerly drinks from a golden cup, tendered to him by a young, villainous-appearing dandy. He falls dead, poisoned by the drink.

The two kings, Ferrex and Porrex, are shown, successively, at their respective seats of government. Ferrex begins to think about the loss of half of the kingdom. He refuses to listen to the advisers his father had given him. He chooses, instead, to feed upon the rebellious thoughts a young ambitious courtier whispers in his ear. Hermon, the young courtier, thinks he should immediately kill his brother. Ferrex thinks, at least, he should be armed and ready for any eventuality. Dordan, the wise old councilor, hastens to inform Gorboduc of approaching trouble.

The scene shifts to Porrex, who has ignored the advice of his wise old councilors and is listening to the poisonous words of young Lyndar. He believes the reports that his brother plans to murder him. Instead of listening to the old adviser, who proposes to find out if there is a plot against him, Porrex decides to invade his brother's kingdom and kill Ferrex. Philander, the old courtier, rushes off to tell Gorboduc and find out if the old father has enough influence left to avoid the dissension.

The *chorus* explains how the events fit the pantomime of the two cups.

## Act III

The *dumb show* presents mourners crossing the stage in black.

The old father receives the bad news from both north and south of the Humber. He calls a council meeting, but before it can act, word arrives of the invasion of Ferrex' lands and of the murder of the elder brother by Porrex.

The *chorus* breaks in with an explanation of the symbolical pantomime.

## Act IV

The *dumb show* presents three furies from Hell, driving before them the rulers of ancient times who had slain their own children. The furies are dripping blood and brandishing snakes, firebrands, and whips.

Queen Videna had always preferred her elder son and had greatly lamented the fact that her husband had deprived him of a part of the kingdom. Now that she hears of the murder of Ferrex, she is furious and swears to avenge the death of her favorite son.

Old Gorboduc has Porrex brought to trial, but before the punishment can be decided upon, word is brought in that his wife has stabbed their son to death in his sleep.

The *chorus* repeats the facts and ties in the murders with the pantomime.

## Act V

The *dumb show* presents men marching in battle array. Bugles and all the noise of war are heard.

The Britons are so stirred up by these atrocities that they rise in rebellion, and in spite of the efforts of the nobles to stop them, kill both Gorboduc and Queen Videna.

The country is now without a ruler. The nobles fear that, if the common people continue in revolt, a foreign army will invade the country and set up its own ruler there. When the nobles meet, one Fergus, Duke of Albany, sees a chance to gain power for himself. He raises an army and prepares to assert his claim. The other nobles realize now that there is little hope of picking a king from among themselves without much bloodshed and civil strife.

## 12.  Thomas Kyd: *The Spanish Tragedy*
Popular Renaissance "revenge" tragedy

*Page 78.  The Spanish Tragedy* (c. 1585) is typical of the melodramatic "bloody thrillers" that sent chills up and down the spines of audiences in the "public" theaters of Elizabethan times. Kyd adapts the rather stiff and academic Senecan tragedy to the popular theater. He used the three conventional devices of Roman tragedy, the ghost, the "revenge" motive, and a good deal of philosophizing in the dialogue. But he adds a thousand tricks of staging, calculated to provide a "thrill a minute." By 1634 this popular play had gone through ten printed editions and countless performances.

### The Prologue

In a war between Spain and Portugal, Don Andrea, a Spanish nobleman had been killed by Balthasar, Prince of Portugal. When his soul reached the lower regions, he was forced to await the crossing of the River Styx until his friend, Don Horatio, could perform his burial rites. While waiting he introduces himself to the Spirit of Revenge:

> When this eternal substance of my soul
> Did live imprisoned in my wanton flesh,
> I was a courtier in the Spanish Court.

Finally Pluto sent Andrea's ghost and Revenge back to earth to see Balthasar slain by Andrea's promised bride, Bel-impera.

### Act I

We learn first that the Spanish have decisively defeated the Portuguese and that Balthasar, Prince of Portugal and slayer of the brave Andrea, has been captured in single combat with Horatio, loyal friend of Andrea and son of Hieronimo, the Spanish general. When the army reaches Spain, the royal prisoner is claimed by two captors, Don Horatio and Don Lorenzo, nephew to the king. The king gives the ransom money to Horatio, but places Balthasar in the custody of Lorenzo as a guest until a truce could be arranged with Portugal.

Meanwhile, in Portugal, the villainous Villuppo persuades the viceroy that a loyal courtier, Alexandro, had killed his son. Alexandro is placed in prison, under sentence of death for slaying Balthasar.

And in Spain, Horatio had reported to Bel-impera how her lover Don Andrea had been killed. She plots revenge and plans to use Horatio to carry it out for her. Meantime, Balthasar, seeing Bel-impera's beauty, has fallen in love with her. She is aware of this and bides her time, bestowing little favors upon Horatio, to win him over thoroughly. Horatio, Lorenzo, and Bel-impera seem to be enjoying themselves, and Balthasar is elated that news has come of the peace that is about to be effected between Spain and Portugal.

Taking the part of a *chorus,* the ghost of Andrea is a bit annoyed to see everyone apparently becoming friends. Revenge assures him that all this friendship and love will soon turn to hate.

## Act II

Lorenzo has become a good friend to Balthasar and sympathizes with the young Prince's love for Bel-impera. He suggests that they discover whom the girl loves. A servant reveals that the object of her affections is apparently Horatio. Balthasar is furious that the man who defeated him in battle should also best him in love. He vows revenge. He and Lorenzo overhear the lovers plan a secret meeting in Hieronimo's garden.

Meanwhile, the King of Spain is bent upon marrying his niece, Bel-impera, to Balthasar, the Portuguese prince, as a further move of diplomacy toward a permanent peace with Portugal.

Lorenzo and Balthasar surprise the lovers and seize Horatio. They hang him and stab his dangling body with swords. Bel-impera recognizes the assassins. She is carried away by them as a safeguard that she will not reveal who they are. Horatio's poor father finds the body of his son and both he and his wife go mad. The father dips his handkerchief in his son's blood and swears revenge.

Again, as a *chorus,* the ghost of Andrea wonders why Horatio is killed and not Balthasar. And after all, he is not there to see Bel-impera, his love, become the property of his enemy! Revenge tells him to have a little more patience.

## Act III

In Portugal, Alexandro is saved from death when word arrives that Balthasar is alive and well. Villuppo, the false tale bearer, is executed in his stead.

In Spain, things are a bit more complex. Hieronimo sets out to avenge his son's death. Lorenzo and Balthasar have one servant murder another, who knew too much for their comfort. The murderous servant is caught and is executed without talking. At least, this is what the two plotters think. In reality, he had written a complete confession before he was killed. Hieronimo had gotten his hands on the paper.

The marriage date has been set for Bel-impera and the prince, with or without her consent. Hieronimo, having recovered from his madness, sees the advantage of continuing to be thought insane. He petitions the king for aid in seeking the murderers, but is so erratic and foolish that Lorenzo easily persuades everyone that the old man is harmless and crazy. Things are working out fine for the culprits.

The ghost of Andrea is about at his ghostly wits end. He calls upon Revenge and all the spirits in Hell to do something. Revenge shows him a pantomime in which a nuptial pair are covered in blood. This quiets the anxiety of the ghost for a bit.

## Act IV

Hieronimo has been biding his time and finally his chance came. Because of his reputation for organizing theatrical entertainments, his help is enlisted by the king to entertain the assemblage at the approaching nuptials of Bel-impera and Balthasar. Hieronimo had written a tragedy and he persuades Bel-impera, Lorenzo, and Balthasar to take parts in it. He convinces them that royal tragedy could be played properly only by royal actors.

In the meantime Hieronimo's wife had stabbed herself, grieving still for her son Horatio. The news but whets Hieronimo's desire to bring his plan to a successful conclusion.

That evening the royal party is assembled and the play begins. Bel-impera plays a beautiful Italian girl, wife of a knight (played by Lorenzo), who is captured by a Turkish sultan, played by

Balthasar. The play finally works around to a point where there
is a general stabbing. Everything is so realistic in Hieronimo's
production that the actors really do stab each other with razor-
sharp blades.

The royal assemblage applauds the very realistic performance.
Hieronimo takes the stage and assures the audience that the
bodies lying around are very real indeed. He then presents the
body of his dead son to the audience and hastens off to hang
himself. He is prevented from doing so, but manages to bite
out his own tongue. He begs for a knife to sharpen a pen so that
he can write out a full account of what has happened. When it is
brought, he quickly stabs Lorenzo's father and himself. His is
the eighth death in this *Spanish Tragedy*.

Andrea's ghost announces that he is finally satisfied that his
enemies have been punished. The Spirit of Revenge tells Andrea
that it is time for them to return to the lower regions and that
Andrea could watch there the further torments which would be
visited upon his enemies. For, as Revenge puts it: "I'll there
begin their endless tragedy."

### 13.  Christopher Marlowe: *Tamburlaine the Great*
#### Renaissance epic drama

*Page 80. Tamburlaine,* first presented about 1587, is a study
of a terrible and ungovernable ambition:

> Threatening the world with high astounding terms,
> And scourging kingdoms with his conquering sword.

Marlowe's poetry is the richest in imagery in English drama
before the plays of Shakespeare. This romantic and epic tragedy
is presented in two parts, each of which is a full-length play. The
setting is Asia in the 14th century.

#### Part I, Act I

Mycetes, King of Persia, is beset with troubles, not the least
of which is the devastation being wrought in his realm by the
bandit Scythian robber chief, Tamburlaine. Mycetes sends a
thousand horsemen to suppress:

> Tamburlaine, that sturdy Scythian thief
> That robs merchants of Persepolis,
> And in confines with his lawless train
> Daily commits incivil outrages.

Cosroe, Mycetes' brother, plans to supplant his weak brother as king and sets out to try to take over the troops which have been sent against the bandit chief.

Meanwhile, Tamburlaine has brought into camp an Egyptian princess, Zenocrate. He feels a tender affection for her and begins to speak to her of his ambitions to conquer Asia and make his name a feared one. He is about to demonstrate his love further to her when the Persian army approaches. Tamburlaine here shows his knowledge of psychology, for his foot soldiers are outnumbered two to one by the horsemen of the Persians. He meets the Persian leader, shows him heaps of loot, and persuades him to bring his men over to his side. He draws plans for world conquest and riches.

## Act II

Cosroe sees the wisdom of enlisting Tamburlaine's aid against Mycetes. Tamburlaine agrees and Mycetes is readily conquered. The petty bandit chieftain is now the "Regent of Persia and General Leftenant of the Armies" and is more than ever convinced that he could be a man of destiny and attain crowns for himself:

> Nature that fram'd us of four elements,
> Warring within our breasts for regiment,
> Doth teach us all to have aspiring minds.
> Our souls, whose faculties can comprehend
> The wondrous architecture of the world . . .
> Wills us to wear ourselves and never rest,
> Until we reach the ripest fruit of all,
> That perfect bliss and sole felicity,
> The sweet fruition of an earthly crown.

Tamburlaine immediately puts his ambitious thoughts into execution and soon Cosroe is killed and the Scythian chief is King of Persia.

## Act III

Zenocrate finds herself falling in love with the crude barbarian warrior, despite the warnings of her noble Median advisers.

Bajazeth, the king of the Turks, becomes alarmed at Tamburlaine's advances. He tries to arrange a truce but the ambitious Tamburlaine spurns the offer. The two armies meet while Zenocrate and Zabina, the wife of the Turkish Emperor, hold their husband's respective crowns and await the outcome. Zabina taunts Zenocrate and calls her the "concubine" of Tamburlaine. The Turk is defeated and Zabina becomes the slave woman of Zenocrate.

## Act IV

Tamburlaine's lust for power is turning him to inhuman cruelties. He makes a public display of Bajazeth, by using him as a footstool. The creeping poison of his ambition now causes him to set out to conquer Damascus. Zenocrate's father, the sultan of Egypt, rouses his men to aid the king of Arabia, in an attempt to stem the overwhelming surge of the barbaric armies of Tamburlaine:

> Awake, ye men of Memphis! hear the clang
> Of Scythian trumpets; hear the basilisks
> That, roaring, shake Damascus' turrets down!

Tamburlaine makes merry and visits inhuman cruelties upon his prisoners as he awaits the inevitable fall of the city:

> His spear, his shield, his horse, his armour plumes,
> And jetty feathers menace death and hell.

As the act ends, Tamburlaine gives us a vivid and terrible picture of his insatiable ambition and the hold it has gotten upon all his faculties:

> We mean to travel to th' antarctic pole,
> Conquering the people underneath our feet,
> And be renown'd as never emperors were.

## Act V

Four young virgins are sent out of Damascus to plead for mercy from the conqueror. He sends his horsemen charging over their bodies.

In the next scene, Tamburlaine is seen as a tender lover.

Zenocrate is now torn emotionally between her love for the fierce warrior and her own horror of the cruelty that underlies his driving ambition. Zenocrate sees the noble Bajazeth dash his brains out against his cage, and his wife Zabina go mad and dash herself against the cage until she also dies. She is beset by a tragic conflict of "shame and duty, love and fear."

The king of Arabia is killed and the sultan of Egypt is brought before Tamburlaine. He spares Zenocrate's father but demands that the daughter become his wife. She accepts and they are united as the curtain falls on Part I.

### Part II.

Marlowe calls his second play *The Bloody Conquests of Mighty Tamburlaine* and explains his purpose in showing the further course of Tamburlaine's ambition:

> The general welcomes *Tamburlaine* received,
> When he arrived last upon our stage,
> Hath made our poet pen his Second Part
> Where Death cuts off the progress of his pomp
> And murderous Fate throws all his triumphs down.

### Act I

The Mohammedan leaders of the East unite and pledge faith with the Christian leaders of Europe against the "rogue of Volga":

> For Tamburlaine, the scourge of God, must die.

Tamburlaine now has three sons, two of whom are brave, but the third is peaceful and to Tamburlaine, a coward.

### Act II

The Mohammedan-Christian alliance does not work out. It seems that Segismund of Hungary and his Christian associates do not accept the binding features of an agreement made with infidels. They break their word and seek to gain power over the Turks. The Turks gain the victory, strangely enough calling upon Christ for aid, rather than upon Mohammed.

Zenocrate becomes ill from her grief and torn allegiances.

She dies and Tamburlaine, refusing to part with her even in death, has her body embalmed and carries it with him wherever he goes. He burns the town in which she died.

## Act III

Callapine, son of Bajazeth, gathers aid from the surrounding countries and prepares to try to stop the conqueror. Tamburlaine attempts to train his sons to the hardships of war by cutting himself and forcing them to bathe their hands in their father's blood. His third son, Calyphus, refuses to have anything to do with war. The opposing armies meet at Aleppo.

## Act IV

Tamburlaine is victorious once more. Calyphus stays in his tent during the battle. Tamburlaine returns from the battlefield and stabs the "effeminate brat." Tamburlaine shows his lack of conscience and beastly primitive qualities at every point during this act. He has captive concubines bury his son and then gives them to his soldiers for their pleasure. He has captive kings hitched to his chariot and beats them unmercifully as they drag him to Babylon.

## Act V

When Babylon is defeated, the lustful Tamburlaine lays waste to the city, permitting his most beastly soldiers to commit every manner of atrocious acts upon its inhabitants. He finally sentences all the remaining citizens to be drowned. He causes all copies of the Koran and evidences of the Moslem religion to be destroyed and burned. He is now completely twisted in his personality and has only one thin sentiment left in his being—his undying affection for the dead Zenocrate.

The deterioration of the mighty barbarian is now practically complete. He suddenly falls ill and is about to die. His mind does not falter in his driving ambition, however. He plans further conquests for his sons. As his life seeps away, Callapine is readied for another attack. Tamburlaine only has enough strength left to hurl defiance in the direction of the approaching enemies. He has his beloved Zenocrate's coffin brought in and dies, bending over it.

## 14. William Shakespeare: *As You Like It*
A romantic pastoral comedy

*Page 89. As You Like It* (c. 1600) is one of Shakespeare's most pleasant and fanciful romances. It is a superb example of the lightness and carefree abandon with which the great dramatist could write. It contains some of the loveliest and most quotable of Shakespearean verse. It aims at no serious purpose except to provide an escape from thinking, a delightful counteraction to worries. The story is laid in the Forest of Arden, in medieval France, during the Middle Ages.

### Act I

Frederick had deposed his elder brother, the Duke of a certain French province, and had caused him to flee for his life into the Forest of Arden. The old duke's beautiful daughter, Rosalind, had remained behind at court as a companion to Celia, Frederick's daughter. Frederick did not approve of this arrangement but Celia insisted that she could not be separated from the gentle Rosalind.

Duke Frederick especially hated young Orlando, the son of an old and loyal supporter of Rosalind's father, the rightful Duke. Orlando was also a special object of hatred for his older brother, Oliver, who wished to see the youth killed so that he might gain the young lad's inheritance.

The Duke suggested that the girls would be amused at a wrestling match between his brawny court wrestler, Charles, and the slender Orlando. It is love at first sight between Rosalind and Orlando. Orlando is determined that the match shall proceed. The false Duke and Oliver persuade the mighty Charles to try to crush the slender Orlando. Under the inspiration of Rosalind's eyes, however, the very nimble Orlando defeats Charles.

When Duke Frederick sees Rosalind give the youth a chain from about her neck, he realizes that she loves the lad. He becomes angry and orders Rosalind banished from the court. Celia resolves to flee into the forest with her dear cousin, where they will seek the old duke. Rosalind will go in the garb of a youth. The faithful court jester, Touchstone, is going with them.

## Act II

Orlando discovers from a courtier that a plot is afoot to do away with him. His father's old servant Adam accompanies him as they flee into the forest.

Rosalind, as Ganymede, and Celia, as the youth's sister, Aliena, enter the forest and purchase a shepherd's hut, sheep, and grazing land from some peasants.

The old duke had gathered about him quite a following and had set up his court under the green trees of Arden Forest. He fancies himself to be like "old Robin Hood of England" with his merry band. He entertains himself royally, and as the audience comes upon him, is enjoying the gloomy philosophy of the melancholy Jacques, who believes that:

> All the world's a stage,
> And all the men and women merely players;
> They have their exits and their entrances;
> And one man in his time plays many parts, . . .

Amiens is a sprightly follower of the old duke, who constantly warbles such ditties as:

> Under the greenwood tree,
> Who loves to lie with me,
> And tune his merry note,
> Unto the sweet bird's throat,
> Come hither, come hither, come hither;
> Here shall he see
> No enemy,
> But winter and rough weather.

Orlando comes upon the supposed band of outlaws and demands food at sword point. The old duke welcomes him and is overjoyed when he finds that Orlando is an old friend's son.

## Act III

Duke Frederick, meanwhile, has told Oliver that his younger brother must be found. The older brother sets out to find Orlando.

At the same time, a delightful and very pastoral confusion

of identities is taking place in the forest glades. Orlando writes verses of love upon the trees, thinking all the time of Rosalind:

> O Rosalind! these trees shall be my books,
> And in their barks my thoughts I'll character,
> That every eye which in this forest looks
> Shall see thy virtue witness'd everywhere . . .

Rosalind is the first to see them and knows that Orlando loves her. But when he comes upon the girls, they depend upon their disguises and tease him about his lovesickness. Rosalind proposes that he pretend that "Ganymede" is Rosalind and make love to "him" daily at his cottage. Orlando agrees to go along with the idea.

The jester Touchstone also falls in love with Audrey, a rude herder of goats, against his better judgment, "I would the gods had made thee poetical." Also Phebe, a shepherd maid, has fallen in love with the supposed youth, Ganymede:

> Who ever lov'd that lov'd not at first sight?

## Act IV

Orlando comes for his first lesson from "Ganymede" on how to fall out of love. The saucy Rosalind instructs him, while dying inside of desire to tell him who she really is and enjoy his love: "Men have died from time to time, and worms have eaten them, but not for love." She tells him to beware of love and marriage: "Men are April when they woo, December when they wed; maids are May when they are maids, but the sky changes when they are wives."

On passing through the forest, Orlando sees a man sleeping under a tree. It is his brother, with a snake coiled around his neck, and nearby is a lioness crouching within a few feet of the sleeper. Orlando saves his evil brother. Oliver regrets his past deeds and the two brothers become reconciled. Orlando is wounded and Oliver helps him to the glen where the Duke is resting with his merry group.

Oliver takes a handkerchief, soaked in Orlando's blood, and seeks out "Ganymede" to report that Orlando is too weak to visit the cottage that day. Rosalind, at the sight of the bloody handkerchief, promptly faints. Celia (as Aliena) and Oliver begin to fall in love as they revive Rosalind (Ganymede).

## Act V

Oliver pours out his love for the supposed Aliena to his brother as soon as they meet and Orlando swears they will arrange for a wedding ceremony immediately. Rosalind, although she was in a dead faint at the time, seems very clear as to how the two had come to love: ". . . for your brother and my sister no sooner met, but they looked; no sooner looked, but they loved; no sooner loved, but they sighed; no sooner sighed but they asked one another the reason; no sooner knew the reason, but they sought the remedy."

The supposed Ganymede teases Orlando by telling him that if Rosalind can be coaxed into the forest, another marriage can take place immediately. Phebe proposes that Ganymede marry her and the teasing Rosalind tells her: "I will marry you, if ever I marry woman, and I'll be married tomorrow." Phebe finally promises to marry the shepherd Silvius if she cannot have Ganymede. Touchstone continues his romance with Audrey, while the melancholy Jacques remarks about them: "Here comes a pair of very strange beasts, which in all tongues are called fools."

The identities are all straightened out and four marriages take place with great rejoicing in the Forest of Arden, as all the assemblage sing right merrily:

> Wedding is great Juno's crown;
>   Oh blessed bond of board and bed!
> 'Tis Hymen peoples every town;
>   High wedlock then, be honoured;
> Honour, high honour and renown,
> To Hymen, god of every town!

Good news comes to the old duke. Frederick has been converted by a hermit and has become a monk, restoring to his brother all of his rightful possessions.

### 15.  William Shakespeare: An Historical Cycle
(Summaries of *Richard II, Henry IV,* and

*Henry V*—historical drama)

*Page 89.* This cycle of historical plays, covering the rulers of England from 1377 to 1422, includes the best in Shakespearean historical drama. These plays were written between 1593 and

1597. His *Richard II* is a masterpiece of historical tragedy. The two parts of his *Henry IV* are the most interesting of his chronicle plays in that they present for us his immortal comic character, Sir John Falstaff. *Henry V* presents Shakespeare's concept of the ideal English King.

## *Richard II*

Richard is called upon to settle a dispute between Henry Bolinbroke and Thomas Mowbray. Bolinbroke accuses Mowbray of mismanaging state money and Mowbray retaliates by accusing Bolinbroke of being implicated in the death of the Duke of Gloucester. Richard finally banishes both men from the country.

Old John of Gaunt, Richard's uncle and Bolinbroke's father, is dying. He sends for Richard and accuses him of extravagance, waste, and of playing favorites in his reign. Richard, angry, seizes the estates of the old man immediately he is dead, estates which are rightfully the patrimony of Bolinbroke.

Meanwhile, many nobles are deserting Richard and waiting eagerly for Bolinbroke to return from France to lead them. Bolinbroke enters the country and wins battle after battle from the king's forces. Richard is finally captured and sentenced to the Tower.

Richard is made to show his weak will, his tendency to be swayed by favorites, and his selfish extravagance throughout the campaign. In the face of defeat, he gives way to despair and self-pity.

Bolinbroke finally decides to mount the throne as Henry IV. One of Henry's courtiers, having overheard the king express a desire that Richard be put out of the way, enters the prison and kills Richard. Henry pretends to be entirely innocent of any complicity in the crime and vows to make a crusade to the Holy Land to atone for the death of his cousin.

## *Henry IV* (two parts)

The historical events of the two parts of Henry IV are rather drab repetitions of plots and counterplots, struggles for power and favor among the factions for and against the king. Henry IV manages to hold on to the throne and pass it to his son, who proves to be a strong king.

The real interest to the reader and the playgoer in these two plays is Sir John Falstaff, Shakespeare's greatest humorous personality. Falstaff is a liar and a thief, but lovable in both capacities. He is fat and lazy. He is one of the most energetic men to be found. He is one of the stage's greatest enigmas. He is both harmless and wicked; he is both weak and strong. He is a coward, but really brave. He is a knave and a gentleman. In short, he has no admirable qualities, but we admire and love him as a fictional creation. In Henry IV, Shakespeare has successfully combined low comedy and drab history and has raised the combination, by means of his exquisite blank verse, to a high level of dramatic production.

Falstaff and his equally debauched cohorts have a great deal of influence on the young Prince Henry, son of Bolinbroke. Throughout the play the father is worried and grieved at his son's antics, and especially his constant association with low companions.

We watch the character of the prince develop and wonder if his companions are of a worse influence upon a growing lad than would be the lords, conniving and conspiring, that surround his father. Aside from the comedy, Shakespeare is showing that the noble qualities of the prince plus the democracy of his associations are slowly molding a harmonious character, a future king of England who will be democratic and balanced in judgment.

Falstaff's wit is sharp and contagious. As he himself says: "I am not only witty in myself but the cause that wit is in other men." His concepts are both original and earthy:

> Honour pricks me on. Yea, but how if honour prick me off when I come on,—how then? Can honour set to a leg? no: or an arm? no: or take away the grief of a wound? no. Honour hath no skill in surgery, then? no. What is honour? a word. What is in that word honour; what is that honour? air. A trim reckoning! Who hath it? he that died o' Wednesday. Doth he feel it? no. Doth he hear it? no. It is insensible, then? yes, to the dead. But will it not live with the living? no. Why? detraction will not suffer it. Therefore I'll none of it. Honour is a mere scutcheon. And so ends my catechism.

## Henry V

In *Henry V*, Shakespeare has glorified the royalty of England for Englishmen in powerful verse. Henry V is one of the most revered of English sovereigns of all time. Shakespeare built his character for rule in *Henry IV,* showing his balanced judgment and his democracy. Now Shakepeare shows us the king, the epitome of English royalty. Shakespeare defines the relationship of subject and king in words from the mouth of Henry: "Every subject's duty is the king's; but every subject's soul is his own."

Shakespeare strives throughout the play to give the king a sense of humility and to develop a character that is both human and conscious of royal obligations:

> . . . if it be a sin to covet honour,
> I am the most offending soul alive.
>
> . . . . . .
>
> And what have kings that privates have not too,
> Save ceremony—save general ceremony?
>
> . . . . . .
>
> In peace there's nothing so becomes a man
> As modest stillness and humility:
> But when the blast of war blows in our ears,
> Then initiate the action of a tiger;
>
> . . . . . .
>
> There is some soul of goodness in things evil,
> Would men obligingly distil it out;

The basic question developed in the play is Henry's right to rule France. Henry presses his demands as against Charles' claim to hereditary right. Henry decides to press his claim by war. England invades France, and after winning minor battles, comes to the decisive engagement at Agincourt.

Henry's character is brought out during the phases of the development of the action. He wanders among the common soldiers, seeking advice and hearing complaints. He is ever shown to be stern, but just and humane.

The English win, a peace is arranged, and Henry sues for the hand of Katherine, the lively daughter of the French King. Readers of Act V, Scene 2, will be treated to a love scene in which Henry speaks little French and Kate less English, but love provides them with a universal language which brings about an understanding that Katherine is to become England's queen. This is one of the most delicious scenes in Shakespeare:

*K. Henry:* Then I will kiss your lips, Kate.
*Katherine:* Les dames et demoiselles pour être baisées

> devant leur noces, il n'est pas le coutume de
> France.
>
> *K. Henry:* Madam, my interpreter, what says she?
>
> *Alice:* Dat is not be de fashion pour les ladies of
> France—I cannot tell vat is baiser en Anglish.
>
> *K. Henry:* To kiss.
>
> *Alice:* Your majesty entendre bettre que moi.
>
> *K. Henry:* It is not the fashion for the maids in France to
> kiss before they are married, would she say?
>
> *Alice:* Oui, vraiment.
>
> *K. Henry:* O Kate, nice customs court'sy to great kings.
> Dear Kate, you and I cannot be confined within
> the weak list of a country's fashion: we are the
> makers of manners, Kate; and the liberty that
> follows our places stops the mouth of all find-
> faults—as I will do yours for upholding the nice
> fashion of your country in denying me a kiss:
> therefore, patiently and yielding. (He kisses
> her.)

Henry is England, and even in love, he recalls the English cause:

> *Katherine:* Is it possible dat I should love de enemy of
> France?
>
> *K. Henry:* No; it is not possible you should love the enemy
> of France, Kate: but in loving me you should
> love the friend of France; for I love France so
> well that I will not part with a village of it; I
> will have it all mine: and, Kate, when France
> is mine and I am yours, then yours is France
> and you are mine.

### 16.    William Shakespeare: *Romeo and Juliet*
#### Romantic tragedy of love

*Page 90.* Shakespeare's first attempt at tragedy (around 1594) has come to be regarded as one of the world's most tender dramas. His poetry, the fire of youthful passion, and the deeper tones of tragic fate have been woven, with a sure technique, into a powerful and intense story of innocent lovers, caught up in a whirlpool of hate and violence and drawn on to their deaths, powerless to resist. *Romeo and Juliet* is a simple story that the genius of Shakespeare has raised to the level of mature drama, with its fine psychological delineation of character, its keen philosophical treatment of life, and its sympathetic and universally appealing poetic musicality.

## Act I

Two famous families of Verona, in 15th century Italy, are the Montagues and the Capulets. These two noble families have been locked in a deadly feud for many years and men of both factions have fought and died as a result of the stubborn will of both sides to keep the angry fires of hatred burning.

As the play opens a brawl takes place in a Verona public street between servants of the two noble houses. The Prince of Verona orders that this public brawling must cease, under penalty of death.

Young Romeo, a Montague, fancies himself in love with Rosaline and hears that she will be present at a masked ball being given in the Capulet house. He determines to attend and takes his friend Mercutio with him.

Meanwhile, in the Capulet palace, arrangements have been made to marry the young Juliet to Count Paris. The obedient girl promises to follow her father's orders.

At the ball, Romeo quickly forgets his infatuation for the haughty Rosaline when he sees Juliet. Smitten by her beauty he approaches her and they converse. Finally he kisses her and both are overcome with a mutual passion. Young Tybalt, nephew of Lady Capulet, recognizes Romeo and is intent upon violence until old Capulet restrains him. He reluctantly lets Romeo and his friend depart, but swears he will avenge the insult that their presence has brought upon the Capulet house.

Juliet, now in love with this charming stranger, learns from her nurse that her suddenly inspired passion is centered upon Romeo, a Montague:

> My only love sprung from my only hate!
> Too early seen unknown, and known too late!

## Act II

Romeo is determined to see this sweet enemy again and climbs into the Capulet garden. Juliet is upon her balcony murmuring the name of her love and wishing that it were another:

> O be some other name!
> What's in a name? that which we call a rose,
> By any other name would smell as sweet;

Romeo speaks to her and attempts to quiet her fears. Soon they confess their love and Juliet bids him not be fickle but match her love for him by one as true and faithful:

> *Juliet:*  O, swear not by the moon, the inconstant moon,
> That monthly changes in her circled orb,
> Lest that thy love prove likewise variable.
> *Romeo:* What shall I swear by?
> *Juliet:*  Do not swear at all;
> Or, if thou wilt, swear by thy gracious se!f,
> Which is the god of my idolatry,
> And I'll believe thee.

The lovers agree to meet again on the morrow. Romeo will arrange with Friar Laurence to marry them; then come what may. Juliet can hardly bear to see him go:

> Good-night, good-night! parting is such sweet sorrow
> That I shall say good-night till it be morrow.

Friar Laurence is skeptical as to the wisdom of this secret affair but resolves to help the lovers. With Juliet's nurse acting as intermediary, the lovers meet at the holy man's cell to be married.

### Act III

Shortly after the marriage takes place, Tybalt kills Mercutio in a Verona street, after many taunts have been hurled back and forth by the followers of both the warring houses. Romeo is torn between thoughts of his bride and loyalty to his friend. As Tybalt returns through the street, Romeo accosts him and kills him in the duel that follows. The Prince orders Romeo banished from Verona. Friar Laurence consoles him and bids him go to Mantua and he will communicate any news of Juliet to him by messenger.

Meanwhile, old Capulet is resolved to marry Juliet to Paris in three days.

Juliet sends her nurse to the good Friar's cell to bring Romeo secretly into her chamber that night. At dawn the lovers part and Romeo sets out for Mantua.

Capulet bids Juliet prepare for her wedding with Paris. In sorrow, she implores her nurse to give her advice. The pica-resque old nurse suggests that she should go ahead and marry Paris, since an absent lover is as good as dead. Juliet, in des-peration, goes to plead with Friar Laurence to find a solution for her woes.

## Act IV

The Friar gives Juliet a potion to take on the night before her wedding. Its effects will be to give her the appearance of death. Meanwhile, he will send for Romeo to come to the Capulet tomb, where Juliet will be placed. As soon as the effects of the drug wear off, the lovers can flee to Mantua.

Juliet suddenly becomes very obedient to her father's wishes and the wedding date is moved forward a day. The evening before the ceremony was to take place, Juliet swallowed the potion and immediately took on the appearance of death. After the first shock of consternation, the Capulets prepare to place Juliet in the family tomb.

## Act V

Friar Laurence has written to Romeo in Mantua, but a quar-antine restriction has caused the messenger to fail to reach Romeo. At about this time, a retainer of Romeo gives him the report that Juliet is dead. Romeo vows to take poison and ob-tains a potion and hastens to view his beloved once more before taking it.

In the churchyard Romeo meets Paris and kills him. He drags the body of Paris into the Capulet's tomb and bends over the lifeless Juliet:

> Eyes, look your last!
> Arms, take your last embrace! and lips, O you
> The doors of breath, seal with a righteous kiss
> A dateless bargain to engrossing death!

He drinks the poison and dies as the frantic Friar Laurence hastens into the tomb to see if Juliet has awakened from her deathlike sleep. The Friar hears someone walking about the tomb and retires.

At this moment Juliet is becoming conscious. She discovers the bodies of Paris and Romeo. She takes Romeo's dagger and stabs herself, as a watchman enters.

Soon the prince, the Capulets, and the Montagues assemble in the tomb. Over the bodies of the ill-starred lovers the family feud is ended:

> *Montague:*       . . . I will raise her statue in pure gold;
> That while Verona by that name is known,
> There shall no figure at such rate be set
> As that of true and faithful Juliet.
> *Capulet:*    As rich shall Romeo by his lady lie;
> Poor sacrifices of our enmity!

## 17.  William Shakespeare: *The Merchant of Venice*
### Serious comedy of character

*Page 90.* In 1596, Shakespeare produced his first masterful character—Shylock. At the same time, the poet wove around his central figure a completely harmonious series of episodes and subplots that make this one of the best integrated and entertaining serious comedies ever written. The play has tragic implications but never becomes pure tragedy. It is serious, or tragicomedy. Shylock represents commerce of the old school of ethical practice and is convinced that hard practice is just; Antonio, the merchant of Venice, represents a more humane ethic. And, though Shylock plays the villain, he is dealt with sympathetically by the poet. The noble and wise Portia is another of the author's strong character creations. She represents here a modern woman, tempering the old world "eye for an eye" justice with a humane mercy. In this play Shakespeare makes use of three oriental themes in his episodes of the pound of flesh, the rings, and the caskets. In addition to being good entertainment, this comedy is a study in fine character development and a serious treatment of a stern, unbending ethic versus a reasonable and humane one. It is also a study in friendship, loyalty, and love.

### Act I

Bassanio prevails upon his friend, the merchant Antonio, to lend him a rather large sum of money. Bassanio desires to win the hand of Portia, a wealthy and virtuous young woman of

Belmont, and he needs money to conduct his wooing properly. Antonio has all of his ready cash tied up in cargoes on the high seas but is willing to try to borrow the money for his friend.

In Belmont, Portia discusses her suitors with her maid, Nerissa. It seems that her father's will has imposed a rather strange method by which she is to select a husband. He has left her three caskets—of gold, of silver, and of lead. Each suitor must choose a casket. If he picks the correct one, Portia will be his. Portia mentally rejects her suitors one by one until she reaches the name of Bassanio, whom she obviously prefers.

Meanwhile, Antonio has gone to the Jewish moneylender, Shylock, to obtain the loan for his friend. Shylock hates Antonio for his ethical business practice and for his berating of Shylock himself in the public marts. He sees his chance to even scores: "I will feed fat the ancient grudge I bear him." He agrees to make the loan and jestingly suggests that he be permitted to take a pound of Antonio's flesh if the loan is not repaid at the end of the agreed period of time. Antonio, despite the fears of Bassanio, jokingly agrees and the contract is drawn up.

## Act II

Jessica, Shylock's beautiful daughter, is planning to elope with Lorenzo, Bassanio's very good friend. While Bassanio entertains Shylock, his friend and the Jewess flee Shylock's house, taking a goodly casket of jewels with them.

At about the same time, two suitors are trying their luck at winning the hand of the fair and wise Portia. The Prince of Morocco chooses the golden casket and learns:

All that glitters is not gold.

The Prince of Aragon chooses the silver casket and learns that he too has failed.

Antonio learns that his ships have been lost in a storm.

## Act III

Shylock is furious at his daughter's elopement and becomes more bitter toward Antonio, for he believes that the merchant has helped Lorenzo spirit her away:

. . . I am a Jew! Hath not a Jew eyes? hath not a Jew hands, organs, dimensions, senses, affections, passions? fed with the same food, hurt with the same weapons, subject to the same diseases, healed by the same means, warmed and cooled by the same winter and summer as a Christian is? If you prick us, do we not bleed? If you tickle us, do we not laugh? if you poison us, do we not die? and if you wrong us, shall we not revenge? If we are like you in the rest, we will resemble you in that. If a Jew wrong a Christian, what is his humility? revenge. If a Christian wrongs a Jew, what should his sufferance be by Christian example? why, revenge. The villany you teach me I will execute; and it shall go hard but I will better the instruction.

Bassanio enters the lottery and, after careful consideration, picks the casket of lead and reads the scroll which bids him:

> Turn you where your lady is
> And claim her with a loving kiss.

Bassanio receives a ring from his love. Gratiano, his friend who is in love with Portia's maid, Nerissa, also receives a ring from her. The men are sworn never to part with the rings so long as they are faithful to their love. Their joy is short-lived as Bassanio soon receives a message from Antonio to the effect that the merchant ships are lost and he must pay the forfeit. Portia has the double wedding ceremony take place immediately and sends Bassanio to Venice with many times the amount of Antonio's debt to try to placate the grasping Shylock. The Jew refuses all pleas and offers and demands his pound of flesh from Antonio.

Jessica and Lorenzo have come to Belmont. Portia and Nerissa leave them in charge of the household while they rush off to consult with a cousin of Portia, who is a famous lawyer.

### Act IV

The Duke of Venice holds court and Shylock appears to make demand of payment on his contract. He refuses to budge from his demand of a pound of flesh, to be taken nearest Antonio's heart. The Duke delays the proceedings, pending the arrival of the famous Dr. Bellario. Soon a letter arrives in which the noted jurist states that he is sending a very wise young lawyer in his stead, to defend Antonio. The young doctor of laws, is, of course, Portia, dressed in the proper legal robes and disguised. Nerissa is in the disguise of a young clerk.

Portia then addresses her famous plea for mercy to the Jew:

> The quality of mercy is not strain'd;
> It droppeth as the gentle rain from heaven
> Upon the place beneath: it is twice bless'd;
> It blesseth him that gives and him that takes:
> 'Tis mightiest in the mightiest; it becomes
> The throned monarch better than his crown;
> His sceptre shows the force of temporal power,
> The attribute to awe and majesty,
> Wherein doth sit the dread and fear of kings;
> But mercy is above his scepter'd sway,
> It is enthroned in the heart of kings,
> It is an attribute to God himself;
> An earthly power doth then show like God's
> When mercy seasons justice . . .

Shylock demands that the contract be fulfilled to the letter. Portia takes the contract and examines it. After some deliberation, she states that Shylock has an airtight case and is to be allowed to cut from Antonio the pound of flesh. As Shylock gloats, Portia calmly reminds him:

> Tarry a little; there is something else.
> This bond doth give thee here no jot of blood;

Shylock admits defeat but is pressed to plead for mercy himself as he is reminded that a law of Venice requires forfeiture of all wealth and property of a citizen who plots against the life of another. The duke generously allows Shylock to retain half of his wealth, provided that the other half goes to Antonio and that Shylock's will provide that Lorenzo and Jessica be his heirs upon his death. A further stipulation is that Shylock must become a Christian!

Bassanio offers the supposed lawyers payment but all their demands are confined to the two rings Bassanio and Gratiano are wearing. After some hesitation, the men part with the rings.

## Act V

All is merriment at Belmont. Lorenzo and Jessica are enjoying a blissful honeymoon at Portia's palace. Sounds of music and brightly lighted halls greet the returning Portia and Nerissa:

> How far that little candle throws his beams!
> So shines a good deed in a naughty world.

Then follows the delightful scene where Portia and Nerissa demand of their new husbands to see the rings they had given to them when they departed to attend Antonio's trial. After the husbands have exhausted all their excuses, only to be met with mock doubt and jesting taunts and threats by their wives, they are told the truth. Antonio joins in the general merriment as he hears that his ships are safely in port after weathering the storms. The newlyweds retire, with Bassanio and Gratiano swearing to answer faithfully all demands made upon them by the very legal-minded pair of ladies whom they have married.

## 18. William Shakespeare: *Julius Caesar*
### A Roman tragedy

*Page 91.* Written about 1598, this is the most famous of Shakespeare's historical plays. His material is largely derived from Plutarch's *Lives* and his focus of interest is upon Caesar's assassination in 44 B.C. and upon the fate of the chief conspirator in that act, Marcus Brutus. Brutus emerges as the noblest character in this play. Shakespeare's language is simple eloquence at its best.

### Acts I and II

Caesar has just returned victorious from the wars and the populace of Rome has shown that his popularity is such that he could sway the mob in any direction he saw fit. A group of nobles fear his growing power and ambition. As Cassius expressed it:

> . . . he doth bestride the narrow world
> Like a Colossus; and we petty men
> Walk under his huge legs and peep about.

The cautious Brutus is hard to persuade, but gradually, watching Caesar parade about to receive the adulation of the crowd, even he comes to desire Caesar's death. Brutus, popular and respected in Rome, comes to see Caesar as an enemy to the common good:

> . . . 'tis a common proof
> That lowliness is young ambition's ladder,
> Whereto the climber-upward turns his face;

> But when he once attains the utmost round,
> He then unto the ladder turns his back,
> Looks in the clouds, scorning the base degrees
> By which he did ascend.

Many omens have been noted, predicting that dire events are about to take place. A soothsayer has warned Caesar to beware the Ides of March. Strange lights have been seen in the sky and ghosts, walking about the streets at night. Caesar's wife, Calphurnia, has cried out in her sleep that her husband is to be murdered. She tries to persuade him not to go to the Senate, but Caesar at first appears brave:

> Cowards die many times before their deaths;
> The valiant never taste of death but once.
> Of all the wonders that I yet have heard,
> It seems to be most strange that men should fear;
> Seeing that death, a necessary end,
> Will come when it will come.

More portents of disaster are brought to his ears and he decides not to go that day. Decius Brutus, one of the conspirators, flatters him, predicting that he will be offered a crown. This causes him to hasten toward the Capitol.

### Act III

In the Senate chamber the conspirators gather around Caesar to present him with a petition. They then fall upon him and stab him various times. When he turns face to face with Marcus Brutus, who stabs him, he utters his famous, *"Et tu, Brute?"* and dies.

Young Mark Antony, a friend of Caesar, pretends to sympathize with the conspirators, but begs to be allowed to speak a funeral oration over Caesar. Brutus can see little harm in this, as he intends to speak first and persuade the populace that he and his companions acted for freedom and liberty for Rome. He only cautions Antony to speak no ill of the conspirators. Antony promises.

In the most famous scene of the play, Brutus convinces the multitude that the assassins but acted in the common cause:

> Not that I loved Caesar less, but that I loved
> Rome more.

When Antony bears in the body of Caesar, the people are reluctant to listen to him, but Brutus persuades them that Antony will but confirm what he has already told them.

Antony had prepared his speech well and gradually, using his eloquent forcefulness and knowledge of mob psychology, he sways the crowd to his will:

> Friends, Romans, countrymen, lend me your ears;
> I come to bury Caesar, not to praise him,
> The evil that men do lives after them;
> The good is oft interred with their bones;
> So let it be with Caesar . . .
> He was my friend, faithful and just to me:
> But Brutus says he was ambitious;
> And Brutus is an honourable man.
> He hath brought many captives home to Rome,
> Whose ransoms did the general coffers fill:
> Did this in Caesar seem ambitious?
> When that the poor have cried, Caesar hath wept;
> Ambition should be made of sterner stuff.
> Yet Brutus says he was ambitious;
> And Brutus is an honourable man.
> You all did see that on the Lupercal
> I thrice presented him with a kingly crown,
> And he did thrice refuse: was this ambition?

Once Antony has the crowd's ear, he continues to pound home his ironical barbs directed at the conspirators, and his tender convincing arguments that Caesar was the people's friend. He shows them Caesar's will, where the general had left his estates to the people. He points out Caesar's wounds to them:

> For Brutus, as you know, was Caesar's angel;
> Judge, O you gods, how dearly Caesar loved him!
> This was the most unkindest cut of all;
> For when the noble Caesar saw him stab,
> Ingratitude, more strong than traitors' arms,
> Quite vanquish'd him: then burst his mighty heart . . .

The Roman multitude is now aroused to a fever pitch of hatred. Cassius and Brutus flee Rome.

### Acts IV and V

Brutus now becomes the tragic figure in Shakespeare's play. He had acted from what he thought were noble motives and now he must meet adversity without flinching. Antony and young Octavius Caesar are allied against the forces supporting Brutus and Cassius. Brutus receives word that his wife has died. He and Cassius constantly quarrel over minor details of the campaign. Brutus realizes that the only course for him is to meet the consequences of his tragic error with equanimity:

> There is a tide in the affairs of men
> Which, taken at the flood, leads on to fortune;
> Omitted, all the voyage of their life
> Is bound in shallows and in miseries.

Shortly afterward, Brutus is confronted with Caesar's ghost who vows to meet him at Philippi.

On the plains of Philippi the victory is a foregone conclusion. The armies of Octavius and Antony overwhelm those of the conspirators and Cassius and Brutus are compelled to commit suicide to avoid being captured. Antony, who realizes the noble personal motives of Brutus in the entire affair, delivers the speech which rounds out the character of Brutus:

> All the conspirators, save only he,
> Did that they did in envy of great Caesar;
> He only, in a general honest thought,
> And common good to all, made one of them.

## 19. William Shakespeare: *Hamlet, Prince of Denmark*
### Greatest drama of tragedy in modern world literature

*Page 92.* Hamlet, written about 1601, is Shakespeare's greatest play and his thesis here is as broad as mankind. *Hamlet* is both drama and penetrating philosophy. Technically, it is a perfectly worked masterpiece of staging, and poetically, its lines are examples of superb English expression.

### *The tragic fault in Hamlet*

Hamlet presents us with a personality in conflict with himself. In its broadest interpretation, Hamlet's tragic fault is not so much a weakness of will as it is a struggle of the individual temperament with its environment. Hamlet's mind is a modern questioning mind; he does not have all the answers and he knows it. His personal tragedy is that he knows what to do, but does not act. He doubts and hesitates, and he is lost. His troubled hesitancy springs from his very modern exercise of reasoning power. Hamlet cannot control his mind; he cannot act according to his convictions, and yet remain indifferent to consequences. He preconsiders those consequences and sinks deeper into a state of doubt that his convictions are sound:

> . . . there is nothing either
> good or bad, but thinking makes it so.

Thus Hamlet's problem is the problem of every modern man, face to face with his environment, with only his faulty reason to fight it with. Shakespeare poses the question to a modern reasoning mankind with his Hamlet: Should not man gain control over his own doubts and act in accordance with his convictions, indifferent to fate and whatever consequences may result? Is not his salvation his own, with only his capacity to reason as a guide to his actions? Hamlet reasoned out his problem and willed a solution, but his very capacity to bring this about also caused him to be weak and to fail—and to bring tragedy to himself and to those about him, friends and foes.

### Act I

Hamlet, the young Prince of Denmark, is a sensitive lad, deeply shocked at the death of his beloved father, who presumedly had been stung by a serpent. He is shocked further when his mother marries his father's brother, a man whom he detests, scarcely a month after the father's death. Hamlet, touched in the depths of his nature, contemplates suicide.

Following reports from faithful retainers that his father's ghost is appearing at night on the battlements of the castle, Hamlet maintains a vigil and learns from the ghost that the report of the serpent sting is false. His brother had murdered the king by pouring poison in his ear while he slept in the garden. The ghost charged Hamlet with the task of avenging him. Hamlet is reluctant to face the duty with which he has been charged:

> The time is out of joint:—O cursed spite,
> That ever I was born to set it right!

While Hamlet faces his personal problem, the scene has shifted to old Polonius, a courtier, and his children, Laertes and

Ophelia. Laertes, about to depart for France, tells Ophelia that she should not continue to meet Hamlet privately as he fears for her virtue. She suggests that her brother had better look to his own behavior before he considers himself qualified to preach to others:

> Do not as some ungracious pastors do.
> Show me the steep and thorny way to heaven;
> Whilst like a puff'd and reckless libertine,
> Himself the primrose path of dalliance treads,
> And recks not his own read.

After giving his son excellent fatherly advice to bear in mind while he is among strangers, Polonius also warns Ophelia not to be intimate with Hamlet.

## Act II

Hamlet has deliberately feigned madness in order to draw others into expressing themselves before him. He has warned his friends to expect queer actions from him. Gradually, as the act develops, Hamlet begins to catch some of the spirit of his pretended insanity. He becomes more and more melancholy and begins to suspect everyone. His resolution becomes weaker.

Old Polonius consults the king about what he suspects is lovesickness in Hamlet. He fears for Ophelia's honour. Claudius, the king, in a struggle with his own conscience, wonders if Hamlet is in reality mad or simply pretending. Fearing that the prince may cause him trouble, he sets Rosencrantz and Guildenstern to watch Hamlet and to report to him. Hamlet succeeds in playing his part of madman and convinces the two spies, who presumedly are his friends, that he is indeed deranged. He also writes fiery love notes and speaks in riddles to both Ophelia and to her father.

At about this time a wandering company of players comes to Elsinore and a plan slowly crystallizes in Hamlet's mind. The somewhat childlike old Polonius is dancing with joy to think of the entertainment to be provided by the players. His speech in praise of the players gives us a picture of the variety of production available to audiences in Elizabethan times:

> The best actors in the world, either for tragedy, comedy, history, pastoral, pastoral-comical, historical-pastoral, tragical-

historical, tragical-comical-historical-pastoral, scene indivisible,
or poem unlimited: Seneca cannot be too heavy nor Plautus too
light. For the law of writ and liberty, these are the only men.

Hamlet spends some time with the players and resolves to
rehearse them on some additional scenes to fit into their regular
production, which will reproduce the garden scene, representing
the real setting in which his father died:

> . . . the play's the thing
> Wherein I'll catch the conscience of the king.

## Act III

Hamlet continues to meditate suicide as a solution for his
personal tribulation:

> To be or not to be, that is the question:
> Whether 'tis nobler in the mind to suffer
> The slings and arrows of outrageous fortune,
> Or to take up arms against a sea of troubles,
> And by opposing end them? To die, to sleep,
> No more; and by a sleep to say we end
> The heart-ache and the thousand natural shocks
> That flesh is heir to, 'tis a consummation
> Devoutly to be wish'd. To die, to sleep;
> To sleep! perchance to dream: ay, there's the rub;
> For in that sleep of death what dreams may come,
> When we have shuffled off this mortal coil,
> Must give us pause: . . .
> . . . . . .
> And thus the native hue of resolution
> Is sickled o'er with the pale cast of thought;
> And enterprises of great pith and moment,
> With this regard, their currents turn awry,
> And lose the name of action . . .

The king and Polonius plant Ophelia where Hamlet is sure
to come upon her. They hide so as to listen, the king still being
convinced that the prince is not dangerous to his security. In
the meeting that follows, Hamlet convinces Ophelia that he is
indeed mad:

If thou dost marry, I'll give thee this plague for thy dowry,
be thou as chaste as ice, as pure as snow, thou shalt not escape

calumny. Get thee to a nunnery, go: farewell. Or, if thou wilt needs marry, marry a fool; for wise men know well enough what monsters you make of them. To a nunnery, go; and quickly too. Farewell.

Ophelia is deeply hurt, as she loves the prince. The king, still unconvinced, plots with Polonius to have the courtier overhear Hamlet talking to his mother. The king is resolved to send Hamlet to England on some pretense or other.

Hamlet proves to the audience that he is as sane as Shakespeare as he gives final instructions to the players. He also proves that he has all the knowledge of the most seasoned stage director in a very long discourse to the actors on how to deliver their lines, which begins:

Speak the speech, I pray you, as I pronounced it to you, trippingly on the tongue: but if you mouth it, as many of your players do, I had as lief the town-crier spoke my lines. Now do not saw the air too much with your hand, thus; but use all gently: for in the very torrent, tempest, and, as I may say, the whirlwind of passion, you must acquire and beget a temperance that may give it smoothness. . . .

The play is presented before the whole court. Hamlet watches the king and the queen closely. When the actors re-enact the garden scene and the nephew of the play-king pours poison into his ear, as the royal uncle sleeps, the king rises and rushes from the hall, demanding lights. The queen seems undisturbed by what is going on in the play. This convinces Hamlet that she is innocent of complicity in the crime. He resolves to go to her and inform her of the truth of the whole ghastly affair.

Polonius informs the king that Hamlet is going toward his mother's chamber. The king bids him rush and conceal himself there. He does so just as Hamlet enters. The Queen, fearing Hamlet's intentions toward her, screams and Polonius makes a sound. Hamlet quickly draws his sword and thrusts it through the curtains and the body of Polonius. He thinks at first that it is the king who has fallen.

Hamlet cruelly tells his mother the entire story and is seized with a desire to do her bodily harm as the ghost appears to him and bids him leave his mother's punishment to her own conscience. Hamlet bids his mother (who has not seen the ghost, of course) refrain from sharing the king's bed any longer:

Assume a virtue, if you have it not.

## Act IV

The king immediately sends Hamlet to England, accompanied by Rosencrantz and Guildenstern, who hold orders to have the King of England murder him upon their arrival. Hamlet alters the letters so that the two courtiers will be murdered instead. He succeeds in getting off the ship that is carrying him.

Meanwhile, Ophelia, whose poor mind cannot stand the shock of Hamlet's actions toward her and her father's death, has taken to wandering aimlessly about the castle, singing simple songs and plucking weeds which she describes as beautiful flowers. Laertes arrives and Claudius convinces him that Hamlet is the cause of his father's death and Ophelia's madness. The king, having just learned that Hamlet is returning, plots with Laertes to kill him. Laertes is to challenge Hamlet to a friendly fencing match, Laertes' rapier being tipped with poison. If this fails the king will have a poisoned cup of beverage prepared when Hamlet desires to refresh himself after the exertion of fencing. About the same time these plans are being agreed upon, the news comes that Ophelia had drowned herself in the brook. Laertes is firmly convinced that it is but justice to kill Hamlet.

## Act V

Hamlet and his friend Horatio are secretly watching the gravediggers who are making ready for Ophelia's burial. Hamlet picks up a skull which has been unearthed:

> Alas, poor Yorick!—I knew him, Horatio; a fellow of infinite jest, of most excellent fancy: he hath borne me on his back a thousand times. . . .

Laertes tries to throw himself into the grave and Hamlet restrains him. They are about to fight on the spot when the king separates them and suggests they settle their little differences in a friendly fencing match. The king bets on Hamlet to win.

Claudius has carefully planned the match. Laertes' sword is tipped in poison and a poisoned cup is placed where Hamlet can reach it conveniently when he becomes overheated from the exercise. The duel begins and Laertes pinks Hamlet with his rapier. The king puts a pearl in the bottom of Hamlet's cup to try to induce him to drink. But Hamlet prefers to finish the match. The dueling proceeds, and in an exchange of thrusts, the swords are knocked from both contestants' hands. When they are picked up again, Hamlet has Laertes' rapier. Soon afterward he draws blood from Laertes.

Meanwhile, the queen sees the pearl, and since she is thirsty anyway, she drains the cup. She dies instantly. Soon Laertes feels the effects of the poison and tells Hamlet that the King had poisoned both the sword and the cup from which the queen had drunk. Hamlet begins to feel the poison, but has strength enough left to stab the king with the poisoned tip. He dies in Horatio's arms as news arrives that Rosencrantz and Guildenstern have been killed in England. The play ends as the bodies are gathered up and the muskets and cannon are sounding from the battlements, announcing the death of royalty in Denmark.

## 20. **Ben Jonson:** *The Alchemist*
### A satirical classic comedy

*Page 100.* In *The Alchemist* (1610) Jonson produced one of the first truly great satirical comedies of the English stage. It is a masterpiece of artistic construction. It is a modern comedy, an adaptation of Roman models, that has all the robustness of the best of the classic comedies. *The Alchemist* is a study of human gullibility and one of the best that has ever been produced. The characterization is brilliant and the dialogue is lively. Jonson, here, is not satirizing all mankind, but those in all societies who, by quackery and charlatanism, manage to dupe the lazier elements of humankind who seek the easier paths to fortune and fame. *The Alchemist* is one of the finest plays of the English theater.

> Alchemy is a pretty kind of game,
> Somewhat like tricks o' the cards to cheat a man
> With charming . . .

### Act I

One Master Lovewit leaves London during an epidemic of plague. He goes into the country and leaves his butler, Jeremy, in charge of his properties. Jeremy is a rather dubious character with many friends in the underworld. He is known in this tricky company as Face. He decides to use his master's house as headquarters for his knavery. He invites in one Subtle, who is posing as an alchemist seeking the philosopher's stone. Subtle brings along one Dol Common, a prostitute. Jeremy sets his friend up with an impressive lot of laboratory equipment and enters into an agreement to share in the take. The two friends are engaged in an argument as to who is really the "boss" in the enterprise when the first client enters. He is one Dapper, a lawyer's clerk. From this point on in the play, we see various elements of English society pass into the den of fakery—ladies, knights, lawyers, gallants, merchantmen, and even members of the clergy—all wanting some miraculous cure or some sort of supernatural aid in their own swindles or some spirit or device to help them to easy gain in their private enterprises.

Dapper wants a spirit conjured up to aid him to win at his gambling. After getting all of his ready cash, Doctor Subtle promises him luck. A young druggist comes next to receive advice and mysterious mumbo-jumbo predictions for his success in a new shop.

## Act II

Sir Epicure Mammon is after the philosopher's stone by which he can work wonders, burn base metals into gold, restore youth to the aged, and rid the kingdom of the plague. Subtle, a master of fake-scientific gibberish, has Mammon persuaded that he is about to produce the marvelous stone for him. Mammon is convinced and promises to have various of his possessions sent to the house. He is also smitten with Dol, whom he believes to be an aristocratic lady who is being cured of a madness by the fake Doctor.

One Master Surly is unconvinced. He believes the organization to be pure fakery and a cover-up for a bawdy house and promises to make trouble.

A Puritan, Ananias, seeks the stone in order to influence various lords to contribute more to the "glorious cause."

## Act III

The cheats have now built up a thriving business. Drugger, the druggist, returns to be duped further. Ananias comes back with his elder, Tribulation Wholesome, and the two are duped into buying the articles Mammon is sending over to be converted into gold. Clients now arrive so fast that Subtle is obliged to put them in different parts of the house while he goes from one to the other. He finds himself operating a clinic alone and without being entirely able to keep various groups from seeing other groups!

## Act IV

Dame Pliant arrives and captivates both Face and Subtle. She is not only rich but "soft and buxom." Meanwhile, Mammon has returned and is making love to Dol. Things have become rather complicated when a mysterious Spanish nobleman enters (really Surly in disguise). The Spanish don pretends that he speaks no English, so Subtle and Face speak freely before him. The Spaniard is left with Dame Pliant while the swindlers hurry to other customers. Surly reveals to Dame Pliant his true identity and together they denounce Face and Subtle. But all the duped victims refuse to believe Surly and he is about to be thrown out of the house when Dol brings in word that the master of the house has returned home.

## Act V

Lovewit, the owner, has received reports from his neighbors of strange happenings in his home during the past weeks. As he is about to force his way in, Jeremy appears as the perfect butler and is about to persuade everyone that nothing unusual has taken place when Surly and Mammon arrive. Soon all the victims are present, calling for officers to arrest the culprits. Lovewit is finally convinced, but he himself promises not to press the charges if Jeremy will find him a nice wealthy young widow to marry and make him seven years younger. Officers arrive but Face and Subtle run out of the back door. Lovewit, who is now married to Dame Pliant, covers for the swindlers and the victims are unable to get back anything that they have deposited in the house. Lovewit, now having gained personally from the knavery of his servant and his friends, rather admires their brilliant abilities. The victims leave without their possessions, convinced that they have all been dupes and have only their own selfishness and greed to blame for their losses.

### 21.   John Milton: *Paradise Lost*
#### The greatest English epic poem

*Page 125. Paradise Lost,* first published in 1667, is an artistic epic poem in majestic blank verse, in every way equal to the great ancient epic poems of Homer and Vergil. Its time is The Beginning and its setting is Heaven, Hell and Earth, and the infinite ethereal regions between. Its principal characters include God, The Father, Christ, The Son, Lucifer (Satan), and two human beings called Adam and Eve. *Paradise Lost* is the epic of mankind, the fall of Adam and, with him, mankind. Its purpose is, in the words of Milton, to

> . . . assert Eternal Providence,
> And justify the ways of God to men.

## Book I

After stating that the fall of man was due to Satan who, in revenge for being cast from Heaven, took the form of a serpent and tempted the mother of mankind to sin, the poet begins to unfold the events which led up to the expulsion of Adam and Eve from the garden of Eden.

Lucifer led a revolt in Heaven against the supreme authority of God. After suffering defeat, Lucifer and his evil hosts are hurled from the ethereal regions and fall for a period of nine days until they land in a burning lake of pitch. Satan (Lucifer) rises and swears that he will be avenged. He gathers the fallen angels about him and vows that he will dispute the authority of Heaven with the Almighty. He determines to turn disaster into success for evil:

> It is better to reign in hell than serve in heaven.

Under the direction of Mammon, the great hall of Pandemonium is built of bricks of gold. A great council is called by Satan and all the fallen angels crowd into the mighty chamber.

## Book II

In congress assembled, some of the spirits suggest war, others believe they should concentrate upon building the splendors of Hell until they outshine those of Heaven. Beelzebub reports on the creation of Earth, to be inhabited by good creatures, called human beings. He suggests that God can best be attacked through this, His favorite project. This suggestion is approved since Satan, the leader, believes that God can be beaten more effectively by guile and indirect attack than through a mass frontal maneuver. The question arises as to who will be daring enough to undertake the dangerous journey to Earth to investigate the new creation and draw plans for undermining God's authority there. Satan bids the hosts build up the strength of Hell:

> . . . while I abroad
> Through all the coasts of dark destruction seek
> Deliverance for us all: this enterprise
> None shall partake with me . . .

Satan wings his way to the Gates of Hell, where his daughter, Sin, and his son, Death, stand watch. They fling wide the massive portals and he plunges into Chaos and Night. There he contemplates, with the deities of these middle regions, Earth:

> Which hangs from Heaven by a golden chain.

## Book III

God witnesses from Heaven all that takes place in Hell. He glimpses Satan "hovering in the dun air sublime" and watches as he approaches Earth. God predicts to His Son and to the other heavenly hosts that man will fall, deceived by Satan. He adds that man's salvation can be gained only if someone among them volunteers to pay the penalty for the earthly sin. The Son of God offers himself:

> Behold me then, me for him, life for life
> I offer, on me let thine anger fall;
> Account me man: I for his sake will leave
> Thy bosom, and this glory next to thee
> Freely put off, and for him lastly die
> Well pleas'd, on me let Death wreck all his rage;

The Father accepts His Son's sacrifice and proclaims that He shall soon be made to appear on earth in man's form to save at least a portion of the race from the consequences of Adam's fall:

> As in him perish all men, so in thee
> As from a second root, shall be restor'd,
> As many as are restor'd, without thee none.

Meantime, Satan speeds through space. In the disguise of a cherub, he deceives Uriel, the guardian of the sun, who lets him pass. Satan lands on earth and prepares to make a preliminary survey of the situation.

## Book IV

Satan has some feeling of fear now that he realizes that he is again within the precincts of God's authority. But he summons his evil courage, realizing that only by submission could he again enjoy hope:

> So farewell Hope, and with Hope farewell Fear,
> Farewell Remorse: all Good to me is lost;
> Evil be thou my Good; by thee at least
> Divided Empire with Heav'ns King I hold
> By thee, and more than half perhaps will reign;
> As Man ere long, and this new World shall know.

Meanwhile, Uriel, realizing that he has let an angel of Hell pass, warns Gabriel, who sends Michael and bands of angels to circle Paradise and keep the evil one out. They are too late. Adam and Eve have retired to their bower, and Satan, in the form of a toad, is by Eve's ear, influencing her dreams. Two angels discover the toad and put Satan to flight.

## Books V, VI, VII, VIII

The next morning Eve told Adam that she had a strange dream the night before. It seems that she was urged to walk in the garden and to taste the fruit of the Tree of Knowledge. She wanted to resist but could not. She then dreamed she floated up from the garden as Adam awakened her. Adam tried to comfort her as she wept:

> . . . and she was cheered,
> But silently a gentle tear let fall
> From either eye, and wip'd them with her hair;
> Two other precious drops that ready stood,
> Each in their crystal sluice, he ere they fell
> Kiss'd . . .

The Almighty summoned Raphael and sent him to warn Adam of his danger. Raphael talked to Adam "as friend with friend" and told him the complete story of the revolt in Heaven, of how the bad angels were defeated by the good angels and sent to the miseries of Hell. He further related how the Earth was created. He cautioned Adam that man must not be too curious as to the ways of God, that there are many things that man is not supposed to understand.

Adam then related how he first awoke to marvel at the splendors of the Paradise that surrounded him. He explained that he had felt lonely and had complained to the Creator, who fashioned Eve from his rib and married them:

> I now see
> Bone of my Bone, Flesh of my Flesh, my Self
> Before me; Woman is her Name, of Man
> Extracted; for this cause he shall forego
> Father and Mother, and to his Wife adhere;
> And they shall be one Flesh, one Heart, one Soul.
>   She heard me thus, and though divinely brought,
> Yet innocence and Virgin Modesty,
> Her virtue and the conscience of her worth,
> That would be woo'd, and not unsought be won.
> Not obvious, not obtrusive, but retir'd,
> The more desirable, or to say all,
> Nature her self, though pure of sinful thought,
> Wrought in her so, that seeing me, she turn'd;
> I followed her, she what was Honour knew,
> And with obsequious Majesty approv'd
> My pleaded reason. To the Nuptial Bower
> I led her blushing like the Morn. . . .

Adam wished to know of Raphael if the angels in Heaven married. Raphael smilingly replied that none save spiritual communion was necessary there to secure perfect bliss. As the sun set, Raphael departed and Adam rejoined his wife.

## Book IX

The poet now tells us that things have changed between man and his heavenly masters:

> No more talk where God or Angel Guest
> With Man, as with his Friend, familiar us'd
> To sit indulgent, and with him partake
> Rural repast, permitting him the while
> Venial discourse unblam'd: I now must change

> Those Notes to Tragic; foul distrust, and breach
> Disloyal on the part of Man, revolt
> And disobedience: . . .

Satan has circled the earth for seven days and seven nights. He returns to the garden and enters the body of a sleeping serpent. Adam and Eve have separated for their morning's tasks and the serpent finds Eve alone among the roses. He addresses her in human voice and explains that a mere taste of the fruit of the Tree of Knowledge gave him the power of speech. Satan uses his most powerful gifts of eloquence as he persuades Eve to taste of the fruit. She does so and Heaven and Earth tremble. The serpent, his mission fulfilled, slinks away.

Eve determines that Adam shall share death, or whatever consequences may result from the keen delight she experiences at having tasted the forbidden fruit:

> Confirmed then I resolve,
> Adam shall share with me in bliss or woe:
> So dear I love him, that with him all deaths
> I could endure, without him live no life.

She hastens to Adam and attempts to make him share her delights. He is shocked, but soon resolves to partake of her fate:

> And me with thee hath ruined, for with thee
> Certain my resolution is to Die;
> How can I live without thee, how forego
> Thy sweet converse and Love so dearly join'd,
> To live again in these wild Woods forlorn?
> Should God create another *Eve,* and I
> Another Rib afford, yet loss of thee
> Would never from my heart; no, no, I feel
> The Link of Nature draw me: Flesh of Flesh,
> Bone of my Bone thou art, and from thy State
> Mine never shall be parted, bliss or woe.

He eats of the fruit. When they enter the bower, they both know shame for the first time and hasten to the fig tree for leaves to cover their nakedness.

### Book X

The Master is sad when he learns that the inevitable has taken place. He sends Christ to earth to judge mankind. The Son reaches the garden in the cool of evening. Adam and Eve are ashamed to face him. Christ sentences the serpent to be a hated animal for all time. He predicts that Eve will bring forth her children in pain and will be subject forever to her husband's command. He informs Adam that he must earn his daily bread by the sweat of his brow for the earth will provide for him no longer unless he wrests his living from it by toil. Both Adam and Eve are sadly repentant and offer up their contrite prayers.

Sin and Death fashion a broad highway from Earth to Hell. Satan, fresh from his triumphs, enters Pandemonium and is greeted as a conquering hero. He proudly relates to his angels that they all now have a broad superhighway readied for their use in going and coming from Earth. As he finishes, the audience prepares to applaud and scream approval of his deeds, but all they can do is to hiss. All, including Satan himself, have been changed into serpents.

### Books XI, XII

The Redeemer is touched by the geniune humility and repentance of our first parents and intercedes for them in Heaven. The Father promises they shall be forgiven, provided that their repentance is real and lasting, but they must be driven from the garden. Sentence of death is postponed, but they must go forth from Paradise and till the ground, side by side, and take from life whatever content their fallen state will allow.

Michael appears to Adam and Eve and informs them of the judgment from Heaven. They listen sadly, but resolute and contrite, as he relates to them the future course of humankind until the Messiah is to be permitted to descend to Earth through a virgin mother. Then the Saviour will lead all redeemed souls to a Paradise greater than that Adam and Eve have inhabited. Thus many souls, through contrition and love of the Redeemer, will be saved:

> . . . so shall the World go on,
> To good malignant, to bad men benign,
> Under her own weight groaning, til the day
> Appear of respiration to the just,
> And vengeance to the wicked, at return
> Of him so lately promis'd to thy aid,
> The woman's seed, obscurely then foretold,
> Now amplier known thy Saviour and thy Lord,

> Last in the Clouds from Heav'n to be revealed
> In glory of the Father, to dissolve
> Satan with his perverted World, then raise
> From the conflagrant mass, purg'd and refin'd,
> New Heav'ns, new Earth, Ages of endless date
> Founded in righteousness and peace and love,
> To bring forth fruits Joy and eternal Bliss.

At last, sad but hopeful, Adam and Eve leave Paradise:

> The World was before them, where to choose
> Their place of rest, and Providence their guide:
> They hand in hand with wandering steps and slow,
> Through Eden took their solitary way.

## 22. William Congreve: *The Way of the World*
### Restoration comedy of manners

*Page 142. The Way of the World* (1700) is the best of the comedies of manners in an artificial and dissolute high society of the Restoration in England. It is biting satire, redolent of brilliant wit and pointed epigram. Verbal fencing between character and character is carried to the limits of possibility. Congreve's play is a masterpiece of the external details of life among a group who devoted their time to drawing room and coffee house intrigue, who scoffed at the sanctity of the most established of social institutions. For this group, convention was something to be attacked, to be played with, and to serve as the butt of clever banter. Congreve succeeds in bringing to his audiences this false and cynical life of deceitful intrigue with a startling realism. The basic satire here is directed toward the marriage relation and is an analysis, approaching at times the ribald, which the writer weaves into a carefully constructed vehicle for sophisticated audiences. Congreve is an early 18th century precursor of Noel Coward.

### The plot

Young Mrs. Millamant is beseiged with suitors. She is beautiful and wealthy. The lady is particularly impressed with Mirabell, a young man about town. Mirabell is a philanderer and known in upper-class society for his cynical wit. His qualities appeal to Mrs. Millamant, who is reputed to be one of the wittiest ladies of London.

Mrs. Millamant is the niece of Lady Wishfort. Lady Wishfort is opposed to the match as, in reality, she also is infatuated with the young rake. She controls her niece's fortune and feels that she can use that weapon to prevent any such foolishness as marriage between the coquette and the young gallant.

Lady Wishfort's daughter, a Mrs. Fainall, is the current mistress of Mirabell. Mrs. Fainall detests her husband and is angry at Mirabell for having persuaded her to marry him. The young man's reply is that it is an admirable arrangement to "have just so much disgust for your husband as may be sufficient to relish your lover." He also suggests that in an affair such as theirs, it is possible that there may be a child, and "where could you have fixed a father's name with credit but on a husband." Mrs. Fainall is so much in love with Mirabell that she is willing to go along with his plans to marry Mrs. Millamant.

In order to bring Lady Wishfort around to his way of thinking, Mirabell dreams up an imaginary uncle, Sir Rowland. He tells the lady that his uncle has been smitten with her charm and wants to marry her. He gets his servant, Waitwell, to impersonate the fictitious uncle. A meeting is arranged between the servant and the anxious lady.

Mrs. Marwood, a past mistress of Mirabell, and a schemer, overhears the plan and decides to block it and try to get Mirabell back for herself. She plays up to Fainall, who hates Mirabell, and gets him to help. As he says, Mirabell is the cause of his being, "out-witted, out-jilted, out-matrimoney'd!"

Lady Wishfort has been persuaded to press Mrs. Millamant into marrying Sir Wilful Witwoud, a country bumpkin. She eagerly awaits the visit from the supposed uncle of Mirabell. She meets Waitwell, acting as Sir Rowland, in her negligee and they get along famously. But a letter arrives from Mrs. Marwood denouncing the deception just as she is persuaded to marry the ardent fellow right away. She is angry and vows revenge on Mirabell. She swears now that Mirabell will never marry Mrs. Millamant.

Fainall threatens Lady Wishfort with public exposure both for herself and for his wife unless his mother-in-law turns all of Mrs. Fainall's fortune over to him. Mrs. Fainall sides with Mirabell and, having just learned of the relations between Fainall and Mrs. Marwood, she threatenes her husband. Lady Wishfort finally forgives Mirabell for his trickery when he pleads with reason that it was merely "an artifice which love contrived—and errors which love produces have ever been accounted pardon-able." Although she forgives Mirabell his stunt, she is still op-posed to his marriage with Mrs. Millamant. He agrees to save Mrs. Fainall's reputation and fortune if she will agree. When she learns that Mirabell can handle Fainall with threat of exposure and that he is holding Mrs. Fainall's fortune in trust, Lady Wishfort gives in and consents to the match.

In the somewhat practical love scene between Mirabell and Mrs. Millamant, a bargain is made between them as to how tightly the bonds of matrimony will hold either of them within the social code. When each has made concession to the other, they mutually agree to give up their single state, for that is the way of the world, but even in conforming to that way, an in-dividual need not be bound in his private life by too much con-ventional behavior.

### 23. John Bunyan: *The Pilgrim's Progress*
#### Prose allegory of Christianity

*Page 152.* In contrast to Milton's very intellectual *Paradise Lost,* Puritan literature produced a religious masterpiece in prose, *The Pilgrim's Progress from This World to That Which is to Come* (1675). The poor tinker and preacher, John Bunyan, wrote what is considered one of the three greatest allegories in world literatures (the others being Spenser's *The Faerie Queene* and Dante's *The Divine Comedy).* Directed to the common man and written in simple prose and easily understood symbolism, this has proved to be the most popular religious book in English, aside from the *Bible* itself. It is at once allegory, a romance of adventures, and a study in character. It is a direct precursor of the English novel.

## The allegory

As I walked through the wilderness of this world, I lighted on a certain place where was a Den, and I laid me down in that place to sleep: and, as I slept, I dreamed a dream. I dreamed, and behold I saw a man clothed with rags, standing in a cer-tain place, with his face from his own house, a book in his hand, and a great burden upon his back. I looked and saw him open the book and read therein; and, as he read, he wept and trembled; and not being able longer to contain, he brake out with a lamentable cry, saying, "What shall I do?"

The Bible, which the man was reading, had convinced him that the City of Destruction, where he dwelt, was to be destroyed. As he pondered his course, Evangelist came up to him and told him that he should flee from this place and journey to the City of Zion. The man, Christian by name, returned to his home and pleaded with his family to accompany him. Finding they but made fun of him, he resolved to seek his salvation alone.

He began to run away from this condemned city and toward a distant light which he knew to be the place where his burden would be lifted from him. On the way he met Pliable and Obstinate, his neighbors. Struggling to be free of them, he is caught in the Slough of Despond and his burden of sins causes him to sink. Just as he is about to go under, Help comes along and gets him out.

No sooner had this taken place than Christian met Mr. Worldly Wiseman, who suggested an easy way to rid him of his burden. He needed only seek out Legality and his son, Civility. He is about to yield when Evangelist appears once more and upbraids him for turning aside from the rocky but sure path. Christian repents his temptation and makes his way to a place where he meets Good-Will and is led to an inn where he learns from Interpreter the various twists and turns there are in the journey to the Celestial City. He sees a vision of the Day of Judgment.

He goes forth and finally reaches a highway which

> . . . was fenced on either side with a wall, and that wall was called Salvation. Up this way, therefore, did burdened Christian run, but not without great difficulty, because of the load on his back.
>
> He ran thus till he came to a place somewhat ascending, and upon that place stood a cross, and a little below, in the bottom, a sepulcher. So I saw in my dreams, that just as Christian came up with the cross, his burden loosed from off his shoulders, and fell off his back, and began to tumble, and so continued to do, till it came to the mouth of the sepulcher, where it fell in and I saw it no more.
>
> Then was Christian glad and lightsome . . .

He now traveled easier, and as he went, he tried to persuade Simple, Sloth, Presumption, and Hypocrisy that short cuts would avail them nothing. He failed to impress them and went on alone, climbing the Hill of Difficulty. Here, after much confusion, he came to rest for the night in a lodge where he discoursed with the beautiful maidens, Prudence, Discretion, Piety, and Charity. He rested in the chamber of Peace, and when he left, he was provided with the sword and shield of Christian Faith.

It is well that he had good weapons for he descended into the Valley of Humiliation and met the giant monster, Apollyon. This creature, covered with the scales of Pride, almost defeated Christian. Christian finally killed him, after being wounded, and after curing himself with leaves from the Tree of Life, he came finally into the Valley of the Shadow of Death. This was a very lonely place and the only way through it involved entering a very deep Ditch and a Quagmire. Also the mouth of Hell opened its fiery jaws there. Christian's sword was useless and he had to resort to a greater weapon, All-Prayer.

Through this valley, Christian met many dangers. He had to pass the Cave of Pagan and Pope. Around him were the skeletons of many pilgrims who had failed to pass. Finally Christian overtook another neighbor, Faithful, who had left the City of Destruction before him. From here on, they traveled together and shared the dangers in their path. At this point, Evangelist appears again and warns the two travelers of the perils that they will meet in the town of Vanity Fair. He predicted that one of them would not be able to resist the many earthly attractions to be found in that place. The people who dwelt in this town were materialists, cruel and stupid, and would have nothing to do with men of faith. Christian and Faithful were arrested immediately because they would not buy the goods laid before them. Faithful was burned at the stake and Christian succeeded in escaping from his prison cell before the time for his execution. When Hopeful, a young man of the town, saw that Faithful was gathered up by a chariot from Heaven, he was converted and became Christian's companion.

They passed through the Valley of Ease, where they were captured by the giant Despair. They were imprisoned in a dungeon. Christian at last realized that he had the key Promise in his possession. He fitted the key to the lock and they were free.

Soon Hopeful and Christian met four shepherds on the Delectable Mountains: Knowledge, Experience, Watchful, and Sincere. After these guardians had pointed out the way to the Celestial Gate, the pilgrims still had to pass through the Valley of Conceit. There they were met by Ignorance and other distracting characters, such as Flatterer and Atheist. But they succeeded in avoiding any further trouble and proceeded into the very precincts of Heaven.

They found, however, that they could not relax their vigilance even though they could see the pearly gates of Heaven glistening just before them. They had to pass through the very deep and treacherous River of Death. As Christian sank deeper and became afraid, Hopeful shouted to him to have hope and faith. Finally the two weary friends dragged themselves from the river and were met by the Heavenly Host. They were saluted with trumpets and their earthly raiment was changed for garments of Shining Gold. They were given harps and crowns.

So I awoke, and behold it was a Dream.

## 24. **Alexander Pope:** *The Rape of the Lock*
<u>Neoclassic mock-heroic epic</u>

*Page 156.* This poem, written in 1714, in polished heroic couplets, containing 814 lines, is one of world literature's best examples of the mock-heroic epic, a sort of tongue-in-cheek poetic grandeur, involving a theme of no importance, and usually of comic proportions. The poem is one of the finest satirical pieces in English literature. It was written at the instigation of a friend of Pope, who was worried over a family feud between two good Catholic families of London. It seems that Lord Petre had snipped off a lock from the fair head of Miss Arabella Fermor, to the great indignation of the family of the fair lady. Pope's interest was a larger one than merely trying to heal the wounds opened by this playful act. He was intent upon holding up to ridicule the petty vanity and artificiality of the society in which the dastardly deed took place. The poem has been enormously popular, and is indeed a delightful reading experience, with its gay wit, its perfect couplets, its fancy and unmatched mock grandeur.

> What dire offense from amorous causes springs,
> What mighty contests rise from trivial things,
>
> . . . . . .
>
> Sol through white curtains shot a timorous ray,
> and oped those eyes that must eclipse the day;
> Now lap-dogs give themselves the rousing shake,
> And sleepless lovers, just at twelve, awake;

But even then, Belinda, sweet Belinda, did not awake. She still dreamed, and in her dreams the watchful sprite, Ariel, came and warned her of dire things to come, "beware of all, but most beware of man!" About this time, Belinda awakened, awakened at the gentle licking of her lap-dog, Shock. Up she sprang and summoned Betty, her maid, to make her toilet. Upon her natural beauty she added the beauties of the many rows of jars and pots on her dressing table and away to the Thames to go boating. And there she floats while all male eyes devour her from the neighboring boats that circle her own. She smiled upon them all and gave not any particular one a smile sweeter than she bestowed upon another. She smiled and nodded her pretty head:

> The nymph, to the destruction of mankind,
> Nourished two locks, which graceful hung behind
> In equal curls, and well conspired to deck
> With shining ringlets the smooth ivory neck.

Lord Petre, with many tokens of love to his credit, swore to have one of those locks, by fair means or foul. Ariel, who knows the evil fellow's designs, calls his sprites and sylphs together and gives each a station to guard, to prevent harm from befalling the beautiful Belinda.

Now, after the cruise, pretty Belinda, surrounded by suitors, repairs to the palace where she desires to play cards a while. Coffee is served. The sylphs guard every move and every part of Belinda's person and dress to prevent harm from descending upon her. But the coffee went to Lord Petre's head and he devised new schemes to get that lock of fragrant hair. Just then Lady Clarissa draws a pair of scissors from her sewing basket and the Lord takes them. But the sylphs surround Belinda's head and blow the hair away from the Lord's snipping edges. But finally:

> The peer now spreads the glittering forfex wide,
> To inclose the lock; now joins it, to divide.
> Even then, before the fatal engine closed,
> A wretched sylph too fondly interposed;
> Fate urged the shears, and cut the sylph twain,
> (But airy substance soon unites again)
> The meeting points the sacred hair dissever
> From the fair head, forever and forever!
> Then flashed the living lightening from her eyes,
> And screams rend the affrighted skies . . .

The devilish Lord shouts with triumph while poor Belinda rages and Ariel weeps with humiliation at his failure to save her.

Umbriel, a melancholy gnome, calls upon the queen of ill tempers to cast a gloom over Belinda's life. The queen mixed an evil potion and the gnome pours the frightful concoction over Belinda's head. It puts the girl in a terrible rage. Her friend Thalestris fans the flames of her anger even more:

> Gods! shall the ravisher display your hair,
> While the fops envy, and the ladies stare!
> Honor forbid! at whose unrivalled shrine
> Ease, pleasure, virtue, all our sex resign.
> Methinks already I your tears survey,
> Already hear the horrid things they say,
> Already see you a degraded toast,
> And all your honor in a whisper lost!

Sir Plume is called upon to demand return of the lock but the Lord only laughs and brags of his conquest. Gradually the forces are drawn up for battle. Lord Petre is finally defeated when Belinda throws snuff in his face and he is forced to sneeze instead of fight. But the lock cannot be found anywhere. It is certain that it mounted to the skies with those most violent sneezes. Fair Belinda, cease to bemoan your lost tress; it is now among the immortal glories and even after all your other beauties go and you face death, with your eyes dull and lifeless:

> When those fair suns shall set, as set they must,
> And all those tresses shall be laid in dust,
> This lock, the Muse shall consecrate to fame,
> And 'midst the stars inscribe Belinda's name.

### 25. Jonathan Swift: *Gulliver's Travels*
### Greatest English prose satire

*Page 161. Travels into Several Remote Nations of the World, by Lemuel Gulliver* (1726-1727), is one of the world's most outstanding social satires. It is a book that has had a wide appeal to adults because of its caustic commentary on man and his institutions; portions of it have thrilled children of every generation since it was written because of its high adventure and fantasy. Its prose is simple and direct. Swift hated mankind in groups and used his mastery of irony to hold up to ridicule man's folly and gross stupidity, his narrowness and hypocrisy.

The many observations, voiced by Swift's literary mouthpiece, are very sharp indeed.

> I heard a very warm debate between two professors, about the most commodious and effectual ways and means of raising money without grieving the subject. The first affirmed the justest method would be to lay a certain tax upon vices and folly, and the sum fixed upon every man to be rated after the fairest manner by a jury of his neighbors. The second was of an opinion directly contrary, to tax those qualities of body and mind for which men chiefly value themselves, the rate to be more or less according to the degrees of excelling, the decision whereof should be left entirely to their own breast . . . But as to honor, justice, wisdom and learning, they should not be taxed at all, because they are qualifications of so singular a kind that no man will either allow them in his neighbor, or value them in himself.
>
> The women were proposed to be taxed according to their beauty and skill in dressing, wherein they had the same privilege with the men, to be determined by their own judgment. But constancy, chastity, good sense, and good nature were not rated, because they would not bear the cost of collecting.
>
> —From Book III

## Part I.  A Voyage to Lilliput

Here Swift's satire is directed toward mankind of his day in the aggregate. His purpose is to provoke laughter by describing the diminutive and the small in action and thought of the people in human society.

Lemuel Gulliver, a ship's surgeon, is shipwrecked in the South Seas and cast up upon an island. He awakes to find that he is bound to the earth by thousands of minute threads. He soon discovers that he is in the land of Lilliput, peopled by a race not over 6 inches in height. He is carried to their capital on a special wagon drawn by 1500 tiny horses.

At the Lilliputian court Gulliver succeeds in gaining the favor of the king. He learns the language, and at this point begins to take note of the customs, which seem to him to be very similar to those found at home among normal-sized humans. He noted among the religious factions that the point upon which followers were burned at the stake seemed to be whether an egg should be broken at the big end or the little end.

Gulliver joined the forces of Lilliput against the enemy,

Blefuscu. He routed the enemy and became a hero. However, he was in the bad graces of the emperor when he opposed the idea of making the inhabitants of Blefuscu slaves to Lilliput. Gulliver went into Blefuscu and found a boat from a shipwrecked vessel. He repaired the boat and succeeded in maneuvering it into the high seas where he was picked up by an English merchant ship.

## Part II.   The Voyage to Brobdingnag

The satire in this part shows Gulliver, a minute human, in the midst of a race of giants, representing the grossness and the coarseness of the mass, against which a puny civilized individual does not have a chance.

After ten months of leisure, Gulliver once more sets sail, this time for India. On a particular coast, Gulliver wandered away from a landing party and found himself among a race of giants. He was treated by them as a domestic pet. He became a fixture in the household of a farmer, who grew wheat forty-five feet high, and became the special charge of the daughter, a nine-year-old child who could look over the top of the growing grain.

Gulliver became a sideshow curiosity in this land and was exhibited publicly until he was near death from exhaustion. Finally the queen took him as a pet. He became a subject for scientific study in this land with rats the size of lions, apples the size of barrels, and wasps the size of hawks. The king amused himself by discussing with Gulliver the relative merits of the respective governments of Brobdingnag and England. The king was not particularly impressed with the past century of English history, nor with the entire race that made up human society:

> He was perfectly astonished with the historical account I gave him of our affairs during the last century, protesting it was only a heap of conspiracies, rebellions, murders, massacres, revolutions, banishments, the very worst effects that avarice, faction, hypocrisy, perfidiousness, cruelty, rage, madness, hatred, envy, lust, malice, or ambition could produce.
>
> .  .  .  .  .  .
>
> ".  .  . you have clearly proved that ignorance, idleness and vice are the proper ingredients for qualifying a legislator: that laws are best explained, interpreted, and applied by those whose interest and abilities lie in perverting, confounding, and eluding them. .  .  . But by what I have gathered from your own relation, and the answers I have with much pains wringed and

extorted from you, I cannot but conclude the bulk of your natives to be the most pernicious race of little odious vermin that nature ever suffered to crawl upon the surface of the earth."

Soon afterward Gulliver's living quarters was lifted up by a huge bird and dropped into the ocean, where he was picked up by a ship bound for England.

## Part III.  A voyage to Laputa, Balnibarbi, Luggnagg, Glubbdubdribb, and Japan

In this part, Gulliver visits various lands where the inhabitants are all scholars and devote themselves to research and speculation. He is here satirizing the scientific spirit of his day and the hypocrisies to be found in learning and education. This part shows Swift has lost the carefree fancy and humor of the first two parts. Here the tone becomes bitter and the statements are morbid and vengeful.

On this voyage Gulliver's ship is attacked by pirates and he is cast adrift in a small boat. A huge flying island picks him up and he finds himself among the intellectuals of Laputa, who dwell in a world of the abstract. All are absent-minded and have to keep servants constantly with them to remind them of what they are doing and saying. One professor has devoted the past eight years to the attempt to extract sunbeams from cucumbers. This is not a happy people:

> These people are under continual disquietudes, never enjoying a minute's peace of mind; and their disturbances proceed from causes which very little affect the rest of mortals. Their apprehensions arise from several changes they dread in the celestial bodies . . .
>
> They are so perpetually alarmed with the apprehensions of these and like impending dangers that they can neither sleep quietly in their beds, nor have any relish for the common pleasures or amusements of life. When they meet an acquaintance in the morning, the first question is about the sun's health, how he looked at his setting and rising, and what hopes they have to avoid the stroke of the approaching comet. This conversation they are apt to run into with the same temper that boys discover, in delighting to hear terrible stories of spirits and hobgoblins, which they greedily listen to, and dare not go to bed for fear.

Gulliver visits the great academy and marvels at the non-sensical and impractical directions the intellectuals take in their pursuit of solutions for the ills and improvements of societies. He visits various lands that the flying island passes and interviews sorcerers and magicians whose minds are as fantastic as they are intellectual. Finally he is dropped upon Japan, from whence he again sails for England.

## Part IV.   The voyage to the land of the Houyhnhnms

This is the most vicious satire of the entire work, in which Gulliver is cast upon an island where very rational horses rule over a race of very disgusting human creatures, the Yahoos. The horses are disgusted to learn that in England, the Yahoos rule over the sensible horses and use them purely for their muscular strength. In this part, Swift dwells upon Gulliver's great admiration for the noble "horse sense" he finds in this land, the peaceful and practical social developments and the pursuit of decency and virtue. He finds the Yahoos represent the opposite of these admirable qualities, the slime and vulgarity, the folly and vice, the degeneracy and the filth of human relations.

The Grand Assembly of the horse kingdom decrees that Gulliver is to be exiled or must join the Yahoos. Gulliver builds a canoe and sadly leaves this land. He is picked up and returned to England. He is moved to revulsion by contact with his own family and takes up his abode in the stable, among his noble and companionable four-footed friends.

## 26.   **Daniel Defoe:** *The Adventures of Robinson Crusoe*
### Greatest precursor of the English novel

*Page 163. Robinson Crusoe* (1719) is a pure tale of adventure and the greatest precursor of the English novel. This book, which is adventure for adventure's sake, delves little more than into the externals of character. It attained instant popularity and never has lost it since. For more than a century it was what amounted to required reading for every English-speaking schoolboy.

It was the first of the "dime novels" and the only one to have such universal appeal. Its theme is a monotonous one, some twenty-four years out of the life of a shipwrecked sailor, but it reaches epic proportions as a relation of the struggle of an average lone man to survive against raw nature and to build up his own rather comfortable, and private, economy.

## A narrative based on fact

*Robinson Crusoe* is based on the real adventures of one Alexander Selkirk, who was wrecked or abandoned on one of the islands of the Juan Fernández group, off the coast of South America in 1705. This sailor lived a solitary life there until he was picked up and returned to England in 1709.

The story takes the form of autobiography and relates the desire of young Robinson Crusoe, a middle-class English lad, for a life on the sea. Against the desires of his parents, who planned for him a life as a merchant, young Robinson slipped away from home and took his first voyage in a ship that was wrecked not far from port. Robinson and his companions succeeded in making the English coast. He vowed that he was through with the sea, but soon his longing came upon him again and he shipped out, this time, for the coast of Africa.

The ship was captured by Turkish pirates and Robinson is brought to the Moroccan coast where he is sold as a slave to a rich Moor. He sets out in a small boat of his master and is picked up by a Portuguese merchant ship bound for the coast of Brazil. In Brazil he acquires a rich plantation. But he soon tires of that quiet life and joins an English merchantman, bound for Africa for a cargo of negro slaves.

This was Robinson's fateful voyage, for the ship ran into a frightful storm and went to pieces off the northern coast of South America and only Robinson Crusoe was saved of the entire crew. He regained consciousness the following morning on the beach of an uninhabited island and here began his minutely described day-to-day existence as a lone human castaway, aided only by Providence.

He first constructed a raft and succeeded in bringing from the broken hulk a good supply of firearms, powder, food, clothing, tools, lumber, liquors, and all manner of miscellaneous gear. His first home in his new environment was a sailcloth tent. From this humble beginning, he gradually built a cabin near a cave where he stored most of his gear and provisions. He added to his new abode through the weeks that followed.

He kept a diary with materials that he had brought from the wreck, and recorded the most minute details of his new life. He domesticated wild goats, captured parrots, and with the companionship of the wild birds and sea animals, gradually became accustomed to being without human company.

His food problem resolved itself in time. He succeeded in supplying himself from the ocean and from the small game and birds on the island. He grew corn, barley, and rice. By the twenty-fourth year of his island existence, he had built up quite a comfortable establishment. The human voice had become but a memory to him, except for his own and for that of his parrot. On one occasion, when he had swum around the island and had fallen exhausted on the beach:

> . . . but judge you, if you can, that read my story, what a surprise I must be in when I was waked out of my sleep by a voice calling me by name several times, 'Robin, Robin, Robin Crusoe, poor Robin Crusoe! Where are you, Robin Crusoe? Where are you? Where have you been?' Dozing between sleeping and waking, I thought I dreamed that someone spoke to me . . . and was at first dreadfully frightened. But no sooner were my eyes open but I saw my Poll sitting on the top of the hedge, and immediately knew that it was he that spoke to me; for in just such bemoaning language I had used to talk to him, and teach him; and he had learned it so perfectly, that he would sit upon my finger and lay his bill close to my face and cry, 'Poor Robin Crusoe! Where are you? Where have you been? How come you here?' and such things as I had taught him . . .

About this time he began to notice that a band of cannibals visited the island occasionally. Finally, one day he rescued a prisoner from them, frightening the Indians away with his musket fire. He at last had a human companion. He named the savage Friday to commemorate the day on which he found him. Gradually he taught his new-found friend and servant to speak English. Friday told him that a number of white men had been captured by the Indians on the neighboring island.

One day the savages returned to Robinson's island with a Spanish prisoner and with Friday's old father. Robinson and Friday rescued them. At last an English ship anchored by the island. It had been taken over by a group of mutineers. Robinson succeeds in releasing the legitimate crew and the mutineers are left behind on the island as, at last, Robinson Crusoe and the ship's crew sail the ship to England. After thirty-five years of absence, Robinson at last comes home.

Part II, a very inferior sequel, relates how, after eight years of quiet living, and following the death of his wife, Robinson returns to his island. There he found that mutineers had taken native women from the neighboring islands and had started quite a numerous colony of little ones. Robinson Crusoe hastens to get the ship's priest to marry the mutineers to the native women, and, satisfied in his pious English pride, sets sail for Brazil. On the way the ship is attacked by natives and Friday is killed:

> Poor honest Friday! We buried him with all the decency and solemnity possible, by putting him into a coffin and throwing him into the sea; and I caused them to fire eleven guns for him; and so ended the life of the most grateful, faithful, honest, and most affectionate servant that man ever had.

Robinson Crusoe eventually visits China, Siberia, and returns to England. He is now old and is content to live out his remaining years in a quiet and prayerful manner.

### 27. Samuel Richardson: *Pamela* and *Clarissa Harlowe*
Sentimental romances—early novels of character

*Pages 167 and 168. Pamela* (1740) is the first modern English novel of character. Both it and *Clarissa Harlowe* (1748) are among the greatest of early English novels. Both are written in the epistolary form. All characterization and plot are revealed to the reader by means of letters written by various characters to each other. Both novels reveal a vivid impression of life in the 18th century and the moral code then prevalent in English society. *Clarissa Harlowe,* usually considered Richardson's masterpiece, was particularly influential upon the development of the European novel in the late 18th and early 19th centuries. In France, Rousseau imitated *Clarissa* in his *La Nouvelle Héloïse* (1756), also written in epistolary form.

Richardson is the first English novelist to reach the heart, especially of his women characters. He is thus the father of the modern English novel. In Pamela, Richardson draws for us a poor, humble servant girl, whose virtue is rewarded through her practical prudence. Today Pamela would appear to us a rather absurd heroine, one who trades upon her virtue to acquire a very practical reward—a husband. Clarissa Harlowe, on the other hand, is a young woman of the gentry, whose decision is to die rather than marry the libertine who has seduced her. Both novels are highly sentimental in their dealing with these two women, but they are both penetrating in their search into the feminine emotions. Both present characters who live and breathe. Both novels did much to pave the way for the modern masterpieces in psychological delineation of character, of the depiction of elemental interests of individual human beings and of their passions.

## *Pamela, or Virtue Rewarded*

Pamela has been the servant girl of Lady B for many years. She is now grown from a young girl and is much grieved by her mistress' recent death. When Mr. B, the son, wishes her to remain in the household, she accepts with gratitude. But it soon becomes apparent that Mr. B's intentions toward her virtue are less than honorable. When he kisses her one day, she prepares to build up her defenses against him.

Pamela's trials and tribulations with the young master are revealed in her long and familiar letters to her parents. "This gentleman has degraded himself to offer freedoms to his poor servant." The young scamp intercepts many of her letters. She is humble and contrite, despite his persistent attentions and his cruel humiliating treatment of her. "It is for you, sir, to say what you please, and for me only to say, God bless your honor!"

Pamela soon realizes that she loves the rascal in spite of herself. "Lucifer is always ready to promote his own work and workmen." She continues to remain firm. He once hid in the closet in her bedroom. In the scene that followed, she threw herself on the bed in a fit, and upon recovering, served her notice. "My soul is of equal importance to the soul of a princess, though my quality is inferior to that of the meanest slave."

Mr. B offers her his coach to take her home and she accepts. But the bribed coachman drives her to Mr. B's country home. There she is virtually a prisoner, but her resolution is strong. She resists the young fellow's advances with fits of emotion. Finally, Mr. B asks her forgiveness and promises to be good. She has softened him and her virtue is about to be rewarded:

> I fear not, sir, the grace of God supporting me, that any acts of kindness would make me forget what I owe to my virtue; but . . . my nature is too frank and open to make me wish to be ungrateful; and if I should be taught a lesson I never yet learnt, with what regret should I descend to the grave, to think that I could not hate my undoer; and that, to the last great day, I must stand up as an accuser of the poor unhappy soul, that I could wish it in my power to save!

At last Mr. B loves her for her virtuous qualities and proposes marriage. She and Mr. B are married and everyone rejoices. That is, everyone is overjoyed except Mrs. Davers, Mr. B's sister. Pamela takes over the household and acts the part of the model housewife, in spite of the insults and abuses she is compelled to endure from Mrs. Davers. Mr. B apparently is not yet a model husband, for at times he is not so faithful as he might be. But Pamela goes forward, never remiss in her duties, bears him a child, and finally, by dint of her persistent faith and virtue, wins him completely and exacts from him sincere promises to devote the remainder of his days to his virtuous wife.

## Clarissa Harlowe, or Virtue Triumphant

Clarissa is constantly at odds with her family. She has inherited money from her grandfather and her brother and sister resent it. Her father tries to bend her strong will to his wishes but she maintains herself independent and an individual in her own right. The entire family want her to marry Mr. Solmes, an elderly rich gentleman, with little of refined taste. She resists the pressures brought to bear upon her by the entire family. Her mother asks, "Who at the long run must submit? all of us to you, or you to all of us?" But it is vain to try to sway the strong-willed, virtuous Clarissa. Insults and pleading will not avail.

Young Robert Lovelace is introduced into the household by an uncle. The family is now bent upon arranging a marriage between the young gentleman and Clarissa's sister, Arabella, but the young fellow is smitten with Clarissa's beauty. She is cool toward his attentions. She sets down, in one of her letters, his merits and faults:

> That such a husband might unsettle me in all my own principles and hazard my future hopes. That he has a very immoral character to women. That, knowing this, it is a high degree of impurity to think of joining in wedlock with such a man. . . .

The family begins to put pressures upon young Lovelace to keep him away from Clarissa and push him into Arabella's arms. He secretly resolves to seduce Clarissa by fair means or foul, to revenge himself upon them all.

Clarissa, finally, to escape her domineering father, agrees to go with Lovelace. He is to take her to the home of a relative for protection until she can come to an agreement with her family, but he takes her to a house of ill-fame where she is virtually a prisoner of a Mrs. Sinclair.

Meanwhile, her family has disowned her and she is forced to depend more and more upon Lovelace. He persists in wooing her, now ignoring his earlier promises of marriage. She runs from him but he catches up with her. He has Mrs. Sinclair and two other women, posing as his cousins, induce her to take drugs. While she is under the influence of the dope, he forces her virtue.

After Clarissa realizes her true situation, she manages to escape from Mrs. Sinclair. She is protected by a friend of Lovelace and by a kindly old couple. She keeps writing letters, to try to effect a reconciliation with her family. She refuses to see Lovelace. He now is very sincerely in love with her.

Gradually, Clarissa declines in health, still refusing to have anything to do with the repentant Lovelace, who pleads with her to marry him. She goes to an undertaker, orders her own coffin and has inscribed upon it the date of her death—the day she left her father's house.

All efforts fail to move Clarissa's resolution to die. The family forgives her. Her cousin begs her to marry Lovelace. All in vain; Clarissa dies. She is buried at the feet of her grandfather.

Lovelace is sad and repentant. Colonel Morden, Clarissa's cousin, follows him to France and challenges him to a duel. Mortally wounded, Lovelace prays that his death will atone in part for the wrong he has done to Clarissa Harlowe.

## 28. Henry Fielding: *The History of Tom Jones, a foundling*
### Greatest novel of the century

*Page 170. Tom Jones* (1749) is the greatest of the early English novels and one of the world's masterpieces in the novel. Fielding's attitudes toward human behavior are not dated, as those of Richardson. Fielding is concerned with a more modern and a more universal ethic. His has a true moral attitude, one which stresses an inner goodness of heart, goodness for the sake of peace of mind, and not virtue held in the hope of material gain. *Tom Jones* is a supreme accomplishment in character portrayal and in the human realism of its situations. It is a novel filled with the follies of human nature, treated sympathetically and humorously. Fielding provokes mankind to laugh at its own weaknesses. He does not condemn mankind and he does not praise its shortcomings. He reveals them, the motives behind them, the very human qualities of the people who are responsible for them. He is impartial in his treatment of human nature; he lets each character work out his own destiny, according to his own nature. He presents things as they are; he does not try to force them into his preconceived mold.

*Tom Jones* is robust and healthy. Fielding is a moralist, but not one with a personal axe to grind. He represents no institution nor code rigidly imposed by some particular self-interested group. He views deceit, self-interest, cruelty, and hypocrisy as the greatest of human sins, wherever they may be found. In the absence of these, he views human error with kindness and humorous tolerance.

Fielding's plot is a skilful interweaving of small details into an almost perfectly integrated pattern. He is a careful observer and presents the developments in the lives of his characters in a direct, sincere, and simple style, in a logical and natural sequence. *Tom Jones* is a cut from 18th century life, raised to a level of artistic perfection.

Fielding reveals the entire tone of the long novel, humorous and tolerant, in his first pages. We are first introduced to Tom Jones, the foundling, as the kindly and whimsical old Squire Allworthy returns to his country estate one evening from a trip into London:

> . . . He came to his house very late in the evening, and after a short supper with his sister, retired much fatigued to his chamber. Here, having spent some minutes on his knees—a custom which he never broke through on any account—he was preparing to step into bed, when, upon opening the cloathes, to his great surprise he beheld an infant, wrapt up in some coarse linen, in a sweet and profound sleep, between his sheets. He stood some time lost in astonishment at this sight; but, as good nature had always the ascendant in his mind, he soon began to be touched with sentiments of compassion for the little wretch before him . . .

When he calls in his 52-year-old housekeeper, the baby's apparently illegitimate innocence provokes quite a different reaction. Here he, unknowingly, faces self-righteous convention, personified by Mrs. Deborah Wilkins:

> . . . nor could she refrain from crying out, with great horror of accent as well as look, "My good sir! what's to be done? . . . and I hope your worship will send out your warrant to take up the hussy its mother, for she must be one of the neighborhood; and I should be glad to see her committed to Bridewell, and whipt at the cart's tail. Indeed, such wicked sluts cannot be too severely punished. . . . Faugh! how it stinks! It doth not smell like a Christian. . . ."
>
> There were some strokes in this speech which perhaps would have offended Mr. Allworthy, had he strictly attended to it; but he had now got one of his fingers into the infant's hand, which, by its gentle pressure, seeming to implore his assistance, had certainly outpleaded the eloquence of Mrs. Deborah, had it been ten times greater than it was. . . .

And once Mrs. Deborah's real nature got hold of her, shorn of her hypocrisy and conventional deceit, she

> . . . took the infant under her arms, without any apparent disgust at the illegality of its birth; and declaring it was a sweet little infant, walked off with it to her own chamber.
>
> Allworthy here betook himself to those pleasing slumbers which a heart that hungers after goodness is apt to enjoy when thoroughly satisfied. As these are possibly sweeter than what are occasioned by any other hearty meal, I should take more pains to display them to the reader, if I knew any air to recommend him to for the procuring such an appetite.

Miss Bridget, the Squire's sister, after making the conventional remarks about the infant's parentage, consents to care for the boy. Shortly afterward, she marries a Captain Blifil, who is counting on inheriting the Allworthy estate. He dies, however, soon after his wife gave birth to a son.

A Jenny Jones was assumed to be the mother of the foundling. She had been a servant in the house of a schoolmaster, named Partridge, who was believed to be the father. Squire Allworthy sent Jenny away. The child was named Tom.

The village assumed that Tom would come to a bad end. By the time he was fourteen he had been accused of many evil things, stealing, picking pockets, etc. The Reverend Mr.

Thwackum, a very pious and good man, instructed the two boys, giving all his favors to the legitimate young Blifil and all his abuse to young Tom.

When Tom was twenty he was in love with the daughter of Squire Western and she was greatly taken with him. He knew, however, that Sophia's father would never consent to their marriage. About this time, the good Allworthy became very ill and suddenly had a seemingly miraculous recovery. Tom was so overjoyed that he imbibed a bit too freely in celebration and became very drunk. As a result of the complications, involving a certain Molly, the truth came out, and Squire Western resolved to marry Sophia to young Blifil. Tom and Sophia continued to meet secretly. Upon discovering this fact, Squire Western hastened to Squire Allworthy with his very wrong suspicions about the young people's relations. The good Squire Allworthy, already angry at Tom because young Blifil had told him that Tom was drunk when the good old man was lying at the point of death, banished Tom from the house.

Tom, having had all his money stolen, sets out upon the open road with Partridge, who had fallen upon evil times after having been banned from teaching jobs because of the suspicion that he was Tom's father. He convinces Tom that there was no truth in the accusation in the first place.

Sophia, meanwhile, found that her marriage with young Blifil was set for the next day. She fled and wound up at the same inn where Tom was having some difficulties with some ladies. He was perfectly innocent in the matter but Sophia believed the worst and left hastily.

Tom and Sophia, traveling apart, encountered many adventures and hardships before they again became reunited. They met in London and became reconciled about the time that Squire Western and Squire Allworthy were hastening there to bring about the marriage between Sophia and young Blifil. Tom is cast in prison at this time because of an altercation with a jealous husband who, in reality, had no cause to be suspicious.

Appearances point to the belief that Tom is involved with a Mrs. Waters, who in reality is Jenny Jones. Jenny explains the situation, however, and further demonstrates that Tom's real mother was Squire Allworthy's own sister, Bridget, who had died some years before. Jenny had been paid by Bridget to take the blame. The Squire also learns that Bridget, just before her death, had written him a letter telling him that Tom was her son—hers and that of a young student who had stayed for a while at the house. Young Blifil had destroyed the letter.

Squire Allworthy now banishes young Blifil from his sight and takes Tom back into his good graces. Delighted with this new turn of events, Squire Western welcomes Tom as his own son as well, and Tom Jones and his Sophia are married with the blessings of all.

## 29. Oliver Goldsmith: *The Vicar of Wakefield*
### Most popular of early English novels

*Page 173.* Goldsmith produced, not the greatest novel of the period, but the most popular in his century and one of the English language's most read books ever since. *The Vicar of Wakefield* (1766) is not a particularly strong novel but has features that have endeared it to readers for many generations. It is short; it is written in simple and clear prose; and it is full of the little problems of daily existence. The vicar is a lovable soul who maintains a calm front in the face of all difficulty. He wins through, without having his faith in God and his fellow man disrupted. The little novel is sentimental, but real. The characters are conventional types that are made to live as human individuals by Goldsmith's genius to handle the commonplace in an artistic manner. The continuous optimistic outlook of the characters, the purity of thought and the absence of morbid satire or dependence upon racy incidents give this novel a wholesome middle-class appeal that few novels have possessed in any literature. It is simply a well-written, folksy tale of the joys and sorrows of the Primrose family.

Charles Primrose, the vicar, tells the story and he begins, and ends, a simple, lovable figure, who struggles (and succeeds) in maintaining his high ideals for human behavior. Typical of his character is the beginning of his family and his reactions to the minor disturbances which early begin to touch the household:

> I was ever of the opinion that the honest man who married and brought up a large family did more service than he who continued single and only talked of population. From this motive, I had scarcely taken orders a year before I began to think seriously of matrimony, and chose my wife as she did her wedding gown, not for a fine glossy surface, but such qualities as would wear well. To do her justice, she was a good-natured woman; and as for breeding there were few country ladies who

could show more. She could read any English book without much spelling, but for pickling, preserving, and cookery, none could excel her. She prided herself also upon being an excellent contriver in housekeeping; though I could never find that we grew richer with all her contrivances.

However, we loved each other tenderly, and our fondness increased as we grew old. There was, in fact, nothing that could make us angry with the world or with each other. We had an elegant house, situated in a fine country, and a good neighborhood. The year was spent in moral or rural amusements, in visiting our rich neighbors, and relieving such as were poor. We had no revolutions to fear, nor fatigues to undergo; all our adventures were by the fireside, and all our migrations from the blue bed to the brown.

. . . Thus we lived many years in a state of much happiness; not but that we sometimes had those little rubs which Providence sends to enhance the value of its favors. My orchard was often robbed by school boys, and my wife's custards plundered by the cats or the children. The squire would sometimes fall asleep in the most pathetic parts of my sermon, or his lady return my wife's civilities at church with a mutilated courtesy. But we soon got over the uneasiness caused by such accidents, and usually in three or four days began to wonder how they vexed us.

The vicar and his wife, Deborah, had five lovely children. Olivia and Sophia were beautiful girls. The real troubles that were to beset the family begin when Dr. Primrose learns that his fortune has dissolved into thin air when a nefarious merchant, who had charge of his investments, absconded with the money. A quarrel immediately breaks out between the vicar and his son George's future father-in-law. The wedding is called off. In his reduced financial condition, the vicar is forced to seek a more humble position.

All of the troubles that now beset the family are domestic ones but they pile up, one upon the other, until they seem overwhelming. It seems that nothing else could happen, but it does. The vicar is very strict in his attitudes (at least they would seem so today) and is bothered endlessly with fears that his daughters are indiscreet and that various men have evil designs upon them.

His fears are confirmed in one quarter when his daughter Olivia is seduced by Squire Thornhill, after a mock wedding ceremony. As he approaches the house with his wayward daughter, he watches his home burn to the ground. The Primroses are now penniless and forced to live in some outbuildings on the squire's estate. Young Squire Thornhill, not succeeding in keeping Olivia as his mistress, sends Dr. Primrose to debtor's prison for nonpayment of rent.

George, the eldest son, attacks the evil squire and is sentenced to be hanged for attempted murder. At about this time, when Dr. Primrose thinks that he has heard the ultimate in bad news, Sophia is kidnaped.

At last, and quite suddenly, the clouds clear and the sun shines brightly upon the Primroses. Sophia is saved by Sir William Thornhill, the good uncle of the young rake. He wishes to marry the girl. George is reunited with his former sweetheart. It is discovered that Olivia had been married to young Thornhill by a real priest, and not the false one that the young scamp thought he had hired. The uncle disinherits the nephew and gives a generous portion of the estate to Olivia:

> "Thy vices, crimes and ingratitude deserve no compassion; but a bare competence shall be supplied thee, and thy wife shall possess a third part of that fortune which once was thine."

The vicar's broker was apprehended with the stolen funds and Dr. Primrose once more finds himself in the possession of his former modest fortune. Everything now seems to be very bright for the vicar. He only hopes that his gratitude for his good fortune can exceed his ability to be submissive when adversity overwhelmed him.

### 30.  Neoclassic Drama: *Three 18th Century Comedies of Manners*
Oliver Goldsmith: *She Stoops to Conquer*
Richard Brinsley Sheridan: *The Rivals*
Richard Brinsley Sheridan: *The School for Scandal*

*Pages 181, 183.* The three plays being summarized here are the best English plays since the Restoration drama of the turn of the century and the only plays which are outstanding in the age of a declining neoclassicism. All were written in the same decade (1773-1777). All three plays follow the lines laid down in the artificial comedy of manners of the Restoration period (See Congreve's *The Way of the World* [1700] p. 270 above).

And all three contain some of the satirical vein that characterized the earlier period.

## Restoration and 18th century drama compared

But there are a number of differences to be observed in this recurrence of the comedy of manners in the latter part of the 18th century. Social values are a little more stable and a new age is just over the horizon. Goldsmith's comedy has much of the new sentimentalism of the later age. It is gay and racy but its humor is less mordant and it depends more on clever situations than on biting wit. *She Stoops to Conquer* presents a more cheerful and optimistic world than did Congreve and his contemporaries. At times the situations are highly realistic, but the over-all effect is that of the idyl and of light romantic comedy. The idealism in Goldsmith was totally absent in Congreve.

Sheridan's plays also have the elements of Restoration drama, but again, his humor is more clean and his satire is less biting. He is bent on revealing the frivolous artificiality of the world of fashion of his day but he is interested in the reality of his characters and in the creation of amusing situations. His plays are satire but of a lighter nature. There is less of the pessimism, of the open flaunting of convention in Sheridan. He wishes to create an amusing mock world. His characters are caricatures of real people, but they have the essence of reality; but they are less important than the intrigues in which they are involved. Both Sheridan and Goldsmith are master stage craftsmen and they never let the audience forget that it is all just a play, that we are with them only in stageland. We must not take them too seriously. There is some of the atmosphere here of the Shakespearean light comedy. They allow their characters to flirt with fire, but they will never permit anyone to get burned seriously.

## Contemporary popularity of the comedies

These three comedies have persisted in popularity until today. They still attract and amuse audiences. They are laid in the late 18th century, but almost 200 years later, their lines sound strikingly modern and their situations are applicable in today's society. The lively wit and the unforgettable comic characterizations still cause the most sophisticated of modern audiences to rock with laughter and to leave the theater with a feeling that the cares and burdens of the day have been left behind in the empty theater seats.

## *She Stoops to Conquer* (1773)

*Page 181.* Kate Hardcastle is in a dither of excitement, for young Marlow is coming to see her. Marlow is Kate's father's choice for her for a husband and the young girl is anxious to see what he looks like, in spite of the fact that she has heard that he is shy and retiring. Hastings, in love with Kate's dearest friend Constance, is to come with Marlow. Mrs. Hardcastle had hoped that her son, Kate's half-brother, Tony Lumpkin, a lazy and spoiled fellow, would be a match for Constance, but the dear children hate each other.

Marlow and Hastings have lost their way and stop at the Three Pigeons Tavern. The lazy Tony Lumpkin happens to be there, loafing and flirting with the barmaids. He learns the identity and the destination of the two young men and decides to play a practical joke on them. He tells them that they can never reach the Hardcastle home that night but that, since this inn is so crowded, they should stop at an inn a bit further up the road, the Buck's Head. He has, in reality, guided them to the Hardcastle home.

Hastings and Marlow arrive, thinking that Hardcastle is the innkeeper, and begin to order the family around. They demand supper and a room. Constance meets Hastings and the two laugh over the joke but decide not to tell Marlow, since he is so shy and sensitive that he will leave in shame if he finds out the hoax. Hastings and Constance plan to elope if she can get her hands on her jewelry. Tony, who comes home about this time, plans to go into Mrs. Hardcastle's room and get the jewels for her. Meanwhile, Kate had heard of the two brazen and rude guests and decides not to dress in other than her ordinary house dress to meet them. When Marlow sees her he decides she must be "a female of the other class," for it seems he was not at all bashful with barmaids. Kate has a hard time keeping his hands from her person. She twits him about Miss Hardcastle and he replies: "Who cares for Miss Hardcastle? A mere awkward, squinting thing! . . . But you. . . ." Hardcastle comes in and sees the scene and orders Marlow from the house. Marlow, in a huff, demands his bill. Kate thinks that it is about time to clear things up and tells Marlow that he is at the Hardcastle home and she is a "poor relation." Marlow is very embarrassed, but realizes that he is in love with the poor maid. Kate begins to imagine also that Marlow is not so bad after all.

Tony, who had stolen the jewels, turned them over to Marlow. He, in turn, to insure their safekeeping, had turned them over to the supposed wife of the innkeeper, Mrs. Hardcastle. Now knowing of her niece's intended elopement, she decides to send the girl packing off to her Aunt Pedigree. Tony drives them away in the coach.

Sir Charles, Marlow's father, arrives and he and Hardcastle have a hearty laugh over the whole confusion, not realizing that Marlow still thinks that the maid and Kate are different persons. When Hardcastle twits him about embracing his daughter, Marlow replies: "By all that's just and true, sir, I never gave Miss Hardcastle the slightest mark of my attachment." Kate tells her father that Marlow had made love to her.

At the final denouement, things are becoming rather strained as Hardcastle grows angry: "You can address a lady in private and deny it in public; you have one story for us and another for my daughter." Kate appears and reveals the truth, and the couple are happily betrothed.

Tony, instead of taking Mrs. Hardcastle and her niece to the aunt's drove them around in the rain and through mud puddles and finally they wind up back at the Hardcastle home. By that time, Mrs. Hardcastle had gotten over her anger and consents that Constance and Hastings marry. Tony is relieved that it is now not he who must face that responsibility.

## The Rivals (1775)

*Page 183.* Lydia Languish lives with her aunt, Mrs. Malaprop. Lydia is so fed up with romantic novels that she wants to marry someone far below her position. Young Captain Jack Absolute has arrived in Bath to pay court to Lydia. He has previously masqueraded before her as Ensign Beverley since he knows her antipathy for young men of her class. Mrs. Malaprop has read some letters from the supposed Beverley and resents him because of a reference to her as a "she-dragon." A Sir Lucius O'Trigger is in love with Mrs. Malaprop, with whom he has corresponded, thinking her to be Lydia.

Sir Anthony Absolute had consulted with Mrs. Malaprop about a possible marriage between his son and Lydia. Mrs. Malaprop sees a way to avoid her niece's alliance with the insufferable and poor Beverley. In discussing the education of women, Sir Anthony asks Mrs. Malaprop what she would have

a girl know. Mrs. Malaprop (famous in drama for her misuse
of the English language) replies:

"Observe me, Sir Anthony. I would by no means wish a
daughter of mine to be a progeny of learning; I don't think so
much learning becomes a young woman: for instance, I would
never let her meddle with Greek, or Hebrew, or algebra, or
simony, or fluxions, or paradoxes, or such inflammatory
branches of learning—neither would it be necessary for her to
handle your mathematical, astronomical, diabolical instruments.
But, Sir Anthony, I would send her, at nine years old, to a
boarding-school, in order to learn a little ingenuity and artifice.
Then, sir, she should have a supercilious knowledge in accounts;
and as she grew up, I would have her instructed in geometry,
so she might know something of the contagious countries; but
above all, Sir Anthony, she should be mistress of orthodoxy,
that she might not miss-pell, and mis-pronounce words so
shamefully as girls usually do; and likewise that she might
reprehend the true meaning of what she is saying. This, Sir
Anthony, is what I would have a woman know; and I don't
think there is a superstitious article in it."

Jack Absolute, not knowing whom his father has chosen for
him, refuses to have anything to do with the arranged marriage.
Meanwhile, Jack's friend Faulkland is having a considerable
amount of misgivings in his wooing of Lydia's cousin, Julia.
Jack finds out who his father intends for him and consents to
meet the girl. At the meeting he whispers to Lydia that he is in
reality Ensign Beverley, posing as Jack Absolute.

Lydia has another suitor in the person of the country squire,
Bob Acres. He learns that he has a rival in Ensign Beverley and
sends a challenge to him through his friend, Sir Lucius O'Trigger. He, never having seen the Ensign, gives the challenge to
Jack Absolute to deliver.

Learning that Jack is Ensign Beverley causes Lydia to re-
nounce the whole affair as being very unromantic. Mrs. Malaprop is becoming very irked at Lydia's apparently fickle attitude:
"Oh, there's nothing to be hoped for from her! She's as head-
strong as an allegory on the banks of the Nile."

Jack is now challenged to a duel by Sir Lucius O'Trigger for
that evening. He states that he also must act as second on the
same evening for his friend Bob Acres in a duel with an Ensign
Beverley. When Lydia found that Jack was to duel for her, he
assumed quite a different aspect in her mind and she hurries to

get her aunt and rush to the field to stop the duel.

On the dueling field Sir Lucius is giving Bob Acres instructions in the proper method of fighting with pistols, in preparation for his duel with Ensign Beverley:

> *Sir Lucius:* Let him see the broadside of your front—there—now a ball or two may pass clean through your body, and never do any harm at all.
>
> *Acres:* Clean through me!—a ball or two clean through me!
>
> *Sir Lucius:* Ay, may they—and it is much the genteelest attitude into the bargain.
>
> *Acres:* Look'ee! Sir Lucius—I'd just as lieve be shot in an awkward posture as a genteel one; so, by my valor! I will stand edgeways.
>
> . . . . . .
>
> *Acres:* . . . my dear Sir Lucius but I-I-I don't feel quite so bold, somehow, as I did.
>
> *Sir Lucius:* O fy!—consider your honor.
>
> *Acres:* Ay—true—my honor. Do, Sir Lucius, edge in a word or two every now and then about my honor. . . .

Everyone arrives at the field and young Absolute tells Bob Acres that he is Beverley. Acres is relieved that he is not to fight. Sir Lucius and Jack begin to duel with swords when Mrs. Malaprop admits that she has been writing all the letters to Sir Lucius herself. Sir Lucius stalks off and leaves Mrs. Malaprop, while Jack and Lydia fall into each other's arms.

The subplot in which Faulkland alternates between mad love and mad jealousy of Julia is finally resolved when Jack Absolute persuades his friend that he must forget his mad sentimentality and become more realistic. Faulkland agrees to accept Julia's love for the wholesome thing it is and to cease his imaginings. Sheridan is using the character of Faulkland to satirize the sentimentality of his times. Early in the play he has Julia puzzling about this strange lover of hers:

> . . . Unused to the fopperies of love, he is negligent of the little duties expected of a lover—but being unhackneyed in the passion, his affection is ardent and sincere; and as it engrosses his whole soul, he expects every thought and emotion of his mistress to move in unison with his. Yet though his pride calls for this full return, his humility makes him undervalue those qualities in him, which would entitle him to it; and not feeling why he should be loved to the degree he wishes,

he still suspects that he is not loved enough. This temper, I must own, has cost me many unhappy hours. . . .

## The School for Scandal (1777)

*Page 183.* Lady Sneerwell had been gossiped about quite a good deal in her youth. Now that she has established herself in society, she resolves to retaliate. She organizes a regular group of ladies and gentlemen who come to her house for the express purpose of reducing reputations and assassinating characters. At present the group is engaged in working on the reputations of Charles and Joseph Surface and Sir Peter and Lady Teazle.

The two Surface brothers are wooing Maria, ward of Sir Peter Teazle. Charles is really in love with her; Joseph is more in love with Sir Peter's money. Sir Peter is susceptible to the flattery of Joseph and favors him over Charles in the suit. He also suspects Charles and his young wife, a lass recently from the country, and hence unused to city ways.

Sir Oliver Surface, recently returned to London after fifteen years absence, is the uncle to the two boys. He is anxious to test them to find where his fortune will be more secure when he dies.

Lady Teazle is an enthusiastic pupil at the School for Scandal at Lady Sneerwell's house. Sir Peter visits but receives the impression that the group is more given to dreaming up scandal about their friends than about their enemies. He leaves in disgust. The guests gradually leave the room to play cards. Joseph is alone with Lady Teazle and finds that he is smitten with her.

Meanwhile, Sir Oliver is receiving conflicting reports about his nephews. Sir Peter denounces Charles in favor of Joseph. Rowley, Sir Peter's servant, seems to think Charles has more character than Joseph. He resolves to visit each, under an assumed name. He goes to Charles as Mr. Premium, a banker. Charles begs for a loan and offers as security the family portraits. He, however, refuses to part with the portrait of his uncle, Sir Oliver: "No, hang it! I'll not part with poor Noll! The old fellow has been very good to me and, egad, I'll keep his picture as long as I can find a place for it." Sir Oliver is convinced that Charles is a waster, but honorable and affectionate toward him.

He goes to Joseph to beg for money for a poor relative. Joseph pleads that he is impoverished. Upon being reminded that Sir Oliver sends him large sums from India, Joseph expresses the opinion: "You are misinformed. Sir Oliver is a worthy man but he is old, and avarice is a vice of old age." Sir Oliver decides to leave his fortune to Charles.

Sir Peter accuses his wife of misconduct with Charles. In a huff, she goes to Joseph's rooms for advice. Sir Peter shows up and Lady Teazle hides behind a screen. Sir Peter berates Charles and hastily hides in a closet as Charles, himself, enters. Joseph, in attempting to get Charles to say something complimentary about Lady Teazle so that Sir Peter can overhear it, gets caught in his own trap as Charles shouts: "Who I? O Lud, not I, upon my word! Why, it's you, Joseph. Don't you remember one day, when I called, and found you together?" Joseph, in trying to quiet Charles, indicates that Sir Peter is in the closet. Charles drags the elderly gentleman out and tries to cover for Joseph by explaining that he was just playing a joke on Joseph. Sir Peter, who previously had seen a bit of skirt outside the screen and had been told by Joseph that it belonged to a milliner who was visiting him, tells Charles that Joseph is quite a rake, he knows, for he has "a little French milliner hidden there right now." Charles topples over the screen and reveals Lady Teazle.

Lady Teazle makes a clean breast of it all as Joseph tries to make excuses: "Don't listen to the hypocrite. I came here, seduced by his insidious arguments, at least to listen to his pretended passion, if not to sacrifice your honor. But I have recovered my senses. Sir Peter, the tenderness you expressed for me, when you did not know I was listening, has penetrated my heart. . . ." Sir Peter forgives her and takes her to his breast.

Lady Sneerwell and other members of the School for Scandal arrive and find that there is simply no scandal about. Sir Peter and Lady Teazle are reconciled; Charles, in his uncle's good graces, has the consent to marry Maria. There is nothing for Lady Sneerwell and Joseph Surface to do but to sneak out, mid the banter and laughter of all concerned:

> For laughter is the weapon of the wise;
> When malice meets with mirth, then scandal dies.

# *Appendix B*

# DICTIONARY
# OF LITERARY TERMS

The following glossary of terms includes brief, simple definitions of the terms indicated by an asterisk ( * ) in the main section. In addition, the student will find defined here many other terms dealing with literature which he might have seen in literary histories or anthologies or might have heard in lectures dealing with the early periods of English literature, leading to romanticism.

**Accent.** The stress given to a syllable in a word or a phrase. A series of accents, according to a predetermined pattern, gives the line of poetry a definite poetic rhythm. *See also* Poetry.

**Adage.** A saying which has become familiar through long usage. Example: "Here today, gone tomorrow."

**Adaptation.** The term used in literatures to indicate the attempt to achieve individual expression through use of already created materials. For instance: Chaucer *adapted* a well-known Oriental framework to give unity and form to his *Canterbury Tales.*

**Age.** A rather long, but indefinite, period of political or cultural history, distinguished by real or fictitious characteristics, and usually named for particular important characteristics or for real or imaginary personages. Examples: *The Age of Chaucer, The Middle Ages, The Age of Milton, The Restoration Age.*

**Alexandrine.** A verse line with twelve syllables or six feet, with usually a break (or caesura) after the sixth syllable. This line was used in Old French metrical romances and was never very popular in English poetry. However, Spenser used it as the final line to his eight-line stanzas. *See* Spenserian stanza, *also* Poetry. Pope, in his *Essay on Criticism,* mocked the Alexandrine line:

A needless Alexandrine ends the song,

Which, like a wounded snake,—drags its slow length along.

**Allegory.** A device used in narrative by which objects, incidents, or people are represented indirectly to the reader by means of personification or symbolism. A veiled or hidden meaning is metaphorically implied, but not expressly stated. The reader is intended, therefore, to understand not only the expressed events in the narrative but also the hidden truths or meanings. Many *parables* and *fables* are found in ancient literatures. In the English Middle Ages all the morality plays and beast epics are allegorical. Spenser's *The Faerie Queene* presents a complicated moral-theological-political allegory. Bunyan's *Pilgrim's Progress* is a famous Christian allegory. Swift's *Gulliver's Travels* is equally famous as satirical allegory. Most English allegory is very moral and religious.

**Alliterative verse.** A poetic device in which the initial letters or sounds in adjacent words or associated words in a line of poetry are merely repetitions of the same sound. Alliterative verse is found extensively in early Anglo-Saxon and Middle English verse. It is also used by modern poets. A line from Langland's *Piers Plowman* will illustrate the device:

> In a somer seson whan soft was the sonne,

Many cultured poets have ridiculed the primitively simple, but appealing, device. Shakespeare, in *A Midsummer Night's Dream,* has his rustic actors describe Pyramus' death:

> Whereat with blade, with bloody blameful blade,
> He bravely broach'd his boiling bloody breast;

**Amphibrach.** *See* Poetry.

**Anapest.** *See* Poetry.

**Antithesis.** A figure of speech in which there is an opposition or contrast of ideas by the use of words of strongly contrasting meaning. Example: "Man proposes, God disposes." Such contrasting ideas as "fair and foul," "heavenly and earthly," "foreign and domestic," etc. would form anthithesis.

**Apologue.** A short narrative, in prose or poetry, relating events, either true or fictional, with the principal objective of teaching a moral lesson. The moral may be deduced from allegorical happenings or it may be directly stated. The apologue is always simple and familiar in language and tone. It may utilize animals, gods, or even inanimate objects as characters. The apologue and the parable are variants of the fable. The apologue is of Oriental origin.

**Arcadia, Arcadian.** Refers to a district of ancient Greece which, according to tradition, was inhabited by simple shepherds and was the home of pastoral simplicity and happiness. *See* Pastoral.

**Arthurian romance.** *See* Romance, medieval.

**Artificiality.** In literature, this term would mean any writing which is deliberately and consciously affected and artistic. In form, the expression would be elaborate, ornate, and courtly or aristocratic. In theme, such writing would deal with unrealistic or fantastic subject matter. *See* Comedy of manners.

**Augustan Age.** A period of high literary attainment and general culture. So called because the age of the Roman Emperor Augustus Caesar (27 B.C. to 14 A.D.) was one of extreme cultural attainment in Rome, including such notable writers as Ovid, Vergil, Horace, Tibullus, etc. Such a period is also known as a Golden age (especially in Spanish literature from about 1550-1650). Both the Elizabethan age and the age of Dryden, Pope, and the classical writers are known as Augustan ages in English literature.

**Ballad.**   A form of folk verse, usually always narrative and employing a very direct and simple metrical form. The popular or folk ballad was composed to be recited or sung and treated some dramatic or timely episode in the lives or fancies of the common people during European Middle Ages. Most English popular ballads were produced from about 1250-1550 and dealt with themes of everyday life. They were transmitted by oral tradition and were memorized and recited as individual or community entertainment, by people who were free from the more aristocratic literary influences. Few were written until 16th century humanists became interested in the rich folk literature and began to collect and publish them. The most famous English ballads were collected on the borders between England and Scotland. The "literary" ballad is a composition of a cultured poet in imitation of the simple charm of the early popular form. The age of Romanticism is particularly rich in this artistic form.

**Ballade.**   A medieval French verse form, inherited from older Provençal poetry. It was a highly aristocratic form and should not be confused with the popular folk ballad.

**Baroque.**   A term applied to the overbold, startling, fantastic, and overdecorative in art. It was first applied to the architectural style which replaced the classic during the Renaissance, and flourished as the dominant style during the 17th and 18th centuries. In literature this tendency manifested itself especially with the Spanish Góngora and the English Lyly, and became commonly known as *gongorism* and *euphuism* (from Lyly's novels about Euphues), respectively. In literature, the term is often used to refer to the overly florid stylistic characteristics of the age of Góngora and Lyly. Hence the literature of this period might be called baroque literature.

**Bestiary, beast epics.**   Favorite literary form during the medieval period in which tales about animals and their characteristics were used to teach moral lessons or to satirize some phase of the church or state. These *bestiaries* gave to animals human attributes. Many of them purported to be scientific studies, but in reality, the method of study of the animals was purely a fabulous one and the characteristics of the animals were made to fit a moral pattern. These tales were composed both in prose and in verse. The French beast epics tended to take the form of verse and were highly satirical, e.g., *Roman de Renard*. The English bestiaries were usually prose tales used by Christian preachers to illustrate dogma.

**Blank verse.**   A form of rhymeless poetry, the lines usually consisting of ten syllables each, with accents on the even-numbered syllables (iambic pentameter). This form was used almost exclusively by Shakespeare and Milton. It has been popular throughout English literature for dramatic poetry and for long poems of a dramatic, philosophical, or narrative nature. It was first used by the Earl of Surrey. *See* Poetry.

**Broadside.**   Term given to narrative poems, ballads, and other popular songs, printed on one side only of a single sheet of paper and sold on street corners, at fairs, or other gatherings, for a penny or two during the 16th and 17th centuries. They were usually the work of hack poets and dealt with all manner of sensational subject matter such as murders, executions, freakish occurrences, political happenings, etc. The broadside was used for religious propaganda during the

Catholic-Protestant controversies in England. Many of these broadsides contained old folk ballads and songs and some indicated the music to which the contents were to be sung.

**Burlesque.** In literature, the term is usually applied to any composition in which serious matter is treated with ridiculous exaggeration, the purpose being to mock and to make absurd matter which, in itself, is sublime or dedicated to honest thought and emotion. *Parody* is often used as a term to indicate that the burlesque efforts have been directed to rephrasing or rewriting a serious work, giving it a frivolous or a nonsensical treatment. Burlesque, in common usage today, indicates stage entertainment in which there is much low comedy, obscene dancing, and exposure of nakedness.

**Caesura.** A pause or a break in a line of verse, usually near the middle of the line. *See* Poetry.

**Canto.** A section or a division of a long, usually narrative, poem. In early epic poetry it indicated a section which was considered of convenient length to be sung or recited by a minstrel at one time. Spenser's *The Faerie Queene* is divided into cantos; on the other hand, Milton's *Paradise Lost* is divided into books.

**Chapbook.** A book or pamphlet, cheaply printed and bound, carried about by chapmen or peddlers during the 16th, 17th, and 18th centuries. The books were sold on the streets or in small bookshops in large quantities at a few pennies. Many of the medieval romances, the first "thriller" novels, and popular ballads were sold in this manner. Also the chapbook became a favorite instrument for the dissemination of religious propaganda.

**Chaucerian stanza.** *See* rime royal, also Poetry.

**Chivalric romance.** *See* Romance of chivalry.

**Chorus.** In the ancient Greek drama of the 5th and 6th centuries before Christ, the chorus consisted in groups of dancers and singers, or the songs themselves. The chorus finally became an integral part of the plays themselves, being used to comment upon the action or to give the audience certain information which the lines of the drama itself did not reveal. The Elizabethan theater developed the chorus in various ways. Sackville and Norton, in *Gorboduc,* used the chorus for pantomime to indicate symbolically certain events to come. Shakespeare used often a single character who gave a prologue and an epilogue commenting upon the import of the entire drama, such as Prospero in *The Tempest.* Often a character, within the action itself, would be used by the author to explain certain aspects of the action. The fool, in Shakespeare's *King Lear,* is used for this purpose.

**Chronicle.** The term implies a sort of historical miscellany which purports to be comprehensive and universal in its scope. It lacks the documentation and critical attitude of historians, and is often incomplete and sketchy. At times the writer maintains an impartial attitude, and at other times he becomes very partisan and emotional. In many cases, the chronicle reports that which is simply legendary. *The Anglo-Saxon Chronicle,* begun by King Alfred in the 9th century, is the most-known English example. This book reports events back to 60 B.C. and was continued by various followers of Alfred to 1154. The *chronicle play* has a purely historical theme, the early Elizabethan examples being based upon Holinshed's *Chronicle of England and Scotland* (1577). The chronicle play often departed considerably from its historical thread and treated material that was purely fictional. The most famous series of chronicle plays are those of Shakespeare.

**Classicism.** As applied to literatures, the term usually refers to the meaning attached to it among the Renaissance writers, who considered only the great works of Greek and Roman literatures as being of sufficient importance to imitate and emulate in their own efforts. Therefore the form and content of those works was *classical* and anything produced in imitation of that form and content was also *classical*. Therefore, from this angle, the term would mean a return to the form and ideals of the ancients. The term, then, would imply "disciplined" literature, emphasis on form rather than content, technical perfection rather than experimentation, precision and objectivity over emotional expressiveness and individuality, rational thinking over imaginative and wild fantasy. The style must be clear, lucid and restrained, controlled and intellectual, moderated and decorous.

The modern works, thus produced on ancient models, would then become "classics" in themselves and later periods which imitated either the modern or the ancient *classics,* would also be termed classic, e.g., the period of neoclassicism with Pope, Dryden, Swift, and Johnson. Broadly, then, the term would cover any piece of literature which, in the opinions of critics over the years, has achieved a solid and recognized position for its excellent qualities. This would be true even for *romantic* works.

In the late 17th and early 18th centuries, the famous controversies of the "battle of the books" variety, was centered on the question of the values of classic versus modern writings. The "modern" group maintained that the classic ideas were unchristian, pagan, low, and vulgar. They maintained that the ancients' style was obsolete and that modern literatures should become less interested in what the past did and be more concerned with modern men, their thoughts and feelings, expressed in new and brighter styles. The "classic" group maintained, of course, that the style and content of the ancients were unsurpassed and that moderns could learn the solid values only from them. It was thus a battle between *discipline* and *inspiration* in literary endeavor. This basic difference between the manner in which the human mind may approach material for thought and expression is, of course, always with us. It is only when large groups of writers lean radically toward the *classic* or the *romantic* extremes that such labels as *neoclassicism, romantic school,* etc. are attached to them.

**Closet drama.** This term is applied to drama which is not written for the purpose of being acted on the stage. It is designed for reading only and does not concern itself with stage technique. It is usually very philosophical and there is little action; it would therefore be little suitable for presentation to large groups. Milton's *Samson Agonistes* is an oustanding English example. Seneca's *Tragedies* provide us with the most famous of ancient examples.

**Comedy.** Comedy is opposed, in idea, to tragedy. Comedy is a light form of drama and is designed to amuse and entertain, and almost invariably ends happily, at least for the admirable characters. A play which ends without any deaths has traditionally been considered comedy. However, tragedy does not necessarily imply that there will be bodies lying around the stage; it simply implies deep conflicts, with a great deal of serious sorrow and sadness prevalent in the action. We may call plays *tragicomedies* when there is a mixture of the tragic and the comic. Comedy may be fantasy, on an utterly idealized plane, with no connection with human lives, or it may involve serious human psychological and social problems. Comedies may be highly exaggerated matter, designed to thrill in a sensational manner (melodrama) or they may be somewhat realistic exposures of the customs of social groups, such as the *comedy of manners* or the *satirical comedy*. They may be analyses of the inner workings of the human mind, such as *psychological comedy*, or descriptions of the inner working of family relationships, such as *domestic comedies*. The line between comedy and tragedy is not a hard and fast one. The Spanish have always called both comedy and tragedy by the term *comedia*. Comedy which is designed to appeal somewhat to the intelligence and is more subtle and sophisticated, and not designed to provoke raucous laughter (such as would the *farce comedy*), is designated "high" comedy; comedy which is bawdy and broad in its grotesque and exaggerated characterization and crude lines, is designated "low". *See* Drama, Tragedy.

**Couplet.** A pair of verse lines in which the end words rhyme. In English literature, the best examples of the form are called the *heroic couplet*, because it was adapted during the 17th and 18th centuries for poems of an epic nature. In poems without the implications of grandeur and serious purpose, the couplet is quite often known as simply *rimed couplet*. Pope was a master of the couplet and always insisted that each couplet express a complete thought. *See* Poetry.

> Lo, the poor Indian! whose untutor'd mind
> Sees God in clouds, or hears him in the wind;

**Dactyl.** *See* Poetry.

**Dark ages.** Usually refers to the earlier centuries of the Middle Ages (about the 5th to the 11th centuries). The term is used to indicate the lack of intellectual or artistic activity in Europe during that period. It is a very loose term, however, since there are evidences of such activity in isolated spots during this period. *See* Medieval.

**Didactic poetry.** Verse which is essentially dedicated to teaching lessons or moral truths. All verse, of course, to a certain extent will contain truth. This term, however, is only applied when the beauties of poetic expression are used as a specific vehicle for teaching. Much of medieval poetry was written to illustrate Christian truths. Pope's *Essay on Man* or his *Essay on Criticism* are famed examples of didactic poetry.

**Doggerel.** Any ill-constructed verse of loose, poorly executed rhyme and rhythm. Many known poets have used doggerel verse to burlesque and satirize literary fads in writing or certain literary compositions. Chaucer's *Sir Thopas* is an outstanding example of the use of doggerel with the deliberate attempt of satirize the verse romances of the poet's age.

**Drama.** As applied to literary forms, drama requires a story, or series of actions, a setting and actors to impersonate the characters in the story. According to Aristotle, drama is "imitated human action." As applied to the theater, drama covers all types of work designed for performance. Therefore its most elementary expression is in mimic of actions and of vocal expression (both as to emotion and dialogue) of the characters involved in the dramatic composition.

Most literary works, which relate some narrative action involving conflict, contain dramatic elements in the broad sense of there being a sufficient emotional content to produce a conflict. Therefore dramatic literature may not necessarily be designed to be presented before an audience. It may even involve action presented in dialogue (*see* Closet drama) but be written exclusively for the reader who may simply visualize the action. Drama may pantomime action, with no spoken words, or it may depend almost exclusively upon the content of dialogue for its effects. It may involve very elaborate scenery and music or singing. It has then entered the realm of opera, musical comedy, pageant, or masque. But to be an actable play or theatrical piece, the composition must be a representation of life, presented by means of a succession of events, related by dialogue and pantomime action.

**Dream allegory.** A type of allegory in which the author sees the events he relates in a dream or a vision. Famed examples of the allegory in which the author acquired his materials in this way are Dante's *Divine Comedy*, Bunyan's prose allegory, *Pilgrim's Progress*, and Langland's *Piers Plowman*. A famed allegory in which this method is not employed is Spenser's *The Faerie Queene*. *See* Allegory.

**Droll.** During the time of the Commonwealth in England—when the Puritan laws forbade the production of stage plays—there developed a form of short dramatic sketches, which were presented privately or on temporary platforms, in lieu of full-length productions. These were quite often scenes taken from longer plays; at times they were original comic pieces, involving songs and dances. These short pieces acquired the names of "droll," "droll humour," or "drollery."

**Dumb show.** A form of pantomime, or silent acting, integrated usually as a part of a major play. The purpose of the "dumb show," in the Elizabethan theater was to illustrate symbolically some phase of the main action. A famed example of the use of this symbolic scenic device is in Sackville and Norton's *Gorboduc*. The dumb show was quite often employed in masques to represent some allegorical dream or imagined scene. In Shakespeare's *Hamlet*, the dumb show is used to represent the production of the actors at the court of Denmark. Uusally, there were no speaking lines in the dumb show; it was purely pantomime.

**Ecologue.** The term came to be applied to the pastoral poems of Vergil. The ecologue was a poem in which two shepherds converse, each perhaps describing his love. Other ecologue versions involved a lament for a dead shepherd, or the sad complaints of a shepherd over the loss of a sweetheart. Sometimes the ecologue had music and involved a type of singing contest between shepherds. Whatever form the ecologue took, the necessary ingredients were: a pastoral setting, flocks of sheep, and shepherds. A famed English example of ecologues is Spenser's *The Shepherd's Calendar,* made up of one ecologue for each month in the year.

**Elegy.** Usually a poem in which the content is a lament for the dead. However, any lyric expression of sorrowful thoughts upon the subject of death is considered an elegy. A famed English example is Gray's *Elegy Written in a Country Churchyard* (1750).

**Enlightenment.** This term is generally applied to the distinctly philosophical movement in western Europe during the later years of the 17th and almost all of the 18th centuries. It was a movement that was largely concerned in making reason the sole ruler of human life. All authority, Church and State, was to be questioned in the light of a new and modern experimental type of reasoning. In England, the term "enlightenment" is seldom used in connection with literature, although it is true that English philosophers (Bacon, Hobbes, and Locke) actually preceded the great French and German movements which bear the name. In England, this questioning attitude became part and parcel of the neoclassical period in such writers as Pope and Swift, whose writings show a constant questioning of the *status quo* of the social institutions of their time, and at times a very nasty, cynical, and hard-boiled attitude. Outside the realm of purely didactic philosophy, the English development of "enlightenment" largely took the form of mordant and bitter satire—a firm resolve to hold up contemporary society to ridicule in the hopes of reforming it before it was too late.

**Epic poetry.** This term has been used in literatures to designate long narrative poems of a dramatic character dealing with the real or fictitious story of notable actions carried out in an heroic manner under the inspiration of some powerful social or supernatural force. In literary history, two types of epic poem have been recognized. In the *folk epic,* one principal hero bears upon his shoulders a powerful national or group honor. This epic developed from popular songs or ballads relating various great deeds of the central hero. When, as early as the 5th century, various European groups began to gain a civic conscience and a feeling for the group which went beyond individual material gain, there began to develop various of these crude "folk" epics. Most of these early epic efforts have been lost to us, but there is ample evidence that they existed throughout European areas from Scandinavia to Spain. These "folk" epics developed independently of the knowledge of these peoples of the great epics of the ancient classical world: the *Iliad* and *Odyssey* of Homer and *Aeneid* of Vergil. As vernacular languages developed among these early European folk groups, these poems received written form and a few have survived nearly in their original forms. Notable examples are: the Anglo-Saxon *Beowulf,* the French *Chanson de Roland,* the Germanic *Nibelungenlied,* and the Spanish *Poem of the Cid.*

The popularity of the folk epic was killed, perhaps, by the introduction of more and more elements of love and fantastic exaggeration in the metrical romances of the 13th century forward and the rise of prose as a narrative form. The long, majestic, and heroic epic poem was not seen again until cultured poets of the late medieval period and the Renaissance began to produce the new *artistic epic* (also known as *literary epic, art epic*). These *artistic epics* have a single known author, but are written in the same grandiose style as the folk epic. Dante's *Divine Comedy* and Milton's *Paradise Lost* are the noblest of these *art epics,* using Christianity as the ennobling theme. Ariosto's *Orlando Furioso* is a noble example of the burlesque epic, employing all the exaggeration of the medieval romance. The outstanding English example of the use of a modern theme of no importance within the framework of noble grandeur and heroic atmosphere is the mock-heroic epic of Pope: *The Rape of the Lock.*

**Epigram.** Any writing which, in very brief prose or verse form, achieves completeness of thought in a witty, pithy, and pointed manner. Epigrams tend to be humorous and ironical, usually defining some human foible or social weakness in a terse, satirical manner. The epigram was popular in classic Roman literature and received its greatest modern revival in English literature in the neoclassic period. Pope, especially, was a master of the epigram in heroic couplets:

> To observations which ourselves we make,
> We grow more partial for th' observer's sake.
>
> . . . . .
>
> Who builds a church to God and not to fame,
> Will never mark the marble with his name.

**Epistle, epistolary novel.** A letter which, in literature, is given a formal, didactic, elegant, or stylistic treatment. A novel in which the narrative is carried forward by a series of letters between the characters is called an *epistolary novel.* The first epistolary novel in English is Richardson's *Pamela* (1740). He followed it in 1747 with *Clarissa Harlowe,* which influenced the European novel considerably. Rousseau wrote his *La Nouvelle Héloïse* (1761) in the epistolary form. Smollett's *Humphrey Clinker* (1771) and Burney's *Evelina* (1778) were also written in the form of letters.

**Essay.** The term is not easily distinguished with exactitude. The word *essay,* as first used by Montaigne in 1571-1580, was a volume of short, reflective observations on human life and institutions. The English Bacon immediately adapted this word to his own more cold scientific observations on life. The word, then, is loosely used to cover any piece of literature, preferably prose, which, in its purpose, is expository and informative. Since Francis Bacon (1561-1626), the essay has been a highly developed form of English writing and has taken many styles (Pope's *Essays,* for instance, are written in heroic couplets). But, generally, the following characteristics define the essay: (1) it is reflective in its approach to matter, (2) it is brief, (3) it does not tell a story, but may employ narrative episodes to further the didactic purpose, (4) it may be "informal" in that it reflects viewpoints, tastes, and feelings of the author in a whimsical, humorous, or warm-hearted manner, or it may be "formal" in that it is a serious study of almost any phase of human interest, but it does not require either plot or characterization and does not require any particular completeness or unity of structure.

**Euphuism.** Gabriel Harvey, a contemporary of Lyly, first used the term "euphuism" to describe the prose style employed by Lyly in his novels, *Euphues: or the Anatomy of Wit* (1579) and *Euphues and his England* (1580). Euphuism is, then, an elaborated and affected prose style, depending on strings of similes and complicated patterns of antithesis, alliteration, and metaphorical comparisons for its effects. The effect of euphuistic writing tends to be monotonous, with its planned variations of pitch and rhythm and its systematically built paragraphs. But Lyly's stilted and elegant style persisted for more than two hundred years in English prose, much as a contagious literary disease, and prevented it from becoming clear, simple, and direct, The *baroque* style of prose, of which *euphuism* is merely the English manifestation, is common to all European literatures of the late 16th and early 17th centuries. In Spanish literature we know it as *gongorism* (*conceptism or culteranism*); in Italian literature as *Marinism* (*concettism* or *secentism*); in French, the same tendency is shown in *preciosité*, and in German, *schwulst*. In England, this style is also apparent in the *metaphysical* poetry of the 17th century.

**Fabliau** (plural **fabliaux**). Short, usually obscene or ribald, stories of the medieval period, of a highly satirical nature. This type of short tale in verse flourished during the 12th and 13th centuries in France and was widespread among the Norman-French in England. The form was popular with the common people and usually concerned domestic intrigue, adultery, the foibles and weaknesses of the clergy, and was full of simple and crassly indecent jokes and tricks. Chaucer used the basis of the *fabliau* for his *Miller's Tale*.

**Farce.** Usually applied to any humorous play in which the plot and the incidents are grossly exaggerated as to provoke raucous laughter on the part of the audiences. The incidents tend to go beyond reality in their ludicrous and grotesque development and the dialogue is racy and full of broad and comic expression. *See* Comedy.

**Foot.** *See* Poetry.

**Gnomic verse.** Verse which deals in an aphoristic and moralistic way with ethical questions. In English literature, this term is particularly applied to the great body of short verse (often only maxims or riddles) in Old English which dealt, in a sententious way, with the wisdom of the Bible. The poets of the 6th century B.C. in ancient Greece, who wrote a great deal of short sayings, or maxims, of a moral nature, are designated "the gnomic poets of antiquity."

**Gothic, Gothic romance, Gothic novel.** The term, in literature, is used to designate a type of novel which flourished from about 1765 to 1820. In medieval times the radical departure in architecture, the nonclassic style which medieval churches and ecclesiastical building took from about the 11th to the 16th centuries, was designated Gothic. This architectural style features pointed arches and vaults, slender spires and buttresses. The 18th century neoclassics looked upon these old castles and churches, with their bat-infested vaults, their dungeon keeps, and their eerie passageways and towers, as something frightful and to be associated with ghosts and fiendish murder. Added to this, the neoclassics looked upon the ancient Gothic tribes as having been savages and barbarians.

The Gothic romance or novel, then, is so named to indicate any such writing which offended the classic taste of simplicity and dignity, that dealt with horror, violence, murder, and the mysterious workings of exaggerated fancy. This type of novel began in England, but its popularity soon spread to the continent and to America. Especially popular in Germany, this novel became a tale of terror and supernatural and weird effects, usually always laid in a medieval setting of an old Gothic castle. Horace Walpole's *Castle of Otranto* (1764) is one of the first and one of the best of these Gothic novels. During the romantic school, in the early 19th century, there was a *Gothic revival,* in which attention turned once more to medieval, primitive, and wild settings for the novel. This is one of the outstanding phases of the romantic movement.

**Graveyard poetry.** The term "graveyard school" is usually applied to a group of poets, during the last half of the 18th century, who became preoccupied with thoughts of death and immortality, and whose verse reflected a gloomy, melancholic, and morbid tone. This preromantic group of poets chose graveyards and cemeteries as their favorite settings. Gray's *Elegy* and the *Night Thoughts* of Edward Young are superb examples, written about mid-18th century.

**Heptameter.** *See* Poetry.

**Heroic age, heroic verse.** The term refers basically, to a hero, one of superhuman strength and of noble aspirations. The term has come to be applied to the age of Homer and the ancient Greek heroes about whom he wrote in his *Iliad* and *Odyssey.* Hence, any other primitive age in which heroes are sung about, is known as a "heroic age." Such an age was that of *Beowulf,* in the northern Baltic lands, about the 5th and 6th centuries. Heroic verse is generally that verse in which heroic epics are written, the pattern being the hexameter verse (a line of six metrical feet) of ancient Greek and Latin heroic epics. More modernly, epics are written in *blank verse,* such as Milton's *Paradise Lost,* or the heroic couplet (iambic pentameter lines), in which were written the heroic plays of the Restoration period in England. This so-called "heroic" couplet dominated English poetry from 1600 to 1800. In Renaissance Italian heroic verse, the form became an eight-syllable line (instead of the English ten) and is known as the *ottava rima.* Ariosto's *Orlando Furioso* is written entirely in this Italian version of the "heroic" verse form. *See* Poetry for definition of *heroic couplet, hexameter, iambic pentameter.*

**Hexameter.** *See* Poetry.

**Humanism.** The term suggests any attitude tending to exalt the human interests, as opposed to the supernatural or to the gross, animal elements. Humanism, then, means a devotion to those studies which promote the advancement and enjoyment of life upon this earth. In our use, during the Renaissance period, the term is applied to the state of mind which, in Europe, began to put emphasis upon the individual and this earth, rather than upon the medieval scholastic attitude with its total emphasis upon the life to come in the other world. The Renaissance humanists took as their models and inspiration the learning and literatures of the ancient Greek and Roman world, and attempted to mold a new world by imitation, adaptation, and experimentation. (See pp. 44-45 for a more detailed discussion.)

**"Humours," comedy of humours.** The medieval theories of the human body assigned to man's physical structure four humours: blood, phlegm, yellow and black biles. These corresponded to the four elements of nature, outside of man: air, fire, water, and earth. It was believed that disturbances of the physical earth were caused by an upsetting of the balance of its four elements. Likewise, it was believed that man's temperament depended upon the state of his "humours." In Elizabethan times, the medieval theory was applied to character delineation, both in drama and the essay. By 1600, actions and disposition of characters were described and explained by the particular balance or "unbalance" of their humours. Thus a good-natured man showed a perfect balance between his humours. Disordered states of disposition, mood, or pronounced character traits were explained by particular dominance of one of the humours. This "humours" theory had a very great influence upon late Elizabethan and early Stuart literature in the many essays of "character" which were written and the great many *comedies of "character"* or *comedies of "humours"* which were presented. Ben Jonson's two comedies, *Every Man in His Humour* and *Every Man Out of His Humour* (1598-1602) are illustrative of the best of the comedies which exploited this quaint theory. The movement contributed a great deal toward the development of the *comedy of manners*.

**Hyperbole.** A figure of speech consisting in exaggerated statement for the purpose of giving an effect, not intended to be taken literally. Example: *a sea of mud; waves mountain high*.

**Iambic, iambic pentameter, iambic tetrameter.** *See* Poetry.

**Interlude.** This term is generally used to designate specifically the short skits, or dramatic sketches or short, farcical plays, very popular during the early 16th century. These little plays were performed in the court, at schools, and at feasts or fetes at the estates of the nobility. The interlude formed an important link between the medieval miracle and morality plays and the full-fledged comedies of the later Elizabethan age.

**Jacobean literature.** The term which is applied to the particular characteristics which literature showed, following the reign of Elizabeth and during that of James I in England (1603-1625). This period was one of transition, from the high Renaissance to an age of Puritan dominance. The literature of this period is also often called *Stuart* literature (particularly the plays) as contrasted with the term *Tudor,* used in connection with the age of Elizabeth Tudor. Under *Jacobean* would come the late works of Shakespeare, those of Jonson, Bacon, Donne, and others. The tendency in this age is definitely toward a more intellectual and scientific tone and away from the purely colorful and sensual. A tendency toward the satirical and the critical is also noted. The term *Jacobean* comes from the Latin form of *Jacobus,* or James.

**Liturgical drama.** A term usually applied to the early phases of the dramatization of portions of the Bible within the Church itself, beginning sometime around the 9th century. Particularly, the liturgy pertaining to the Easter season was dramatized for the congregations by scenic representations, with priests acting the various biblical roles. Gradually, liturgical drama came to include any material from the New Testament. Also it moved from the cathedral to the market-place and the local lay organizations began to provide actors and to write the scripts. Thus the liturgical drama gradually became the miracle and the mystery play of the later Middle Ages, a thoroughly secularized drama.

**Lyric poetry.** The term *lyric* in poetry always implies a musical qual-ity, since all early lyric poetry was intended to be sung. Lyric poetry today is any verse which is highly personal and emotional and which is a sincere expression of feeling. There may be ideas or thought, or even narrative elements, in lyric poetry, but they are definitely subordinate to the expression of the subjective emotion of the poet, couched in a metrical language, which is designed to appeal to the emotional, rather than the intellectual, in the mind of the reader or hearer.

**Masque.** This form of entertainment was an elaborate, costly, and spectacular aristocratic entertainment which reached its heights of popularity during the latter part of the reign of Elizabeth, and during the reigns of James I and Charles I. The masque depended mainly upon color and spectacular scenery, dramatic tableaux, and music. The literary masque combined a story with all this color, and pro-duced such outstanding examples as Milton's *Comus.* The first masques came to England from Italy. Shakespeare introduces one in his *Love's Labour's Lost.* Many of the late Elizabethan and the Jacobean writers vied with each other in the production of masques. Ben Jonson was, perhaps, the most successful writer of this form of elab-orate, and expensive, entertainment. It is obvious that the masque was an early precursor of the opera.

**Medieval.** Of or pertaining to the Middle Ages, the transition between the early and the later ages, the early age of the glories of antiquity (roughly to 400 A.D.) and the glories of the Renaissance period (roughly beginning about 1400) and the death of feudalism and scholasticism as systems.

**Melodrama.** A play or dramatic spectacle which employs startling and sensational action and lurid, emotional, and exaggerated language in order to play upon the emotional and sentimental reactions of the audience. Integration of plot, character development, and dramatic motivation are definitely secondary to the exaggerated incidents of the action, designed to inspire horror, joy, deep feelings of pity and sorrow. This type of play is usually full of hairbreath escapes, op-pressive villains, noble heroes, and sorrowing families who are rescued, usually, in the nick of time, with all ending happily for the good people and sadly for the bad ones. The term *melodramatic* may be applied to any form of writing in which the sensational and the spectacular predominate.

**Metaphysical poetry.** The term "metaphysical" was first applied by Samuel Johnson, in his *Lives of the Poets,* to a group of early 17th century poets who attempted to analyze their inner and spiritual feel-ings in their verse. The poetry of this group is distinguished by its striking imagery, its development of startling figures of speech and conceits of idea, in the effort to reveal psychological effects of love and spiritual inspiration. Initiated by John Donne, this often grotesque and strange verse was written by a number of other English poets of the time, including George Herbert, Henry Vaughn, Thomas Traherne, Abraham Cowley, and Richard Crashaw.

**Meter.** *See* Poetry.

**Metrical romance.** *See* Romance.

**Miracle and mystery plays.** The chief forms that medieval drama took in Europe. The mystery play originated in the liturgy of the Church and revolved around depiction of the Nativity, the Passion, and the Resurrection. The term *mystère* was given to these early religious plays by the French to denote the religious *ministerium,* or function of the drama. Later, when these plays began to become secularized and to treat various themes or miracles, derived from nonbiblical sources, such as the lives of saints and the various legends of the miraculous workings of the Virgin, these little plays came to be known as "miracles." The English continued to refer to all manner of little religious pieces as "miracle plays" until well into the 15th century. The mystery play, then, was one that adhered strictly to the scriptural subjects. However, this distinction is hard to maintain, since various cycles of these plays show a mixed nature. Modernly, most authorities lump all of this medieval sacred drama under the term "miracle."

**Monometer.** *See* Poetry.

**Morality plays.** The moralities developed from the earlier mystery or miracle plays and are noted in the 15th and 16th centuries. These little religious plays are distinguished by their use of dramatized allegory, in which virtues and vices are personified in their struggle for the soul of man. Where the earlier plays portrayed characters taken from the Bible or from the lives of saints and medieval legend, these moralities portrayed directly such "deadly" sins as avarice, lechery, pride, wrath, envy, sloth, gluttony, covetousness, in their realistic attempts to gain man for themselves. Allied against them were such characters as faith, mercy, conscience, etc. These moralities tended to be very realistic and often involved very heated and humorous debates between virtues and vices. Gradually, as the Protestant Reformation gained ground in the 16th century, these little plays began to be filled with ethical and social questions; the didactic elements began to obscure the dramatic and the realistically racy dialogue of the earlier moralities. It was in the late 16th century that the English comedy, with its broad realistic humor in a Roman sense, replaced the morality play in popular taste.

**Mystery play.** *See* Miracle play.

**Mystical literature.** Much of English writing (notably the metaphysical school of the 17th century, Bunyan's *Pilgrim's Progress,* and much of the Puritan Age in general) concerned itself with man's attempts to communicate directly with the divine spirit. The expression of this faith of man's contact with the spiritual elements of Nature or with some concept of deity is known in literatures generally as *mysticism.* English writers have shown varying aspects of this expression of spiritual communication. Some have inclined to religion, others to philosophy, while still others have communicated directly with the beauties of nature. All have expressed their personal reactions in more or less symbolic language. John Bunyan's allegorical approach is simple and direct; that of William Blake presents us with a highly abstruse and complex expression of poetic mysticism.

**Neoclassicism.** *See* Classicism. The revival of classicism in the Restoration period and in 18th century England is usually known as *neo-* or *pseudo-* classicism since, in reality, it was a conscious attempt at a revival, in a modern interpretation, of the ideals of ancient literatures, particularly that of Rome. In reality, the conventional approach of the modern classic school was one of imagined, rather than real, classic concepts in the "ancient" sense. The modern revival of the ancient spirit of Horace and Vergil was based upon order and reason, decorum and dignity, clarity and moderation, and loftiness of purpose. These ideals were simply reactions against very modern excesses of imagination and flights of fancy assigned to the Renaissance writers. Furthermore, the English neoclassicism was not based directly upon the Roman models at all, but rather on contemporary French attitudes and pronouncements as to what constituted "revival" of the spirit of the classic writers. In fact, all the modern revivals of "classic" spirit are simply returns to more order and discipline in writing and less of the individual and imaginative spirit that characterizes periods of romanticism. Classic writing, in a modern sense, tends to be colorless and unimaginative, but intellectual and clever. Entire groups of writers follow the same rules (usually following some literary "dictator," such as Dryden, Pope, or Johnson) and produce material with a permeating sameness. The spirit of English neoclassicism was definitely satirical and mordant, but clever and witty. It was a literature that reflected discouragement of individual expression in art. It was a literature devoted to correctness and "good taste"—the "good taste" of the dominant literary groups, such as the coffee-house society of Pope and Johnson.

**Novel.** A novel is usually considered a fictitious prose tale, of considerable length, in which an integrated plot, professing to be a cut from real life, is woven around characters and actions. This definition, of course, is highly inadequate, since we classify as novels many fictional works which do not tell a story and which have very little action. But, by and large, the novel is written to entertain, to present a problem or enlarge upon some ethical question, or to present a realistic cut from real life. It tends to be long (from 80,000 words up) and to be an integrated whole as to plot, characterization, and purpose. The modern novel is an 18th century development with Defoe and Richardson in England. In Spain, Cervantes wrote the first modern novel with his *Don Quijote* (1605-1615). Many *fictional* forms existed in ancient literatures with what could, roughly, be called a novelistic pattern. But, from *Robinson Crusoe, Pamela,* etc. forward to the present day, the novel has been the most popular form of literature and many have been the modern attempts to inject into this form the elements of poetry, drama, and the essay. For the most part, the novel has continued to treat adventure and love as the two major themes, but many novels are written for the purposes of propaganda, to develop social issues, to analyze character, or to teach truth.

**Novella.** Early Italian literature developed a short fictional genre, taking the form of a short tale or story and having little interest in character development, which became popular there as *novella*. This form was adapted by other European literatures and became highly popular in the English Renaissance period. It continued to be a short prose narrative tale. Cervantes' *Novelas ejemplares* (1614) is an outstanding European example of a collection of these tales, patterned upon the Italian models of Boccaccio, Bandello, and others. In Spanish, Italian, and English literatures the term came later to apply to the longer forms of prose fiction (*see* Novel). But the term *romance* (referring to the medieval tales of chivalry, *see* Romance) continued to form the basis for the term to describe the longer fictional works in France and Germany, e.g., the German *romanz* and the French *roman*.

**Octameter.** *See* Poetry.

**Octave.** *See* Poetry.

**Octosyllabic couplet.** *See* Poetry.

**Ode.** The ode, as invented by the ancient Greek writers, was a type of lyric poem, intended to be set to music and sung. Modernly, the ode is any exalted lyric composition, characterized by nobility of sentiment and dignity of style. The ode has one progressive theme and very often this single theme is named in the title, e.g., Collins: *Ode to Liberty*.

**Ottava rima.** *See* Poetry.

**Parody.** A literary composition in imitation of the form or content of another work, another author, or a particular literary style. The *parody* is almost always written for the purpose of ridicule. Pope's *Rape of the Lock* is a parody of the grandeur of heroic epic themes and style. Fielding's *Joseph Andrews* was begun as a parody of the exaggerated sentimentality of Richardson's *Pamela*. Thus, quite often, parodies become literary masterpieces in themselves.

**Pastoral.** The term may be applied to any composition in which the principal theme is woven around a rural setting, with shepherds, flocks of sheep, and country swains and their maidens. The genre developed from the *Bucolics* of Theocritus, a Greek writer of 3rd century B.C. It was given further development in Roman literature by Vergil. The form received Renaissance development in Italy. During the 16th and 17th centuries France, England, and Spain developed the form as a very aristocratic genre both in the novel and in poetry. Montemayor's *Diana* and the poetry of Garcilaso and Boscán are notable Spanish examples. In England Sidney's *Arcadia* (1590) and Lodge's *Rosalynde* are examples of the pastoral romance; Fletcher's *Faithful Shepherdess* and Jonson's *Sad Shepherd* are examples of the pastoral drama. Shakespeare's *As You Like It* is a notable example of a pastoral romance in drama, in imitation of Lodge's novel. The *pastoral ecologue* is represented by Spenser's *Shepherds' Calendar*. Milton's *Lycidas* is an outstanding *pastoral elegy*. *See* Ecologue and Elegy. This pastoral literature is, of course, not realistic. It is simply the fancy and sentimental nostalgic longings of the lords and ladies of the courts for the simple rural existence, expressed in highly elaborated prose or verse.

**Pentameter.** *See* Poetry.

**Picaresque.** The term is derived from the Spanish *pícaro,* a young rogue whose main interest in life was in filling his stomach by means of trickery and clever and amusing frauds, usually perpetrated upon his various masters. Beginning with *Lazarillo de Tormes* (1553), the Spanish developed the picaresque novel into one of their major literary genres. Even today, both Spanish and Spanish American writers continue to exploit this form. In England, Thomas Nash's *The Unfortunate Traveller, or the Life of Jack Wilton* (1594) began a series of picaresque novels which culminated in a wave of popularity for this type of adventure fiction during the 18th century. All the picaresque novels, whether Spanish or English, tend to be autobiographical, with very little sustained plot, but rather a loosely connected series of episodes. They tend to be satirically humorous and give valuable exposés of trickery and chicanery present in the social setting within which the anti-hero's adventures unfold. In English writing, the picaresque novel has come also to be known as the *rogue novel.*

**Poetry, poetic figures, meter, forms and classifications.** Poetry embodies the most imaginative expression of writing. Its language is distinguished by its patterns of rhythmical words and phrases. It is the crystallization in language of the beauty and the musicality of imaginative thought and of the poet's powerful emotional reaction to the sensory impressions which life and fancy have engraved upon his mind. Poetry is ethereal and imaginative, and hence any exact definition of it is likely to be equally ethereal. Thousands of poets have attempted to define their own medium; perhaps Wordsworth came as close as any of them in defining this form of literature which is least subject to being imprisoned in any set formula: ". . . the spontaneous overflow of powerful feelings recollected in tranquillity." But there are certain aspects of form, meter, classification, and technique which have come to be accepted as properties which the body of English poetry manifests. Briefly and nontechnically, these observable aspects are:

**Language of English poetry:** To build up musicality, fancy, and imaginative ideas, the poet resorts often to symbolic expressions to carry his meanings outside the realm of pure reality, these expressions being known as *figures of speech.* The most common of these are:

1. *Simile.* A comparison, where a resemblance between two things is noted with *as* or *like,* e.g., *like silk is her hair.*

2. *Metaphor.* An implied comparison, where a word or phrase, actually denoting characteristics of one thing, are used in reference to another thing to suggest a likeness or analogy between the two things, e.g., *to see the world in a grain of sand or heaven in a flower.*

3. *Synecdoche.* A figure which uses a more comprehensive term to represent a less comprehensive one, or *vice versa,* e.g., *now, all hands to the task.*

4. *Metonymy.* The substitution of one object or thought for

another, closely associated with it because of some common quality assigned to both, e.g., *the pen is mightier than the sword.*

5. *Personification.* Where human characteristics are given to inanimate objects or ideas, e.g., *See how my sword weeps for the poor king's death.*

6. *Alliteration.* A repetition of the same sound in consecutive or almost consecutive words, e.g., *the moan of doves in immemorial elms, and murmuring of innumerable bees.*

7. *Hyperbole.* An exaggeration for the sake of emphasis, e.g., *Falstaff sweats to death, and lards the earth as he walks along.*

8. *Antithesis.* The balancing of one opposing term against another for the purpose of heightening effect through contrast, e.g., *fair is foul, and foul is fair.*

The above common figures show a few of the many devices by which the language of poetry is made to appeal to the feelings and the emotional reactions of the reader through molding the vocabulary of the language into imaginative thoughts and ideas.

**Meter.** A second essential to verse is the rise and fall of stress in a poetic line which produce the melody or the rhythmical groupings in the flow of poetic language. The verse of a skilled poet follows a certain definite pattern of stress called *meter.* A single metrical unit in English poetry is called a *foot.* A *foot* may contain from one to three syllables. Each type of foot bears a special name, according to the arrangement of the stressed or unstressed syllables it contains. When one counts the poetic feet in a line of poetry (a process called *scansion*) he may indicate the unstressed syllable with a *breve* ( ‿ ) and the stressed syllable with a *macron* ( – ). The common poetic feet used in English poetry are:

| | |
|---|---|
| *Iambus* ‿ – | *Spondee* – – |
| *Trochee* – ‿ | *Pyrrhic* ‿ ‿ |
| *Anapest* ‿ ‿ – | *Amphibrach* ‿ – ‿ |
| *Dactyl* – ‿ ‿ | |

Poetic lines are classified according to the number of feet in a line:

| | |
|---|---|
| *Monometer,* one foot | *Pentameter,* five feet |
| *Dimeter* two feet | *Hexameter,* six feet |
| *Trimeter,* three feet | *Heptameter,* seven feet |
| *Tetrameter,* four feet | *Octameter,* eight feet |

The meter of most of the lines from the great poets of English literature may be scanned by some combination or combinations of the above elements. For instance, Shakespeare was a master of the *iambus* used in a *pentameter* line, e.g.,

‿ – ‿ – ‿ – ‿ – ‿ –
If af | ter ev | ery tem | pest come | such calms,

‿ – ‿ – ‿ – ‿ – ‿ –
May the | winds blow | till they | have wak | ened death!

The lines thus produced are known in poetic parlance as *iambic pentameter* lines. Poets, although they tend to follow some one of the possible schemes of regular meter, occasionally use irregular combinations for their effects. For instance, Burns uses here in his *tetrameter* line, three *amphibrach* feet, and an *iambus:*

$$\text{U} \quad - \text{U} \quad \text{U} \quad - \text{U} \quad \text{U} \quad - \quad \text{U} \quad \text{U} \quad -$$
Flow gently, | sweet Afton, | among thy | green braes,

The *Alexandrine* is an example of a particular line of verse which has received a special name through the fact that it was used in Old French poems about Alexander. An example from Spenser's *The Faerie Queene* will show the *Alexandrine* to be an *hexameter* line:

$$\text{U} \quad - \quad \text{U} \quad - \quad \text{U} \quad - \quad \text{U} \quad - \quad \text{U} - \quad \text{U} \quad -$$
Fierce warres | and faith | full loves | shall mor | al ize | my song.

**Melody and caesura.** In addition to the technical aspects noted above, the poet is also concerned with the melody or the over-all tone quality of the poetic line. In order to give the line the flow of language or the swing he desires, he must be careful in his choice of words and phrases which will have the proper combinations of vowels and consonants to give the mood he intends to create in the reader. Thus, not only his ideas but the very choice of words will give impressions of sadness, gentle delicacy, roughness, gayety, or madness.

Also, in almost every line of poetry of three or more feet, there is provided a slight rhythmical pause, indicated by the poet by a pause in the sense of the line. This pause is known as a *caesura*. If the pause follows an accented syllable, the *caesura* is called *masculine;* if it follows an unaccented syllable, it is known as *feminine*. The following two lines from Milton show the two uses of *caesura* in *iambic pentameter* lines:

$$\text{U} \quad - \quad \text{U} \quad - \qquad \text{U} \quad - \text{U} \quad - \text{U} \quad -$$
Vain war with Heaven; || and, by suc cess un taught,

$$\text{U} \quad - \quad \text{U} \quad -\text{U} - \quad \text{U} \quad - \quad \text{U} \quad -$$
His proud im ag i na tions || thus dis played.

**Stanza forms.** A number of poetic lines *(verses)* make up a division *(stanza)* of the entire poem. Of course, a stanza may be the entire poem, or the entire composition may comprise many stanzas and not necessarily of the same length in number of lines. Stanzas are commonly known by the number of verses they contain:

> Couplet, two-line stanza
> Triplet, three-line stanza
> Quatrain, four-line stanza
> Quintet, five-line stanza
> Sestet, six-line stanza
> Septet, seven-line stanza
> Octave, eight-line stanza
> Nine-line stanza

In most of the above combinations, *rhyme* is considered necessary. Much famous poetry has been written, however, in which there is no end rhyme. This is called *blank verse*. Conventional rhyme in English is secured almost invariably by a repetition of sound produced by similarity of sounds (same vowels and consonants) in two or more words *(swallow-follow; love-above)* placed at the ends of two or more lines of the stanza. Occasionally poets have had rhyme occur within lines. When a two-lined stanza has end rhyme, it is then a *rhymed couplet*. Traditionally, when rhymed couplets are written in iambic pentameter, they are called *heroic couplets*. An entire poem composed of heroic couplets would then be known as *heroic verse*. When each couplet contains a complete idea or thought, it is sometimes also known as a *closed couplet*. Pope is famous in English for his *rhymed couplets,* which are, at the same time, *heroic couplets* and often *closed couplets.*

> 'Tis education forms the common mind:
> Just as the twig is bent the tree's inclined.

When a stanza contains more than two lines, we usually look for the rhyme pattern by assigning letters of the alphabet to the end-rhyming words. Thus, a three-line stanza, ending *love-home-above,* would rhyme *aba;* an eight-line stanza with lines ending *eyes-mine-cup-wine-rise-divine-sup-thine* would rhyme *abcbabcb* (see page 68, Jonson's *Song to Celia*).

Following are traditional names assigned to special rhyme schemes in stanzas of more than two lines.

1. *Terza rima.* A form invented by Dante and used throughout European poetry, where the triplets (or *tercets*) interlace or interlink in the following scheme: *love-moon-dove soon-run-June, aba bcb,* etc.

2. The quatrain, rhyming *abcb* formed the most popular *ballad* stanza (see *Sweet William,* p. 40).

3. The quatrain, rhyming *abab,* has been a favorite stanza among elegy writers and is often known as the *heroic quatrain* or *elegaic tanza (see* Gray's *Elegy,* p. 188).

4. The seven-line stanza, of course, may be rhymed in varied combinations, using couplets, quatrains, and triplets. The most famous English septet is known as the *Chaucerian stanza* or the *rime royal* (ababbcc) *(see* digest of *Troilus and Crysede,* p. 214).

5. The stanza of eight lines, rhyming *abababcc,* and borrowed from the Italians, is known as *ottava rima.* It is invariably in iambic pentameter lines.

6. The *Spenserian stanza* uses eight iambic pentameter lines, followed by one iambic hexameter line *(see* digest of *The Faerie Queene* p. 222).

7. A favorite rhyme scheme in English poetry is the so-called *tail-rime stanza,* where two short lines (usually in a total of six) rhyme with each other and the longer lines also rhyme with each other *(see* Burns' *To a Mouse,* p. 192 for four tetrameter lines and two dimeter lines).

Certain more or less fixed classifications of poetry (in addition to those already mentioned) are:

1. *The sonnet:* The Italian, or Petrarchan, form of the fourteen-line poem known as a sonnet consists of an octave of two quatrains *(abba abba)* and a sestet (with *cde cde* or *cd cd cd*). This form was used by many of the early English sonneteers and is very popular recently. However, many early poets revised the form of Petrarch. Spenser, for

instance, used *abab bcbc cdcd,* and concluded with a couplet *ee.* This is known as the *Spenserian Sonnet.* The most notable English form was popularized by Shakespeare and is known as the *English sonnet* or *Shakespearean sonnet (abab cdcd efef gg) (see* Sonnet 116, p. 64).

2. Many French forms, adapted into English poetry, could be mentioned. Chaucer wrote several *ballades,* the first in English. The *ballade (not* ballad) was an aristocratic form which consists of three or four stanzas, each stanza containing eight or ten lines of various rhyme schemes. The ballade usually ended with an *envoi,* a short added stanza of usually four lines. Other French forms which were adapted early into English poetry are the *rondel,* the *villanelle,* the *triolet,* the *lai,* the *rondolet,* the *rondeau,* the *douzet,* and others, all aristocratic French court forms.

Poetry may also be classified according to content. These classifications would serve to cover most poetic composition in English literature: *lyric, narrative* and *dramatic* poetry. (All these general types have been discussed in other portions of this section and in the main discussion section. *Narrative* poetry was discussed under *ballad, epic, pastoral.* Any narrative poetry would, of course, tell a story.)

**Poulter's measure.** A popular Renaissance metrical pattern which consisted of couplets of alternating Alexandrines and fourteen-syllable lines. It was so called for the practice of poultrymen in giving an even dozen eggs to the customer who only bought one dozen and fourteen to the one who took a second dozen. This measure was common in early Elizabethan times with such poets as Wyatt, Surrey, Sidney, and Brooke. Swift and Cowper used it for comic effect.

**Pyrrhic.** *See* Poetry.

**Quatrain.** *See* Poetry.

**Realism.** In literature, this is an attitude adopted by the author by which he attempts to present in his work things as they actually are in life. His work purports to depict life and to picture nature as faithfully as possible. Realism does not reject beauties of language and poetic expression, but it does reject any theme which idealizes or is fanciful and imaginative. The term is thus opposed to *romanticism* and idealism. It opposes any attitude which tends to escape into a fanciful world or into a world of idea and thought which is not actual and present to men of a particular epoch. Realism, as a conscious literary trend, may be said to have begun in English Literature with Defoe, Fielding, and Smollett. In the 19th century, realism, as a literary trend, was to sweep through world literatures in the novel and produce such great works as those of Dickens, Dostoevski, Balzac, Zola, Galdós, and others.

**Reformation.** *See* main section, pp. 45-46.

**Reformation literature.** The Protestant Reformation in England and Scotland produced a mass of so-called "Reformation" literature, in the 16th century. This body of writing consisted mostly of tracts, sermons, and disputations. Occasionally popular works in the somewhat aesthetic range were produced, such as allegorical plays, satirical verse, and moral essays. The effects of the Reformation, of course, tinged certain works of the better known aesthetic writers, such as

Spenser, Surrey, and others. In addition, the Reformation (and its didactic writing) inspired many of the Puritan writers of the 17th century to produce masterpieces of more or less moral and intellectual content, e.g., Bunyan and Milton.

**Renaissance.** *See* main section, pp. 41-44.

**Restoration literature.** In English history, the Restoration refers to the period following the time of Cromwell and the Commonwealth, when the Stuart dynasty returned to the throne of England with Charles II (1660). It was a period of reaction against Puritan ideas and one of French aristocratic influence. It was a period characterized by licentiousness and the flaunting of convention in its high society. In literature the effects were felt in two ways; on the one hand, literature was very sophisticated and produced a great period of productivity in the drama. These plays were full of wit and naughtiness, but reflected well the conditions within the aristocratic society which catered to them. Thus they contributed much to the development of a *comedy of manners* in English drama. Dryden and Congreve were outstanding contributors to this drama. Also, in the period, we have a number of diaries of sophisticates which reflect the rich artificiality of society, e.g., Pepys and Evelyn. This Restoration literature is marked by satire and by a highly polished, sharp, and witty expression.

**Rhyme.** *See* Poetry.

**Rime royal.** *See* Poetry.

**Romance, medieval romance, metrical romance, romance of chivalry.** Applied to language, *romance* came to refer to the vernacular languages which developed from the Latin spoken in the provinces of the Roman Empire in Europe. And applied to literature, the term passed over to the type of tale which began to be developed in the courts of these provinces in the new vernacular *romance*. This tale, either in verse or in prose. was one of knights and the ideals of chivalry. It spoke of love and of refined living, of monsters and of adventures, of nobility and courtesy. The romantic tale in verse started among the French courts of the 12th century and spread into Spain, Germany, and England. In addition to themes of Charlemagne, of Arthur, and of Tristram, this *medieval romance* or *metrical romance* (if it were in verse) treated themes of the ancient Greek and Roman world, notably that of Alexander the Great. As the Middle Ages wore on, both the *metrical romance* and the *romances of chivalry* became more popular and now included many new themes, the most notable in England being the development of the various knights of King Arthur's court. The English *romance* which has been considered the masterpiece of the genre is *Sir Gawain and the Green Knight,* written by The Pearl Poet in about 1370.

The term *romance* continued in literatures in the 16th and 17th centuries to be used for any fanciful tales in verse or prose which dealt with subjects and incidents remote from those of a daily realistic life. In English literature, the term has continued to have that meaning in writing. In France and Germany, the equivalent word *(roman, romanz)* has come to designate a novel of any type.

The *medieval romance* replaced the older *folk epic* as a longer fictional work; the modern *novel* has replaced the *romance* in popular favor. In modern literatures the *short story* has almost entirely replaced the *ballad* to convey brief fictional incidents. And in both cases, story telling in modern literatures has come to be almost entirely couched in prose.

**Romanticism.** Romanticism in philosophy is a tendency to inspiration and away from discipline. In literature, it is a tendency away from life as it is and toward a world of the imagination and fancy. *Romanticism* is thus opposed to *realism* in subject matter and to *classicism* with regard to the ordered systems, rules, and decorum of ancient or modern classical periods. The term *romanticism* or *romantic revival, romantic school,* etc., is applied to the world movement in the arts during the late years of the 18th century and the first half of the 19th, in which all phases of art reacted violently against the orthodox and formal *neoclassicism* of the preceding period. In literature, as in the other arts, much was new in this rebellion and much was a survival or revival of the earlier Renaissance period with its individualism, color, imagination, and fancy. In addition, a revived interest centered in the period of medieval European life and one phase of 19th century *romanticism* was a return to the chivalric ideals of medieval *romance. See* Romance.

**Runes.** Characters in the ancient Germanic alphabet of the Anglo-Saxons. These characters were developed during the 2nd or 3rd centuries and were fairly widespread among all the northern Germanic tribes of Europe. The characters were a modification of Greek and Roman letters and were carved into wooden tablets. They were also engraved on horns, weapons, and stones. Some runes were used for magical purposes, to avoid danger, to lay curses upon enemies, to convey messages of love, and to provide healing formulas. "Rune" also came to be synonymous with "poem" or "epic." Runic writing came to England with the Angles and the Saxons and was gradually replaced during the 6th, 7th, and 8th centuries by the Latin alphabet.

**Satire.** Literary satire is writing intended to incite contempt, amusement, or disgust on the part of the reader toward some theme which the author is holding up to ridicule and mordant criticism. A true satirist will attempt to improve institutions by pointing out their weaknesses, and by means of humor and wit, lightly prod and prick at those weaknesses until readers who have influence over such conditions seek to improve the institutions. Hence satire may take a very light, humorous, and mischievous direction and provoke laughter even on the part of those being satirized. On the other hand, satire may take the direction of bitterness and libelous ideas; it may be malicious, vindictive, and abusive. Satire has been common to all literatures from ancient times to the present day. But occasionally there are periods which seem to produce a flood of satirical writing. Such an age was that of the Restoration and the period of neoclassicism in English literature. The period of Dryden, Pope, Swift, Addison, Steele, and Fielding was England's golden age of satire.

**Scansion.** *See* Poetry.

**Scholasticism.** The system of Christian education during the medieval period. Based upon Aristotle's system of logic combined with Christian doctrine, this system of teaching became more and more devoted to argumentation and debate in an attempt to systematize and prove traditional beliefs. The Schoolmen, with few exceptions, neglected the arts and the exploration for new truth. Teaching came to be devoted to trivialities and lifeless argumentation. By 1620 the humanists had undermined the strictly *deductive* method of scholasticism and introduced the *inductive* method which has led to the achievements of modern science. Today our most advanced educational methods attempt to harmonize the best aspects of both scholasticism and the humanism which overthrew it.

**Senecan tragedy.** The Latin tragedies of Seneca (a Spanish Roman philosopher who lived in the 1st century) were imitative of the Greek plays of Euripides. The principal difference lies in the fact that Euripides wrote his plays to be acted, whereas Seneca wrote his to be recited. The Senecan play was full of philosophy and rhetorical argumentation. It was crammed with murders and gore of every description. There was almost always the "revenge" motive, with some member of a family avenging some affront to his particular clan. There was a great deal of action in a Senecan tragedy but it was not intended to be staged. Seneca employed a ghostly messenger who told of much of the tragic happenings; also he employed the *chorus* to discuss the psychological and philosophical aspects of the problem. *See* Chorus.

The humanists of the Renaissance became interested in Seneca and soon Seneca was being imitated in Elizabethan plays. *See Gorboduc* and *The Spanish Tragedy* in Appendix A. Here the blood and gore of Seneca were presented on the stage. Seneca's plays were translated and imitated throughout the Renaissance period in Italy, France, and England. The importance of the Roman Seneca's plays in the development of English drama is very great indeed.

**Sentimentalism.** In literature, this quality would denote an excess of emotional appeal in writing, a mawkish tear-jerking type of writing which deliberately places characters in positions calculated to cause intense emotional reactions on the part of readers (or audiences, in the case of drama). Where the Senecan "revenge" tragedy of the Elizabethan and Jacobean periods were calculated to thrill and horrify audiences, the wave of 18th century *sentimentality* was deliberately aimed to produce effects of sadness, tearfulness, and melancholy on the part of readers and audiences. It was perhaps a natural reaction in English literature against the hardness and cynical wittiness of the literature of the Restoration and also of the satirical bitterness of the neoclassic school. In the sentimental novels of Richardson and others, the characters are distinguished by their excessive piety and goodness or by their evil and malicious badness. At about the same period there was a wave in England of sentimental drama, such as Steele's *The Tender Husband, The Funeral,* and *The Lying Lover* (all written shortly after 1700). The poets of the late neoclassic years also indulged in nostalgic sentimentality, e.g., Goldsmith's *The Deserted Village*. During the late years of the century there was a reaction against this tear-producing literature. Drama became a more true *comedy of manners;* the novel became more realistic and poetic description became less nostalgic and more realistically beautiful, e.g.,

Crabbe's *The Village,* a good contrasting study to Goldsmith's poem, written only thirteen years before.

**Sestet.** *See* Poetry.

**Shakespearean "rime," Shakespearean sonnet.** *See* Poetry.

**Simile.** *See* Poetry.

**Sins (seven deadly sins).** Medieval literature is full of these seven evils which preyed upon the souls of men. A great deal of English medieval literature, some Renaissance allegory, and later Puritan writing is concerned with the struggle of various virtues to overcome the effects of the seven deadly sins and to regain the souls of men for Paradise. The seven cardinal sins were: pride, envy, wrath, lechery (lust), avarice (covetousness), gluttony, and sloth. From a close perusal of medieval literature, it becomes evident that these seven combatants for the soul of man provided far more entertaining reading than did the literature concerning the seven cardinal virtues: meekness, charity, chastity, industry, abstinence, generosity, and patience.

**Sonnet.** *See* Poetry.

**Spenserian stanza.** *See* Poetry.

**Spondee.** *See* Poetry.

**Symbolism.** Symbolism, as a literary movement, does not attain importance until about 1870 in English literature. Therefore it will be treated fully in Volume II. But symbolism, as an attitude of the human mind in approaching material of idea and thought, has existed since the beginnings of writings. Symbolism is the presentation of ideas, objects, and life in general through means of imagery, metaphor, and beauty and musicality of language. As such, symbolism is opposed to *realism,* in that realism presents things as they are and symbolism presents things through indirect impressions. Most of the beauty of poetry is achieved through some form of symbolism. In theme, all allegory is symbolic. *See* Allegory, Poetry, Metaphysical.

**Tercet.** *See* Poetry.

**Terza rima.** *See* Poetry.

**Tragedy.** Aristotle first defined tragedy as "dramatic representation of some serious action, arousing pity and fear." This basic idea of tragedy has changed little through the years. It is now considered that tragedy is a struggle and conflict of wills which ends disastrously for a leading personality or personalities. The struggle might be a conflict of wills of different individuals, a conflict of will with circumstances or even an inner conflict of will and desire, or the revelation of some fundamental weakness of will of the "tragic" personality, e.g., *Hamlet.* Despite the attitude of early modern tragedians (influenced unduly by the Senecan school—*See* Senecan tragedy) this form does not require that there be deaths and murders. It is sufficient that the conflicts be very serious and the consequences be deadly important. There may be comic moments in tragedy but they are interspersed to lighten, for a brief time, the attention of the audience to the serious conflict being unfolded. The audience reaction to tragedy is intended to be thoughtful, sad or pitying. *See* Comedy for Tragicomedy.

**Trimeter.** *See* Poetry.

**Trochee.** *See* Poetry.

**Tudor literature.** The House of Tudor came to the throne of England with Henry VII (1485-) and ended its reign with Elizabeth (1558-1603). Tudor literature, then, would refer to the great Renaissance period of English literature, or as it is during the reign of Elizabeth that the great writers of the Augustan age came to the fore, the period of greatest variety and accomplishment is usually referred to as the *Elizabethan age*. Such terms as this are not exact, of course, for it would be wrong to believe that there was any immediate change noted from the reign of the Tudors to that of the Stuarts, beginning with James I in 1603. The actual changing of the tone of literature toward one of more serious purpose and intellectual appeal had already begun before Elizabeth died. The cause is the rise of Puritanism and a controlling middle-class morality, combined with the new humanistic-scientific attitudes, rather than the change in ruling houses.

**Unities (classic).** The three dramatic "unities" of *time, place,* and *action* are, modernly, but interpretations of Aristotle's statements in regard to drama in his *Poetics*. As strictly interpreted, the unity of *time* would force the action of a play to take place within a twenty-four hour period; the unity of *place* would force the action to transpire in one setting (at least in one town or the area closely surrounding one place); the unity of *action* would dictate that there should be one main plot and no subplots in a play, and that comedy and tragedy must not be mixed in the same play. These strict interpretations of Aristotle's generalizations were largely those of one Castelvetro, a 16th century Italian scholar and critic. Actually, Aristotle pleaded only for organic unity in plot, an integration between incidents, and that "tragedy endeavors, as far as possible, to confine itself to a single revolution of the sun, or but slightly to exceed this limit." This was interpreted to mean one day, and although Aristotle did not mention place, it followed that an action could not go beyond immediate limits of one place in a day, with the transportation facilities being what they were in 16th century Italy.

This modern version of the so-called *Aristotelean unities* became a fighting point in dramatic criticism and discussion for many years. Many great Renaissance plays follow them, but generally speaking, most English and Spanish Augustan Age plays violate one or all of them. They were revived in the classical age and were much argued. In general, the great French classic drama of the 17th century followed them. They were followed halfheartedly by English neoclassic writers. The romantic school disregarded them entirely, and today they are ignored and largely serve as aids in interpreting the drama of the past.

**Villanelle.** *See* Poetry.

**"Wheel" construction, framework construction.** Terms referring to collections of tales, each story being independent and complete in itself, but an integral part of an over-all plot or intrigue. This arrangement may be compared to a wheel, the spokes of which are individual stories, and the rim and axle forming the frame which holds each spoke in place in the whole work. This method of story telling is apparently Oriental in development and was adapted into European literatures first in Spain. The best known Oriental construction of this sort is found in the collection known as *The Arabian Nights*. In Spain, several of these Oriental "framework" collections were translated by the 13th century. In the 14th century three great original European collections of tales employed this "wheel" arrangement: *El libro de Patronio* of Juan Manuel (Spain-1335), *Il Decamerone* of Boccaccio (Italy-1353), and *The Canterbury Tales* of Chaucer (1391). It was not until Richardson, Fielding, and Smollett that the early European novels lost this tendency to offer isolated incidents or episodes, held together loosely by a main character or central scheme.

# *Appendix C*

# CHRONOLOGICAL TABLE OF CIVILIZATION AND LITERATURE

## From 55 B.C. to 1798 A.D.

The following four-column table is arranged to indicate highlights or mileposts in English and world historical, literary, and general cultural achievements. The left-hand page gives data relating to England and the right-hand page contains references to the principal world civilizations, outside of England. In so far as is practical, the items are matched as to date of occurrence, so that the student, by glancing across both pages, can gain a comparative view of world literary accomplishment, and of the political and social setting for the literary works. Naturally, a table of such scope can be only an aid to study, and in itself cannot be comprehensive. Only major items are included for a particular period. The over-all purpose is to show the student the ebb and flow of cultural achievement, the productive as well as the nonproductive periods, and the change and transition in attitudes, spirit, and form, from age to age.

These abbreviations are used: b.—born; d.—died; c.—date is approximate.

## CHRONOLOGICAL OUTLINE

### English

| General History and Culture | Literature |
|---|---|
| To 55 B.C. Celtic Britain. | No literature from this period. |
| 55 B.C. Caesar invades Britain. | |
| 43 A.D. Invasion by Claudius. | |
| 410 Romans withdraw. | |
| 449 Germanic invasions under Hengist and Horsa. | 450-700 Probable period of composition of Old English poems: *Beowulf, Widsith, Deor's Lament, Finnsburg, Waldhere, The Wanderer, The Seafarer, The Wife's Complaint, The Husband's Message.* |
| 597 Augustine brings Christianity to Britain. | |
| 604 St. Paul's founded by Ethelbert. | |
| 617 St. Peter's founded, now Westminster Abbey. | 547 Gildas: *History.* |
| | c. 670 Caedmon *Hymns*—first known English poet. |
| 690 The name England first used. | 640-709 Aldhelm: Latin works— his English poems lost. |
| | 673-735 Bede: *De Natura Rerum, De Ratione Temporum, De Arte Metrica, Historia Ecclesiastica* (c. 731). |
| | c. 750 Cynwulf: *Christ, Saint Julian, Saint Helen, Saint Andreas, Judith, Fall of the Angels, Dream of the Rood, Phoenix.* |
| 787 First Danish invasion. | c. 800 Nennius: *History of the Britons.* First mention of Arthur. |
| 837 Battle of Brunanburh. | |
| 871-901 Reign of Alfred the Great. | 871-901 Alfred the Great: Translations into English of Bede's *Ecclesiastical History*, Gregory's *Pastoral Care*, Boethius' *Consolation of Philosophy*, Osorius' *Universal History.* |

## CHRONOLOGICAL OUTLINE

### Foreign

| **General History and Culture** | **Literatures** |
|---|---|
| 51 B.C. Caesar conquers Gaul. | 51 B.C. Julius Caesar: *Commentaries*. |
| 44 B.C. Caesar assassinated. | 70-19 B.C. Vergil: *Georgics, Aeneid*. |
| 30 A.D. Christ crucified. | 27 B.C.-14 A.D. Augustus Caesar —Age of Vergil, Ovid, Horace. |
| 476 Fall of Rome. | |
| 527 Justinian Code of Laws. | 475-525 Boethius: *De Consolatione Philosophiae*. |
| | 600-1100 Arabic culture flourishes. *Fables of Bidpai, Arabian Nights,* lyric poetry, mathematics, architectural advances. |
| 625-640 Mohammedanism sweeps Jerusalem, Antioch, and Alexandria. | 634 Mohammed: *Koran*. |
| 698 Christianity gains in Germanic nations but loses Africa to Mohammedans. | |
| 711 Arabs invade Spain. | |
| 732 Saracens defeated at Tours. | |
| 778 Battle of Roncesvalles. | 800-1200 Composition of poems forming the *Eddas* in Iceland. Age of the *saga* in Scandinavian countries. |
| 800 Charlemagne founds the Western Empire of Italy, Germany, and France. | 800-814 Renaissance of learning in France under Charlemagne. |
| By 850 feudal system established in Europe. | c. 830 *The Heliand:* German epic of Christianity in alliterative verse. |
| 912 Northmen occupy Normandy in France. | 850-900 Liturgical drama begins to flower in Europe. |

## CHRONOLOGICAL OUTLINE

### English

| General History and Culture | Literature |
|---|---|
| 890 Oxford University founded by Alfred. | 850-900 *Anglo-Saxon Chronicle* revised and extended back to Hengist and Horsa. |
| 900-1100 Age of Chivalry established. | |
| 915 University of Cambridge founded. | 937 Heroic poem: *The Battle of Brunanburh.* |
| 952 Malcolm I becomes King of Scotland. | 950 *Junius Manuscript:* contains poems by Caedmon. |
| 960 Dunstan becomes Archbishop of Canterbury. Attempts reform of Church. | 971 *Blickling Homilies.* |
| | 952-1022 Aelfric: *Lives of Saints, Colloquium, Homilae Catholicae.* |
| 985 Danish invasions. | |
| | 991 Heroic poem: *The Battle of Maldon.* |
| | 1000 First romance: translation of *Appolonius of Tyre.* |
| 1016 Canute the Dane becomes King. | 1025 *The Exeter Book:* manuscript containing many early poems. |
| 1034 Duncan is King of Scotland. | 1000-1100 *The Vercelli Book:* contains Anglo-Saxon poems, including *Dream of the Rood.* |
| 1039 Macbeth murders Duncan. | |
| 1042 Saxon rule restored. | |
| 1066 Battle of Hastings (Cenlac). Norman conquest. William I is King of England. | |
| 1070 Feudal system introduced. | |
| | 1086 *Doomsday Book:* contains English census. |
| 1100 Henry I unites Normans and Saxons. | c. 1100 *Play of St. Catherine:* first miracle play in England. |
| | c. 1136 Geoffrey of Monmouth: *History of the Kings of Britain.* First mention of Arthur's Round Table. |
| | 1121-1154 *English Chronicle.* |

## CHRONOLOGICAL OUTLINE

### Foreign

**General History and Culture**

**Literatures**

940 Cordova, in Spain, famous as center of science, learning, and commerce.

1002 Churches being built in Gothic style of architecture.

950-1050 Arabic numerals in use in Europe. French language takes written form. Signs of art in Italy. Six-note musical scale invented. Paper is made of cotton rags.

1050 Rise of scholastic philosophy.

1065 Jerusalem taken by Saracens.

1073 First known booksellers.

1000 Firdausi, the Persian Homer, writes *Shah Namah (Book of Kings)*.

1070 Troubadour poetry in Provence.

1000-1100 French *Chansons de Geste* and Spanish epics probably in a period of flowering. No copies extant from this period.

1096 The First Crusade.

1099 The Cid dies in Valencia.

1100 New impulse to study of theology.

1120 Intense rivalry builds up between England and France.

1147 Second Crusade.

1090-1100 Anselm: *Cur Deus Homo, De Voluntate, Proslogium,* etc.

1100-1300 Lyric poetry flourishes in southern France.

1100-1250 Age of famed Icelandic sagas: *Volsungsaga,* etc.

1100- Great period of *Chansons de Geste* in France. *Chanson de Roland* (c. 1125). First great troubadour, William de Poitiers.

## CHRONOLOGICAL OUTLINE

### English

**General History and Culture**

1154 House of Plantaganet. Henry II is King of England. French and Latin the language of the court. Center of learning.

1158-1164 Thomas à Becket is Archbishop of Canterbury.

1158 Woolen manufacturing in England.

1172 Henry II takes Ireland.

1189 Richard I "Coeur de Lion" is king. Takes part in Third Crusade.

1193 John attempts to rule in absence of Richard. Becomes king in 1200.

1215 John forced to sign Magna Carta at Runnymede.

1216 Henry III is king.

1246 Henry marries Eleanor of Provence.

1265 First regular Parliament.

1272 Edward I; 1307 Edward II; 1327 Edward III.

1285 Courts of law established.

1297 Scotland and England at war.

**Literature**

1150-1200 Many French poets in England, Crétien de Troyes, Marie de France, Benôit de Ste. More, etc. French romance stresses courtly ideals. Ancient themes of Alexander and Troy treated.

c. 1170 *Poema Morales:* didactic poem.

1150-1200 French versions of *Brut, Havelock the Dane,* and *Waltheof* are circulated. Now lost.

1100-1500 Period of flourishing of Irish sagas.

c. 1205 Layamon: *Brut.*

From 1200 Many religious tracts, history, and chronicle are being written in Latin.

1200-1250 Romances of *King Horn* and *Beves of Hampton.* First English metrical romances with English themes.

c. 1250 English "debate" poetry and folk lyric evident. *The Owl and the Nightingale. Sumer is Icumen in.* Middle English gaining influence.

c. 1250 *Gesta Romanorum:* tales in Latin.

c. 1250 *The Bestiary.*

c. 1267 Roger Bacon: *Opus Majus, Opus Minus, Opus Tertium* (Christian education, history, and scientific thought).

14th century. *Guy of Warwick.*

# CHRONOLOGICAL OUTLINE

## Foreign

| General History and Culture | Literatures |
| --- | --- |

**General History and Culture**

1100-1150 Scholastic philosophy reaches new heights under Abelard. Logic of Aristotle popular. Gratian organizes canon law. Magnetic needle used in Italy. Italy establishes banking houses.

1139 Portugal becomes kingdom under Henry I.

1141 Fighting breaks out between Guelphs and Ghibellines in Italy.

1167 Frederick Barbarossa takes Rome.

1168 Colleges of law, theology, and philosophy at Paris.

1200 University of Bologna has 10,000 students. 1206 Univ. of Paris established.

1202 Fourth Crusade, Constantinople taken.

b. 1220 Pisano, Italian sculptor.

1222 University of Padua.

1227 University of Salamanca.

b. 1240 Cembrai, Italian painter.

b. 1267 Giotto, Italian painter and architect.

1252-84 Alfonso The Wise of Castile, leader of a minor Renaissance in literature and science.

1300-1400 High point of Gothic architecture.

**Literatures**

1133 *The Younger Edda* (prose and verse) by Snorri Sturleson. Norse masterpiece.

1140 *Nibelungenlied:* first great epic in Germany.

1140 *The Cid:* only surviving great epic poem from Spain.

1150-1200 *Aucassin et Nicolette:* one of best French medieval romances. *Roman de Renard.* Crétien de Troyes: *Erec et Enide.* Epic of *Gudrun* in Germany.

1200- Period of *troubadours* in France, *minnesingers* in Germany, *minstrels* in England, *juglares* in Spain, *jongleurs* in France.

c. 1230-1270 Guillaume de Lorris and Jean de Meun: *Roman de la Rose.*

c. 1215-1260 *The Fall of Adam:* Anglo-Norman French mystery play. Jean Bodel: *Play of St. Nicholas,* c. 1250- Anglo-Norman French miracle play.

1265-1321 Dante: *Vita Nouva,* 1294, *The Divine Comedy* (1307-1321).

1304 Birth of Petrarch.

## CHRONOLOGICAL OUTLINE

### English

**General History and Culture**

1306 Robert Bruce is king of Scotland. Scotland wins independence in 1327.

1338-1456 Hundred Years' War for French crown.

1348, 1361-69 The Black Death.

1362 Middle English used in courts and in Parliament.

1373 Winchester College established.

1377 Reformation begins in England with John Wyclif and the Lollards.

1377 Richard II is king.

1381 The Peasants' Revolt (Tyler's Rebellion).

c. 1385 English replaces French in the schools.

1399 Richard II deposed. Henry IV of Lancaster is king.

**Literature**

1310 *Havelock the Dane:* Middle English verse romance.

1340 Birth of Chaucer.

1362 William Langland: *Piers the Plowman.*

1370 *The Pearl.*

To 1372 Chaucer's Period of French Influence: *Romance of the Rose, The Book of the Duchess, ABC, Complaint unto Pity, Complaint to His Lady.*

1375 The Pearl Poet: *Patience, Sir Gawain and the Green Knight* (best English metrical romance).

1372-1385 Chaucer's period of Italian influence: *Boece, The House of Fame, Troilus and Criseyde, The Parliament of Fowls, The Legend of Good Women, The Complaint of Mars, Chaucer's Words unto Adam, To Rosemounde, Womanly Noblesse, Anelida and Arcite.*

1380-1382 Wyclif's *Bible,* first complete Bible in English.

1385-1400 Chaucer's period of English influence: *The Canterbury Tales* (1387-1400); five ballades, *The Complaint of Venus, L'Envoy de Chaucer à Scogan, L'Envoy de Chaucer à Bukton, The Complaint of Chaucer to His Empty Purse.*

## CHRONOLOGICAL OUTLINE

### Foreign

**General History and Culture**

1300-1350 Invention flourishes: gunpowder, clocks, mariner's compass, etc.

1303-1308 New universities of Avignon, Orleans, Perugia, and Coimbra.

From 1350 Italian Renaissance, upsurge of humanism and development in the arts.

b. 1377 Brunelleschi, Italian architect.

b. 1387 Fra Angelico, Italian painter.

b. 1390 Jan Van Eyck, Flemish painter, invents oil paint.

1370-1400 Tamerlane devastating the East.

**Literatures**

1313 Birth of Boccaccio.

1336 Juan Manuel of Spain: *Libro de Polonio* (first European short story collection).

1341 Petrarch, great sonneteer, honored in Rome. Boccaccio is writing *Ameto,* first pastoral.

1343 Juan Ruiz: *El libro de buen amor (Book of Good Love).*

1350 Boccaccio: *The Decameron;* Petrarch's eclogues and some sonnets to Laura.

From 1350 Both verse and prose romances of chivalry are written in France, Spain, and Italy. The popular ballad especially flowers in England, Scotland, and Spain during the period. The miracle and morality plays increase in popularity throughout the Catholic world. Vernacular languages are well established for literature in Italy, France, England, Spain, and Portugal. Oriental literature has declined. Courtly literature continues to achieve new heights in France.

## CHRONOLOGICAL OUTLINE

### English

**General History and Culture**

1413 Henry V is king. Wins Battle of Agincourt in 1415 and claims French crown.

1422 Henry VI is king.

c. 1425 Minor humanist activity. Many English students attend Italian universities. Some translations.

1444 Truce with France. Marriage of Henry to Margaret of Anjou.

1453-1485 War of the Roses between Houses of York and Lancaster.

1461 House of York places Edward IV on throne.

1476 Caxton introduces printing press into England.

1483 Richard III of York.

1490-1520 The "Oxford Reformers," famed group of humanists, including Colet, More, Grocyn, and Linacre. Erasmus joins group in 1499 and teaches at Cambridge (1511-1514).

**Literature**

1410-1500 Many imitators of Chaucer during the century. Mostly weak and thin. English imitators were: John Lydgate, *Troy Book* and others; Thomas Hoccleve, *The Regiment of Princes* and others; John Skelton, *The Bouge of Court* and others. The main Scottish imitators were: James I, *The Kings Quair, The Testament of Cresseid,* and others; William Dunbar, *The Dance of the Sevin Deidly Synnis* and others.

1449 English translation of Sir John Mandeville's *Voyage and Travel* from the French. Early example of clear, simple English prose.

1469 Sir Thomas Malory completes his *Morte d'Arthur* (pub. 1485).

1400-1500 Many sermons, tracts and histories date from the century. The popular ballad is especially strong in the age.

1475 to 1500 Famous cycles of miracle plays. *The Chester Cycle* with some 25; *The York Cycle* with 48; *The Wakefield* (or *Towneley) Cycle* with 32 plays, including the most famous of all English miracle plays, *The Second Shepherds' Play.*

## CHRONOLOGICAL OUTLINE

### Foreign

| General History and Culture | Literatures |
| --- | --- |

1406-1469 Fra Lippo Lippi, Italian painter.

1431 Joan of Arc burned at the stake.
1434 Invention of printing at Mayence.

1431 François Villon born.

1453 Capture of Constantinople by the Turks.
From 1450: Great age in the arts in Italy: Leonardo Da Vinci, Raphael, Michael Angelo, Tintoretto, Correggio, Veccio, Sanzio, Andrea del Sarto.

1455 Gutenberg's *Bible*.

1469 Marriage of Ferdinand of Aragon and Isabella of Castile.

1469-1492 Lorenzo de Medici supreme in struggle against aristocracy in Italy.

1471 Thomas à Kempis: *De Imitatione Christi*.

b. 1471 Dürer, German painter.

1490 Sannazzaro: *Arcadia* (much imitated pastoral romance).

b. 1497 Holbein, German painter.

## CHRONOLOGICAL OUTLINE

### English

| General History and Culture | Literature |
|---|---|
| 1485 The House of Tudor. Henry VII. | |
| | 1500 *Everyman:* finest of the morality plays. |
| | 1503-1542 Sir Thomas Wyatt. Early Renaissance poet. |
| 1509 Henry VIII | 1509 Erasmus: *The Praise of Folly* (social satire); Barclay: *Ship of Fools* (social satire); Hawes: *Pastime of Pleasure* (allegorical *romance*). |
| 1516 Linacre founds the Royal College of Physicians. | 1516 Sir Thomas More: *Utopia.* |
| | Use of Roman comedies of Terence and Plautus in teaching of Latin in English schools. |
| | 1516 Skelton: *Magnificence* (morality play, involving social satire). |
| | 1519 Rastell: *The Four Elements* (first published interlude). |
| | 1525 Tyndale: *New Testament.* |
| | 1530- Heywood is writing Interludes. The *New Poetry* of Wyatt and Surrey, imitating Italian models. |
| 1532 The King marries Ann Boleyn. | |
| 1533 Separation of the English Church from Rome. | 1531 Elyot: *The Governor.* |
| 1535 Henry is excommunicated by the Pope. Suppression of the monasteries and execution of Sir Thomas More. | 1535 Coverdale: First complete *Bible* printed in English. |
| | 1539 Cramer: *Bible.* |
| 1536 Execution of Tyndale. | |
| | 1543 *Book of Common Prayer.* |

## CHRONOLOGICAL OUTLINE

### Foreign

| General History and Culture | Literatures |
|---|---|
| 1492 Discovery of America by Christopher Columbus. | |
| 1492 Moors surrender Granada to Ferdinand and Isabella. | 1499 *La Celestina* begins great age of Spanish Literature. |
| 1498 Vasco da Gama reaches India around Cape of Good Hope. | |
| 1513 Discovery of the Pacific by Balboa. | |
| | 1516 Ariosto: *Orlando Furioso* (Italian romantic epic). |
| 1517 Beginnings of Protestantism. Martin Luther proclaims his 95 theses. | 1517 Machiavelli: *The Prince;* Hans Sachs initiates German drama. |
| 1519 Cortés invades Mexico. | 1519 *Amadis of Gaul* translated into Spanish. |
| 1521 Luther before the Diet of Worms. | |
| 1521 Circumnavigation of the globe by Magellan. | |
| | 1523 Ronsard is born. Luther: *New Testament.* |
| | 1524 Camoëns is born. |
| | 1528 Castiglione: *The Courtier.* |
| 1533 Pizarro invades Peru. | 1533 Rabelais: *Pantagruel.* |
| 1540 Lisbon becomes the major commercial port of the world. Society of Jesus founded by Loyola. | 1542 Montemayor: *Diana.* |
| | 1544 Tasso is born. |

## CHRONOLOGICAL OUTLINE

### English

| General History and Culture | Literature |
|---|---|
| 1547 Formal establishment of Protestantism. Edward VI is king. Surrey is executed. | |
| 1553 Mary, "Bloody Mary," is Queen of England. Attempts to restore Catholicism.<br>1554-55 Persecution of Protestants. Lady Jane Grey is executed. | 1553 *Ralph Roister Doister.* |
| 1558 Elizabeth I is Queen of England.<br>1559 John Knox in Scotland.<br>Rise of the Puritans in this epoch. Italianism is dominant in poetry and the Roman classic comedy is dominant in drama. Intense spirit of nationalism and patriotism is evident in England. | 1557 Tottel's *Miscellany.*<br>1558 Knox: *First Blast of the Trumpet.* |
| | 1562 *Gorboduc. Gammer Gurton's Needle.*<br>1564 Birth of Shakespeare. Birth of Marlowe.<br>1566 Gascoigne: *Jocasta.*<br>1576 First theater established (called The Theatre). |
| 1577 Sir Francis Drake's voyage around the world. | |
| | 1579 Lyly: *Euphues;* Spenser: *Shepherd's Calendar;* North's translation of Plutarch's *Lives.* |

## CHRONOLOGICAL OUTLINE

### Foreign

| General History and Culture | Literatures |
|---|---|
| 1545 Fabulous mines at Potosi discovered. | |
| 1545 Vasalius makes important revelations in field of anatomy. | |
| 1547-1571 Turks reach height of military power. | 1547 Cervantes is born. |
| | 1549 Du Bellay: *Defense de la Langue Française* (lays poetic foundation for *The Pléiade*. |
| | 1550 Ronsard: *Odes*. |
| | 1552 Jodelle: *Cléopâtre* (tragedy). Ronsard: *Amours* (sonnets). |
| 1554 Siberia discovered. | 1554 *Lazarillo de Tormes* (influential Spanish picaresque novel). Bandello: *Novelle*. |
| | 1557 Surrey employs blank verse for translation of two books of the *Aeneid*. |
| | 1562-1635 Lope de Vega, best-known Spanish dramatist. |
| 1564 Spanish name Philippines for Philip II. | |
| 1571 Battle of Lepanto. Spanish decisively defeat Turks in navy battle. | |
| 1572 Massacre of St. Bartholomew in France. | 1572 Camoëns: *The Lusiads* (great Portuguese epic poem). |
| 1575-1642 Guido Reni, Italian painter. | 1573 Tasso: *Aminta*. |
| c. 1576 El Greco comes to Toledo. | |
| 1577-1640 Rubens, Flemish painter. | |
| 1580-1666 Franz Hals, Dutch painter. | |

## CHRONOLOGICAL OUTLINE

### English

| General History and Culture | Literature |
|---|---|
| 1573-1632 Inigo Jones, famed architect. | 1580 Lyly: *Alexander and Campaspe* (a court comedy).<br>1581 Sir Philip Sidney: *Apology for Poesie;* Peele: *Arraignment of Paris* (a masque).<br>1584 *Handful of Pleasant Delights* (a ballad anthology). |
| 1584 Ralegh's expedition to Virginia. | 1586 Kyd: *The Spanish Tragedy*<br>1587 Marlowe: *Tamburlaine.* |
| 1587 Mary, Queen of Scots, executed.<br>1588 England defeats the Spanish Armada. First newspaper. | 1588 Marlowe: *Doctor Faustus.*<br>1590 Lodge: *Rosalynde;* Sidney: *Arcadia;* Spenser: *The Faerie Queene.*<br>1591-96 Famous cycles of sonnets: Daniel, Drayton, Sidney, Lodge, Spenser, Shakespeare, etc. Spenser: *Complaints;* Sidney: *Astrophel and Stella.* |
| The age of Elizabeth established England's independence from all foreign powers. The English Church became firmly established. Industry and commerce boomed. Feudalism was dead. Intense nationalism characterized the era. Under Hawkins, Drake, Raleigh, Davis, and Baffin, the British Navy became a force in world influence. Exploration and plans were completed for an extensive colonization program. An era of material prosperity and the rise of middle-class industrial group. Living standards were raised to a much higher level than ever before. | To 1595 Shakespeare's early plays.<br>1592 Constable: *Diana;* Daniel: *Delia;* Lyly: *Galatea, Midas.*<br>1593 Shakespeare: *Venus and Adonis.*<br>1594 Greene: *Friar Bacon and Friar Bungay;* Nashe: *The Unfortunate Traveler.*<br>1595-1600 Shakespeare's historical plays and romantic comedies. Spenser: *Amoretti.*<br>1596 *Romeo and Juliet.* Ralegh: *Discovery of Guiana.*<br>1597 Francis Bacon: *Essays. The Merchant of Venice.* |

## CHRONOLOGICAL OUTLINE

### Foreign

| General History and Culture | Literatures |
|---|---|
| 1579 Republic of Holland. | |
| | 1580 Montaigne: *Essays.* |
| | 1581 Tasso: *Jerusalem Delivered,* Italian epic poem. |

1586 Tobacco introduced into Europe.

1590 Telescope invented by Jansen; Napier invents logarithms.

1592 The Rialto and the Piazza di San Marco built in Venice.

1593-1678 Jordaens, Flemish painter.

1594-1665 Pousin, French painter.

1599-1641 Van Dyck, Flemish painter.

1600-1682 Claude Lorrain, French painter.

The final decade of the sixteenth century found Europe in a period of political and economic transition. The powers of Portugal and of Spain were on the decline. These two nations had dominated discovery and exploration for a century and a half. Now England was to be the dominant power on the seas. The Dutch approach a period of commercial and artistic greatness. The French, following an artistic decline, are soon to assume a diplomatic and an aristocratic leadership among nations. By 1600 European Christianity appears secure at last from Mohammedan threat. Italy

The final decade of the sixteenth century found all European literatures in a period of transition, except for English and Spanish. The Augustan age of Italian literature, which began with Dante, Petrarch, and Boccaccio, was definitely over. In France, *The Pléiade* ended a period of romance which had started early in the medieval period. She was now gearing herself for a great period of classicism, to begin shortly after 1600. The Italian Renaissance effects were scarcely felt in Germany. There, perhaps, the Reformation, with its leaning to the didactic, the philosophical and the theological, could be said to have produced its own particular type of Renaissance. Germany had produced little of the romantic in literature. Portugal had experienced its Augustan age from about 1385 to Camoëns (1572). The Oriental literatures now produced little of interest to the

## CHRONOLOGICAL OUTLINE

### English

| General History and Culture | Literature |
|---|---|
| | 1598 Jonson: *Every Man in His Humour*. Shakespeare: *Julius Caesar*. Chapman: Translation of *Iliad*. |
| | 1599 Shakespeare's "happy" comedies: *Much Ado About Nothing*, *As You Like It*, *Twelfth Night*. Shakespeare's company is performing in the Globe Theatre. |
| 1600 East India Company formed. | 1600-1604 *Hamlet, Prince of Denmark*. Dekker: *Shoemaker's Holiday*. Hakluyt: *Voyages and Discoveries*. |
| 1603 Elizabeth dies. James I is king. Scotland and England united. Divine right of kings proclaimed. | |
| | 1602-1603 Shakespeare: The bitter comedies: *Measure for Measure, All's Well That Ends Well, Troilus and Cressida*. |
| | 1604 *Othello, Moor of Venice*. |
| | 1605 Bacon: *Advancement of Learning*. |
| 1606 Plymouth and London Companies founded for colonization. | 1606 *Macbeth* and *King Lear*. |
| 1607 Settlement at Jamestown, Virginia. | 1607 *Antony and Cleopatra*. |
| | In this period scores of plays are being written and produced in "private" and "public" theaters. |
| | 1610 Ben Jonson: *The Alchemist*. Donne: *Anatomy of the World*. |
| | 1611 *Authorized Version of the Bible* under direction of James I. |
| | 1613 Browne: *Britannia's Pastorals*. |
| | 1614 Webster: *Duchess of Malfi*. |

## CHRONOLOGICAL OUTLINE

### Foreign

**General History and Culture**

and Germany fail to achieve national status until the 19th century. A new world is open for exploration and colonization. The English, the Dutch, and the French are to join Spain and Portugal in competition for its development.

1598 Edict of Nantes: official toleration is agreed upon for Protestants.

1599-1660 Velásquez, Spanish painter.

**Literatures**

Western World. Spanish America had produced little as yet except chronicle. North American literature was yet over the horizon. Spain's golden age was to produce its greatest works around 1600 and England's high level was to maintain itself, with brief weak periods, until this century. Germany was to wait until the 19th century, and Russia until the mid-1800's, for their Augustan ages of literature.

1600-1681 Calderón de la Barca, last great dramatist of Spain's golden age.

1600 Peri: *Euridice* (first Italian opera).

1604 French in Nova Scotia.

1605 Cervantes: Part I of *Don Quijote de la Mancha.*

1606 Gilbert makes his discoveries in electricity.

1606 Corneille, great French classic dramatist, is born.

1607-1669 Rembrandt, Dutch painter.

1608 Champlain founds Quebec.

1609 Champlain discovers lake that bears his name. Henry Hudson explores Hudson river. Galileo works with telescope.

From 1610-1625 Luis de Góngora in Spain writes in style known as *gongorism.*

1615 Cervantes: Part II of *Don Quijote de la Mancha.*

## CHRONOLOGICAL OUTLINE

### English

| General History and Culture | Literature |
|---|---|
| 1616 Deaths of England's greatest writer, Shakespeare and of Spain's greatest writer, Cervantes. | 1616 Capt. John Smith: *A Description of New England.* |
| | 1616 Great age of drama declines under Puritan pressure. |
| | 1616 Chapman translates *Odyssey* in heroic couplets. |
| 1618 Ralegh executed. | |
| 1619 First American legislative assembly at Jamestown. Negro slavery in Virginia. | |
| 1620 Mayflower carries Puritans to Massachusetts (Plymouth). | 1620 Bacon: *Novum Organum.* |
| | 1620- Donne, Taylor, and others write sermons. |
| | 1621 Burton: *Anatomy of Melancholy.* |
| | 1623 First edition of Shakespeare's plays. |
| 1625 Charles I is king. | 1625 Bacon: *Essays* (final edition). |
| | 1625-1650 Cavalier lyric is competing with Puritan writing, metaphysical poetry abounds, especially with John Donne and Herbert. |
| | 1629 Milton's first poem: *Ode on the Nativity.* |
| 1629 Parliament dissolved by Charles. | 1633 Herbert: *The Temple* (metaphysical lyrics). |
| 1596-1662 Henry Lawes, first famed English musician. | 1633 Milton: *L'Allegro* and *Il Penseroso.* |
| 1632-1723 Sir Christopher Wren, English architect. | 1634 Milton: *Comus* (a masque). Devenant: *The Temple of Love.* Chapman dies. |
| 1634 Maryland settled by English. | |
| 1635 Roger Williams is banished from Massachusetts. | |
| 1636 Williams founds Providence. Tolerance to all faiths. Harvard College founded. | 1636 Jacobean drama continues, despite restrictions. Devenant: *Platonic Lovers* and *The Wits.* |

## CHRONOLOGICAL OUTLINE

### Foreign

**General History and Culture**  **Literatures**

1618-1648 Thirty Years' War: Protestants versus Catholics.
1618 Murillo, Spanish painter. Harvey discovers circulation of the blood.
1620 Thermometers invented by Drebel.

1621 La Fontaine is born.
1622 Molière is born.
1623 Pascal is born.

1626 Peter Minuit founds New Amsterdam. Kepler's laws discovered.

1628 Malherbe: *Works* (foremost early advocate for French classicism).

1630 Massachusetts Bay Colony founded at Salem by non-Separatist dissenters.
1632-1675 Van der Meer, Dutch painter.

1635 French Academy founded.

1636 Corneille: *Le Cid* (classic tragicomedy).
1637 Descartes: *Discours de la Methode.*

## CHRONOLOGICAL OUTLINE

### English

| General History and Culture | Literature |
|---|---|
| 1639 Baptist Church founded in America by Williams. Printing press in Cambridge, Mass.<br>1640 The Long Parliament. | 1639 Milton: *Lycidas* (a pastoral elegy). |
| 1642 Theaters closed. Civil War. | 1642 Browne: *Religio Medici* (prose innovations).<br><br>1644 *Aeropagitica* by Milton. A plea for freedom of expression. |
| 1649 Execution of Charles I. Beginning of Commonwealth under Cromwell.<br>c. 1650 Many Cavaliers are migrating to Virginia.<br><br>1652 Quaker movement underway. War with Holland.<br>1656 Quakers arrive in Mass. | c. 1650 French romances and novels, translated into English.<br>1651 Milton: *Defense of the English People*. (Milton defends the execution of Charles I.) Hobbes: *Leviathan* (defense of monarchy).<br>1653 Walton: *The Compleat Angler*.<br>1658 Dryden: *Stanzas on the Death of Cromwell*. |
| 1660 Commonwealth ended. The Stuarts are restored to power with Charles II. | 1660 Theaters reopened and the age of Restoration drama begins.<br>1660-1669 Period covered by Pepys's *Diary*. |
| | 1663 Butler: *Hudibras* (mock epic, satirizing Puritans).<br><br>1664 Heroic plays popular. Dryden: *The Indian Queen*, (1665) *The Indian Emperor*. |
| 1665 Plague in London. | |

## CHRONOLOGICAL OUTLINE

### Foreign

| General History and Culture | Literatures |
|---|---|
| | 1639 Racine born. |
| 1640 Portugal regains independence. *Bay Psalm Book.* (First book printed in the Americas, north of Mexico.) | 1641 Descartes: *Meditationes.* |
| | 1643 Corneille: *Le Menteur.* |
| | 1645 Corneille: *Théodore.* |
| 1648 Treaty of Westphalia. | |
| 1654 Air pumps invented. | 1652 Milton becomes blind. |
| | 1659 Molière: *Les Précieuses Ridicules.* |
| | 1660 Spain's golden age is over and the classic age of French literature is well under way with Corneille and the first plays of Molière. American colonial literature is still restricted almost entirely to history, chronicle and religious tracts. |
| 1662 Baptist Church founded in Boston. | 1662 La Fontaine: *Contes.* Molière: *L'Ecole des Femmes.* |
| | 1665 La Rochefoucauld: *Maxims.* |

## CHRONOLOGICAL OUTLINE

### English

| General History and Culture | Literature |
|---|---|
| 1666 Great fire in London. | |
| | 1667 Milton: *Paradise Lost*. |
| | 1670 Dryden made Poet Laureate. |
| | 1671 Milton: *Paradise Regained. Samson Agonistes*. |
| | 1675 Wycherley: *The Country Wife*. |
| | 1678 John Bunyan: *The Pilgrim's Progress*. |
| 1679 Rise of the Whig and Tory parties. | |
| | 1681 Dryden: *Absolom and Achitophel*. |
| 1682 Penn settles Pennsylvania. | |
| 1685 James II is king. | |
| | 1687 Sir Isaac Newton: *Principia* (law of gravitation). Dryden: *The Hind and the Panther*. |
| 1688 The "Bloodless Revolution" puts Mary II and her husband William III on the throne of England. | |
| 1689 A Bill of Rights passed by Parliament. | |
| 1690 Battle of the Boyne. James is defeated and returns to France. White paper first made. | 1690 Locke: *Essay concerning Human Understanding*. |
| 1692 Witchcraft trials in Salem. First opera in London. | |

## CHRONOLOGICAL OUTLINE

### Foreign

| General History and Culture | Literatures |
|---|---|
| | 1666 Molière: *Le Misanthrope.* |
| | 1667 Molière: *Tartufe.* Racine: *Andromaque.* |
| 1668 The Triple Alliance of England, Sweden, and Holland against France. | 1668 La Fontaine: *Fables.* Molière: *L'Avare.* |
| | 1670 Pascal: *Thoughts.* |
| 1671 Foundation of Academy of Architecture at Paris. | 1673 Boileau: *L'art Poétique.* |
| | 1674 Racine: *Iphigénie.* |
| | 1677 Racine: *Phèdre.* |
| | 1677 Spinoza: *Ethica.* |
| 1680 Alsace seized by France. | |
| 1682 LaSalle explores the Mississippi. | |
| 1684-1721 Watteau, French painter. | |
| 1684-1759 Händel, German composer. | |
| 1685-1750 Bach, German composer. | |
| 1687 Telegraph instrument invented. | |
| | 1688 La Bruyère: *Characters.* |
| 1689 Peter the Great is Czar of Russia. | |
| 1692 Witchcraft executions in Salem, Massachusetts. | |

## CHRONOLOGICAL OUTLINE

### English

| General History and Culture | Literature |
|---|---|
| 1693 William and Mary College founded. Bank of England founded. | 1693 Congreve: *Old Bachelor* and *Double Dealer*. |
| 1695 Press freed from censorship. | 1695 Congreve: *Love for Love*. |
| 1697-1764 Hogarth, English painter. | 1698 Jeremy Collier: *Short View of the Immorality and Profaneness of the English Stage*. |
| 1701-1712 War of the Spanish Succession. Yale University founded. | 1700 Congreve: *The Way of the World*. Farquhar: *Constant Couple*. |
| 1702 First daily newspaper in London. Queen Anne I. | 1701-1729 Steele's works are written. |
| | 1704 Jonathan Swift: *The Battle of the Books; The Tale of a Tub* (satire on human institutions). |
| 1704 Gibraltar taken by the English. | 1704-1719 Addison's works are written. |
| 1706 Benjamin Franklin born. | 1707 Farquhar: *The Beaux' Stratagem*. |
| | 1709 Addison and Steele found *The Tatler*. Alexander Pope: *Pastorals*. |
| 1710 The Whigs lose power. | 1710-1713 Swift: *Journal to Stella*. |
| | 1711 Pope: *Essay on Criticism* (classical criticism, written in heroic couplets). Addison and Steele found *The Spectator*. |
| | 1712 Pope: *The Rape of the Lock* (greatest mock-heroic epic). |
| 1714 House of Hanover. George I is king. | 1714 Mandeville: *Fable of the Bees* (satire on idealistic philosophy). |
| 1721 Inoculation for the dread killer, smallpox, is introduced. | 1719 Daniel Defoe: *Robinson Crusoe*. |
| 1727 George II is king. | 1722 Defoe: *Moll Flanders*. |
| 1723-1792 Sir Joshua Reynolds, English portrait painter. | |

## CHRONOLOGICAL OUTLINE

### Foreign

**General History and Culture**

**Literatures**

1694 Dictionary of the French Academy. Voltaire, great French philosopher and literary figure, is born.

1697 Peter the Great visits England.

1699-1779 Chardin, French painter.

1699 Fénelon: *Télémaque*.

1703-1770 Boucher, French painter.

1707 Spain abandons all possessions in Italy.

1714-1787 Gluck, German composer.

The early years of the 18th century are another transition period for Western literatures. The Renaissance, with its aristocratic paganism and its fantasy and often shallow thought, its search for color and beauty of expression, had given way to a baroque period of an orthodox Christian mentality, a rather heavy ornateness of style and thought. Literature had become moral and satirical. There was little of a happy medium—convention and social institutions were subjected to bitter censure and ridicule in writing or an uncompromising Puritan orthodoxy was evident. Slowly, in this century, philosophy and literature blended. The influence of antiquity became strong and literature adopted a new dignity, moderation, clarity, and rationality, based largely upon early French interpretations of Boileau, Ra-

## CHRONOLOGICAL OUTLINE

### English

| General History and Culture | Literature |
|---|---|
| 1723-1788 Gainsborough, English portrait painter. | 1726 Swift: *Gulliver's Travels.* |
| | 1728 Pope: *Dunciad* (literary satire). Gay: *The Begger's Opera* (burlesque opera). |
| | 1729 Swift: *A Modest Proposal* (bitter social satire). |
| 1730 Methodist Society is formed at Oxford. | |
| 1734-1802 Romney, English portrait painter. | 1733 Pope: *Essay on Man* (attempt to rationalize man's existence—in heroic couplets). |
| 1740 Factories flourish in the manufacture of Irish linen, steel, and cutlery. | 1740 Richardson: *Pamela* (first modern English novel). |
| | 1741 Fielding: *Joseph Andrews* (satirical novel on the sentimentality of Richardson). |
| | 1742 Young: *Night Thoughts* (first of the "graveyard" poets). |
| | 1743 Blair: *The Grave.* |
| | 1744 Death of Pope. |

## CHRONOLOGICAL OUTLINE

### Foreign

**General History and Culture**

1725-1805 Greuze, French painter.

1728 Behring Strait is discovered.

1732-1806 Fragonard, French painter.

1732-1809 Haydn, German composer.

1732 Franklin opens first public library in the Americas in Philadelphia. George Washington is born.

1733 Georgia is settled by Oglethorpe.

1734 Zenger wins victory for freedom of the press.

1740 Frederick the Great becomes King of Poland.

1743 Thomas Jefferson is born.

1746-1828 Goya, Spanish painter.

**Literatures**

cine, and Corneille. Literature became philosophical and realistic, and for the first time, middle class. Molière had pointed the way to realistic interpretation in drama. It remained for Defoe, Richardson, Smollett, Fielding and Sterne to point to a new realistic prose that would form the basis for the great modern novel. But the Renaissance has created the spirit of the modern individual which will not be denied. And this spirit, in the 19th century, is to prove stronger than a new classicism or a new middle class realism in literatures. It is to assert the right of the individual to rebel aesthetically. It is to result in a new height for romanticism in the arts.

1732 Franklin: *Poor Richard's Almanac*.

# CHRONOLOGICAL OUTLINE

## English

| General History and Culture | Literature |
|---|---|
| | 1745 Death of Swift. |
| | 1747 Collins: *Odes* (evidence that the romantic spirit is already in English poetry). |
| | 1748 Richardson: *Clarissa Harlowe*. Smollett: *Roderick Random*. |
| | 1749 Fielding: *Tom Jones* (greatest early English novel). |
| 1751 Clive in India. | 1751 Gray: *Elegy Written in a Country Churchyard*. |
| 1752 Franklin makes discovery that lightning is electric force. The Georgian calendar is adopted. | |
| 1751-1806 Sheraton, English cabinet maker. | 1755 Samuel Johnson: *Dictionary*. |
| 1756-1823 Raeburn, English portrait painter. | |
| 1757-1827 William Blake, painter and engraver. Early romantic poet. | |
| 1758-1860 Hoppner, painter and engraver. | |
| 1757 Clive wins India in Battle of Plassey. | |
| 1759 Wolfe wins Canada for England at Quebec. | 1759 Johnson: *Rasselas*. |
| 1760 George III is king. | 1760-1767 Sterne: *Tristram Shandy* (novel of character). |
| 1765 The Stamp Act. | 1764 Walpole: *Castle of Otranto* (first important Gothic romance). |
| | 1766 Goldsmith: *The Vicar of Wakefield*. |
| 1767 First spinning machine in England. | 1768 Sterne: *Sentimental Journey*. |
| 1769-1830 Laurence, portrait painter. | |
| | 1770 Goldsmith: *The Deserted Village*. William Wordsworth born. |

## CHRONOLOGICAL OUTLINE
### Foreign

| General History and Culture | Literatures |
| --- | --- |

1748-1825 David, French painter.

1748 Montesquieu: *Esprit des Lois (The Spirit of Laws).*

1749 The University of Pennsylvania is founded.

1751- Vol. I of the French *Encyclopaedia.*

1756-1791 Mozart, German composer.

1757 Voltaire: *Candide* (social satire).

1761 Rousseau: *La Nouvelle Héloïse.*

1762 Catherine the Great of Russia.

1762 Rousseau: *Contrat Social.*

1764 Rousseau: *Emile.*
1766 Lessing: *Laokoön* (criticism).
1766-1817 Madame de Staël.

1767 Jesuits expelled from Spain.

1767 Goethe: *Götz Von Berlichingen.*
1767 Lessing: *Minna Von Barnhelm.*

1770 Marie Antoinette is married to the Dauphin.
1770-1827 Beethoven, German composer.

## CHRONOLOGICAL OUTLINE

### English

| General History and Culture | Literature |
|---|---|
| | 1771 Smollett: *Expedition of Humphry Clinker*. Sir Walter Scott is born. |
| | 1772 Samuel Coleridge is born. |
| | 1773 Goldsmith: *She Stoops to Conquer*. |
| 1774 Arkwright invents the spinning jenny. | 1774 Jefferson: *Summary of View of Rights of British America*. |
| 1775-1783 The American Revolution. | 1775 Burke: *Speech on Conciliation*. Sheridan: *The Rivals*. |
| 1776 Franklin in Paris. | 1776 Thomas Paine: *Common Sense*. |
| Thomas Chippendale's factory is turning out fine furniture in this period. | 1776 Gibbon: *Decline and Fall of the Roman Empire*. Adam Smith: *Wealth of Nations*. |
| 1775-1851 Turner, landscape painter. | |
| 1776-1837 Constable, landscape painter. | |
| | 1777 Sheridan: *The School for Scandal*. |
| 1778 France lines up with America. | 1778 Frances Burney: *Evelina*. |
| | 1779 William Cowper: *Olney Hymns*. |
| | 1780- Cowper, Crabbe, Burns, and Blake are writing romantic poetry from this period. |
| 1783 Treaty of Peace grants independence to American colonies. | 1783 Crabbe: *The Village*. |
| 1785 The *London Times* founded. | 1785 Thomas de Quincey is born. |
| | 1785 Cowper: *The Task*. |
| | 1786 Burns: *Poems*. |

## CHRONOLOGICAL OUTLINE

### Foreign

| General History and Culture | Literatures |
|---|---|
| | 1771 Franklin: *Autobiography*. |
| | 1771 First edition of the *Encyclopaedia Britannica*. |
| 1774 First Continental Congress in America. | 1774 Goethe: *Sorrows of Werther* (a morbidly sentimental novel—the first major work of the great period of German writing). |
| 1774 Louis XVI is King of France. Steam engine perfected by Watt and Bolton. | |
| | 1775 Beaumarchais: *Barber of Seville;* 1784: *Marriage of Figaro*. |
| 1776 American Declaration of Independence. | |
| 1777 American Articles of Confederation. | |
| 1778 French Treaty with American colonies. | 1778 Deaths of Rousseau and Voltaire. |
| | 1779 Lessing: *Nathan the Wise*. |
| 1780-1867 Ingres, French painter. | 1781 Kant: *Critique of Pure Reason*. Schiller: *The Robbers*. |
| 1783 The Treaty of Versailles ends the American Revolution. | 1784 Manzoni, Italian romantic novelist, born. |
| | 1785 Philip Freneau: *Poems*. |
| 1786-1826 Weber, German composer; 1791-1863 Meyerbeer, German composer; 1792-1868 Rossini, Italian composer. | |

## CHRONOLOGICAL OUTLINE

### English

| General History and Culture | Literature |
| --- | --- |
| | 1788 Byron is born. |
| | 1789 Blake: *Songs of Innocence*. |
| | 1791 Boswell: *Life of Johnson*. |
| | 1792 Shelley is born. |
| 1793 War with France. | Influence of the German *Sturm und Drang* is strong in England from this period. |
| | 1794 Blake: *Songs of Experience*. |
| | 1795 Keats and Carlyle born. |
| | 1793-1797 Wordsworth, Southey, and Coleridge begin to write. |
| 1797 Nelson destroys French Fleet near Alexandria. | |
| | 1798 Wordsworth and Coleridge: *Lyrical Ballads* (triumph of the "new" romantic poetry). |

## CHRONOLOGICAL OUTLINE

### Foreign

| General History and Culture | Literatures |
|---|---|
| | 1787 Goethe: *Iphigenie*. Schiller: *Don Carlos*. |
| | 1788 St. Pierre: *Paul and Virginia*. Goethe: *Egmont*. |
| 1789-1793 The French Revolution. | |
| 1795-1797 The Reign of Terror of France. Louis and Marie Antoinette beheaded. Napoleon Bonaparte commands the army. | 1795 Goethe: *Wilhelm Meister*. |
| 1796 Napoleon's Italian campaign. | |
| 1796-1875 Carot, French landscape painter; 1797-1828 Schubert, Austrian composer; 1798-1863 Delacroix, French painter. | |
| 1797 Napoleon invades Austria. | |
| 1798 Napoleon invades Egypt. | 1798 Goethe: *Hermann und Dorothea*. Schiller: *Wallenstein*. |

# Index

The comprehensive *Table of Contents* gives references to the major divisions of English Literature and cultural history. This Index locates specific items within those major divisions and draws attention to the portions of the text giving the most concise information for the review of particular subjects. Boldface figures indicate main references. The letter A before a reference indicates a plot summary in Appendix A. The letter B indicates a definition of the particular literary term in Appendix B.